2124C: Programming with C#

Microsoft

Released: 02/2002

Course Number: 2124C
Part Number: X09-90414
Released: 02/2002

END-USER LICENSE AGREEMENT FOR MICROSOFT OFFICIAL CURRICULUM COURSEWARE –STUDENT EDITION

PLEASE READ THIS END-USER LICENSE AGREEMENT ("EULA") CAREFULLY. BY USING THE MATERIALS AND/OR USING OR INSTALLING THE SOFTWARE THAT ACCOMPANIES THIS EULA (COLLECTIVELY, THE "LICENSED CONTENT"), YOU AGREE TO THE TERMS OF THIS EULA. IF YOU DO NOT AGREE, DO NOT USE THE LICENSED CONTENT.

1. **GENERAL.** This EULA is a legal agreement between you (either an individual or a single entity) and Microsoft Corporation ("Microsoft"). This EULA governs the Licensed Content, which includes computer software (including online and electronic documentation), training materials, and any other associated media and printed materials. This EULA applies to updates, supplements, add-on components, and Internet-based services components of the Licensed Content that Microsoft may provide or make available to you unless Microsoft provides other terms with the update, supplement, add-on component, or Internet-based services component. Microsoft reserves the right to discontinue any Internet-based services provided to you or made available to you through the use of the Licensed Content. This EULA also governs any product support services relating to the Licensed Content except as may be included in another agreement between you and Microsoft. An amendment or addendum to this EULA may accompany the Licensed Content.

2. **GENERAL GRANT OF LICENSE.** Microsoft grants you the following rights, conditioned on your compliance with all the terms and conditions of this EULA. Microsoft grants you a limited, non-exclusive, royalty-free license to install and use the Licensed Content solely in conjunction with your participation as a student in an Authorized Training Session (as defined below). You may install and use one copy of the software on a single computer, device, workstation, terminal, or other digital electronic or analog device ("Device"). You may make a second copy of the software and install it on a portable Device for the exclusive use of the person who is the primary user of the first copy of the software. A license for the software may not be shared for use by multiple end users. An "Authorized Training Session" means a training session conducted at a Microsoft Certified Technical Education Center, an IT Academy, via a Microsoft Certified Partner, or such other entity as Microsoft may designate from time to time in writing, by a Microsoft Certified Trainer (for more information on these entities, please visit www.microsoft.com). WITHOUT LIMITING THE FOREGOING, COPYING OR REPRODUCTION OF THE LICENSED CONTENT TO ANY SERVER OR LOCATION FOR FURTHER REPRODUCTION OR REDISTRIBUTION IS EXPRESSLY PROHIBITED.

3. **DESCRIPTION OF OTHER RIGHTS AND LICENSE LIMITATIONS**

    3.1   *Use of Documentation and Printed Training Materials.*

        3.1.1   The documents and related graphics included in the Licensed Content may include technical inaccuracies or typographical errors. Changes are periodically made to the content. Microsoft may make improvements and/or changes in any of the components of the Licensed Content at any time without notice. The names of companies, products, people, characters and/or data mentioned in the Licensed Content may be fictitious and are in no way intended to represent any real individual, company, product or event, unless otherwise noted.

        3.1.2   Microsoft grants you the right to reproduce portions of documents (such as student workbooks, white papers, press releases, datasheets and FAQs) (the "Documents") provided with the Licensed Content. You may not print any book (either electronic or print version) in its entirety. If you choose to reproduce Documents, you agree that: (a) use of such printed Documents will be solely in conjunction with your personal training use; (b) the Documents will not republished or posted on any network computer or broadcast in any media; (c) any reproduction will include either the Document's original copyright notice or a copyright notice to Microsoft's benefit substantially in the format provided below; and (d) to comply with all terms and conditions of this EULA. In addition, no modifications may made to any Document.

        Form of Notice:

        © 2002. Reprinted with permission by Microsoft Corporation. All rights reserved.

        Microsoft and Windows are either registered trademarks or trademarks of Microsoft Corporation in the US and/or other countries. Other product and company names mentioned herein may be the trademarks of their respective owners.

    3.2   *Use of Media Elements.* The Licensed Content may include certain photographs, clip art, animations, sounds, music, and video clips (together "Media Elements"). You may not modify these Media Elements.

    3.3   *Use of Sample Code.* In the event that the Licensed Content includes sample code in source or object format ("Sample Code"), Microsoft grants you a limited, non-exclusive, royalty-free license to use, copy and modify the Sample Code; if you elect to exercise the foregoing rights, you agree to comply with all other terms and conditions of this EULA, including without limitation Sections 3.4, 3.5, and 6.

    3.4   *Permitted Modifications.* In the event that you exercise any rights provided under this EULA to create modifications of the Licensed Content, you agree that any such modifications: (a) will not be used for providing training where a fee is charged in public or private classes; (b) indemnify, hold harmless, and defend Microsoft from and against any claims or lawsuits, including attorneys' fees, which arise from or result from your use of any modified version of the Licensed Content; and (c) not to transfer or assign any rights to any modified version of the Licensed Content to any third party without the express written permission of Microsoft.

3.5 *Reproduction/Redistribution Licensed Content.* Except as expressly provided in this EULA, you may not reproduce or distribute the Licensed Content or any portion thereof (including any permitted modifications) to any third parties without the express written permission of Microsoft.

4. **RESERVATION OF RIGHTS AND OWNERSHIP.** Microsoft reserves all rights not expressly granted to you in this EULA. The Licensed Content is protected by copyright and other intellectual property laws and treaties. Microsoft or its suppliers own the title, copyright, and other intellectual property rights in the Licensed Content. You may not remove or obscure any copyright, trademark or patent notices that appear on the Licensed Content, or any components thereof, as delivered to you. **The Licensed Content is licensed, not sold.**

5. **LIMITATIONS ON REVERSE ENGINEERING, DECOMPILATION, AND DISASSEMBLY.** You may not reverse engineer, decompile, or disassemble the Software or Media Elements, except and only to the extent that such activity is expressly permitted by applicable law notwithstanding this limitation.

6. **LIMITATIONS ON SALE, RENTAL, ETC. AND CERTAIN ASSIGNMENTS.** You may not provide commercial hosting services with, sell, rent, lease, lend, sublicense, or assign copies of the Licensed Content, or any portion thereof (including any permitted modifications thereof) on a stand-alone basis or as part of any collection, product or service.

7. **CONSENT TO USE OF DATA.** You agree that Microsoft and its affiliates may collect and use technical information gathered as part of the product support services provided to you, if any, related to the Licensed Content. Microsoft may use this information solely to improve our products or to provide customized services or technologies to you and will not disclose this information in a form that personally identifies you.

8. **LINKS TO THIRD PARTY SITES.** You may link to third party sites through the use of the Licensed Content. The third party sites are not under the control of Microsoft, and Microsoft is not responsible for the contents of any third party sites, any links contained in third party sites, or any changes or updates to third party sites. Microsoft is not responsible for webcasting or any other form of transmission received from any third party sites. Microsoft is providing these links to third party sites to you only as a convenience, and the inclusion of any link does not imply an endorsement by Microsoft of the third party site.

9. **ADDITIONAL LICENSED CONTENT/SERVICES.** This EULA applies to updates, supplements, add-on components, or Internet-based services components, of the Licensed Content that Microsoft may provide to you or make available to you after the date you obtain your initial copy of the Licensed Content, unless we provide other terms along with the update, supplement, add-on component, or Internet-based services component. Microsoft reserves the right to discontinue any Internet-based services provided to you or made available to you through the use of the Licensed Content.

10. **U.S. GOVERNMENT LICENSE RIGHTS.** All software provided to the U.S. Government pursuant to solicitations issued on or after December 1, 1995 is provided with the commercial license rights and restrictions described elsewhere herein. All software provided to the U.S. Government pursuant to solicitations issued prior to December 1, 1995 is provided with "Restricted Rights" as provided for in FAR, 48 CFR 52.227-14 (JUNE 1987) or DFAR, 48 CFR 252.227-7013 (OCT 1988), as applicable.

11. **EXPORT RESTRICTIONS.** You acknowledge that the Licensed Content is subject to U.S. export jurisdiction. You agree to comply with all applicable international and national laws that apply to the Licensed Content, including the U.S. Export Administration Regulations, as well as end-user, end-use, and destination restrictions issued by U.S. and other governments. For additional information see <http://www.microsoft.com/exporting/>.

12. **TRANSFER.** The initial user of the Licensed Content may make a one-time permanent transfer of this EULA and Licensed Content to another end user, provided the initial user retains no copies of the Licensed Content. The transfer may not be an indirect transfer, such as a consignment. Prior to the transfer, the end user receiving the Licensed Content must agree to all the EULA terms.

13. **"NOT FOR RESALE" LICENSED CONTENT.** Licensed Content identified as "Not For Resale" or "NFR," may not be sold or otherwise transferred for value, or used for any purpose other than demonstration, test or evaluation.

14. **TERMINATION.** Without prejudice to any other rights, Microsoft may terminate this EULA if you fail to comply with the terms and conditions of this EULA. In such event, you must destroy all copies of the Licensed Content and all of its component parts.

15. **DISCLAIMER OF WARRANTIES. TO THE MAXIMUM EXTENT PERMITTED BY APPLICABLE LAW, MICROSOFT AND ITS SUPPLIERS PROVIDE THE LICENSED CONTENT AND SUPPORT SERVICES (IF ANY) *AS IS AND WITH ALL FAULTS,* AND MICROSOFT AND ITS SUPPLIERS HEREBY DISCLAIM ALL OTHER WARRANTIES AND CONDITIONS, WHETHER EXPRESS, IMPLIED OR STATUTORY, INCLUDING, BUT NOT LIMITED TO, ANY (IF ANY) IMPLIED WARRANTIES, DUTIES OR CONDITIONS OF MERCHANTABILITY, OF FITNESS FOR A PARTICULAR PURPOSE, OF RELIABILITY OR AVAILABILITY, OF ACCURACY OR COMPLETENESS OF RESPONSES, OF RESULTS, OF WORKMANLIKE EFFORT, OF LACK OF VIRUSES, AND OF LACK OF NEGLIGENCE, ALL WITH REGARD TO THE LICENSED CONTENT, AND THE PROVISION OF OR FAILURE TO PROVIDE SUPPORT OR OTHER SERVICES, INFORMATION, SOFTWARE, AND RELATED CONTENT THROUGH THE LICENSED CONTENT, OR OTHERWISE ARISING OUT OF THE USE OF THE LICENSED CONTENT. ALSO, THERE IS NO WARRANTY OR CONDITION OF TITLE, QUIET ENJOYMENT, QUIET POSSESSION, CORRESPONDENCE TO DESCRIPTION OR NON-INFRINGEMENT WITH REGARD TO THE LICENSED CONTENT. THE ENTIRE RISK AS TO THE QUALITY, OR ARISING OUT OF THE USE OR PERFORMANCE OF THE LICENSED CONTENT, AND ANY SUPPORT SERVICES, REMAINS WITH YOU.**

16. **EXCLUSION OF INCIDENTAL, CONSEQUENTIAL AND CERTAIN OTHER DAMAGES. TO THE MAXIMUM EXTENT PERMITTED BY APPLICABLE LAW, IN NO EVENT SHALL MICROSOFT OR ITS SUPPLIERS BE LIABLE FOR ANY SPECIAL, INCIDENTAL, PUNITIVE, INDIRECT, OR CONSEQUENTIAL DAMAGES WHATSOEVER (INCLUDING, BUT NOT**

LIMITED TO, DAMAGES FOR LOSS OF PROFITS OR CONFIDENTIAL OR OTHER INFORMATION, FOR BUSINESS INTERRUPTION, FOR PERSONAL INJURY, FOR LOSS OF PRIVACY, FOR FAILURE TO MEET ANY DUTY INCLUDING OF GOOD FAITH OR OF REASONABLE CARE, FOR NEGLIGENCE, AND FOR ANY OTHER PECUNIARY OR OTHER LOSS WHATSOEVER) ARISING OUT OF OR IN ANY WAY RELATED TO THE USE OF OR INABILITY TO USE THE LICENSED CONTENT, THE PROVISION OF OR FAILURE TO PROVIDE SUPPORT OR OTHER SERVICES, INFORMATION, SOFTWARE, AND RELATED CONTENT THROUGH THE LICENSED CONTENT, OR OTHERWISE ARISING OUT OF THE USE OF THE LICENSED CONTENT, OR OTHERWISE UNDER OR IN CONNECTION WITH ANY PROVISION OF THIS EULA, EVEN IN THE EVENT OF THE FAULT, TORT (INCLUDING NEGLIGENCE), MISREPRESENTATION, STRICT LIABILITY, BREACH OF CONTRACT OR BREACH OF WARRANTY OF MICROSOFT OR ANY SUPPLIER, AND EVEN IF MICROSOFT OR ANY SUPPLIER HAS BEEN ADVISED OF THE POSSIBILITY OF SUCH DAMAGES. BECAUSE SOME STATES/JURISDICTIONS DO NOT ALLOW THE EXCLUSION OR LIMITATION OF LIABILITY FOR CONSEQUENTIAL OR INCIDENTAL DAMAGES, THE ABOVE LIMITATION MAY NOT APPLY TO YOU.

17. **LIMITATION OF LIABILITY AND REMEDIES.** NOTWITHSTANDING ANY DAMAGES THAT YOU MIGHT INCUR FOR ANY REASON WHATSOEVER (INCLUDING, WITHOUT LIMITATION, ALL DAMAGES REFERENCED HEREIN AND ALL DIRECT OR GENERAL DAMAGES IN CONTRACT OR ANYTHING ELSE), THE ENTIRE LIABILITY OF MICROSOFT AND ANY OF ITS SUPPLIERS UNDER ANY PROVISION OF THIS EULA AND YOUR EXCLUSIVE REMEDY HEREUNDER SHALL BE LIMITED TO THE GREATER OF THE ACTUAL DAMAGES YOU INCUR IN REASONABLE RELIANCE ON THE LICENSED CONTENT UP TO THE AMOUNT ACTUALLY PAID BY YOU FOR THE LICENSED CONTENT OR US$5.00. THE FOREGOING LIMITATIONS, EXCLUSIONS AND DISCLAIMERS SHALL APPLY TO THE MAXIMUM EXTENT PERMITTED BY APPLICABLE LAW, EVEN IF ANY REMEDY FAILS ITS ESSENTIAL PURPOSE.

18. **APPLICABLE LAW.** If you acquired this Licensed Content in the United States, this EULA is governed by the laws of the State of Washington. If you acquired this Licensed Content in Canada, unless expressly prohibited by local law, this EULA is governed by the laws in force in the Province of Ontario, Canada; and, in respect of any dispute which may arise hereunder, you consent to the jurisdiction of the federal and provincial courts sitting in Toronto, Ontario. If you acquired this Licensed Content in the European Union, Iceland, Norway, or Switzerland, then local law applies. If you acquired this Licensed Content in any other country, then local law may apply.

19. **ENTIRE AGREEMENT; SEVERABILITY.** This EULA (including any addendum or amendment to this EULA which is included with the Licensed Content) are the entire agreement between you and Microsoft relating to the Licensed Content and the support services (if any) and they supersede all prior or contemporaneous oral or written communications, proposals and representations with respect to the Licensed Content or any other subject matter covered by this EULA. To the extent the terms of any Microsoft policies or programs for support services conflict with the terms of this EULA, the terms of this EULA shall control. If any provision of this EULA is held to be void, invalid, unenforceable or illegal, the other provisions shall continue in full force and effect.

Should you have any questions concerning this EULA, or if you desire to contact Microsoft for any reason, please use the address information enclosed in this Licensed Content to contact the Microsoft subsidiary serving your country or visit Microsoft on the World Wide Web at http://www.microsoft.com.

Si vous avez acquis votre Contenu Sous Licence Microsoft au CANADA :

DÉNI DE GARANTIES. Dans la mesure maximale permise par les lois applicables, le Contenu Sous Licence et les services de soutien technique (le cas échéant) sont fournis *TELS QUELS ET AVEC TOUS LES DÉFAUTS* par Microsoft et ses fournisseurs, lesquels par les présentes dénient toutes autres garanties et conditions expresses, implicites ou en vertu de la loi, notamment, mais sans limitation, (le cas échéant) les garanties, devoirs ou conditions implicites de qualité marchande, d'adaptation à une fin usage particulière, de fiabilité ou de disponibilité, d'exactitude ou d'exhaustivité des réponses, des résultats, des efforts déployés selon les règles de l'art, d'absence de virus et d'absence de négligence, le tout à l'égard du Contenu Sous Licence et de la prestation des services de soutien technique ou de l'omission de la 'une telle prestation des services de soutien technique ou à l'égard de la fourniture ou de l'omission de la fourniture de tous autres services, renseignements, Contenus Sous Licence, et contenu qui s'y rapporte grâce au Contenu Sous Licence ou provenant autrement de l'utilisation du Contenu Sous Licence. PAR AILLEURS, IL N'Y A AUCUNE GARANTIE OU CONDITION QUANT AU TITRE DE PROPRIÉTÉ, À LA JOUISSANCE OU LA POSSESSION PAISIBLE, À LA CONCORDANCE À UNE DESCRIPTION NI QUANT À UNE ABSENCE DE CONTREFAÇON CONCERNANT LE CONTENU SOUS LICENCE.

EXCLUSION DES DOMMAGES ACCESSOIRES, INDIRECTS ET DE CERTAINS AUTRES DOMMAGES. DANS LA MESURE MAXIMALE PERMISE PAR LES LOIS APPLICABLES, EN AUCUN CAS MICROSOFT OU SES FOURNISSEURS NE SERONT RESPONSABLES DES DOMMAGES SPÉCIAUX, CONSÉCUTIFS, ACCESSOIRES OU INDIRECTS DE QUELQUE NATURE QUE CE SOIT (NOTAMMENT, LES DOMMAGES À L'ÉGARD DU MANQUE À GAGNER OU DE LA DIVULGATION DE RENSEIGNEMENTS CONFIDENTIELS OU AUTRES, DE LA PERTE D'EXPLOITATION, DE BLESSURES CORPORELLES, DE LA VIOLATION DE LA VIE PRIVÉE, DE L'OMISSION DE REMPLIR TOUT DEVOIR, Y COMPRIS D'AGIR DE BONNE FOI OU D'EXERCER UN SOIN RAISONNABLE, DE LA NÉGLIGENCE ET DE TOUTE AUTRE PERTE PÉCUNIAIRE OU AUTRE PERTE

DE QUELQUE NATURE QUE CE SOIT) SE RAPPORTANT DE QUELQUE MANIÈRE QUE CE SOIT À L'UTILISATION DU CONTENU SOUS LICENCE OU À L'INCAPACITÉ DE S'EN SERVIR, À LA PRESTATION OU À L'OMISSION DE LA 'UNE TELLE PRESTATION DE SERVICES DE SOUTIEN TECHNIQUE OU À LA FOURNITURE OU À L'OMISSION DE LA FOURNITURE DE TOUS AUTRES SERVICES, RENSEIGNEMENTS, CONTENUS SOUS LICENCE, ET CONTENU QUI S'Y RAPPORTE GRÂCE AU CONTENU SOUS LICENCE OU PROVENANT AUTREMENT DE L'UTILISATION DU CONTENU SOUS LICENCE OU AUTREMENT AUX TERMES DE TOUTE DISPOSITION DE LA U PRÉSENTE CONVENTION EULA OU RELATIVEMENT À UNE TELLE DISPOSITION, MÊME EN CAS DE FAUTE, DE DÉLIT CIVIL (Y COMPRIS LA NÉGLIGENCE), DE RESPONSABILITÉ STRICTE, DE VIOLATION DE CONTRAT OU DE VIOLATION DE GARANTIE DE MICROSOFT OU DE TOUT FOURNISSEUR ET MÊME SI MICROSOFT OU TOUT FOURNISSEUR A ÉTÉ AVISÉ DE LA POSSIBILITÉ DE TELS DOMMAGES.

<u>LIMITATION DE RESPONSABILITÉ ET RECOURS.</u> MALGRÉ LES DOMMAGES QUE VOUS PUISSIEZ SUBIR POUR QUELQUE MOTIF QUE CE SOIT (NOTAMMENT, MAIS SANS LIMITATION, TOUS LES DOMMAGES SUSMENTIONNÉS ET TOUS LES DOMMAGES DIRECTS OU GÉNÉRAUX OU AUTRES), LA SEULE RESPONSABILITÉ 'OBLIGATION INTÉGRALE DE MICROSOFT ET DE L'UN OU L'AUTRE DE SES FOURNISSEURS AUX TERMES DE TOUTE DISPOSITION DEU LA PRÉSENTE CONVENTION EULA ET VOTRE RECOURS EXCLUSIF À L'ÉGARD DE TOUT CE QUI PRÉCÈDE SE LIMITE AU PLUS ÉLEVÉ ENTRE LES MONTANTS SUIVANTS : LE MONTANT QUE VOUS AVEZ RÉELLEMENT PAYÉ POUR LE CONTENU SOUS LICENCE OU 5,00 $US. LES LIMITES, EXCLUSIONS ET DÉNIS QUI PRÉCÈDENT (Y COMPRIS LES CLAUSES CI-DESSUS), S'APPLIQUENT DANS LA MESURE MAXIMALE PERMISE PAR LES LOIS APPLICABLES, MÊME SI TOUT RECOURS N'ATTEINT PAS SON BUT ESSENTIEL.

À moins que cela ne soit prohibé par le droit local applicable, la présente Convention est régie par les lois de la province d'Ontario, Canada. Vous consentez Chacune des parties à la présente reconnaît irrévocablement à la compétence des tribunaux fédéraux et provinciaux siégeant à Toronto, dans de la province d'Ontario et consent à instituer tout litige qui pourrait découler de la présente auprès des tribunaux situés dans le district judiciaire de York, province d'Ontario.

Au cas où vous auriez des questions concernant cette licence ou que vous désiriez vous mettre en rapport avec Microsoft pour quelque raison que ce soit, veuillez utiliser l'information contenue dans le Contenu Sous Licence pour contacter la filiale de succursale Microsoft desservant votre pays, dont l'adresse est fournie dans ce produit, ou visitez écrivez à : Microsoft sur le World Wide Web à http://www.microsoft.com

Contents

Introduction

Course Materials..2
Prerequisites 3
Course Outline...4
Microsoft Certified Professional Program..7
Facilities 10

Module 1: Overview of the Microsoft .NET Platform

Overview 1
Introduction to the .NET Platform...2
Overview of the .NET Framework 5
Benefits of the .NET Framework 7
The .NET Framework Components..8
Languages in the .NET Framework..14
Review..16

Module 2: Overview of C#

Overview 1
Structure of a C# Program 2
Basic Input/Output Operations 9
Recommended Practices..15
Compiling, Running, and Debugging...22
Lab 2.1: Creating a Simple C# Program..36
Review..44

Module 3: Using Value-Type Variables

Overview 1
Common Type System 2
Naming Variables..8
Using Built-in Data Types..14
Creating User-Defined Data Types 22
Converting Data Types..26
Lab 3.1: Creating and Using Types 30
Review..34

Module 4: Statements and Exceptions

Overview 1
Introduction to Statements...2
Using Selection Statements 6
Using Iteration Statements..17
Using Jump Statements 29
Lab 4.1: Using Statements..32
Handling Basic Exceptions..42
Raising Exceptions 52
Lab 4.2: Using Exceptions...62
Review..72

Module 5: Methods and Parameters

Overview 1
Using Methods...2
Using Parameters...16
Using Overloaded Methods...29
Lab 5.1: Creating and Using Methods 37
Review...48

Module 6: Arrays

Overview 1
Overview of Arrays 2
Creating Arrays...10
Using Arrays..17
Lab 6.1: Creating and Using Arrays 29
Review...40

Module 7: Essentials of Object-Oriented Programming

Overview 1
Classes and Objects 2
Using Encapsulation 10
C# and Object Orientation..21
Lab 7.1: Creating and Using Classes..39
Defining Object-Oriented Systems...52
Review...61

Module 8: Using Reference-Type Variables

Overview 1
Using Reference-Type Variables...2
Using Common Reference Types 15
The Object Hierarchy 23
Namespaces in the .NET Framework 29
Lab 8.1: Defining And Using Reference-Type Variables 35
Data Conversions..44
Multimedia: Type-Safe Casting..57
Lab 8.2: Converting Data 58
Review...63

Module 9: Creating and Destroying Objects

Overview 1
Using Constructors 2
Initializing Data..13
Lab 9.1: Creating Objects...32
Objects and Memory 40
Resource Management 46
Lab 9.2: Managing Resources 55
Review...58

Module 10: Inheritance in C#

Overview 1
Deriving Classes 2
Implementing Methods 10
Using Sealed Classes 27
Using Interfaces 29
Using Abstract Classes 42
Lab 10.1: Using Inheritance to Implement an Interface 52
Review 70

Module 11: Aggregation, Namespaces, and Advanced Scope

Overview 1
Using Internal Classes, Methods, and Data 2
Using Aggregation 11
Lab 11.1: Specifying Internal Access 22
Using Namespaces 28
Using Modules and Assemblies 49
Lab 11.2: Using Namespaces and Assemblies 57
Review 63

Module 12: Operators, Delegates, and Events

Overview 1
Introduction to Operators 2
Operator Overloading 6
Lab 12.1: Defining Operators 19
Creating and Using Delegates 37
Defining and Using Events 47
Demonstration: Handling Events 53
Lab 12.2: Defining and Using Events 54
Review 63
Course Evaluation 65

Module 13: Properties and Indexers

Overview 1
Using Properties 2
Using Indexers 17
Lab 13.1: Using Properties and Indexers 33
Review 42

Module 14: Attributes

Overview 1
Overview of Attributes 2
Defining Custom Attributes 13
Retrieving Attribute Values 22
Lab 14.1: Defining and Using Attributes 26
Review 34
Course Evaluation 36

Appendix A: Resources for Further Study

Resources for C# 1

About This Course

This section provides you with a brief description of the course, audience, suggested prerequisites, and course objectives.

Description

This five-day instructor-led course provides students with the knowledge and skills needed to develop C# applications for the Microsoft® .NET Platform. The course focuses on C# program structure, language syntax, and implementation details.

Audience

This course is intended for experienced developers who already have programming experience in C, C++, Microsoft Visual Basic®, or Java. These developers will be likely to develop enterprise business solutions.

Student Prerequisites

This course requires that students meet the following prerequisites:

- Experience programming in C, C++, Visual Basic, Java, or another programming language

- Familiarity with the Microsoft .NET strategy as described on the Microsoft .NET Web site (http://www.microsoft.com/net/)

- Familiarity with the .NET Framework as described on the MSDN® Web site (http://msdn.microsoft.com/library/default.asp?url=/library /en-us/cpguidnf/html/cpovrintroductiontonetframeworksdk.asp)

Course Objectives

After completing this course, the student will be able to:

- List the major elements of the .NET Framework, and explain how C# fits into the .NET Platform.
- Analyze the basic structure of a C# application, and be able to debug, compile, and run a simple application.
- Create, name, and assign values to variables.
- Use common statements to implement flow control, looping, and exception handling.
- Create methods (functions and subroutines) that can return values and take parameters.
- Create, initialize, and use arrays.
- Explain the basic concepts and terminology of object-oriented programming.
- Use common objects and references types.
- Create, initialize, and destroy objects in a C# application.
- Build new C# classes from existing classes.
- Create self-contained classes and frameworks in a C# application.
- Define operators and add event specifications.
- Implement properties and indexers.
- Use predefined and custom attributes.

Student Materials Compact Disc Contents

The Student Materials compact disc contains the following files and folders:

- *Autorun.exe*. When the CD is inserted into the CD-ROM drive, or when you double-click the autorun.exe file, this file opens the CD and allows you to browse the Student Materials compact disc.

- *Autorun.inf*. When the compact disc is inserted into the compact disc drive, this file opens Autorun.exe.

- *Default.htm*. This file opens the Student Materials Web page. It provides students with resources pertaining to this course, including additional reading, review and lab answers, lab files, multimedia presentations, and course-related Web sites.

- *Readme.txt*. This file explains how to install the software for viewing the Student Materials compact disc and its contents and how to open the Student Materials Web page.

- *2124C_ms.doc*. This file is the Classroom Setup Guide. It contains a description of classroom requirements, classroom setup instructions, and the classroom configuration.

- *Democode*. This folder contains demonstration code.

- *Flash*. This folder contains the installer for the Macromedia Flash 5.0 browser plug-in.

- *Fonts*. This folder contains fonts that are required to view the Microsoft PowerPoint presentation and Web-based materials.

- *Labs*. This folder contains files that are used in the hands-on labs. These files may be used to prepare the student computers for the hands-on labs.

- *Media*. This folder contains files that are used in multimedia presentations for this course.

- *Mplayer*. This folder contains the setup file to install Microsoft Windows Media™ Player.

- *Webfiles*. This folder contains the files that are required to view the course Web page. To open the Web page, open Windows Explorer, and in the root directory of the compact disc, double-click **Default.htm** or **Autorun.exe**.

- *Wordview*. This folder contains the Word Viewer that is used to view any Word document (.doc) files that are included on the compact disc.

Document Conventions

The following conventions are used in course materials to distinguish elements of the text.

Convention	Use
◆	Indicates an introductory page. This symbol appears next to a topic heading when additional information on the topic is covered on the page or pages that follow it.
bold	Represents commands, command options, and syntax that must be typed exactly as shown. It also indicates commands on menus and buttons, dialog box titles and options, and icon and menu names.
italic	In syntax statements or descriptive text, indicates argument names or placeholders for variable information.
Title Capitals	Indicate domain names, user names, computer names, directory names, and folder and file names, except when specifically referring to case-sensitive names. Unless otherwise indicated, you can use lowercase letters when you type a directory name or file name in a dialog box or at a command prompt.
ALL CAPITALS	Indicate the names of keys, key sequences, and key combinations—for example, ALT+SPACEBAR.
`monospace`	Represents code samples or examples of screen text.
[ ]	In syntax statements, enclose optional items. For example, [*filename*] in command syntax indicates that you can choose to type a file name with the command. Type only the information within the brackets, not the brackets themselves.
{ }	In syntax statements, enclose required items. Type only the information within the braces, not the braces themselves.
|	In syntax statements, separates an either/or choice.
▶	Indicates a procedure with sequential steps.
…	In syntax statements, specifies that the preceding item may be repeated.
. . .	Represents an omitted portion of a code sample.

msdn training

Introduction

Contents

Introduction	1
Course Materials	2
Prerequisites	3
Course Outline	4
Microsoft Certified Professional Program	7
Facilities	10

Introduction

- Name
- Company Affiliation
- Title / Function
- Job Responsibility
- Programming Experience
- C, C++, Visual Basic, or Java Experience
- Expectations for the Course

Course Materials

- **Name Card**
- **Student Workbook**
- **Student Materials Compact Disc**
- **Course Evaluation**

The following materials are included with your kit:

- *Name card.* Write your name on both sides of the name card.

- *Student workbook.* The student workbook contains the material covered in class, in addition to the hands-on lab exercises.

- *Student Materials compact disc.* The Student Materials compact disc contains the Web page that provides you with links to resources pertaining to this course, including additional readings, review and lab answers, lab files, multimedia presentations, and course-related Web sites.

Note   To open the Web page, insert the Student Materials compact disc into the CD-ROM drive, and then in the root directory of the compact disc, double-click **Autorun.exe** or **Default.htm**.

- *Course evaluation.* To provide feedback on the course, training facility, and instructor, you will have the opportunity to complete an online evaluation near the end of the course.

  To provide additional comments or inquire about the Microsoft Certified Professional program, send e-mail to mcphelp@msprograms.com.

Prerequisites

- **Experience programming in C, C++, Visual Basic, or Java**
- **Familiarity with the Microsoft .NET strategy**
- **Familiarity with the Microsoft .NET Framework**

This course requires that you meet the following prerequisites:

- Experience programming in C, C++, Microsoft® Visual Basic®, Java, or another programming language

- Familiarity with the Microsoft .NET strategy as described on the Microsoft .NET Web site (http://www.microsoft.com/net/)

- Familiarity with the .NET Framework as described on the Microsoft MSDN® Web site: http://msdn.microsoft.com/library/default.asp?url=/library /en-us/cpguidnf/html/cpovrintroductiontonetframeworksdk.asp

Course Outline

- **Module 1: Overview of the Microsoft .NET Platform**
- **Module 2: Overview of C#**
- **Module 3: Using Value-Type Variables**
- **Module 4: Statements and Exceptions**
- **Module 5: Methods and Parameters**

Module 1, "Overview of the Microsoft .NET Platform," describes the rationale and features that provide the foundation for the .NET Platform, including the .NET components. The purpose of this module is to build an understanding of the .NET Platform for which you will be developing C# code. After completing this module, you will be able to describe the components of the .NET Platform.

Module 2, "Overview of C#," describes the basic structure of a C# application. This module provides a simple working example for you to analyze to learn how to use the **Console** class to perform some basic input and output operations and to learn best practices for handling errors and documenting your code. After completing this module, you will be able to compile, run, and debug a C# application.

Module 3, "Using Value-Type Variables," describes how to use value-type variables in C#. This module explains how to specify the type of data that variables will hold, how to name variables according to standard naming conventions, how to assign values to variables, and how to convert existing variables from one data type to another. After completing this module, you will be able to use value-type variables in C#.

Module 4, "Statements and Exceptions," explains how to use some common statements in C#. This module also describes how to implement exception handling in C#. After completing this module, you will be able to throw and catch errors.

Module 5, "Methods and Parameters," describes how to create static methods that take parameters and return values, how to pass parameters to methods in different ways, and how to declare and use overloaded methods. After completing this module, you will be able to use methods and parameters.

Course Outline *(continued)*

- **Module 6: Arrays**
- **Module 7: Essentials of Object-Oriented Programming**
- **Module 8: Using Reference-Type Variables**
- **Module 9: Creating and Destroying Objects**
- **Module 10: Inheritance in C#**

Module 6, "Arrays," explains how to group data into arrays. After completing this module, you will be able to create, initialize, and use arrays.

Module 7, "Essentials of Object-Oriented Programming," explains the terminology and concepts required to create and use classes in C#. This module also explains abstraction, encapsulation, inheritance, and polymorphism. After completing this module, you will be able to explain some of the common concepts of object-oriented programming.

Module 8, "Using Reference-Type Variables," describes how to use reference-type variables in C#. This module explains a number of reference types, such as string, that are built into the C# language and the common language runtime. After completing this module, you will be able to use reference-type variables in C#.

Module 9, "Creating and Destroying Objects," explains what happens in the runtime when an object is created and how to use constructors to initialize objects. This module also explains what happens when an object is destroyed and how the garbage collector reclaims memory. After completing this module, you will be able to create and destroy objects in C#.

Module 10, "Inheritance in C#," explains how to derive a class from a base class. This module also explains how to implement methods in a derived class by defining them as virtual methods in the base class and overriding or hiding them in the derived class, as required. This module explains how to seal a class so that it cannot be derived from and how to implement interfaces and abstract classes. After completing this module, you will be able to use inheritance in C# to derive classes and to define virtual methods.

Course Outline *(continued)*

- **Module 11: Aggregation, Namespaces, and Advanced Scope**
- **Module 12: Operators, Delegates, and Events**
- **Module 13: Properties and Indexers**
- **Module 14: Attributes**
- **Appendix A: Resources for Further Study**

Module 11, "Aggregation, Namespaces, and Advanced Scope," describes how to group classes together into larger, higher-level classes and how to use namespaces to group classes together inside named spaces and to create logical program structures beyond individual classes. This module also explains how to use assemblies to group collaborating source files together into a reusable, versionable, and deployable unit. After completing this module, you will be able to make code accessible at the component or assembly level.

Module 12, "Operators, Delegates, and Events," explains how to define operators and how to use delegates to decouple a method call from a method implementation. It also explains how to add event specifications to a class. After completing this module, you will be able to implement operators, delegates, and events.

Module 13, "Properties and Indexers," explains how to create properties to encapsulate data within a class and how to define indexers to gain access to classes by using array-like notation. After completing this module, you will be able to use properties to enable field-like access and indexers to enable array-like access.

Module 14, "Attributes," describes the purpose of attributes and the role they play in C# applications. This module explains attribute syntax and how to use some predefined attributes in the .NET environment. After completing this module, you will be able to create custom user-defined attributes and use these custom attributes to query attribute information at run time.

Appendix A, "Resources for Further Study," serves as a reference that you can use after attending the course for further study and to help you locate the latest news and information about C# and the .NET Framework.

Microsoft Certified Professional Program

The Microsoft Certified Professional program is a leading certification program that validates your experience and skills to keep you competitive in today's business environment. The following table describes each certification in more detail.

Certification	Description
MCSA on Microsoft Windows® 2000	The Microsoft Certified Systems Administrator (MCSA) certification is designed for professionals who implement, manage, and troubleshoot existing network and system environments based on Microsoft Windows 2000 platforms, including the Windows .NET Server family. Implementation responsibilities include installing and configuring parts of the systems. Management responsibilities include administering and supporting the systems.
MCSE on Microsoft Windows 2000	The Microsoft Certified Systems Engineer (MCSE) credential is the premier certification for professionals who analyze the business requirements and design and implement the infrastructure for business solutions based on the Microsoft Windows 2000 platform and Microsoft server software, including the Windows .NET Server family. Implementation responsibilities include installing, configuring, and troubleshooting network systems.
MCSD	The Microsoft Certified Solution Developer (MCSD) credential is the premier certification for professionals who design and develop leading-edge business solutions with Microsoft development tools, technologies, platforms, and the Microsoft Windows DNA architecture. The types of applications that MCSDs can develop include desktop applications and multi-user, Web-based, N-tier, and transaction-based applications. The credential covers job tasks ranging from analyzing business requirements to maintaining solutions.
MCDBA on Microsoft SQL Server™ 2000	The Microsoft Certified Database Administrator (MCDBA) credential is the premier certification for professionals who implement and administer Microsoft SQL Server databases. The certification is appropriate for individuals who derive physical database designs, develop logical data models, create physical databases, create data services by using Transact-SQL, manage and maintain databases, configure and manage security, monitor and optimize databases, and install and configure SQL Server.

(*continued*)

Certification	Description
MCP	The Microsoft Certified Professional (MCP) credential is for individuals who have the skills to successfully implement a Microsoft product or technology as part of a business solution in an organization. Hands-on experience with the product is necessary to successfully achieve certification.
MCT	Microsoft Certified Trainers (MCTs) demonstrate the instructional and technical skills that qualify them to deliver Microsoft Official Curriculum through Microsoft Certified Technical Education Centers (Microsoft CTECs).

Certification Requirements

The certification requirements differ for each certification category and are specific to the products and job functions addressed by the certification. To become a Microsoft Certified Professional, you must pass rigorous certification exams that provide a valid and reliable measure of technical proficiency and expertise.

For More Information   See the Microsoft Training and Certification Web site at http://www.microsoft.com/traincert/.

You can also send e-mail to mcphelp@msprograms.com if you have specific certification questions.

Acquiring the Skills Tested by an MCP Exam

Microsoft Official Curriculum (MOC) and MSDN Training Curriculum can help you to develop the skills that you need to do your job. They also complement the experience that you gain while working with Microsoft products and technologies. However, no one-to-one correlation exists between MOC and MSDN Training courses and MCP exams. Microsoft does not expect or intend for the courses to be the sole preparation method for passing MCP exams. Practical product knowledge and experience is also necessary to pass the MCP exams.

To help prepare for the MCP exams, use the preparation guides that are available for each exam. Each Exam Preparation Guide contains exam-specific information, such as a list of the topics on which you will be tested. These guides are available on the Microsoft Training and Certification Web site at http://www.microsoft.com/traincert/.

Facilities

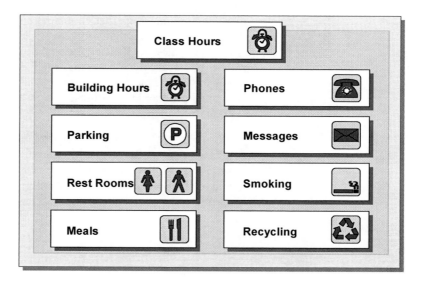

msdn®training

Module 1: Overview of the Microsoft .NET Platform

Contents

Overview	1
Introduction to the .NET Platform	2
Overview of the .NET Framework	5
Benefits of the .NET Framework	7
The .NET Framework Components	8
Languages in the .NET Framework	14
Review	16

Microsoft®

Overview

- ■ **Introduction to the .NET Platform**
- ■ **Overview of the .NET Framework**
- ■ **Benefits of the .NET Framework**
- ■ **The .NET Framework Components**
- ■ **Languages in the .NET Framework**

The Microsoft® .NET Platform provides all of the tools and technologies that you need to build distributed Web applications. It exposes a language-independent, consistent programming model across all tiers of an application while providing seamless interoperability with, and easy migration from, existing technologies. The .NET Platform fully supports the Internet's platform-neutral, standards-based technologies, including Hypertext Transfer Protocol (HTTP), Extensible Markup Language (XML), and SOAP.

C# is a new language specifically designed for building .NET applications. As a developer, you will find it useful to understand the rationale and features that provide the foundation for the .NET Platform before you start writing C# code.

After completing this module, you will be able to:

- ■ Describe the .NET Platform.
- ■ List the main elements of the .NET Platform.
- ■ Describe the .NET Framework and its components.
- ■ Explain the language support in the .NET Framework.

Introduction to the .NET Platform

- **The .NET Framework**
- **.NET My Services**
- **The .NET Enterprise Servers**
- **Visual Studio .NET**

The .NET Platform provides several core technologies, as shown on the slide. These technologies are described in the following topics.

The .NET Framework

The .NET Framework is based on a new common language runtime. The common language runtime provides a common set of services for projects built in Microsoft Visual Studio® .NET, regardless of the language. These services provide key building blocks for applications of any type, across all application tiers.

Microsoft Visual Basic®, Microsoft Visual C++®, and other Microsoft programming languages have been enhanced to take advantage of these services. Microsoft Visual J#™ .NET has been developed for Java-language developers who want to build applications and services using the .NET Framework. Third-party languages that are written for the .NET Platform also have access to the same services. The .NET Framework is explained in greater detail later in this module.

.NET My Services

.NET My Services is a set of user-centric XML Web services. With .NET My Services, users receive relevant information as they need it, delivered to the devices they are using, and based on preferences they have established. Using .NET My Services, applications can communicate directly by using SOAP and XML from any platform that supports SOAP.

Core .NET My Services include:

- .NET Passport authentication
- The ability to send alerts and manage preferences for receiving alerts
- The storage of personal information (including contacts, e-mail, calendar, profile, lists, electronic wallet, and physical location)
- The ability to maintain document stores, save application settings, record favorite Web sites, and note devices owned.

The .NET Enterprise Servers

The .NET Enterprise Servers provide scalability, reliability, management, integration within and across organizations, and many other features, as described in the following table.

Server	Description
Microsoft SQL Server™	Includes rich XML functionality, support for Worldwide Web Consortium (W3C) standards, the ability to manipulate XML data by using Transact SQL (T-SQL), flexible and powerful Web-based analysis, and secure access to your data over the Web by using HTTP.
Microsoft BizTalk™ Server	Provides enterprise application integration (EAI), business-to-business integration, and the advanced BizTalk Orchestration technology to build dynamic business processes that span applications, platforms, and organizations over the Internet.
Microsoft Host Integration Server	Provides the best way to embrace Internet, intranet, and client/server technologies while preserving investments in existing earlier systems.
Microsoft Exchange Enterprise Server	Builds on the powerful Exchange messaging and collaboration technology by introducing several important new features and further increasing the reliability, scalability, and performance of its core architecture. Other features enhance the integration of Exchange with Microsoft Windows®, Microsoft Office, and the Internet.
Microsoft Application Center	Provides a deployment and management tool for high-availability Web applications.
Microsoft Internet Security and Acceleration Server	Provides secure, fast, and manageable Internet connectivity. Internet Security and Acceleration Server integrates an extensible, multilayer enterprise firewall and a scalable high-performance Web cache. It builds on Windows security and directory for policy-based security, acceleration, and management of internetworking.
Microsoft Commerce Server	Provides an application framework, sophisticated feedback mechanisms, and analytical capabilities.
Microsoft SharePoint™ Portal Server	Provides the ability to create corporate Web portals with document management, content searching, and team collaboration features.
Microsoft Mobile Information Server	Integrates with the Microsoft .NET Enterprise Servers and Microsoft Windows® to provide secure communications and data exchange with mobile devices. High reliability, scalability, and performance are achieved by using clustering, replication, load balancing, and content delivery.
Microsoft Content Management Server	Offers complete feature sets for content contribution and delivery, site development, and enterprise site management to enable businesses to effectively create, deploy, and manage Internet, intranet, and extranet Web sites.

Visual Studio .NET

Visual Studio .NET provides a development environment for building applications on the .NET Framework. It provides important enabling technologies to simplify the creation, deployment, and ongoing evolution of secure, scalable, highly available Web applications and XML Web services.

Overview of the .NET Framework

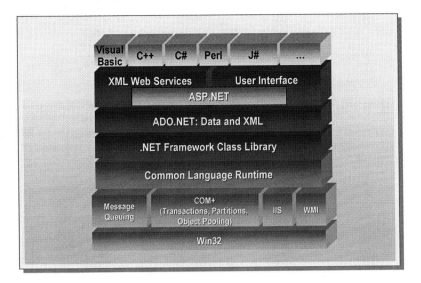

The .NET Framework

The .NET Framework provides the necessary compile-time and run-time foundation to build and run .NET-based applications.

Platform Substrate

The .NET Framework must run on an operating system. Currently, the .NET Framework is built to run on the Microsoft Win32® operating systems. In the future, the .NET Framework will be extended to run on other platforms, such as Microsoft Windows® CE.

Application Services

When running on Windows, application services, such as Component Services, Message Queuing, Windows Internet Information Server (IIS), and Windows Management Instrumentation (WMI), are available to the developer. The .NET Framework exposes application services through classes in the .NET Framework class library.

Common Language Runtime

The common language runtime simplifies application development, provides a robust and secure execution environment, supports multiple languages, and simplifies application deployment and management.

The common language runtime environment is also referred to as a managed environment, in which common services, such as garbage collection and security, are automatically provided.

.NET Framework Class Library

The .NET Framework class library exposes features of the runtime and provides other services that every developer needs. The classes simplify development of .NET-based applications. Developers can extend them by creating their own libraries of classes.

ADO.NET

ADO.NET is the next generation of Microsoft ActiveX® Data Objects (ADO) technology. ADO.NET provides improved support for the disconnected programming model. It also provides rich XML support.

ASP.NET

Microsoft ASP.NET is a programming framework that is built on the common language runtime. ASP.NET can be used on a server to build powerful Web applications. ASP.NET Web Forms provide an easy and powerful way to build dynamic Web user interfaces (UI).

XML Web Services

XML Web services are programmable Web components that can be shared among applications on the Internet or the intranet. The .NET Framework provides tools and classes for building, testing, and distributing XML Web services.

User Interfaces

The .NET Framework supports three types of user interfaces:

- Web Forms, which work through ASP.NET

- Windows Forms, which run on Win32 client computers

- Console Applications, which, for simplicity, are used for most of the labs in this course

Languages

Any language that conforms to the common language specification (CLS) can run on the common language runtime. In the .NET Framework, Microsoft provides Visual Basic, Visual C++, Microsoft Visual C#™, Visual J#, and Microsoft JScript® support. Third parties can provide additional languages.

Benefits of the .NET Framework

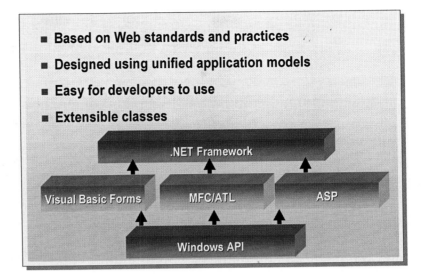

- Based on Web standards and practices
- Designed using unified application models
- Easy for developers to use
- Extensible classes

In this section, you will learn about some of the benefits of the .NET Framework. The NET Framework was designed to meet the following goals:

- **Based on Web standards and practices**

  The .NET Framework fully supports the existing Internet technologies, including Hypertext Markup Language (HTML), XML, SOAP, Extensible Stylesheet Language for Transformations (XSLT), XML Path Language (XPath), and other Web standards. The .NET Framework favors loosely connected, stateless XML Web services.

- **Designed using unified application models**

  The functionality of a .NET class is available from any .NET-compatible language or programming model.

- **Easy for developers to use**

  In the .NET Framework, code is organized into hierarchical namespaces and classes. The .NET Framework provides a common type system, referred to as the unified type system, which is used by any .NET-compatible language. In the unified type system, all languages elements are objects. There are no variant types, there is only one string type, and all string data is Unicode. The unified type system is described in more detail in later modules.

- **Extensible classes**

  The hierarchy of the .NET Framework is not hidden from the developer. You can access and extend .NET classes (unless they are sealed) through inheritance. You can also implement cross-language inheritance.

◆ The .NET Framework Components

- **Common Language Runtime**
- **.NET Framework Class Library**
- **ADO.NET: Data and XML**
- **Web Forms and XML Web Services**
- **User Interface for Windows**

In this section, you will learn about the Microsoft .NET Framework. The .NET Framework is a set of technologies that form an integral part of the Microsoft .NET Platform. It provides the basic building blocks for developing Web applications and XML Web services.

After completing this module, you will be able to:

- Describe the common language runtime.
- Describe the Base Class Library.
- Describe Web Forms and XML Web services.
- Work with the user interface.

Common Language Runtime

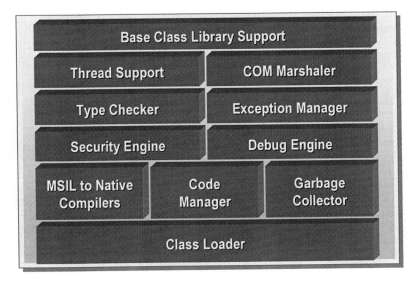

The common language runtime simplifies application development, provides a robust and secure execution environment, supports multiple languages, and simplifies application deployment and management. The environment is also referred to as a *managed environment*, one in which common services, such as garbage collection and security, are automatically provided. The common language runtime features are described in the following table.

Component	Description
Class loader	Manages metadata, in addition to the loading and layout of classes.
Microsoft intermediate language (MSIL) to native compiler	Converts MSIL to native code (Just-in-time).
Code manager	Manages code execution.
Garbage collector (GC)	Provides automatic lifetime management of all of your objects. This is a multiprocessor, scalable garbage collector.
Security engine	Provides evidence-based security, based on the origin of the code in addition to the user.
Debug engine	Allows you to debug your application and trace the execution of code.
Type checker	Will not allow unsafe casts or uninitialized variables. MSIL can be verified to guarantee type safety.
Exception manager	Provides structured exception handling, which is integrated with Windows Structured Exception Handling (SEH). Error reporting has been improved.
Thread support	Provides classes and interfaces that enable multithreaded programming.
COM marshaler	Provides marshaling to and from COM.
Base Class Library (BCL) support	Integrates code with the runtime that supports the BCL.

.NET Framework Class Library

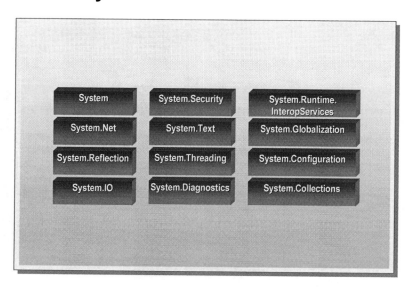

The .NET Framework class library exposes features of the runtime and provides other high-level services that every programmer needs by means of namespaces.

System Namespaces

The **System** namespace contains fundamental classes and base classes that define commonly-used value and reference data types, events and event handlers, interfaces, attributes, and processing exceptions. Other classes provide services supporting data type conversion, method parameter manipulation, mathematics, remote and local program invocation, application environment management, and supervision of managed and unmanaged applications.

The **System.Collections** namespace provides sorted lists, hash tables, and other ways to group data. The **System.IO** namespace provides file input /output (I/O), streams, and so on. The **System.Net** namespace provides Transmission Control Protocol/Internet Protocol (TCP/IP) and sockets support.

For more information about namespaces, see the .NET Framework SDK documentation.

ADO.NET: Data and XML

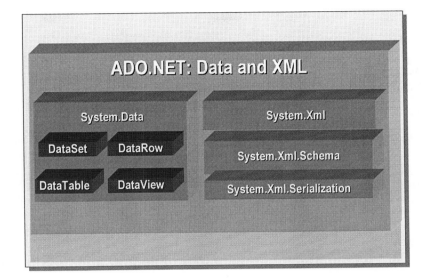

ADO.NET, the next generation of ADO technology, provides improved support for the disconnected programming model. It also provides rich XML support in the **System.Xml** namespace.

System.Data Namespace

The **System.Data** namespace consists of classes that constitute the ADO.NET object model. At a high level, the ADO.NET object model is divided into two layers: the connected layer and the disconnected layer.

The **System.Data** namespace includes the **DataSet** class, which represents multiple tables and their relations. These **DataSets** are completely self-contained data structures that can be populated from a variety of data sources. One data source could be XML, another could be OLEDB, and a third data source could be the direct adapter for SQL Server.

System.Xml Namespace

The **System.Xml** namespace provides support for XML. It includes an XML parser and a writer, which are both W3C-compliant. The Extensible Stylesheet Language (XSL) transformation is provided by the **System.Xml.Xsl** namespace. The **System.Xml.Serialization** namespace contains classes that are used to serialize objects into XML format documents or streams.

Web Forms and XML Web Services

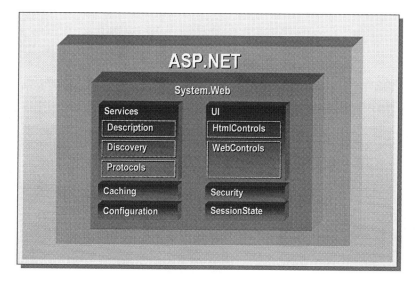

ASP.NET is a programming framework built on the common language runtime that can be used on a server to build powerful Web applications. ASP.NET Web Forms provide an easy and powerful way to build dynamic Web user interfaces (UIs). ASP.NET XML Web services provide the building blocks for constructing distributed Web-based applications. XML Web services are based on open Internet standards, such as HTTP and XML.

The common language runtime provides built-in support for creating and exposing XML Web services by using a programming abstraction that is consistent and familiar to both Active Server Pages (ASP) Web Forms and Visual Basic developers. The resulting model is both scalable and extensible. This model is based on open Internet standards (HTTP, XML, SOAP, SDL) so that it can be accessed and interpreted by any client computer or Internet-enabled device.

System.Web

In the **System.Web** namespace, there are lower-level services such as caching, security, configuration, and others that are shared between XML Web services and Web user interface (UI).

System.Web.Services

The **System.Web** namespace supplies classes and interfaces that enable communication between browsers and servers.

System.Web.UI

The **System.Web.UI** namespace provides classes and interfaces that allow you to create controls and pages that will appear in your Web applications as the user interface on a Web page.

User Interface for Windows

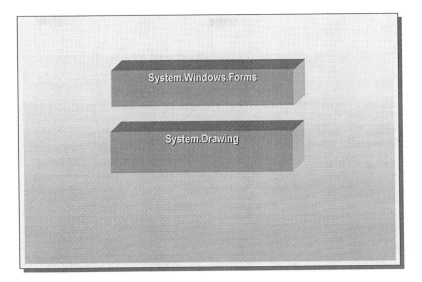

System.Windows.Forms Namespace

You can use the **System.Windows.Forms** namespace classes to build the client UI. This class lets you implement the standard Windows UI in your .NET-based applications. Many functions that were previously only accessible by means of application programming interface (API) calls are now available as part of the forms themselves, making development much easier and more powerful.

System.Drawing Namespace

The **System.Drawing** namespace provides access to GDI+ basic graphics functionality. More advanced functionality is provided in the **System.Drawing.Drawing2D**, **System.Drawing.Imaging**, and **System.Drawing.Text** namespaces.

Languages in the .NET Framework

- **C# – Designed for .NET**
  New component-oriented language
- **Managed Extensions to C++**
  Enhanced to provide more power and control
- **Visual Basic .NET**
  New version of Visual Basic with substantial language innovations
- **JScript .NET**
  New version of JScript that provides improved performance and productivity
- **J# .NET**
  .NET Java-language support enabling new development and Java migration
- **Third-party Languages**

The .NET Framework provides support for several programming languages. C# is the programming language specifically designed for the .NET Platform, but C++ and Visual Basic have also been upgraded to fully support the .NET Framework.

Language	Description
C#	C# was designed for the .NET Platform and is the first modern component–oriented language in the C and C++ family. It can be embedded in ASP.NET pages. Some of the important features of this language include classes, interfaces, delegates, boxing and unboxing, namespaces, properties, indexers, events, operator overloading, versioning, attributes, unsafe code, and XML documentation generation. No header or Interface Definition Language (IDL) files are needed.
Managed Extensions to C++	The managed C++ is a minimal extension to the C++ language. This extension provides access to the .NET Framework that includes garbage collection, single-implementation inheritance, and multiple-interface inheritance. This upgrade also eliminates the need to write plumbing code for components. It offers low-level access where useful.
Visual Basic .NET	Visual Basic .NET provides substantial language innovations over previous versions of Visual Basic. Visual Basic .NET supports inheritance, constructors, polymorphism, constructor overloading, structured exceptions, stricter type checking, free threading, and many other features. There is only one form of assignment—no **Let** or **Set** methods. New rapid application development (RAD) features, such as XML Designer, Server Explorer, and Web Forms designer, are available to Visual Basic from Visual Studio .NET. With this release, Visual Basic Scripting Edition provides full Visual Basic functionality.
JScript .NET	JScript .NET is rewritten to be fully .NET aware. It includes support for classes, inheritance, types, and compilation, and it provides improved performance and productivity features. JScript .NET is also integrated with Visual Studio .NET. You can take advantage of any .NET Framework class in JScript .NET.

(continued)

Language	Description
Visual J# .NET	Visual J# .NET is a development tool for Java-language developers who want to build applications and services on the .NET Framework. Visual J# .NET is fully .NET-aware and includes tools to automatically upgrade and convert existing Visual J++ 6.0 projects and solutions to the new Visual Studio .NET format. Visual J# .NET is part of the Java User Migration Path to Microsoft .NET (JUMP to .NET) strategy.
Third-party languages	Several third-party languages are supporting the .NET Platform. These languages include APL, COBOL, Pascal, Eiffel, Haskell, ML, Oberon, Perl, Python, Scheme, and Smalltalk.

Review

■ **Introduction to the .NET Platform**

■ **Overview of the .NET Framework**

■ **Benefits of the .NET Framework**

■ **The .NET Framework Components**

■ **Languages in the .NET Framework**

1. What is the .NET Platform?

2. What are the core technologies in the .NET Platform?

3. List the components of the .NET Framework.

4. What is the purpose of the common language runtime?

5. What is the purpose of common language specification?

6. What is an XML Web service?

7. What is a managed environment?

msdn training

Module 2:
Overview of C#

Contents

Overview	1
Structure of a C# Program	2
Basic Input/Output Operations	9
Recommended Practices	15
Compiling, Running, and Debugging	22
Lab 2.1: Creating a Simple C# Program	36
Review	44

Overview

- **Structure of a C# Program**
- **Basic Input/Output Operations**
- **Recommended Practices**
- **Compiling, Running, and Debugging**

In this module, you will learn about the basic structure of a C# program by analyzing a simple working example. You will learn how to use the **Console** class to perform some basic input and output operations. You will also learn about some best practices for handling errors and documenting your code. Finally, you will compile, run, and debug a C# program.

After completing this module, you will be able to:

- Explain the structure of a simple C# program.
- Use the **Console** class of the **System** namespace to perform basic input/output operations.
- Handle exceptions in a C# program.
- Generate Extensible Markup Language (XML) documentation for a C# program.
- Compile and execute a C# program.
- Use the debugger to trace program execution.

◆ Structure of a C# Program

- **Hello, World**
- **The Class**
- **The Main Method**
- **The using Directive and the System Namespace**
- **Demonstration: Using Visual Studio to Create a C# Program**

In this lesson, you will learn about the basic structure of a C# program. You will analyze a simple program that contains all of the essential features. You will also learn how to use Microsoft® Visual Studio® to create and edit a C# program.

Hello, World

```
using System;

class Hello
{
  public static void Main()
  {
    Console.WriteLine("Hello, World");
  }
}
```

The first program most people write when learning a new language is the inevitable Hello, World. In this module, you will get a chance to examine the C# version of this traditional first program.

The example code on the slide contains all of the essential elements of a C# program, and it is easy to test! When executed from the command line, it simply displays the following:

```
Hello, World
```

In the following topics, you will analyze this simple program to learn more about the building blocks of a C# program.

The Class

- **A C# application is a collection of classes, structures, and types**

- **A class Is a set of data and methods**

- **Syntax**

```
class name
{
    . . .
}
```

- **A C# application can consist of many files**

- **A class cannot span multiple files**

In C#, an application is a collection of one or more classes, data structures, and other types. In this module, a class is defined as a set of data combined with methods (or functions) that can manipulate that data. In later modules, you will learn more about classes and all that they offer to the C# programmer.

When you look at the code for the Hello, World application, you will see that there is a single class called **Hello**. This class is introduced by using the keyword **class**. Following the class name is an open brace ({). Everything up to the corresponding closing brace (}) is part of the class.

You can spread the classes for a C# application across one or more files. You can put multiple classes in a file, but you cannot span a single class across multiple files.

Note for Java developers   The name of the application file does not need to be the same as the name of the class.

Note for C++ developers   C# does not distinguish between the definition and the implementation of a class in the same way that C++ does. There is no concept of a definition (.hpp) file. All code for the class is written in one file.

The Main Method

- When writing Main, you should:
  - Use an uppercase "M", as in "Main"
  - Designate one **Main** as the entry point to the program
  - Declare **Main** as **public static void Main**
- **Multiple classes can have a Main**
- **When Main finishes, or returns, the application quits**

Every application must start somewhere. When a C# application is run, execution starts at the method called **Main**. If you are used to programming in C, C++, or even Java, you are already familiar with this concept.

Important   The C# language is case sensitive. **Main** must be spelled with an uppercase "M" and with the rest of the name in lowercase.

Although there can be many classes in a C# application, there can only be one entry point. It is possible to have multiple classes each with **Main** in the same application, but only one **Main** will be executed. You need to specify which one should be used when the application is compiled.

The signature of **Main** is important too. If you use Visual Studio, it will be created automatically as **static void**. (You will learn what these mean later in the course.) Unless you have a good reason, you should not change the signature.

Tip   You can change the signature to some extent, but it must always be static, otherwise it might not be recognized as the application's entry point by the compiler.

The application runs either until the end of **Main** is reached or until a **return** statement is executed by **Main**.

The using Directive and the System Namespace

- **The .NET Framework provides many utility classes**
  - Organized into namespaces
- **System is the most commonly used namespace**
- **Refer to classes by their namespace**

```
System.Console.WriteLine("Hello, World");
```

- **The using directive**

```
using System;
...
Console.WriteLine("Hello, World");
```

As part of the Microsoft .NET Framework, C# is supplied with many utility classes that perform a range of useful operations. These classes are organized into *namespaces*. A namespace is a set of related classes. A namespace may also contain other namespaces.

The .NET Framework is made up of many namespaces, the most important of which is called **System**. The **System** namespace contains the classes that most applications use for interacting with the operating system. The most commonly used classes handle input and output (I/O). As with many other languages, C# has no I/O capability of its own and therefore depends on the operating system to provide a C# compatible interface.

You can refer to objects in namespaces by prefixing them explicitly with the identifier of the namespace. For example, the **System** namespace contains the **Console** class, which provides several methods, including **WriteLine**. You can access the **WriteLine** method of the **Console** class as follows:

```
System.Console.WriteLine("Hello, World");
```

However, using a fully qualified name to refer to objects can be unwieldy and error prone. To ease this burden, you can specify a namespace by placing a **using** directive at the beginning of your application before the first class is defined. A **using** directive specifies a namespace that will be examined if a class is not explicitly defined in the application. You can put more than one **using** directive in the source file, but they must all be placed at the beginning of the file.

With the **using** directive, you can rewrite the previous code as follows:

```
using System;
...
Console.WriteLine("Hello, World");
```

In the Hello, World application, the **Console** class is not explicitly defined. When the Hello, World application is compiled, the compiler searches for **Console** and finds it in the **System** namespace instead. The compiler generates code that refers to the fully qualified name **System.Console**.

Note   The classes of the **System** namespace, and the other core functions accessed at run time, reside in an assembly called mscorlib.dll. This assembly is used by default. You can refer to classes in other assemblies, but you will need to specify the locations and names of those assemblies when the application is compiled.

Demonstration: Using Visual Studio to Create a C# Program

In this demonstration, you will learn how to use Visual Studio to create and edit C# programs.

◆ Basic Input/Output Operations

- ■ **The Console Class**
- ■ **Write and WriteLine Methods**
- ■ **Read and ReadLine Methods**

In this lesson, you will learn how to perform command-based input/output operations in C# by using the **Console** class. You will learn how to display information by using the **Write** and **WriteLine** methods, and how to gather input information from the keyboard by using the **Read** and **ReadLine** methods.

The Console Class

- **Provides access to the standard input, standard output, and standard error streams**
- **Only meaningful for console applications**
  - Standard input – keyboard
  - Standard output – screen
  - Standard error – screen
- **All streams may be redirected**

The **Console** class provides a C# application with access to the standard input, standard output, and standard error streams.

Standard input is normally associated with the keyboard—anything that the user types on the keyboard can be read from the standard input stream. Similarly, the standard output stream is usually directed to the screen, as is the standard error stream.

Note These streams and the **Console** class are only meaningful to console applications. These are applications that run in a Command window.

You can direct any of the three streams (standard input, standard output, standard error) to a file or device. You can do this programmatically, or the user can do this when running the application.

Write and WriteLine Methods

- **Console.Write and Console.WriteLine display information on the console screen**
  - **WriteLine** outputs a line feed/carriage return
- **Both methods are overloaded**
- **A format string and parameters can be used**
  - Text formatting
  - Numeric formatting

You can use the **Console.Write** and **Console.WriteLine** methods to display information on the console screen. These two methods are very similar; the main difference is that **WriteLine** appends a new line/carriage return pair to the end of the output, and **Write** does not.

Both methods are overloaded. You can call them with variable numbers and types of parameters. For example, you can use the following code to write "99" to the screen:

```
Console.WriteLine(99);
```

You can use the following code to write the message "Hello, World" to the screen:

```
Console.WriteLine("Hello, World");
```

Text Formatting

You can use more powerful forms of **Write** and **WriteLine** that take a format string and additional parameters. The format string specifies how the data is output, and it can contain markers, which are replaced in order by the parameters that follow. For example, you can use the following code to display the message "The sum of 100 and 130 is 230":

```
Console.WriteLine("The sum of {0} and {1} is {2}", 100, 130,
100+130);
```

Important The first parameter that follows the format string is referred to as parameter zero: {0}.

You can use the format string parameter to specify field widths and whether values should be left or right justified in these fields, as shown in the following code:

```
Console.WriteLine("\"Left justified in a field of width 10:
{0, -10}\"", 99);
Console.WriteLine("\"Right justified in a field of width 10:
{0,10}\"", 99);
```

This will display the following on the console:

"Left justified in a field of width 10: 99   "

"Right justified in a field of width 10:   99"

> **Note** You can use the backward slash (\) character in a format string to turn off the special meaning of the character that follows it. For example, "\{" will cause a literal "{" to be displayed, and "\\" will display a literal "\". You can use the at sign (@) character to represent an entire string verbatim. For example, @"\\server\share" will be processed as "\\server\share."

Numeric Formatting

You can also use the format string to specify how numeric data is to be formatted. The full syntax for the format string is {N,M:FormatString}, where N is the parameter number, M is the field width and justification, and FormatString specifies how numeric data should be displayed. The table below summarizes the items that may appear in **FormatString**. In all of these formats, the number of digits to be displayed, or rounded to, can optionally be specified.

Item	Meaning
C	Display the number as currency, using the local currency symbol and conventions.
D	Display the number as a decimal integer.
E	Display the number by using exponential (scientific) notation.
F	Display the number as a fixed-point value.
G	Display the number as either fixed point or integer, depending on which format is the most compact.
N	Display the number with embedded commas.
X	Display the number by using hexadecimal notation.

The following code shows some examples of how to use numeric formatting:

```
Console.WriteLine("Currency formatting - {0:C}   {1:C4}", 88.8,
➥-888.8);
Console.WriteLine("Integer formatting - {0:D5}", 88);
Console.WriteLine("Exponential formatting - {0:E}", 888.8);
Console.WriteLine("Fixed-point formatting - {0:F3}",
➥888.8888);
Console.WriteLine("General formatting - {0:G}", 888.8888);
Console.WriteLine("Number formatting - {0:N}", 8888888.8);
Console.WriteLine("Hexadecimal formatting - {0:X4}", 88);
```

When the previous code is run, it displays the following:

```
Currency formatting - $88.80   ($888.8000)
Integer formatting - 00088
Exponential formatting - 8.888000E+002
Fixed-point formatting - 888.889
General formatting - 888.8888
Number formatting - 8,888,888.80
Hexadecimal formatting - 0058
```

Note For more information on formatting, search "formatting strings" in Microsoft MSDN® Help.

Read and ReadLine Methods

- **Console.Read and Console.ReadLine read user input**
  - **Read** reads the next character
  - **ReadLine** reads the entire input line

You can obtain user input from the keyboard by using the **Console.Read** and **Console.ReadLine** methods.

The Read Method

Read reads the next character from the keyboard. It returns the **int** value −1 if there is no more input available. Otherwise it returns an **int** representing the character read.

The ReadLine Method

ReadLine reads all characters up to the end of the input line (the carriage return character). The input is returned as a string of characters. You can use the following code to read a line of text from the keyboard and display it to the screen:

```
string input = Console.ReadLine( );
Console.WriteLine("{0}", input);
```

◆ Recommended Practices

- **Commenting Applications**
- **Generating XML Documentation**
- **Demonstration: Generating and Viewing XML Documentation**
- **Exception Handling**

In this lesson, you will learn some recommended practices to use when writing C# applications. You will be shown how to comment applications to aid readability and maintainability. You will also learn how to handle the errors that can occur when an application is run.

Commenting Applications

- **Comments are important**
  - A well-commented application permits a developer to fully understand the structure of the application
- **Single-line comments**

```
// Get the user's name
Console.WriteLine("What is your name? ");
name = Console.ReadLine( );
```

- **Multiple-line comments**

```
/* Find the higher root of the
   quadratic equation */
x = (...);
```

It is important to provide adequate documentation for all of your applications. Provide enough comments to enable a developer who was not involved in creating the original application to follow and understand how the application works. Use thorough and meaningful comments. Good comments add information that cannot be expressed easily by the code statements alone—they explain the "why" rather than the "what." If your organization has standards for commenting code, then follow them.

C# provides several mechanisms for adding comments to application code: single-line comments, multiple-line comments, and XML-generated documentation.

You can add a single-line comment by using the forward slash characters (//). When you run your application, everything following these two characters until the end of the line is ignored.

You can also use block comments that span multiple lines. A block comment starts with the /* character pair and continues until a matching */ character pair is reached. You cannot nest block comments.

Generating XML Documentation

```
/// <summary> The Hello class prints a greeting
/// on the screen
/// </summary>
class Hello
{
  /// <remarks> We use console-based I/O.
  /// For more information about WriteLine, see
  /// <seealso cref="System.Console.WriteLine"/>
  /// </remarks>
  public static void Main( )
  {
    Console.WriteLine("Hello, World");
  }
}
```

You can use C# comments to generate XML documentation for your applications.

Documentation comments begin with three forward slashes (///) followed by an XML documentation tag. For examples, see the slide.

There are a number of suggested XML tags that you can use. (You can also create your own.) The following table shows some XML tags and their uses.

Tag	Purpose
<summary> ... </summary>	To provide a brief description. Use the <remarks> tag for a longer description.
<remarks> ... </remarks>	To provide a detailed description. This tag can contain nested paragraphs, lists, and other types of tags.
<para> ... </para>	To add structure to the description in a <remarks> tag. This tag allows paragraphs to be delineated.
<list type="..."> ... </list>	To add a structured list to a detailed description. The types of lists supported are "bullet," "number," and "table." Additional tags (<term> ... </term> and <description> ... </description>) are used inside the list to further define the structure.
<example> ... </example>	To provide an example of how a method, property, or other library member should be used. It often involves the use of a nested <code> tag.
<code> ... </code>	To indicate that the enclosed text is application code.

(*continued*)

Tag	Purpose
<c> ... </c>	To indicate that the enclosed text is application code. The <code> tag is used for lines of code that must be separated from any enclosing description; the <c> tag is used for code that is embedded within an enclosing description.
<see cref="*member*"/>	To indicate a reference to another member or field. The compiler checks that "member" actually exists.
<seealso cref="*member*"/>	To indicate a reference to another member or field. The compiler checks that "member" actually exists. The difference between <see> and <seealso> depends upon the processor that manipulates the XML once it has been generated. The processor must be able to generate See and See Also sections for these two tags to be distinguished in a meaningful way.
<exception> ... </exception>	To provide a description for an exception class.
<permission> ... </permission>	To document the accessibility of a member.
<param name="*name*"> ... </param>	To provide a description for a method parameter.
<returns> ... </returns>	To document the return value and type of a method.
<value> ... </value>	To describe a property.

You can compile the XML tags and documentation into an XML file by using the C# compiler with the /doc option:

```
csc myprogram.cs /doc:mycomments.xml
```

If there are no errors, you can view the XML file that is generated by using a tool such as Internet Explorer.

Note   The purpose of the /doc option is only to generate an XML file. To render the file, you will need another processor. Internet Explorer displays a simple rendition that shows the structure of the file and allows tags to be expanded or collapsed, but it will not, for example, display the <list type="bullet"> tag as a bullet.

Demonstration: Generating and Viewing XML Documentation

In this demonstration, you will see how to compile the XML comments that are embedded in a C# application into an XML file. You will also learn how to view the documentation file that is generated.

Exception Handling

```
using System;
public class Hello
{
   public static void Main(string[ ] args)
   {
      try{
          Console.WriteLine(args[0]);
          }
      catch (Exception e) {
          Console.WriteLine("Exception at
         ➥{0}", e.StackTrace);
      }
   }
}
```

A robust C# application must be able to handle the unexpected. No matter how much error checking you add to your code, there is inevitably something that can go wrong. Perhaps the user will type an unexpected response to a prompt, or will try to write to a file in a folder that has been deleted. The possibilities are endless.

When a run-time error occurs in a C# application, the operating system throws an exception. Trap exceptions by using a **try-catch** construct as shown on the slide. If any of the statements in the **try** part of the application cause an exception to be raised, execution will be transferred to the **catch** block.

You can find out information about the exception that occurred by using the **StackTrace**, **Message**, and **Source** properties of the **Exception** object. You will learn more about handling exceptions in a later module.

Note   If you print out an exception, by using **Console.WriteLine** for example, the exception will format itself automatically and display the **StackTrace**, **Message**, and **Source** properties.

Tip It is far easier to design exception handling into your C# applications from the start than it is to try to add it later.

If you do not use exception handling, a run-time exception will occur. If you want to debug your program using Just-in-time debugging instead, you need to enable it first. If you have enabled Just-in-time debugging, depending upon which environment and tools are installed, Just-in-time debugging will prompt you for a debugger to be used.

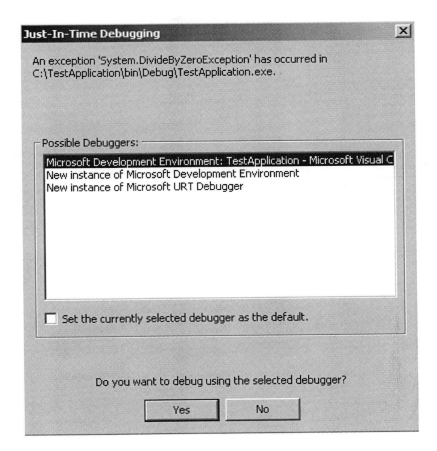

To enable Just-in-time debugging, perform the following steps:

1. On the **Tools** menu, click **Options**.

2. In the **Options** dialog box, click the **Debugging** folder.

3. In the **Debugging** folder, click **Just-In-Time Debugging**.

4. Enable or disable Just-in-time (JIT) debugging for specific program types, and then click **OK**.

You will learn more about the debugger later in this module.

◆ Compiling, Running, and Debugging

- ■ **Invoking the Compiler**

- ■ **Running the Application**

- ■ **Demonstration: Compiling and Running a C# Program**

- ■ **Debugging**

- ■ **Demonstration: Using the Visual Studio Debugger**

- ■ **The SDK Tools**

- ■ **Demonstration: Using ILDASM**

In this lesson, you will learn how to compile and debug C# programs. You will see the compiler executed from the command line and from within the Visual Studio environment. You will learn some common compiler options. You will be introduced to the Visual Studio Debugger. Finally, you will learn how to use some of the other tools that are supplied with the Microsoft .NET Framework software development kit (SDK).

Invoking the Compiler

- **Common Compiler Switches**
- **Compiling from the Command Line**
- **Compiling from Visual Studio**
- **Locating Errors**

Before you execute a C# application, you must compile it. The compiler converts the source code that you write into machine code that the computer understands. You can invoke the C# compiler from the command line or from Visual Studio.

Note Strictly speaking, C# applications are compiled into Microsoft intermediate language (MSIL) rather than native machine code. The MSIL code is itself compiled into machine code by the Just-in-time (JIT) compiler when the application is run. However, it is also possible to compile directly to machine code and bypass the JIT compiler using the Native Image Generator (Ngen.exe) utility. This utility creates a native image from a managed assembly and installs it into the native image cache on the local computer. Running Ngen.exe on an assembly allows the assembly to load faster, because it restores code and data structures from the native image cache rather than generating them dynamically.

Common Compiler Switches

You can specify a number of switches for the C# compiler by using the **csc** command. The following table describes the most common switches.

Switch	Meaning
/?, /help	Displays the compiler options on the standard output.
/out	Specifies the name of the executable.
/main	Specifies the class that contains the **Main** method (if more than one class in the application includes a **Main** method).
/optimize	Enables and disables the code optimizer.
/warn	Sets the warning level of the compiler.
/warnaserror	Treats all warnings as errors that abort the compilation.
/target	Specifies the type of application generated.

(continued)

Switch	Meaning
/checked	Indicates whether arithmetic overflow will generate a run-time exception.
/doc	Processes documentation comments to produce an XML file.
/debug	Generates debugging information.

Compiling from the Command Line

To compile a C# application from the command line, use the **csc** command. For example, to compile the Hello, World application (Hello.cs) from the command line, generating debug information and creating an executable called Greet.exe, the command is:

```
csc /debug+ /out:Greet.exe Hello.cs
```

Important   Ensure that the output file containing the compiled code is specified with an .exe suffix. If it is omitted, you will need to rename the file before you can run it.

Compiling from Visual Studio

To compile a C# application by using Visual Studio, open the project containing the C# application, and click **Build Solution** on the **Build** menu.

Note   By default, Visual Studio opens the debug configuration for projects. This means that a debug version of the application will be compiled. To compile a release build that contains no debug information, change the solution configuration to release.

You can change the options used by the compiler by updating the project configuration:

1. In Solution Explorer, right-click the project icon.
2. Click **Properties**.
3. In the **Property Pages** dialog box, click **Configuration Properties**, and then click **Build**.
4. Specify the required compiler options, and then click **OK**.

Locating Errors

If the C# compiler detects any syntactic or semantic errors, it will report them.

If the compiler was invoked from the command line, it will display messages indicating the line numbers and the character position for each line in which it found errors.

If the compiler was invoked from Visual Studio, the Task List window will display all lines that include errors. Double-clicking each line in this window will take you to the respective error in the application.

Tip   It is common for a single programming mistake to generate a number of compiler errors. It is best to work through errors by starting with the first ones found because correcting an early error may automatically fix a number of later errors.

Running the Application

- **Running from the Command Line**
  - Type the name of the application
- **Running from Visual Studio**
  - Click **Start Without Debugging** on the **Debug** menu

You can run a C# application from the command line or from within the Visual Studio environment.

Running from the Command Line

If the application is compiled successfully, an executable file (a file with an .exe suffix) will be generated. To run it from the command line, type the name of the application (with or without the .exe suffix).

Running from Within Visual Studio

To run the application from Visual Studio, click **Start Without Debugging** on the **Debug** menu, or press CTRL+F5. If the application is a Console Application, a console window will appear automatically, and the application will run. When the application has finished, you will be prompted to press any key to continue, and the console window will close.

Demonstration: Compiling and Running a C# Program

In this demonstration, you will see how to compile and run a C# program by using Visual Studio. You will also see how to locate and correct compile-time errors.

Debugging

- **Exceptions and JIT Debugging**
- **The Visual Studio Debugger**
  - Setting breakpoints and watches
  - Stepping through code
  - Examining and modifying variables

Exceptions and JIT Debugging

If your application throws an exception and you have not written any code that can handle it, common language runtime will instigate JIT debugging. (Do not confuse JIT debugging with the JIT compiler.)

Assuming that you have installed Visual Studio, a dialog box will appear giving you the choice of debugging the application by using the Visual Studio Debugger (Microsoft Development Environment), or the debugger provided with the .NET Framework SDK.

If you have Visual Studio available, it is recommended that you select the Microsoft Development Environment debugger.

Note The .NET Framework SDK provides another debugger: cordbg.exe. This is a command-line debugger. It includes most of the facilities offered by the Microsoft Development Environment, except for the graphical user interface. It will not be discussed further in this course.

Setting Breakpoints and Watches in Visual Studio

You can use the Visual Studio Debugger to set breakpoints in your code and examine the values of variables.

To bring up a menu with many useful options, right-click a line of code. Click **Insert Breakpoint** to insert a breakpoint at that line. You can also insert a breakpoint by clicking in the left margin. Click again to remove the breakpoint. When you run the application in debug mode, execution will stop at this line and you can examine the contents of variables.

The Watch window is useful for monitoring the values of selected variables while the application runs. If you type the name of a variable in the **Name** column, its value will be displayed in the **Value** column. As the application runs, you will see any changes made to the value. You can also modify the value of a watched variable by typing over it.

Important To use the debugger, ensure that you have selected the Debug solution configuration rather than Release.

Stepping Through Code

Once you have set any breakpoints that you need, you can run your application by clicking **Start** on the **Debug** menu, or by pressing F5. When the first breakpoint is reached, execution will halt.

You can continue running the application by clicking **Continue** on the **Debug** menu, or you can use any of the single-stepping options on the **Debug** menu to step through your code one line at a time.

Tip The breakpoint, stepping, and watch variable options are also available on the **Debug** toolbar.

Examining and Modifying Variables

You can view the variables defined in the current method by clicking **Locals** on the **Debug** toolbar or by using the Watch window. You can change the values of variables by typing over them (as you can in the Watch window).

Demonstration: Using the Visual Studio Debugger

This demonstration will show you how to use the Visual Studio Debugger to set breakpoints and watches. It will also show you how to step through code and how to examine and modify the values of variables.

The SDK Tools

- **General Tools and Utilities**
- **Windows Forms Design Tools and Utilities**
- **Security Tools and Utilities**
- **Configuration and Deployment Tools and Utilities**

The .NET Framework SDK is supplied with a number of tools that provide additional functionality for developing, configuring, and deploying applications. These tools can be run from the command line.

General Tools and Utilities

You may find some of the following general-purpose tools useful.

Tool name	Command	Description
Runtime Debugger	cordbg.exe	The command-line debugger.
MSIL Assembler	ilasm.exe	An assembler that takes MSIL as input and generates an executable file.
MSIL Disassembler	ildasm.exe	A disassembler that can be used to inspect the MSIL and metadata in an executable file.
PEVerify	peverify.exe	Validates the type safety of code and metadata prior to release.
Window Forms Class Viewer	wincv.exe	Locates managed classes and displays information about them.

Windows Forms Design Tools and Utilities

You can use the following tools to manage and convert ActiveX® controls and Microsoft Windows® Forms controls.

Tool name	Command	Description
Windows Forms ActiveX Control Importer	aximp.exe	The ActiveX Control Importer converts type definitions in a COM type library for an ActiveX control into a Windows Forms control.
License Compiler	lc.exe	The License Compiler reads text files that contain licensing information and produces a .licenses file that can be embedded in a common language runtime executable as a resource.
Resource File Generation Utility	ResGen.exe	Produces a binary .resources file for managed code from text files that describe the resources.
Windows Forms Resource Editor	winres.exe	The Windows Forms Resource Editor is a visual layout tool that helps localization experts localize Windows Forms forms. The .resx or .resources files that are used as input to the Winres.exe are typically created using a visual design environment such as Visual Studio .NET.

Security Tools and Utilities

You can use the following tools to provide security and encryption features for assemblies and classes in .NET.

Tool name	Command	Description
Code Access Security Policy Utility	caspol.exe	The Code Access Security Policy tool enables users and administrators to modify security policy for the machine policy level, the user policy level, and the enterprise policy level.
Software Publisher Certificate Test Utility	cert2spc.exe	Creates a Software Publisher's Certificate from an X.509 certificate. This tool is used only for testing purposes.
Certificate Creation Utility	makecert.exe	An enhanced version of cert2spc.exe. It is also used only for testing purposes.
Certificate Manager Utility	certmgr.exe	Maintains certificates, certificate trust lists, and certificate revocation lists.
Certificate Verification Utility	chktrust.exe	Verifies the validity of a signed file.
Permissions View Utility	permview.exe	Views the permissions requested for an assembly.
Secutil Utility	SecUtil.exe	Locates public key or certificate information in an assembly.
Set Registry Utility	setreg.exe	Modifies registry settings related to public key cryptography.
File Signing Utility	signcode.exe	Signs an executable file or assembly with a digital signature.
Strong Name Utility	Sn.exe	Helps create assemblies that have strong names. It guarantees name uniqueness and provides some integrity. It also allows assemblies to be signed.

Configuration and Deployment Tools and Utilities

Many of the following tools are specialized tools that you will use only if you are integrating .NET Platform managed code and COM classes.

Tool name	Command	Description
Assembly Generation Utility	al.exe	Generates an assembly manifest from MSIL and resource files.
Assembly Registration Tool	RegAsm.exe	Enables .NET Platform managed classes to be called transparently by COM components.
Services Registration Tool	RegSvcs.exe	Makes managed classes available as COM components by loading and registering the assembly and by generating and installing a COM+ type library and application.
Assembly Cache Viewer	shfusion.dll	Views the contents of the global cache. It is a shell extension used by Microsoft Windows Explorer.
Isolated Storage Utility	storeadm.exe	Manages isolated storage for the user that is currently logged on.
Type Library Exporter	TlbExp.exe	Converts a .NET assembly into a COM type library.
Type Library Importer	Tlbimp.exe	Converts COM type library definitions into the equivalent metadata format for use by .NET.
XML Schema Definition Tool	xsd.exe	The XML Schema Definition tool generates XML schema or common language runtime classes from XDR, XML, and XSD files, or from classes in a runtime assembly.

Demonstration: Using ILDASM

In this demonstration, you will learn how to use Microsoft Intermediate Language (MSIL) Disassembler (ildasm.exe) to examine the manifest and MSIL code in a class.

Lab 2.1: Creating a Simple C# Program

Objectives

After completing this lab, you will be able to:

- Create a C# program.
- Compile and run a C# program.
- Use the Visual Studio Debugger.
- Add exception handling to a C# program.

Estimated time to complete this lab: 60 minutes

Exercise 1
Creating a Simple C# Program

In this exercise, you will use Visual Studio to write a C# program. The program will ask for your name and will then greet you by name.

▶ **To create a new C# console application**

1. Start **Microsoft Visual Studio .NET**.
2. On the **File** menu, point to **New**, and then click **Project**.
3. Click **Visual C# Projects** in the **Project Types** box.
4. Click **Console Application** in the **Templates** box.
5. Type **Greetings** in the **Name** box.
6. Type *install folder*\Labs\Lab02 in the **Location** box and click **OK**.
7. Type an appropriate comment for the summary.
8. Change the name of the class to **Greeter**.
9. Save the project by clicking **Save All** on the **File** menu.

▶ **To write statements that prompt and greet the user**

1. In the **Main** method, after the TODO: comments, insert the following line:

   ```
   string myName;
   ```

2. Write a statement that prompts users for their name.
3. Write another statement that reads the user's response from the keyboard and assigns it to the *myName* string.
4. Add one more statement that prints "Hello *myName*" to the screen (where *myName* is the name the user typed in).
5. When completed, the **Main** method should contain the following:

   ```
   static void Main(string[ ] args)
   {
     string myName;

     Console.WriteLine("Please enter your name");
     myName = Console.ReadLine( );
     Console.WriteLine("Hello {0}", myName);
   }
   ```

6. Save your work.

▶ **To compile and run the program**

1. On the **Build** menu, click **Build Solution** (or press CTRL+SHIFT+B).

2. Correct any compilation errors and build again if necessary.

3. On the **Debug** menu, click **Start Without Debugging** (or press CTRL+F5).

4. In the console window that appears, type your name when prompted and press **ENTER**.

5. After the hello message is displayed, press a key at the "Press any key to continue" prompt.

Exercise 2
Compiling and Running the C# Program from the Command Line

In this exercise, you will compile and run your program from the command line.

▶ **To compile and run the application from the command line**

1. From the Windows **Start** button, point to **All Programs**, then click **Visual Studio .NET**, then click **Visual Studio .NET Tools**, and then click **Visual Studio .NET Command Prompt**.

2. Go to the *install folder*\Labs\Lab02\Greetings folder.

3. Compile the program by using the following command:

```
csc /out:Greet.exe Class1.cs
```

4. Run the program by entering the following:

```
Greet
```

5. Close the Command window.

Exercise 3
Using the Debugger

In this exercise, you will use the Visual Studio Debugger to single-step through your program and examine the value of a variable.

▶ **To set a breakpoint and start debugging by using Visual Studio**

1. Start **Visual Studio .NET** if it is not already running.

2. On the **File** menu, point to **Open**, and then click **Project**.

3. Open the Greetings.sln project in the *install folder*\Labs\Lab02\Greetings folder.

4. Click in the left margin on the line containing the first occurrence of **Console.WriteLine** in the class **Greeter**.

   A breakpoint (a large red dot) will appear in the margin.

5. On the **Debug** menu, click **Start** (or press F5).

   The program will start running, a console window will appear, and the program will then halt at the breakpoint.

▶ **To watch the value of a variable**

1. On the **Debug** menu, point to **Windows**, point to **Watch**, and then click **Watch 1**.

2. In the Watch window, add the variable *myName* to the list of watched variables.

3. The *myName* variable will appear in the Watch window with a value of **null**.

▶ **To single-step through code**

1. On the **Debug** menu, click **Step Over** (or press F10) to run the first **Console.WriteLine** statement.

2. Single-step the next line containing the **Console.ReadLine** statement by pressing F10.

3. Return to the console window and type your name, and then press the RETURN key.

   Return to Visual Studio. The value of *myName* in the Watch window will be your name.

4. Single-step the next line containing the **Console.WriteLine** statement by pressing F10.

5. Bring the console window to the foreground.

   The greeting will appear.

6. Return to Visual Studio. On the **Debug** menu, click **Continue** (or press F5) to run the program to completion.

Exercise 4
Adding Exception Handling to a C# Program

In this exercise, you will write a program that uses exception handling to trap unexpected run-time errors. The program will prompt the user for two integer values. It will divide the first integer by the second and display the result.

▶ **To create a new C# program**

1. Start Visual Studio .NET if it is not already running.
2. On the **File** menu, point to **New,** and then click **Project.**
3. Click **Visual C# Projects** in the **Project Types** box.
4. Click **Console Application** in the **Templates** box.
5. Type **Divider** in the **Name** box.
6. Type *install folder*\Labs\Lab02 in the **Location** box and click **OK.**
7. Type an appropriate comment for the summary.
8. Change the name of the class to **DivideIt.**
9. Save the project by clicking **Save All** on the **File** menu.

▶ **To write statements that prompt the user for two integers**

1. In the **Main** method, write a statement that prompts the user for the first integer.
2. Write another statement that reads the user's response from the keyboard and assigns it to a variable named *temp* of type **string.**
3. Add a statement to convert the string value in *temp* to an integer and to store the result in *i* as follows:

   ```
   int i = Int32.Parse(temp);
   ```

4. Add statements to your code to:

   a. Prompt the user for the second integer.

   b. Read the user's response from the keyboard and assign it to *temp.*

   c. Convert the value in *temp* to an integer and store the result in *j.*

   Your code should look similar to the following:

   ```
   Console.WriteLine("Please enter the first integer");
   string temp = Console.ReadLine( );
   int i = Int32.Parse(temp);

   Console.WriteLine("Please enter the second integer");
   temp = Console.ReadLine( );
   int j = Int32.Parse(temp);
   ```

5. Save your work.

▶ **To divide the first integer by the second and display the result**

1. Write code to create a new integer variable *k* that is given the value resulting from the division of *i* by *j*, and insert it at the end of the previous procedure. Your code should look like the following:

    ```
    int k = i / j;
    ```

2. Add a statement that displays the value of *k*.

3. Save your work.

▶ **To test the program**

1. On the **Debug** menu, click **Start Without Debugging** (or press CTRL+F5).

2. Type **10** for the first integer value and press ENTER.

3. Type **5** for the second integer value and press ENTER.

4. Check that the value displayed for *k* is 2.

5. Run the program again by pressing CTRL+F5.

6. Type **10** for the first integer value and press ENTER.

7. Type **0** for the second integer value and press ENTER.

8. The program causes an exception to be thrown (divide by zero).

9. Click No to clear the Just-In-Time Debugging dialog.

▶ **To add exception handling to the program**

1. Place the code in the **Main** method inside a **try** block as follows:

    ```
    try
    {
        Console.WriteLine (...);
        ...
        int k = i / j;
        Console.WriteLine(...);
    }
    ```

2. Add a **catch** statement to **Main**, after the try block. The **catch** statement should print a short message, as is shown in the following code:

    ```
    catch(Exception e)
    {
        Console.WriteLine("An exception was thrown: {0}" , e);
    }
    ...
    ```

3. Save your work.

4. The completed **Main** method should look similar to the following:

```
public static void Main(string[ ] args)
{
  try {
     Console.WriteLine ("Please enter the first integer");
     string temp = Console.ReadLine( );
     int i = Int32.Parse(temp);

     Console.WriteLine ("Please enter the second integer");
     temp = Console.ReadLine( );
     int j = Int32.Parse(temp);

     int k = i / j;
     Console.WriteLine("The result of dividing {0} by {1}
       ↪is {2}", i, j, k);
  }
  catch(Exception e) {
     Console.WriteLine("An exception was thrown: {0}", e);
  }
}
```

► **To test the exception-handling code**

1. Run the program again by pressing CTRL+F5.

2. Type **10** for the first integer value and press ENTER.

3. Type **0** for the second integer value and press ENTER.

   The program still causes an exception to be thrown (divide by zero), but this time the error is caught and your message appears.

Review

- Structure of a C# Program
- Basic Input/Output Operations
- Recommended Practices
- Compiling, Running, and Debugging

1. Where does execution start in a C# application?

2. When does application execution finish?

3. How many classes can a C# application contain?

4. How many **Main** methods can an application contain?

5. How do you read user input from the keyboard in a C# application?

6. What namespace is the **Console** class in?

7. What happens if your C# application causes an exception to be thrown that it is not prepared to catch?

msdn® training

Module 3: Using Value-Type Variables

Contents

Overview	1
Common Type System	2
Naming Variables	8
Using Built-in Data Types	14
Creating User-Defined Data Types	22
Converting Data Types	26
Lab 3.1: Creating and Using Types	30
Review	34

Overview

- **Common Type System**
- **Naming Variables**
- **Using Built-in Data Types**
- **Creating User-Defined Data Types**
- **Converting Data Types**

All applications manipulate data in some way. As a C# developer, you need to understand how to store and process data in your applications. Whenever your application needs to store data temporarily for use during execution, you store that data in a variable. Before you use a variable, you must define it. When you define a variable, you reserve some storage for that variable by identifying its data type and giving it a name. After a variable is defined, you can assign values to that variable.

In this module, you will learn how to use value-type variables in C#. You will learn how to specify the type of data that variables will hold, how to name variables according to standard naming conventions, and how to assign values to variables. You also will learn how to convert existing variables from one data type to another and how to create your own variables.

After completing this module, you will be able to:

- Describe the types of variables that you can use in C# applications.
- Name your variables according to standard C# naming conventions.
- Declare a variable by using built-in data types.
- Assign values to variables.
- Convert existing variables from one data type to another.
- Create and use your own data types.

◆ Common Type System

- **Overview of CTS**
- **Comparing Value and Reference Types**
- **Comparing Built-in and User-Defined Value Types**
- **Simple Types**

Every variable has a data type that determines what values can be stored in the variable. C# is a type-safe language, meaning that the C# compiler guarantees that values stored in variables are always of the appropriate type.

The common language runtime includes a Common Type System (CTS) that defines a set of built-in data types that you can use to define your variables.

After completing this lesson, you will be able to:

- Describe how the CTS works.
- Choose the appropriate data types for your variables.

Overview of CTS

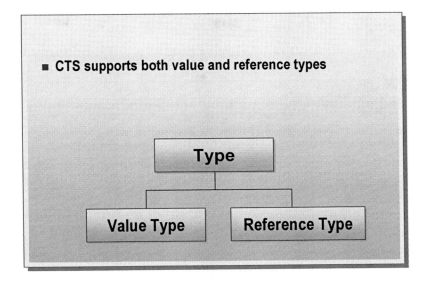

- CTS supports both value and reference types

When you define a variable, you need to choose the right data type for your variable. The data type determines the allowable values for that variable, which, in turn, determine the operations that can be performed on that variable.

CTS

CTS is an integral part of the common language runtime. The compilers, tools, and the runtime itself share CTS. It is the model that defines the rules that the runtime follows when declaring, using, and managing types. CTS establishes a framework that enables cross-language integration, type safety, and high-performance code execution.

In this module, you will learn about two types of variables:

- Value-type variables.
- Reference-type variables.

Comparing Value and Reference Types

- **Value types:**
  - Directly contain their data
  - Each has its own copy of data
  - Operations on one cannot affect another

- **Reference types:**
  - Store references to their data (known as objects)
  - Two reference variables can reference same object
  - Operations on one can affect another

Value Types

Value-type variables directly contain their data. Each value-type variable has its own copy of the data, so it is not possible for operations on one variable to affect another variable.

Reference Types

Reference-type variables contain references to their data. The data for reference-type variables is stored in an object. It is possible for two reference-type variables to reference the same object, so it is possible for operations on one reference variable to affect the object referenced by another reference variable.

Note   All of the base data types are defined in the **System** namespace. All types are ultimately derived from **System.Object**. Value types are derived from **System.ValueType**.

For more information about reference types, see Module 8, "Using Reference-Type Variables," in Course 2124C, *Programming with C#*.

Comparing Built-in and User-Defined Value Types

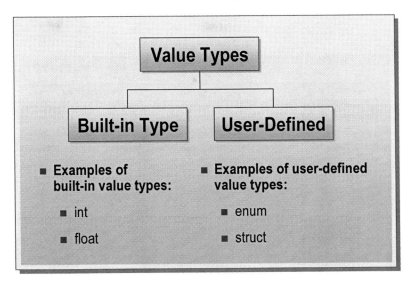

Value types include built-in and user-defined data types. The difference between built-in and user-defined types in C# is minimal because user-defined types can be used in the same way as built-in ones. The only real difference between built-in data types and user-defined data types is that you can write literal values for the built-in types. All value types directly contain data, and they cannot be **null**.

You will learn how to create user-defined data types such as enumeration and structure types in this module.

Simple Types

> ■ **Identified through reserved keywords**
>
> - int // Reserved keyword
>
> - or -
>
> - **System.Int32**

Built-in value types are also referred to as basic data types or simple types. Simple types are identified by means of reserved keywords. These reserved keywords are aliases for predefined struct types.

A simple type and the struct type it aliases are *completely indistinguishable*. In your code, you can use the reserved keyword or you can use the struct type. The following examples show both:

```
byte // Reserved keyword
```

—Or—

```
System.Byte // struct type
```

```
int // Reserved keyword
```

—Or—

```
System.Int32 // struct type
```

For more information about the sizes and ranges of built-in value types, search for "Value Types" in the Microsoft® Visual Studio® .NET Help documents.

The following table lists common reserved keywords and their equivalent aliased struct type.

Reserved keywords	Alias for struct type
sbyte	System.SByte
byte	System.Byte
short	System.Int16
ushort	System.UInt16
int	System.Int32
uint	System.UInt32
long	System.Int64
ulong	System.UInt64
char	System.Char
float	System.Single
double	System.Double
bool	System.Boolean
decimal	System.Decimal

◆ Naming Variables

- ■ **Rules and Recommendations for Naming Variables**
- ■ **C# Keywords**
- ■ **Quiz: Can You Spot Disallowed Variable Names?**

To use a variable, you first choose a meaningful and appropriate name for the variable. Each variable has a name that is also referred to as the *variable identifier*.

When naming variables, follow the standard naming conventions recommended for C#. You also need to be aware of the C# reserved keywords that you cannot use for variable names.

After completing this lesson, you will be able to:

- ■ Identify C# standard reserved keywords.
- ■ Name your variables according to standard C# naming conventions.

Rules and Recommendations for Naming Variables

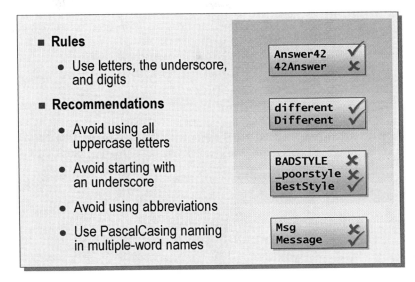

When you name variables, observe the following rules and recommendations.

Rules

The following are the naming rules for C# variables:

- Start each variable name with a letter or underscore character.
- After the first character, use letters, digits, or the underscore character.
- Do not use reserved keywords.
- If you use a disallowed variable name, you will get a compile-time error.

Recommendations

It is recommended that you follow these recommendations when naming your variables:

- Avoid using all uppercase letters.
- Avoid starting with an underscore.
- Avoid using abbreviations.
- Use PascalCasing naming in multiple-word names.

PascalCasing Naming Convention

To use the PascalCasing naming convention, capitalize the first character of each word. Use PascalCasing for classes, methods, properties, enums, interfaces, read only and constant fields, namespaces, and properties, as shown in the following example:

```
void InitializeData( );
```

camelCasing Naming Convention

To use the camelCasing naming convention, capitalize the first character of each word except for the first word. Use camelCasing for variables that define fields and parameters, as shown in the following example:

```
int loopCountMax;
```

For more information about naming conventions, see "Naming Guidelines" in the .NET Framework Software Development Kit (SDK) Help documents.

C# Keywords

- **Keywords are reserved identifiers**

  ```
  abstract, base, bool, default, if, finally
  ```

- **Do not use keywords as variable names**
  - Results in a compile-time error
- **Avoid using keywords by changing their case sensitivity**

  ```
  int INT;  // Poor style
  ```

Keywords are reserved, which means that you cannot use any keywords as variable names in C#. Using a keyword as a variable name will result in a compile-time error.

Keywords in C#

The following is a list of keywords in C#. Remember, you cannot use any of these words as variable names.

abstract	as	base	bool	break
byte	case	catch	char	checked
class	const	continue	decimal	default
delegate	do	double	else	enum
event	explicit	extern	false	finally
fixed	float	for	foreach	goto
if	implicit	in	int	interface
internal	is	lock	long	namespace
new	null	object	operator	out
override	params	private	protected	public
readonly	ref	return	sbyte	sealed
short	sizeof	stackalloc	static	string
struct	switch	this	throw	true
try	typeof	uint	ulong	unchecked
unsafe	ushort	using	virtual	void
volatile	while			

Quiz: Can You Spot the Disallowed Variable Names?

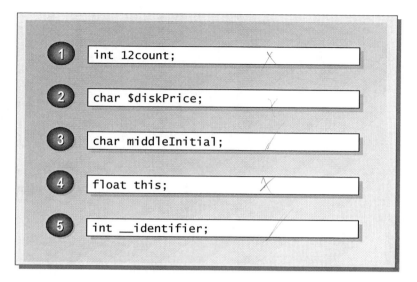

Quiz Answers

1. **Disallowed**. Variable names cannot begin with a digit.

2. **Disallowed**. Variable names must start with a letter or an underscore.

3. **Allowed**. Variable names can start with a letter.

4. **Disallowed**. Keywords (**this**) cannot be used to name variables.

5. **Allowed**. Variable names can start with an underscore.

◆ Using Built-in Data Types

- **Declaring Local Variables**
- **Assigning Values to Variables**
- **Compound Assignment**
- **Common Operators**
- **Increment and Decrement**
- **Operator Precedence**

To create a variable, you must choose a variable name, declare your variable, and assign a value to your variable, unless it has already been automatically assigned a value by C#.

After completing this lesson, you will be able to:

- Create a local variable by using built-in data types.
- Use operators to assign values to variables.
- Define read-only variables and constants.

Declaring Local Variables

- **Usually declared by data type and variable name:**

```
int itemCount;
```

- **Possible to declare multiple variables in one declaration:**

```
int itemCount, employeeNumber;
```

--or--

```
int itemCount,
    employeeNumber;
```

Variables that are declared in methods, properties, or indexers are called local variables. Generally, you declare a local variable by specifying the data type followed by the variable name, as shown in the following example:

```
int itemCount;
```

You can declare multiple variables in a single declaration by using a comma separator, as shown in the following example:

```
int itemCount, employeeNumber;
```

In C#, you cannot use uninitialized variables. The following code will result in a compile-time error because the *loopCount* variable has not been assigned an initial value:

```
int loopCount;
Console.WriteLine ("{0}", loopCount);
```

Assigning Values to Variables

- **Assign values to variables that are already declared:**

```
int employeeNumber;
employeeNumber = 23;
```

- **Initialize a variable when you declare it:**

```
int employeeNumber = 23;
```

- **You can also initialize character values:**

```
char middleInitial = 'J';
```

You use assignment operators to assign a new value to a variable. To assign a value to a variable that is already declared, use the assignment operator (=), as shown in the following example:

```
int employeeNumber;
employeeNumber = 23;
```

You can also initialize a variable when you declare it, as shown in the following example:

```
int employeeNumber = 23;
```

You can use the assignment operator to assign values to character type variables, as shown in the following example:

```
char middleInitial = 'J';
```

Compound Assignment

- **Adding a value to a variable is very common**

```
itemCount = itemCount + 40;
```

- **There is a convenient shorthand**

```
itemCount += 40;
```

- **This shorthand works for all arithmetic operators**

```
itemCount -= 24;
```

Adding a Value to a Variable Is Very Common

The following code declares an **int** variable called *itemCount*, assigns it the value 2, and then increments it by 40:

```
int itemCount;
itemCount = 2;
itemCount = itemCount + 40;
```

There Is a Convenient Shorthand

The code to increment a variable works, but it is slightly cumbersome. You need to write the identifier that is being incremented twice. For simple identifiers this is rarely a problem, unless you have many identifiers with very similar names. However, you can use expressions of arbitrary complexity to designate the value being incremented, as in the following example:

```
items[(index + 1) % 32] = items[(index + 1) % 32] + 40;
```

In these cases, if you needed to write the same expression twice you could easily introduce a subtle bug. Fortunately, there is a shorthand form that avoids the duplication:

```
itemCount += 40;
items[(index + 1) % 32] += 40;
```

This Shorthand Works for All Arithmetic Operators

```
var += expression; // var = var + expression
var -= expression; // var = var - expression
var *= expression; // var = var * expression
var /= expression; // var = var / expression
var %= expression; // var = var % expression
```

Common Operators

Common Operators	Example
· **Equality operators**	== !=
· **Relational operators**	< > <= >= is
· **Conditional operators**	&& || ?: *(and)*
· **Increment operator**	++ *(or)*
· **Decrement operator**	- -
· **Arithmetic operators**	+ - * / %
· **Assignment operators**	= *= /= %= += -= <<= >>= &= ^= |=

Expressions are constructed from *operands* and *operators*. The operators of an expression indicate which operations to apply to the operands.

Examples of operators include the concatenation and addition operator (+), the subtraction operator (-), the multiplication operator (*), and the division operator (/). Examples of operands include literals, fields, local variables, and expressions.

Common Operators

Some of the most common operators used in C# are described in the following table.

Type	Description
Assignment operators	Assign values to variables by using a simple assignment. For the assignment to succeed, the value on the right side of the assignment must be a type that can be implicitly converted to the type of the variable on the left side of the assignment.
Relational logical operators	Compare two values.
Logical operators	Perform bitwise operations on values.
Conditional operator	Selects between two expressions, depending on a Boolean expression.
Increment operator	Increases the value of the variable by one.
Decrement operator	Decreases the value of the variable by one.
Arithmetic operators	Performs standard arithmetic operations.

For more information about the operators available in C#, see "Expressions" in the C# Language Specification in the Visual Studio .NET Help documents.

Increment and Decrement

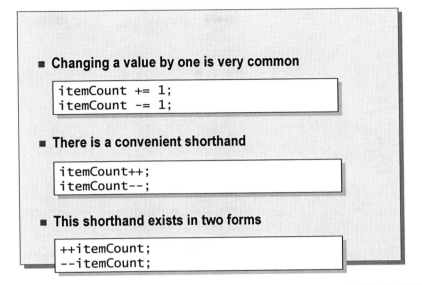

- ■ **Changing a value by one is very common**
  ```
  itemCount += 1;
  itemCount -= 1;
  ```

- ■ **There is a convenient shorthand**
  ```
  itemCount++;
  itemCount--;
  ```

- ■ **This shorthand exists in two forms**
  ```
  ++itemCount;
  --itemCount;
  ```

[Handwritten margin notes: ^ excl or | or ?: lif(',^,y) % modulus &= → x &=y x= x &y]

Changing a Value by One is Very Common

You often want to write a statement that increments or decrements a value by one. You could do this as follows:

```
itemCount = itemCount + 1;
itemCount = itemCount - 1;
```

However, as just explained, there is a convenient shorthand for this:

```
itemCount += 1;
itemCount -= 1;
```

Convenient Shorthand

Incrementing or decrementing a value by one is so common, that this shorthand method has an even shorter shorthand form!

```
itemCount++; // itemCount += 1;
itemCount--; // itemCount -= 1;
```

The ++ operator is called the increment operator and the – operator is called the decrement operator. You can think of ++ as an operator that changes a value to its successor and – as an operator that changes a value to its predecessor.

Once again, this shorthand is the preferred idiomatic way for C# programmers to increment or decrement a value by one.

Note C++ is called C++ because it was the successor to C!

This Shorthand Exists in Two Forms

You can use the ++ and – operators in two forms.

1. You can place the operator symbol *before* the identifier, as shown in the following examples. This is called the *prefix* notation.

```
++itemCount;
--itemCount;
```

2. You can place the operator symbol *after* the identifier, as shown in the following examples. This is called the *postfix* notation.

```
itemCount++;
itemCount--;
```

In both cases, the *itemCount* is incremented (for ++) or decremented (for --) by one. So why have two notations? To answer this question, you first need to understand assignment in more detail:

An important feature of C# is that assignment is an operator. This means that besides assigning a value to a variable, an assignment expression itself has a value, or outcome, which is the value of the variable after the assignment has taken place. In most statements the value of the assignment expression is discarded, but it can be used in a larger expression, as in the following example:

```
int itemCount = 0;
Console.WriteLine(itemCount = 2); // Prints 2
Console.WriteLine(itemCount = itemCount + 40); // Prints 42
```

Compound assignment is also an assignment. This means that a compound assignment expression, besides assigning a value to a variable, also has a value—an outcome itself. Again, in most statements the value of the compound assignment expression is discarded, but it can be used in a larger expression, as in the following example:

```
int itemCount = 0;
Console.WriteLine(itemCount += 2); // Prints 2
Console.WriteLine(itemCount -= 2); // Prints 0
```

Increment and decrement are also assignments. This means, for example, that an increment expression, besides incrementing a variable by one, also has a value, an outcome itself. Again, in most statements the value of the increment expression is discarded, but it can be used again in a larger expression, as in the following example:

```
int itemCount = 42;
int prefixValue = ++itemCount;  // prefixValue == 43
int postfixValue = itemCount++; // postfixValue = 43
```

The value of the increment expression differs depending on whether you are using the prefix or postfix version. In both cases *itemCount* is incremented. That is not the issue. The issue is what the value of the increment expression is. The value of a prefix increment/decrement is the value of the variable *after* the increment/decrement takes place. The value of a postfix increment/decrement is the value of the variable *before* the increment/decrement takes place.

Operator Precedence

- **Operator Precedence and Associativity**
  - Except for assignment operators, all binary operators are left-associative
  - Assignment operators and conditional operators are right-associative

Operator Precedence

When an expression contains multiple operators, the precedence of the operators controls the order in which the individual operators are evaluated. For example, the expression x + y * z is evaluated as x + (y * z) because the multiplicative operator has higher precedence than the additive operator. For example, an *additive-expression* consists of a sequence of *multiplicative-expressions* separated by + or - operators, thus giving the + and - operators lower precedence than the *, /, and % operators.

Associativity

When an operand occurs between two operators with the same precedence, the *associativity* of the operators controls the order in which the operations are performed. For example, x + y + z is evaluated as (x + y) + z. This is particularly important for assignment operators. For example, x = y = z is evaluated as x = (y = z).

- Except for the assignment operators, all binary operators are *left-associative*, meaning that operations are performed from left to right.

- The assignment operators and the conditional operator (?:) are *right-associative*, meaning that operations are performed from right to left.

You can control precedence and associativity by using parentheses. For example, x + y * z first multiplies y by z and then adds the result to x, but (x + y) * z first adds x and y and then multiplies the result by z.

◆ Creating User-Defined Data Types

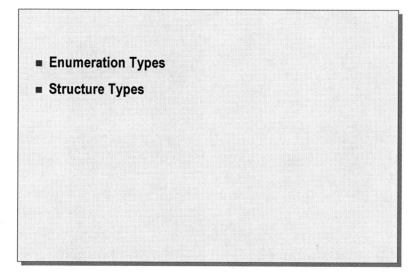

- Enumeration Types
- Structure Types

In your applications, you will need to know how to create user-defined **enumeration (enum)** and **structure (struct)** data types.

After completing this lesson, you will be able to:

- Create user-defined **enum** data types.
- Create user-defined **struct** data types.

Enumeration Types

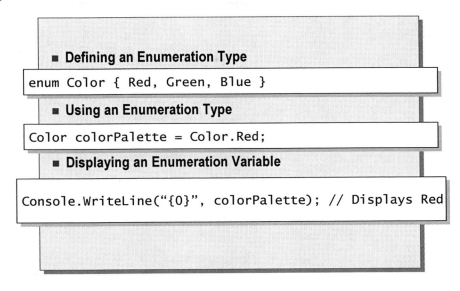

■ **Defining an Enumeration Type**

```
enum Color { Red, Green, Blue }
```

■ **Using an Enumeration Type**

```
Color colorPalette = Color.Red;
```

■ **Displaying an Enumeration Variable**

```
Console.WriteLine("{0}", colorPalette); // Displays Red
```

Enumerators are useful when a variable can only have a specific set of values.

Defining an Enumeration Type

To declare an enumeration, use the **enum** keyword followed by the enum variable name and initial values. For example, the following enumeration defines three integer constants, called enumerator values.

```
enum Color { Red, Green, Blue }
```

By default, enumerator values start from 0. In the preceding example, *Red* has a value of 0, *Green* has a value of 1, and *Blue* has a value of 2.

You can initialize an enumeration by specifying integer literals.

Using an Enumeration Type

You can declare a variable *colorPalette* of **Color** type by using the following syntax:

```
Color colorPalette;        // Declare the variable
colorPalette = Color.Red; // Set value
```

- Or -

```
colorPalette = (Color)0; // Type casting int to Color
```

Displaying an Enumeration Value

To display an enumeration value in readable format, use the following statement:

```
Console.WriteLine("{0}", colorPalette);
```

Structure Types

- **Defining a Structure Type**

```
public struct Employee
{
    public string firstName;
    public int age;
}
```

- **Using a Structure Type**

```
Employee companyEmployee;
companyEmployee.firstName = "Joe";
companyEmployee.age = 23;
```

You can use structures to create objects that behave like built-in value types. Because structs are stored inline and are not heap allocated, there is less garbage collection pressure on the system than there is with classes.

In the .NET Framework, simple data types such as **int**, **float**, and **double** are all built-in structures.

Defining a Structure Type

You can use a structure to group together several arbitrary types, as shown in the following example:

```
public struct Employee
{
    public string firstName;
    public int   age;
}
```

This code defines a new type called **Employee** that consists of two elements: first name and age.

Using a Structure Type

To access elements inside the struct, use the following syntax:

```
Employee companyEmployee;            // Declare variable
companyEmployee.firstName = "Joe";   // Set value
companyEmployee.age = 23;
```

◆ Converting Data Types

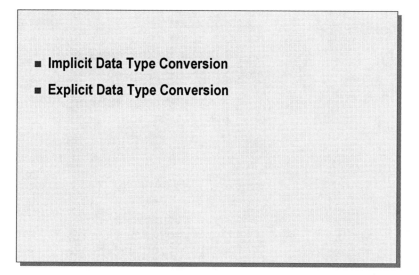

- **Implicit Data Type Conversion**
- **Explicit Data Type Conversion**

In C#, there are two types of conversion:

- Implicit data type conversion.
- Explicit data type conversion.

After completing this lesson, you will be able to:

- Perform implicit data conversion.
- Perform explicit data conversion.

Implicit Data Type Conversion

- **To Convert int to long:**

```
using System;
class Test           public ?
{
    static void Main( )
    {
        int intValue = 123;
        long longValue = intValue;
        Console.WriteLine("(long) {0} = {1}", intValue,
    ↪longValue);
    }
}
```

- **Implicit conversions cannot fail**
  - May lose precision, but not magnitude

Converting from an **int** data type to a **long** data type is implicit. This conversion always succeeds, and it never results in a loss of information. The following example shows how to convert the variable *intValue* from an **int** to a **long**:

```
using System;
class Test
{
    static void Main( )
    {
        int intValue = 123;                        123
        long longValue = intValue;
        Console.WriteLine("(long) {0} = {1}", intValue,
    ↪longValue);
    }                                              123
}
```

Explicit Data Type Conversion

upscaling

> ■ **To do explicit conversions, use a cast expression:**
>
> ```
> using System;
> class Test
> {
>     static void Main( )
>     {
>         long longValue = Int64.MaxValue;
>         int intValue = (int) longValue;
>         Console.WriteLine("(int) {0} = {1}", longValue,
>     ⇥intValue);
>     }
> }
> ```

You can convert variable types explicitly by using a cast expression. The following example shows how to convert the variable *longValue* from a **long** data type to an **int** data type by using a cast expression:

```
using System;
class Test
{
    static void Main( )
    {
        long longValue = Int64.MaxValue;
        int intValue = (int) longValue;
        Console.WriteLine("(int) {0} = {1}", longValue,
    ⇥intValue);
    }
}
```

Because an overflow occurs in this example, the output is as follows:

```
(int) 9223372036854775807 = -1
```

To avoid such a situation, you can use the **checked** statement to raise an exception when a conversion fails, as follows:

```
using System;
class Test
{
  static void Main( )
  {
    checked
    {
      long longValue = Int64.MaxValue;
      int intValue = (int) longValue;
      Console.WriteLine("(int) {0} = {1}", longValue,
➥intValue);
    }
  }
}
```

Lab 3.1: Creating and Using Types

Objectives

After completing this lab, you will be able to:

- Create new data types.
- Define and use variables.

Prerequisites

Before working on this lab, you should be familiar with the following:

- The Common Type System.
- Value-type variables in C#.

Scenario

In Exercise 1, you will write a program that creates a simple **enum** type and then sets and prints the values by using the **Console.WriteLine** statement.

In Exercise 2, you will write a program that uses the **enum** type declared in Exercise 1 in a **struct**.

If time permits, you will add input/output functionality to the program you wrote in Exercise 2.

Starter and Solution Files

There are starter and solution files associated with this lab. The starter files are in the *install folder*\Labs\Lab03\Starter folder and the solution files are in the *install folder*\Labs\Lab03\Solution folder.

Estimated time to complete this lab: 35 minutes

Exercise 1
Creating an enum Type

In this exercise, you will create an enumerated type for representing different types of bank accounts (checking and savings). You will create two variables by using this **enum** type, and set the values of the variables to Checking and Deposit. You will then print the values of the variables by using the **System.Console.WriteLine** function.

▶ **To create an enum type**

1. Open the BankAccount.sln project in the *install folder*\Labs\Lab03\Starter\BankAccount folder.

2. Open the Enum.cs file and add an **enum** called **AccountType** before the class definition as follows:

   ```
   public enum AccountType { Checking, Deposit }
   ```

   This **enum** will contain Checking and Deposit types.

3. Declare two variables of type **AccountType** in **Main** as follows:

   ```
   AccountType goldAccount;
   AccountType platinumAccount;
   ```

4. Set the value of the first variable to Checking and the value of the other variable to Deposit as follows:

   ```
   goldAccount = AccountType.Checking;
   platinumAccount = AccountType.Deposit;
   ```

5. Add two **Console.WriteLine** statements to print the value of each variable as follows:

   ```
   Console.WriteLine("The Customer Account Type is {0}"
   ↪,goldAccount);
   Console.WriteLine("The Customer Account Type is {0}"
   ↪,platinumAccount);
   ```

6. Compile and run the program.

Exercise 2
Creating and Using a Struct Type

In this exercise, you will define a **struct** that can be used to represent a bank account. You will use variables to hold the account number (a **long**), the account balance (a **decimal**), and the account type (the **enum** that you created in Exercise 1). You will create a **struct** type variable, populate the **struct** with some sample data, and print the result.

▶ **To create a struct type**

1. Open the StructType.sln project in the
   install folder\Labs\Lab03\Starter\StructType folder.

2. Open the Struct.cs file and add a **public struct** called **BankAccount** that contains the following fields.

Type	Variable
public long	*accNo*
public decimal	*accBal*
public AccountType	*accType*

3. Declare a variable *goldAccount* of type **BankAccount** in **Main**.

   ```
   BankAccount goldAccount;
   ```

4. Set the *accType*, *accBal*, and *accNo* fields of the variable *goldAccount*.

   ```
   goldAccount.accType = AccountType.Checking;
   goldAccount.accBal = (decimal)3200.00;
   goldAccount.accNo = 123;
   ```

5. Add **Console.WriteLine** statements to print the value of each element in the struct variable.

   ```
   Console.WriteLine("Acct Number  {0}", goldAccount.accNo);
   Console.WriteLine("Acct Type    {0}", goldAccount.accType);
   Console.WriteLine("Acct Balance ${0}",goldAccount.accBal);
   ```

6. Compile and run the program.

If Time Permits
Adding Input/Output functionality

In this exercise, you will modify the code written in Exercise 2. Instead of using the account number 123, you will prompt the user to enter the account number. You will use this number to print the account summary.

▶ **To add input/output functionality**

1. Open the StructType.sln project in the
   install folder\Labs\Lab03\Starter\Optional folder.

2. Open the Struct.cs file and replace the following line:

   ```
   goldAccount.accNo = 123; //remove this line and add code
   below
   ```

   with a `Console.Write` statement to prompt the user to enter the account number:

   ```
   Console.Write("Enter account number: ");
   ```

3. Read the account number by using a **Console.ReadLine** statement. Assign this value to *goldAccount.accNo*.

   ```
   goldAccount.accNo = long.Parse(Console.ReadLine());
   ```

   Note You need to use the **long.Parse** method to convert the string read by the **Console.ReadLine** statement into a decimal value before assigning it to *goldAccount.accNo*.

   ---

4. Compile and run the program. Enter an account number when prompted.

Review

- **Common Type System**
- **Naming Variables**
- **Using Built-in Data Types**
- **Creating User-Defined Data Types**
- **Converting Data Types**

1. What is the Common Type System?

2. Can a value type be **null**?

3. Can you use uninitialized variables in C#? Why?

4. Can there be loss of magnitude as a result of an implicit conversion?

msdn training

Module 4: Statements and Exceptions

Contents

Overview	1
Introduction to Statements	2
Using Selection Statements	6
Using Iteration Statements	17
Using Jump Statements	29
Lab 4.1: Using Statements	32
Handling Basic Exceptions	42
Raising Exceptions	52
Lab 4.2: Using Exceptions	62
Review	72

Microsoft

Overview

- ■ **Introduction to Statements**
- ■ **Using Selection Statements**
- ■ **Using Iteration Statements**
- ■ **Using Jump Statements**
- ■ **Handling Basic Exceptions**
- ■ **Raising Exceptions**

One of the fundamental skills required to use a programming language is the ability to write the statements that form the logic of a program in that language. This module explains how to use some common statements in C#. It also describes how to implement exception handling in C#.

In particular, this module shows how to throw errors as well as catch them, and how to use **try-finally** statement blocks to ensure that an exception does not cause the program to abort before cleaning up.

After completing this module, you will be able to:

- ■ Describe the different types of control statements.
- ■ Use jump statements.
- ■ Use selection statements.
- ■ Use iteration statements.
- ■ Handle and raise exceptions.

◆ Introduction to Statements

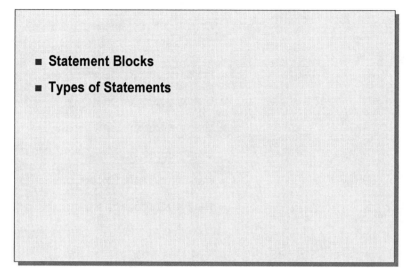

- **Statement Blocks**
- **Types of Statements**

A program consists of a sequence of statements. At run time, these statements are executed one after the other, as they appear in the program, from left to right and from top to bottom.

After completing this lesson, you will be able to:

- Group a set of statements together in C#.
- Use the different types of statements available in C#.

Statement Blocks

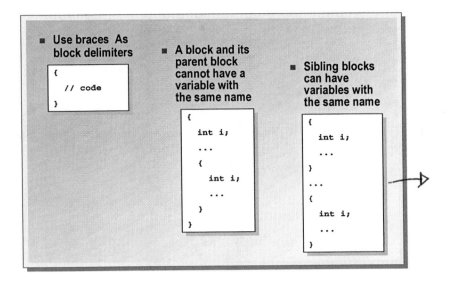

When developing C# applications, you need to group statements together just as you do in other programming languages. To do so, you use the syntax of languages such as C, C++, and Java, which means that you enclose groups of statements in braces: { and }. You do not use keyword matched delimiters such as the **If** ... **End If** of Microsoft® Visual Basic® for grouping statements.

Grouping Statements into Blocks

A group of statements enclosed between braces is referred to as a block. A block can contain a single statement or another block that is nested within it.

Each block defines a scope. A variable that is declared in a block is called a local variable. The scope of a local variable extends from its declaration to the right brace that ends its enclosing block. It is good practice to declare a variable in the innermost block possible because the restricted visibility of the variable helps to make the program clearer.

Using Variables in Statement Blocks

In C#, you cannot declare a variable in an inner block with the same name as a variable in an outer block. For example, the following code is not allowed:

```
int i;
{
    int i; // Error: i already declared in parent block
    ...
}
```

However, you can declare variables with the same name in *sibling* blocks. Sibling blocks are blocks that are enclosed by the same parent block and are nested at the same level. The following is an example:

```
{
    int i;
    ...
}
...
{
    int i;
    ...
}
```

You can declare variables anywhere in a statement block. Given this freedom, you can easily follow the recommendation of initializing a variable at the point of declaration.

Types of Statements

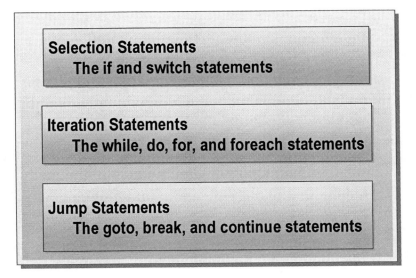

As the complexity of the problem being solved by a program increases, so does the complexity of the logic of the program. Consequently, the program requires structured flow control, which you can achieve by using higher-level constructs or statements. These statements can be grouped into the following categories:

- Selection statements

    The **if** and **switch** statements are known as selection statements. They make choices based on the value of expressions and selectively execute statements based on those choices.

- Iteration statements

    The **while, do, for,** and **foreach** statements execute repeatedly while a specific condition is true. They are also known as looping statements. Each of these statements is appropriate for a certain style of iteration.

- Jump statements

    The **goto, break,** and **continue** statements are used to unconditionally transfer control to another statement.

◆ Using Selection Statements

- **The if Statement**
- **Cascading if Statements**
- **The switch Statement**
- **Quiz: Spot the Bugs**

The **if** and **switch** statements are known as selection statements. They make choices based on the value of expressions and selectively execute statements based on those choices.

After completing this lesson, you will be able to:

- Use the **if** statement in C#.
- Use the **switch** statement in C#.

The if Statement

- **Syntax:**

```
if ( Boolean-expression )
   first-embedded-statement
else
   second-embedded-statement
```

- **No implicit conversion from int to bool**

```
int x;
...
if (x) ...       // Must be if (x != 0) in C#
if (x = 0) ... // Must be if (x == 0) in C#
```

The **if** statement is the primary decision-making statement. It can be coupled with an optional **else** clause, as shown:

```
if ( Boolean-expression )
    first-embedded-statement
else
    second-embedded-statement
```

The **if** statement evaluates a Boolean expression to determine the course of action to follow. If the Boolean expression evaluates to **true**, the control is transferred to the first embedded statement. If the Boolean expression evaluates to **false**, and there is an **else** clause, the control is transferred to the second embedded statement.

Examples

You can use a simple embedded **if** statement such as the following:

```
if (number % 2 == 0)
    Console.WriteLine("even");
```

Although braces are not required in embedded statements, many style guides recommend using them because they make your code less error prone and easier to maintain. You can rewrite the previous example with braces as follows:

```
if (number % 2 == 0) {
    Console.WriteLine("even");
}
```

You can also use an **if** statement block such as the following:

```
if (minute == 60) {
    minute = 0;
    hour++;
}
```

Converting Integers to Boolean Values

Implicit conversion from an integer to a Boolean value is a potential source of bugs. To avoid such conversion-related bugs, C# does not support integer to Boolean value conversion. This is a significant difference between C# and other similar languages.

For example, the following statements, which at best generate warnings in C and C++, result in compilation errors in C#:

```
int x;
...
if (x) ...      // Must be x != 0 in C#
if (x = 0) ... // Must be x == 0 in C#
```

Cascading if Statements

```
enum Suit { Clubs, Hearts, Diamonds, Spades }
Suit trumps = Suit.Hearts;
if (trumps == Suit.Clubs)
    color = "Black";
else if (trumps == Suit.Hearts)
    color = "Red";
else if (trumps == Suit.Diamonds)
    color = "Red";
else
    color = "Black";
```

You can handle cascading **if** statements by using an **else if** statement. C# does not support the **else if** statement but forms an **else if**-type statement from an **else** clause and an **if** statement, as in C and C++. Languages such as Visual Basic support cascading **if** statements by using an **else if** statement between the initial **if** statement and the final **else** statement.

By using the **else if** construct, you can have any number of branches. However, the statements controlled by a cascading **if** statement are mutually exclusive, so that only one statement from the set of **else if** constructs is executed.

Nesting if Statements

Nesting one **if** statement within another **if** statement creates a potential ambiguity called a *dangling else*, as shown in the following example:

```
if (percent >= 0 && percent <= 100)
    if (percent > 50)
        Console.WriteLine("Pass");
else
    Console.WriteLine("Error: out of range");
```

The **else** is indented to the same column as the first **if**. When you read the code, it appears that the **else** does not associate with the second **if**. This is dangerously misleading. Regardless of the layout, the compiler binds an **else** clause to its nearest **if** statement. This means that the compiler will interpret the above code as follows:

```
if (percent >= 0 && percent <= 100) {
    if (percent > 50)
        Console.WriteLine("Pass");
    else
        Console.WriteLine("Error: out of range");
}
```

One way you can make the **else** associate with the first **if** is to use a block, as follows:

```
if (percent >= 0 && percent <= 100) {
    if (percent > 50)
        Console.WriteLine("Pass");
} else {
    Console.WriteLine("Error: out of range");
}
```

Tip It is best to format cascading **if** statements with proper indentation; otherwise, long decisions quickly become unreadable and trail off the right margin of the page or screen.

The switch Statement

- Use switch statements for multiple case blocks

- Use break statements to ensure that no fall through occurs

```
switch (trumps) {
case Suit.Clubs :
case Suit.Spades :
    color = "Black"; break;
case Suit.Hearts :
case Suit.Diamonds :
    color = "Red"; break;
default:
    color = "ERROR"; break;
}
```

The **switch** statement provides an elegant mechanism for handling complex conditions that would otherwise require nested **if** statements. It consists of multiple case blocks, each of which specifies a single constant and an associated **case** label. You cannot group a collection of constants together in a single **case** label. Each constant must have its own **case** label.

A **switch** block can contain declarations. The scope of a local variable or constant that is declared in a **switch** block extends from its declaration to the end of the **switch** block, as is shown in the example on the slide.

Execution of switch Statements

A **switch** statement is executed as follows:

1. If one of the constants specified in a **case** label is equal to the value of the **switch** expression, control is transferred to the statement list following the matched **case** label.

2. If no **case** label constant is equal to the value of the **switch** expression, and the **switch** statement contains a **default** label, control is transferred to the statement list following the **default** label.

3. If no **case** label constant is equal to the value of the **switch** expression, and the **switch** statement does not contain a **default** label, control is transferred to the end of the **switch** statement.

You can use a **switch** statement to evaluate only the following types of expressions: any integer type, a **char**, an **enum**, or a **string**. You can also evaluate other expression types by using the **switch** statement, as long as there is exactly one user-defined implicit conversion from the disallowed type to one of the allowed types.

Note   Unlike in Java, C, or C++, the governing type of a **switch** statement in C# can be a string. With a string expression, the value **null** is permitted as a **case** label constant.

For more information about conversion operators, search for "conversion operators" in the Microsoft .NET Framework SDK Help documents.

Grouping Constants

To group several constants together, repeat the keyword **case** for each constant, as shown in the following example:

```
enum MonthName { January, February, ..., December }
MonthName current;
int monthDays;
...
switch (current) {
case MonthName.February :
    monthDays = 28;
    break;
case MonthName.April :
case MonthName.June :
case MonthName.September :
case MonthName.November :
    monthDays = 30;
    break;
default :
    monthDays = 31;
    break;
}
```

You use the **case** and **default** labels only to provide entry points for the control flow of the program based on the value of the **switch** expression. They do not alter the control flow of the program.

The values of the **case** label constants must be unique. This means that you cannot have two constants that have the same value. For example, the following example will generate a compile-time error:

```
switch (trumps) {
case Suit.Clubs :
case Suit.Clubs : // Error: duplicate label
    ...
default :
default : // Error: duplicate label again
    ...
}
```

Using break in switch Statements

Unlike in Java, C, or C++, C# statements associated with one or more **case** labels cannot silently fall through or continue to the next **case** label. A *silent fall through* occurs when execution proceeds without generating an error. In other words, you must ensure that the last statement associated with a set of **case** labels does not allow the control flow to reach the next set of **case** labels.

Statements that help you to fulfill this requirement, known as the *no fall through rule*, are the **break** statement (probably the most common), the **goto** statement (very rare), the **return** statement, the **throw** statement, and an infinite loop.

The following example will generate a compile-time error because it breaks the no fall through rule:

```
string suffix = "th";
switch (days % 10) {
case 1 :
    if (days / 10 != 1) {
        suffix = "st";
        break;
    }
    // Error: fall through here
case 2 :
    if (days / 10 != 1) {
        suffix = "nd";
        break;
    }
    // Error: fall through here
case 3 :
    if (days / 10 != 1) {
        suffix = "rd";
        break;
    }
    // Error: fall through here
default :
    suffix = "th";
    // Error: fall through here
}
```

You can fix the error in this example by rewriting the code as follows:

```
switch (days % 10) {
case 1 :
    suffix = (days / 10 == 1) ? "th" : "st";
    break;
case 2 :
    suffix = (days / 10 == 1) ? "th" : "nd";
    break;
case 3 :
    suffix = (days / 10 == 1) ? "th" : "rd";
    break;
default :
    suffix = "th";
    break;
}
```

Using goto in switch Statements

In C#, unlike in Java, C, or C++, you can use a **case** label and a **default** label as the destination of a **goto** statement. You can use a **goto** statement this way to achieve the fall through effect, if necessary. For example, the following code will compile without any problem:

```
switch (days % 10) {
case 1 :
    if (days / 10 != 1) {
        suffix = "st";
        break;
    }
    goto case 2;
case 2 :
    if (days / 10 != 1) {
        suffix = "nd";
        break;
    }
    goto case 3;
case 3 :
    if (days / 10 != 1) {
        suffix = "rd";
        break;
    }
    goto default;
default :
    suffix = "th";
    break;
}
```

Because of the no fall through rule, you can rearrange sections of a **switch** statement without affecting the overall behavior of the **switch** statement.

Quiz: Spot the Bugs

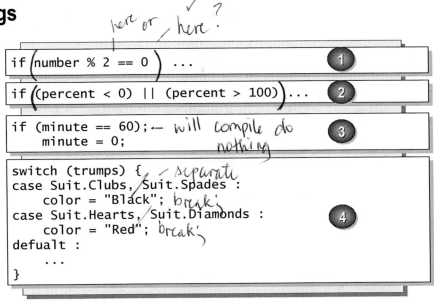

```
here or   here ?

if (number % 2 == 0 ) ...                    1

if ((percent < 0) || (percent > 100))...     2

if (minute == 60); ← will compile do         3
    minute = 0;              nothing

switch (trumps) {  ← separate
case Suit.Clubs, Suit.Spades :
    color = "Black"; break;
case Suit.Hearts, Suit.Diamonds :            4
    color = "Red"; break;
defualt :
    ...
}
```

In this quiz, you can work with a partner to spot the bugs in the code on the slide. To see the answers to this quiz, turn the page.

Answers

1. The **if** statement is not in parentheses. The C# compiler traps this bug as a compile-time error. The corrected code is as follows:

   ```
   if (number % 2 == 0) ...
   ```

2. The **if** statement as a whole is not fully parenthesized. The C# compiler traps this bug as a compile-time error. The corrected code is as follows:

   ```
   if ((percent < 0) || (percent > 100)) ...
   ```

3. The **if** statement has a single semicolon as its embedded statement. A single semicolon is called an empty statement in the C# Language Reference document and a **null** statement in the C# compiler diagnostic messages. It does nothing, but it is allowed. The layout of the statements does not affect how the compiler parses the syntax of the code. Hence, the compiler reads the code as:

   ```
   if (minute == 60)
           ;
   minute = 0;
   ```

   The C# compiler traps this bug as a compile-time warning.

4. The following errors are present:

   a. There is more than one constant in the same **case** label. The C# compiler traps this bug as a compile-time error.

   b. The statements associated with each **case** fall through to the next **case**. The C# compiler traps this bug as a compile-time error.

   c. The keyword **default** has been misspelled. Unfortunately, this is still allowable code, as it creates a simple identifier label. The C# compiler traps this bug as two compile-time warnings: one indicating unreachable code, and another indicating that the **default:** label has not been used.

◆ Using Iteration Statements

- **The while Statement**
- **The do Statement**
- **The for Statement**
- **The foreach Statement**
- **Quiz: Spot the Bugs**

The **while, do, for**, and **foreach** statements are known as iteration statements. You use them to perform operations while a specific condition is true.

After completing this lesson, you will be able to:

- Use iteration statements in C#.
- Identify errors in the use of iteration statements in C#.

The while Statement

- **Execute embedded statements based on Boolean value**
- **Evaluate Boolean expression at beginning of loop**
- **Execute embedded statements while Boolean value Is True**

```
int i = 0;
while (i < 10) {
    Console.WriteLine(i);
    i++;
}
```

```
0 1 2 3 4 5 6 7 8 9
```

The **while** statement is the simplest of all iteration statements. It repeatedly executes an embedded statement *while* a Boolean expression is true. Note that the expression that the **while** statement evaluates must be Boolean, since C# does not support implicit conversion from an integer to a Boolean value.

Flow of Execution

A **while** statement is executed as follows:

1. The Boolean expression controlling the **while** statement is evaluated.

2. If the Boolean expression yields **true**, control is transferred to the embedded statement. When control reaches the end of the embedded statement, control is implicitly transferred to the beginning of the **while** statement, and the Boolean expression is re-evaluated.

3. If the Boolean expression yields **false**, control is transferred to the end of the **while** statement. Therefore, while the controlling Boolean expression is **true**, the program repeatedly executes the embedded statement.

The Boolean expression is tested at the start of the **while** loop. Therefore, it is possible that the embedded statement may never be executed at all.

Examples

You can use a simple embedded statement as shown in the following example:

```
while (i < 10)
    Console.WriteLine(i++);
```

When using embedded statements, you do not need to use braces. Nevertheless, many style guides recommend using them because they simplify maintenance. You can rewrite the previous example with braces as follows:

```
while (i < 10) {
    Console.WriteLine(i++);
}
```

You can also use a **while** statement block as shown in the following example:

```
while (i < 10) {
    Console.WriteLine(i);
    i++;
}
```

Tip Despite being the simplest iteration statement, the **while** statement poses potential problems for developers who are not careful. The classic syntax of a **while** statement is as follows:

```
initializer
while ( Boolean-expression ) {
    embedded-statement
    update
}
```

It is easy to forget the *update* part of the **while** block, particularly if your attention is focused on the Boolean expression.

The do Statement

- Execute embedded statements based on Boolean value

- Evaluate Boolean expression at end of loop

- Execute embedded statements while Boolean value Is True

```
int i = 0;
do {
    Console.WriteLine(i);
    i++;
} while (i < 10);
```
— "while" inside a DO must end with ;

0 1 2 3 4 5 6 7 8 9

A **do** statement is always coupled with a **while** statement. It is similar to a **while** statement, except that the Boolean expression that determines whether to continue or exit the loop is evaluated at the end of the loop rather than at the start. This means that, unlike a **while** statement, which iterates zero or more times, a **do** statement iterates one or more times.

Therefore, a **do** statement always executes its embedded statement at least once. This behavior is particularly useful when you need to validate input before allowing program execution to proceed.

Flow of Execution

A **do** statement is executed as follows:

1. Control is transferred to the embedded statement.

2. When control reaches the end of the embedded statement, the Boolean expression is evaluated.

3. If the Boolean expression yields **true**, control is transferred to the beginning of the **do** statement.

4. If the Boolean expression yields **false**, control is transferred to the end of the **do** statement.

Examples

You can use a simple embedded **do** statement as shown in the following example:

```
do
    Console.WriteLine(i++);
while (i < 10);
```

Just as with the **if** and **while** statements, you do not need to use braces in embedded **do** statements, but it is a good practice to use them.

You can also use a **do** statement block as follows:

```
do {
    Console.WriteLine(i);
    i++;
} while (i < 10);
```

In all cases, you must end a **do** statement with a semicolon, as follows:

```
do {
    Console.WriteLine(i++);
} while (i < 10) // Error no ; here
```

The for Statement

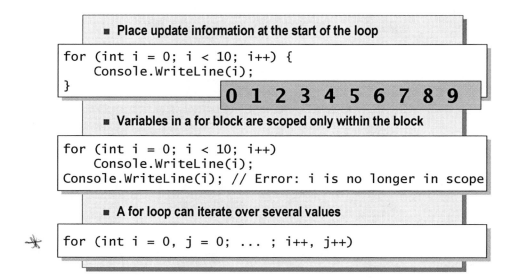

- **Place update information at the start of the loop**

```
for (int i = 0; i < 10; i++) {
    Console.WriteLine(i);
}
```
`0 1 2 3 4 5 6 7 8 9`

- **Variables in a for block are scoped only within the block**

```
for (int i = 0; i < 10; i++)
    Console.WriteLine(i);
Console.WriteLine(i); // Error: i is no longer in scope
```

- **A for loop can iterate over several values**

```
for (int i = 0, j = 0; ... ; i++, j++)
```

When using **while** statements, developers often forget to update the control variable. The following code provides an example of this mistake:

```
int i = 0;
while (i < 10)
    Console.WriteLine(i); // Mistake: no i++
```

This mistake occurs because the developer's attention is focused on the body of the **while** statement and not on the update. Also, the **while** keyword and the update code may be very far apart.

You can minimize these errors by using the **for** statement. The **for** statement overcomes the problem of omitted updates by moving the update code to the beginning of the loop, where it is harder to overlook. The syntax of the **for** statement is as follows:

```
for ( initializer ; condition ; update )
    embedded-statement
```

Important In a **for** statement, the update code precedes the embedded statement. Nevertheless, the update code is executed by the runtime after the embedded statement.

The syntax of the **for** statement is essentially identical to that of the **while** statement, as shown in the following example:

```
initializer
while ( condition ) {
    embedded-statement
    update
}
```

As with all iteration statements, the condition in a **for** block must be a Boolean expression that serves as a continuation condition and not a termination condition.

Examples

The initializer, condition, and update components of a **for** statement are optional. However, an empty condition is considered implicitly **true** and can easily cause an infinite loop. The following code provides an example:

```
for (;;) {
    Console.WriteLine("Help ");
    ...
}
```

As with the **while** and **do** statements, you can use a simple embedded statement or a block statement as shown in the following examples:

```
for (int i = 0; i < 10; i++)
    Console.WriteLine(i);

for (int i = 0; i < 10; i++) {
    Console.WriteLine(i);
    Console.WriteLine(10 - i);
}
```

Declaring Variables

One subtle difference between the **while** statement and the **for** statement is that a variable declared in the initializer code of a **for** statement is scoped only within the **for** block. For example, the following code generates a compile-time error:

```
for (int i = 0; i < 10; i++)
    Console.WriteLine(i);
Console.WriteLine(i); // Error: i is no longer in scope
```

In conjunction with this rule, it is important to note that you cannot declare a variable in a **for** block with the same name as a variable in an outer block. This rule also applies to variables declared in the initializer code of a **for** statement. For example, the following code generates a compile-time error:

```
int i;
for (int i = 0; i < 10; i++) // Error: i is already in scope
```

However, the following code is allowed:

```
for (int i = 0; i < 10; i++) ...
for (int i = 0; i < 20; i++) ...
```

Further, you can initialize two or more variables in the initializer code of a **for** statement, as follows:

```
for (int i = 0, j = 0; ... ; ...)
```

However, the variables must be of the same type. Therefore, the following is not permitted:

```
for (int i = 0, long j = 0; i < 10; i++)
    ...
```

You can also use two or more expression statements separated by a comma or commas in the update code of a **for** statement, as follows:

```
for (int i = 0, j = 0; ... ; i++, j++)
```

The **for** statement is best suited to situations in which the number of iterations is known. They are particularly well suited to modifying each element of an array.

The foreach Statement

- **Choose the type and name of the iteration variable**
- **Execute embedded statements for each element of the collection class**

```
ArrayList numbers = new ArrayList( );
for (int i = 0; i < 10; i++ ) {
    numbers.Add(i);
}
                        ╭ new variable
foreach (int number in numbers) {
    Console.WriteLine(number); ╲ array list
}
```

```
0 1 2 3 4 5 6 7 8 9
```

Collections are software entities whose purpose is to collect other software entities, much as a ledger can be thought of as a collection of bank accounts or a house as a collection of rooms.

The Microsoft .NET Framework provides a simple collection class called **ArrayList**. You can use **ArrayList** to create a collection variable and add elements to the collection. For example, consider the following code:

```
using System.Collections;
...
ArrayList numbers = new ArrayList( );
for (int i = 0; i < 10; i++) {
    numbers.Add(i);
}
```

You can write a **for** statement that accesses and prints each collection element from this collection class in turn:

```
for (int i = 0; i < numbers.Count; i++) {
    int number = (int)numbers[i];
    Console.WriteLine(number);
}
```

This **for** statement contains many individual statements that in combination implement the mechanism used to iterate through each collection element of numbers. However, this solution is not easy to implement and is prone to error.

To address this problem, C# provides the **foreach** statement, which allows you to iterate through a collection without using multiple statements. Rather than explicitly extracting each element from a collection by using syntax specific to the particular collection, you use the **foreach** statement to approach the problem in the opposite way. You effectively instruct the collection to present its elements one at a time. Instead of taking the embedded statement to the collection, the collection is taken to the embedded statement.

By using the **foreach** statement, you can rewrite the previous **for** statement as follows:

```
foreach (int number in numbers)
    Console.WriteLine(number);
```

The **foreach** statement executes the embedded statement for each element of the collection class *numbers*. You only need to choose the type and name of the iteration variable, which in this case are **int** and *number*, respectively.

You cannot modify the elements in a collection by using a **foreach** statement because the iteration variable is implicitly **readonly**. For example:

```
foreach (int number in numbers) {
    number++; // Compile-time error
    Console.WriteLine(number);
}
```

Tip   You can use a **foreach** statement to iterate through the values of an enumerator by using the **Enum.GetValues**() method, which returns an array of objects.

It is important to be cautious when deciding the type of the **foreach** iteration variable. In some circumstances, a wrong iteration variable type might not be detected until run time.

Quiz: Spot the Bugs

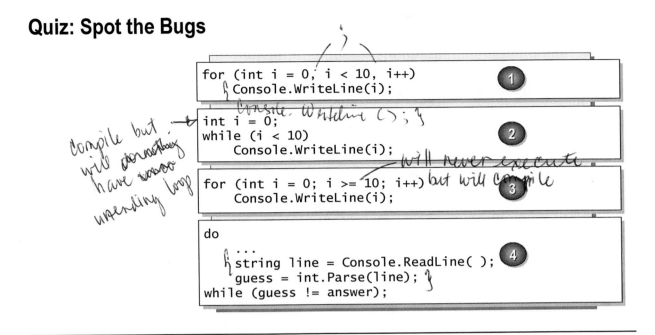

In this quiz, you can work with a partner to spot the bugs in the code on the slide. To see the answers to this quiz, turn the page.

Answers

1. The **for** statement elements are separated by commas rather than semicolons. The C# compiler traps this bug as a compile-time error. The corrected code is as follows:

```
for (int i = 0; i < 10; i++)
    ...
```

2. The **while** statement does not update the continuation expression. It will loop forever. This bug does not generate a warning or an error at compile time. The corrected code is as follows:

```
int i = 0;
while (i < 10) {
    Console.WriteLine(i);
    i++;
}
```

3. The **for** statement has a termination rather than a continuation condition. It will never loop at all. This bug does not generate a warning or an error at compile time. The corrected code is as follows:

```
for (int i = 0; i < 10; i++)
    ...
```

4. The statements between **do** and **while** must be grouped together in a block. The C# compiler traps this bug as a compile-time error. The corrected code is as follows:

```
do {
    ...
    string line = Console.ReadLine( );
    guess = int.Parse(line);
} while (guess != answer);
```

◆ Using Jump Statements

- ■ **The goto Statement**
- ■ **The break and continue Statements**

The **goto**, **break**, and **continue** statements are known as jump statements. You use them to transfer control from one point in the program to another, at any time. In this section, you will learn how to use jump statements in C# programs.

The goto Statement

- **Flow of control transferred to a labeled statement**
- **Can easily result in obscure "spaghetti" code**

```
if (number % 2 == 0) goto Even;
Console.WriteLine("odd");
goto End;
Even:
Console.WriteLine("even");
End: ;
```

The **goto** statement is the most primitive C# jump statement. It transfers control to a labeled statement. The label must exist and must be in the scope of the **goto** statement. More than one **goto** statement can transfer control to the same label.

The **goto** statement can transfer control out of a block, but it can never transfer control into a block. The purpose of this restriction is to avoid the possibility of jumping past an initialization. The same rule exists in C++ and other languages as well.

The **goto** statement and the targeted label statement can be very far apart in the code. This distance can easily obscure the control-flow logic and is the reason that most programming guidelines recommend that you do not use **goto** statements.

Note   The only situations in which **goto** statements are recommended are in **switch** statements or to transfer control to the outside of a nested loop.

The break and continue Statements

- **The break statement jumps out of an iteration**
- **The continue statement jumps to the next iteration**

```
int i = 0;
while (true) {
    Console.WriteLine(i);
    i++;
    if (i < 10)
        continue;
    else
        break;  — similar to 'Exit' of Foxpro
}
```

A **break** statement exits the nearest enclosing **switch, while, do, for**, or **foreach** statement. A **continue** statement starts a new iteration of the nearest enclosing **while, do, for**, or **foreach** statement.

The **break** and **continue** statements are not very different from a **goto** statement, whose use can easily obscure control-flow logic. For example, you can rewrite the **while** statement that is displayed on the slide without using **break** or **continue** as follows:

```
int i = 0;
while (i < 10) {
    Console.WriteLine(i);
    i++;
}
```

Preferably, you can rewrite the previous code by using a **for** statement, as follows:

```
for (int i = 0; i < 10; i++) {
    Console.WriteLine(i);
}
```

Lab 4.1: Using Statements

Objectives

After completing this lab, you will be able to:

- Use statements to control the flow of execution.
- Use looping statements.

Prerequisites

Before working on this lab, you should be familiar with the following:

- Creating variables in C#
- Using common operators in C#
- Creating **enum** types in C#

Estimated time to complete this lab: 30 minutes

Exercise 1
Converting a Day of the Year into a Month and Day Pair

In this exercise, you will write a program that reads an integer day number (between 1 and 365) from the console and stores it in an integer variable. The program will convert this number into a month and a day of the month and then print the result to the console. For example, entering 40 should result in "February 9" being displayed. (In this exercise, the complications associated with leap years are ignored.)

▶ **To read the day number from the console**

1. Open the WhatDay1.sln project in the *install folder*\Labs\Lab04\Starter\WhatDay1 folder. The **WhatDay** class contains a variable that contains the number of days in each month stored in a collection. For now, you do not need to understand how this works.

2. Add a **System.Console.Write** statement to **WhatDay.Main** that writes a prompt to the console asking the user to enter a day number between 1 and 365.

3. Add a statement to **Main** that declares a **string** variable called *line* and initializes it with a line read from the console by the **System.Console.ReadLine** method.

4. Add a statement to **Main** that declares an **int** variable called *dayNum* and initializes it with the integer returned from the **int.Parse** method.

The complete code should be as follows:

```
using System;

class WhatDay
{
    static void Main( )
    {
        Console.Write("Please enter a day number between 1
    and 365: ");
        string line = Console.ReadLine( );
        int dayNum = int.Parse(line);

        //
        // To do: add code here
        //
    }
    ...
}
```

5. Save your work.

6. Compile the WhatDay1.cs program and correct any errors. Run the program.

▶ **To calculate the month and day pair from a day number**

1. Add a statement to **Main** that declares an **int** variable called *monthNum* and initializes it to zero.

2. Ten commented out **if** statement (one for each month from January to October) have been provided for you. Uncomment the ten if statements and add two more similar **if** statements for the months November and December to **Main**.

Tip   Multiple comments can be removed (but their contents retained) by selecting the lines, then choosing **Edit**, **Advanced**, and then **Uncomment Selection**.

---

3. Add an identifier label called **End** to **Main** after the last **if** statement.

4. Add a statement after the **End** label that declares an uninitialized **string** variable called *monthName*.

5. A **switch** statement has been partially provided for you after the **End** label. Ten commented out **case** labels for the months January to October are already present. Uncomment them and add two more similar **case** labels and their contents for the months November and December. Add a **default** label to the **switch** statement. Add a statement to the **default** label that assigns the **string** literal "not done yet" to the variable *monthName*.

6. After the **switch** statement, use the **WriteLine** method to output the values for *dayNum* and *monthName*.

7. The completed program should be as follows:

```
using System;

class WhatDay
{
    static void Main( )
    {
        Console.Write("Please enter a day number between 1
and 365: ");
        string line = Console.ReadLine( );
        int dayNum = int.Parse(line);

        int monthNum = 0;

        if (dayNum <= 31) { // January
            goto End;
        } else {
            dayNum -= 31;
            monthNum++;
        }

        if (dayNum <= 28) { // February
            goto End;
        } else {
            dayNum -= 28;
            monthNum++;
        }

        if (dayNum <= 31) { // March
            goto End;
        } else {
            dayNum -= 31;
            monthNum++;
        }
```
Code continued on following page.

```
                 if (dayNum <= 30) { // April
                     goto End;
                 } else {
                     dayNum -= 30;
                     monthNum++;
                 }

                 if (dayNum <= 31) { // May
                     goto End;
                 } else {
                     dayNum -= 31;
                     monthNum++;
                 }

                 if (dayNum <= 30) { // June
                     goto End;
                 } else {
                     dayNum -= 30;
                     monthNum++;
                 }

                 if (dayNum <= 31) { // July
                     goto End;
                 } else {
                     dayNum -= 31;
                     monthNum++;
                 }

                 if (dayNum <= 31) { // August
                     goto End;
                 } else {
                     dayNum -= 31;
                     monthNum++;
                 }

                 if (dayNum <= 30) { // September
                     goto End;
                 } else {
                     dayNum -= 30;
                     monthNum++;
                 }

                 if (dayNum <= 31) { // October
                     goto End;
                 } else {
                     dayNum -= 31;
                     monthNum++;
                 }

                 if (dayNum <= 30) { // November
                     goto End;
                 } else {
                     dayNum -= 30;
                     monthNum++;
                 }
```

Code continued on following page.

```
            if (dayNum <= 31) { // December
                goto End;
            } else {
                dayNum -= 31;
                monthNum++;
            }

        End:
            string monthName;

            switch (monthNum) {
            case 0 :
                monthName = "January"; break;
            case 1 :
                monthName = "February"; break;
            case 2 :
                monthName = "March"; break;
            case 3 :
                monthName = "April"; break;
            case 4 :
                monthName = "May"; break;
            case 5 :
                monthName = "June"; break;
            case 6 :
                monthName = "July"; break;
            case 7 :
                monthName = "August"; break;
            case 8 :
                monthName = "September"; break;
            case 9 :
                monthName = "October"; break;
            case 10 :
                monthName = "November"; break;
            case 11 :
                monthName = "December"; break;
            default:
                monthName = "not done yet"; break;
            }

            Console.WriteLine("{0} {1}", dayNum, monthName);
        }
        ...
    }
```

8. Save your work.

9. Compile the WhatDay1.cs program and correct any errors. Run the program. Verify that the program is working correctly by using the following data.

Day number	Month and day
32	February 1
60	March 1
91	April 1
186	July 5
304	October 31
309	November 5
327	November 23
359	December 25

▶ **To calculate the name of the month by using an enum**

1. You will now replace the **switch** statement that determines the month name from a month number with a more compact mechanism. Declare an **enum** type called **MonthName** and populate it with the names of the twelve months, starting with January and ending with December.

2. Comment out the entire **switch** statement.

Tip   Multiple lines of code can be commented by selecting the lines, then choosing **Edit**, **Advanced**, and then **Comment Selection**.

---

3. In place of the **switch** statement, add a statement that declares an **enum** **MonthName** variable called *temp*. Initialize *temp* from the *monthNum* **int** variable. You will need the following cast expression:

```
(MonthName)monthNum
```

4. Replace the initialization of *monthName* with the expression

```
temp.ToString( )
```

5. The completed program should be as follows:

```
using System;

enum MonthName
{
    January,
    February,
    March,
    April,
    May,
    June,
    July,
    August,
    September,
    October,
    November,
    December
}

class WhatDay
{
    static void Main( )
    {
        Console.Write("Please enter a day number between 1
and 365: ");
        string line = Console.ReadLine( );
        int dayNum = int.Parse(line);

        int monthNum = 0;

        // 12 if statements, as above

        End:

        MonthName temp = (MonthName)monthNum;
        string monthName = temp.ToString( );

        Console.WriteLine("{0} {1}", dayNum, monthName);
    }
    ...
}
```

6. Save your work.

7. Compile the WhatDay1.cs program and correct any errors. Run the program. Use the preceding table of data to verify that the program is still working correctly.

▶ **To replace the 12 if statements with one foreach statement**

1. You will now replace the 12 statements that calculate the day and month pairs with one **foreach** statement. Comment out all 12 **if** statements. You will replace these statements in the next steps.

2. Write a **foreach** statement that iterates through the provided **DaysInMonths** collection. To do this, add the following statement:

```
foreach (int daysInMonth in DaysInMonths) ...
```

3. Add a block statement as the body of the **foreach** statement. The contents of this block will be very similar to an individual commented-out **if** statement except that the *daysInMonth* variable is used instead of the various integer literals.

4. Comment out the **End** label above the commented-out **switch** statement. Replace the **goto** statement in the **foreach** statement with a **break** statement.

5. The completed program should be as follows:

```
using System;

enum MonthName { ... }

class WhatDay
{
    static void Main( )
    {
        Console.Write("Please enter a day number between 1
↪and 365: ");
        string line = Console.ReadLine( );
        int dayNum = int.Parse(line);

        int monthNum = 0;

        foreach (int daysInMonth in DaysInMonths) {
            if (dayNum <= daysInMonth)
            {
                break;
            }
            else
            {
                dayNum -= daysInMonth;
                monthNum++;
            }
        }
        MonthName temp = (MonthName)monthNum;
        string monthName = temp.ToString( );

        Console.WriteLine("{0} {1}", dayNum, monthName);
    }
    ...
}
```

6. Save your work.

7. Compile the WhatDay1.cs program and correct any errors. Run the program. Use the preceding table of data to verify that the program is still working correctly.

8. Run the program, entering day numbers less than 1 and greater than 365, to see what happens.

◆ Handling Basic Exceptions

- **Why Use Exceptions?**
- **Exception Objects**
- **Using try and catch Blocks**
- **Multiple catch Blocks**

As a developer, you sometimes seem to spend more time checking for errors and handling them than you do on the core logic of the actual program. You can address this issue by using exceptions. Exceptions are designed to handle errors. In this section, you will learn how to catch and handle exceptions in C#.

Why Use Exceptions?

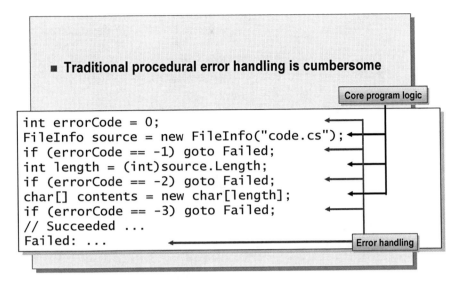

Planning for the unexpected, and recovering if it does happen, is the mark of a good, robust program. Errors can happen at almost any time during the compilation or execution of a program.

The core program logic from the slide is as follows:

```
FileInfo source = new FileInfo("code.cs");
int length = (int)source.Length;
char[ ] contents = new char[length];
...
```

Unfortunately, these core statements are lost in a confusing mass of intrusive error-handling code. This error-handling code obscures the logic of the program in a number of ways:

- Program logic and error-handling code become intermixed.

    The core program statements lose their conceptual wholeness as they become intermixed with alternating error-handling code. The program is then difficult to understand.

- All error code looks alike.

    All of the error-checking statements are similar. All of them test the same error code by using **if** statements. Also, there is a lot of duplicate code, which is always a warning sign.

- Error codes are not inherently meaningful.

    In this code, a number such as –1 does not have an explicit meaning. It could represent "Security error: no read permission," but only the documentation can tell you what –1 represents. Therefore, integer error codes are very "programmatic"; they do not describe the errors they represent.

■ Error codes are defined at the method level.

Every method reports its error by setting the error code to a specific value unique to it. No two methods can use the same value. This means that every method is coupled to every other method. You can clearly see this coupling in effect when the integer error codes are replaced by an enumeration, as in the following code:

```
enum ErrorCode {
    SecurityError = -1,
    IOError = -2,
    OutOfMemoryError = -3,
    ...
}
```

This code is better: An identifier such as FileNotFound is certainly more descriptive than –1. However, when a new named error is added to the **enum**, every method that names its errors in the **enum** will be affected and require recompiling.

■ Simple integers have limited descriptive power.

For example, –1 might be documented to mean "Security error: no read permission," but –1 cannot also provide the name of the file that you do not have permission to read.

■ Error codes are too easy to ignore.

For example, C programmers almost never check the **int** returned by the **printf** function. A **printf** is unlikely to fail, but if it does, it returns a negative integer value (usually –1).

As you can see, you need an alternative to the traditional approach of handling errors. Exceptions provide an alternative that is more flexible, requires less overhead, and produces meaningful error messages.

Exception Objects

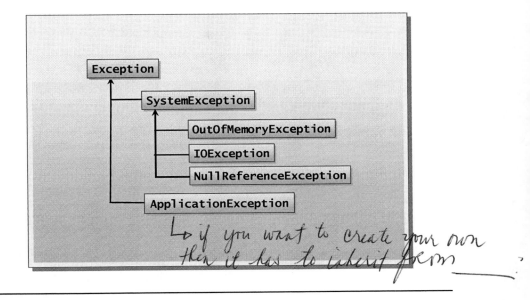

The programmatic error codes used in procedural error-handling code look similar to the following:

```
enum ErrorCode {
    SecurityError = -1,
    IOError = -2,
    OutOfMemoryError = -3,
    ...
}
```

The use of such error codes makes it difficult to supply information that you can use to recover from the error. For example, if an IOError is generated, you do not get information about what kind of error it is. Is it an attempt to write to a read-only file or a non-existent file, or is it a corrupt disk? Additionally, what file is being read from or written to?

To overcome this problem of lack of information about the generated error, the .NET Framework has defined a range of exception classes.

All exceptions derive from the class named **Exception**, which is a part of the common language runtime. The hierarchy between these exceptions is displayed on the slide. The exception classes provide the following benefits:

- Error messages are no longer represented by integer values or enums.

  The programmatic integer values such as -3 disappear. In their place, you use specific exception classes such as **OutOfMemoryException**. Each exception class can reside inside its own source file and is decoupled from all other exception classes.

- Meaningful error messages are generated.

  Each exception class is descriptive, clearly and obviously representing a specific error. Instead of a −3, you use a class called **OutOfMemoryException**. Each exception class can also contain information specific to itself. For example, a **FileNotFoundException** class could contain the name of the file that was not found.

Tip   To use exceptions effectively, you need to maintain a balance between exception classes that are too vague and those that are too precise. If the exception class is too vague, you will not be able to write a useful catch block. On the other hand, do not create an exception class that is so precise that it leaks implementation details and breaks encapsulation.

Using try and catch Blocks

■ **Object-oriented solution to error handling**

- Put the normal code in a **try** block

- Handle the exceptions in a separate **catch** block

```
try {
        Console.WriteLine("Enter a number");
        int i = int.Parse(Console.ReadLine());     Program logic
}
catch (OverflowException caught) ←─── Error handling
{
        Console.WriteLine(caught);
}
```

Can i use more than 1 catch → yes

Object orientation offers a structured solution to error-handling problems in the form of **try** and **catch** blocks. The idea is to physically separate the core program statements that handle the normal flow of control from the error-handling statements. Therefore, the sections of code that might throw exceptions are placed in a **try** block, and the code for handling exceptions in the **try** block is placed in a separate **catch** block.

The syntax of a **catch** block is as follows:

```
catch ( class-type identifier ) { ... }
```

The class type must be **System.Exception** or a type derived from **System.Exception**.

The identifier, which is optional, is a read-only local variable in the scope of the **catch** block.

```
catch (Exception caught) {
    ...
}
Console.WriteLine(caught); // Compile-time error:
                           // caught is no longer in scope
```

The example in the slide shows how to use **try** and **catch** statements. The **try** block encloses an expression that may generate the exception. if the exception occurs, the runtime stops normal execution and starts searching for a **catch** block that can catch the pending exception (based on its type). If an appropriate **catch** block is not found in the immediate function, the runtime will unwind the call stack searching for the calling function. If an appropriate **catch** block is not found there, it will search for the function that called the calling function, and so on, until it finds a **catch** block. (Or until it reaches the end of **Main**. If this happens, the program will shut down.) If it finds a **catch** block, the exception is considered to have been caught, and normal execution starts again, beginning with the body of the **catch** block (which in the slide writes out the message that is contained within the exception object **OverflowException**).

Therefore, if you use **try** and **catch** blocks, the error-handling statements no longer intermix themselves with the core logic statements, and this makes the program easier to understand.

Multiple catch Blocks

- **Each catch block catches one class of exception**
- **A try block can have one general catch block**
- **A try block is not allowed to catch a class that is derived from a class caught in an earlier catch block**

```
try
{
    Console.WriteLine("Enter first number");
    int i = int.Parse(Console.ReadLine());
    Console.WriteLine("Enter second number");
    int j = int.Parse(Console.ReadLine());
    int k = i / j;
}
catch (OverflowException caught) {...}
catch (DivideByZeroException caught) {...}
```

[handwritten: Variable / then what do u / what to do]

A block of code inside a **try** construct can contain many statements. Each statement could raise one or more different classes of exception. Since there are many different exception classes, it is acceptable to have many **catch** blocks, each catching a specific kind of exception.

An exception is caught solely based on its type. The runtime automatically catches exception objects of a particular type in a **catch** block for that type.

To get a better understanding of what is happening in a multiple **try-catch** block, consider the following code:

```
1. try {
2.      Console.WriteLine("Enter first number");
3.      int i = int.Parse(Console.ReadLine());
4.      Console.WriteLine("Enter second number");
5.      int j = int.Parse(Console.ReadLine());
6.      int k = i / j;
7. }
8. catch (OverflowException caught)
9. {
10.     Console.WriteLine(caught);
11. }
12. catch(DivideByZeroException caught)
13. {
14.     Console.WriteLine(caught);
15. }
16. ...
```

Line 3 initializes int i with a value read from the console. This can throw an exception object of class **OverflowException**. If it does, then line 4, 5, and 6 are not executed. Normal sequential execution is suspended, and control transfers to the first **catch** block that can catch that exception. In this example, this **catch** block is line 8. After control is transferred to this statement, it executes to its closing brace, and transfers control to line 16.

On the other hand, line 3 to 5 may not throw an exception. In this case, sequential execution will proceed normally to line 6. This line might throw an exception object of class **DivideByZeroException**. If it does, then control flow jumps to the **catch** block at line 12, this **catch** block executes normally, and control then transfers to line 16.

If none of the statements in the **try** block throw an exception, then the control flow reaches the end of the **try** block and transfers to line 16. Note that the control flow enters a **catch** block only if an exception is thrown.

You can write the statements in a **try** block without being concerned about whether an earlier statement in the **try** block will fail. If an earlier statement does throw an exception, the control flow will not physically reach the statements that follow it in the **try** block.

If the control flow fails to find a suitable **catch** block, it will terminate the current method call and resume its search at the statement from which the method call was invoked. It will continue its search, unwinding the call stack all the way back to **Main** if necessary. If this causes **Main** itself to be terminated, the thread or process that invoked **Main** is terminated in an implementation-defined fashion.

General catch Block

A general **catch** block, also known as a general **catch** clause, can catch any exception regardless of its class and is often used to trap any exceptions that might fall through because of the lack of an appropriate handler.

There are two ways to write a general **catch** block. You can write a simple **catch** statement as shown:

```
catch { ... }
```

You can also write the following:

```
catch (System.Exception) { ... }
```

A **try** block can have only one general **catch** block. For example, the following code will generate an error:

```
try {
    ...
}
catch { ... }
catch { ... } // Error
```

If a general **catch** block is present, it must be the last **catch** block in the program, as follows:

```
try {
    ...
}
catch { ... }
catch (OutOfMemoryException caught) { ... } // Error
```

You will generate a compile time error if you catch the same class twice, as in the following example:

```
catch (OutOfMemoryException caught) { ... }
catch (OutOfMemoryException caught) { ... } // Error
```

You will also generate a compile time error if you try to catch a class that is derived from a class caught in an earlier **catch** block, as follows:

```
catch (Exception caught) { ... }
catch (OutOfMemoryException caught) { ... } // Error
```

This code results in an error because the **OutOfMemoryException** class is derived from the **SystemException** class, which is in turn derived from the **Exception** class.

◆ Raising Exceptions

- **The throw Statement**
- **The finally Clause**
- **Checking for Arithmetic Overflow**
- **Guidelines for Handling Exceptions**

C# provides the **throw** statement and the **finally** clause so that programmers can raise exceptions if required and handle them as appropriate.

After completing this lesson, you will be able to:

- Raise your own exceptions.
- Enable checking for arithmetic overflow.

The throw Statement  *① you want to create new exception*

- **Throw an appropriate exception**
- **Give the exception a meaningful message**

```
throw expression ;
```

```
if (minute < 1 || minute >= 60) {
  throw new InvalidTimeException(minute +
                        " is not a valid minute");
  // !! Not reached !!
}
```

The **try** and **catch** blocks are used to trap errors that are raised by a C# program. You have seen that instead of signaling an error by returning a special value, or assigning it to a global error variable, C# causes execution to be transferred to the appropriate **catch** clause.

System-Defined Exceptions

When it needs to raise an exception, the runtime executes a **throw** statement and raises a system-defined exception. This immediately suspends the normal sequential execution of the program and transfers control to the first **catch** block that can handle the exception based on its class.

Raising Your Own Exceptions

You can use the **throw** statement to raise your own exceptions, as shown in the following example:

```
if (minute < 1 || minute >= 60) {
  string fault = minute + "is not a valid minute";
  throw new InvalidTimeException(fault);
  // !!Not reached!!
}
```

In this example, the **throw** statement is used to raise a user-defined exception, InvalidTimeException, if the time being parsed does not constitute a valid time.

Exceptions typically expect a meaningful message string as a parameter when they are created. This message can be displayed or logged when the exception is caught. It is also good practice to throw an appropriate class of exception.

Caution   C++ programmers will be accustomed to creating and throwing an exception object with a single statement, as shown in the following code:

```
throw out_of_range("index out of bounds");
```

The syntax in C# is very similar but requires the **new** keyword, as follows:

```
throw new FileNotFoundException("...");
```

Throwing Objects

You can only throw an object if the type of that object is directly or indirectly derived from **System.Exception**. This is different from C++, in which objects of any type can be thrown, such as in the following code:

```
throw 42; // Allowed in C++, but not in C#
```

You can use a **throw** statement in a **catch** block to rethrow the current exception object, as in the following example:

```
catch (Exception caught) {
    ...
    throw caught;
}
```

You can also throw a new exception object of a different type:

```
catch (IOException caught) {
    ...
    throw new FileNotFoundException(filename);
}
```

In the preceding example, notice that the **IOException** object, and any information it contains, is lost when the exception is converted into a **FileNotFoundException** object. A better idea is to wrap the exception, adding new information but retaining existing information as shown in the following code:

```
catch (IOException caught) {
    ...
    throw new FileNotFoundException(filename, caught);
}
```

This ability to map an exception object is particularly useful at the boundaries of a layered system architecture.

A **throw** statement with no expression can be used, but only in a **catch** block. It rethrows the exception that is currently being handled. This action is called a rethrow in C++ as well. Therefore, the following two lines of code produce identical results:

```
catch (OutOfMemoryException caught) { throw caught; }
...
catch (OutOfMemoryException) { throw ; }
```

The finally Clause

■ **All of the statements in a finally block are always executed**

```
Monitor.Enter(x);
try {
    ...
}
finally {
    Monitor.Exit(x);
}
```

Any catch blocks are optional

[handwritten notes in left margin:]

① If you don't have CATCH, Finally is mandatory.
If you have CATCH, Finally is optional.

② Finally should always always go with TRY.

C# provides the **finally** clause to enclose a set of statements that need to be executed regardless of the course of control flow. Therefore, if control leaves a **try** block as a result of normal execution because the control flow reaches the end of the **try** block, the statements of the **finally** block are executed. Also, if control leaves a **try** block as a result of a **throw** statement or a jump statement such as **break**, **continue**, or **goto**, the statements of the **finally** block are executed.

The **finally** block is useful in two situations: to avoid duplication of statements and to release resources after an exception has been thrown.

Avoiding Duplication of Statements

If the statements at the end of a **try** block are duplicated in a general **catch** block, the duplication can be avoided by moving the statements into a **finally** block. Consider the following example:

```
try {
    ...
    statements
}
catch {
    ...
    statements
}
```

You can simplify the preceding code by rewriting it as follows:

```
try {
    ...
}
catch {
    ...
}
finally {
    statements
}
```

It is an error for a **break**, **continue**, or **goto** statement to transfer control out of a **finally** block. They can be used only if the target of the jump is within the same **finally** block. However, it is always an error for a **return** statement to occur in a **finally** block, even if the **return** statement is the last statement in the block.

If an exception is thrown during the execution of a **finally** block, it is propagated to the next enclosing **try** block, as shown:

```
try {
    try {
        ...
    }
    catch {
        // ExampleException is not caught here
    }
    finally {
        throw new ExampleException("who will catch me?");
    }
}
catch {
    // ExampleException is caught here
}
```

If an exception is thrown during the execution of a **finally** block, and another exception was in the process of being propagated, then the original exception is lost, as shown:

```
try {
    throw new ExampleException("Will be lost");
}
finally {
    throw new ExampleException("Might be found and caught");
}
```

Checking for Arithmetic Overflow

- **By default, arithmetic overflow is not checked**
  - A checked statement turns overflow checking on

```
checked {
    int number = int.MaxValue;
    Console.WriteLine(++number);
}
```

`OverflowException`

Exception object is thrown.
WriteLine is *not* executed.

```
unchecked {
    int number = int.MaxValue;
    Console.WriteLine(++number);
}
```

MaxValue + 1 is negative?

`-2147483648`

By default, a C# program will not check arithmetic for overflow. The following code provides an example:

```
// example.cs
class Example
{
    static void Main( )
    {
        int number = int.MaxValue;
        Console.WriteLine(++number);
    }
}
```

In the preceding code, *number* is initialized to the maximum value for an **int**. The expression ++*number* increments *number* to –2147483648, the largest negative **int** value, which is then written to the console. No error message is generated.

Controlling Arithmetic Overflow Checking

When compiling a C# program, you can globally turn on arithmetic overflow checking by using the /checked+ command line option, as follows:

```
c:\ csc /checked+ example.cs
```

The resulting executable program will cause an exception of class **System.OverflowException**.

Similarly, you can turn off global arithmetic overflow checking by using the /checked- command line option, as follows:

```
c:\ csc /checked- example.cs
```

The resulting executable program will silently wrap the **int** value to int.MinValue and will not cause an exception of class **System.OverflowException**.

Creating Checked and Unchecked Statements

You can use the **checked** and **unchecked** keywords to create statements that are explicitly checked or unchecked statements:

```
checked   { statement-list }
unchecked { statement-list }
```

Regardless of the compile-time /checked setting, the statements inside a **checked** statement list are *always* checked for arithmetic overflow. Similarly, regardless of the compile-time /checked setting, the statements inside an **unchecked** statement list are *never* checked for arithmetic overflow.

Creating Checked and Unchecked Expressions

You can also use the **checked** and **unchecked** keywords to create checked and unchecked expressions:

```
checked ( expression )
unchecked ( expression )
```

A **checked** expression is checked for arithmetic overflow; an **unchecked** expression is not. For example, the following code will generate a **System.OverflowException**.

```
// example.cs
class Example
{
    static void Main( )
    {
        int number = int.MaxValue;
        Console.WriteLine(checked(++number));
    }
}
```

Guidelines for Handling Exceptions

- **Throwing**
  - Avoid exceptions for normal or expected cases
  - Never create and throw objects of class **Exception**
  - Include a description string in an **Exception** object
  - Throw objects of the most specific class possible
- **Catching**
  - Arrange **catch** blocks from specific to general
  - Do not let exceptions drop off **Main**

Use the following guidelines for handling exceptions:

- Avoid exceptions for normal or expected cases.

- Never create or throw objects of class **Exception**.

  Create exception classes that are derived directly or indirectly from **SystemException** (and never from the root **Exception** class). The following code provides an example:

  ```
  class SyntaxException : SystemException
  {
      ...
  }
  ```

- Include a description string in an **Exception** object.

  Always include a useful description string in an exception object, as shown:

  ```
  string description =
     String.Format("{0}({1}): newline in string constant",
  filename, linenumber);
  throw new SyntaxException(description);
  ```

- Throw objects of the most specific class possible.

  Throw the most specific exception possible when the user might be able to use this specific information. For example, throw a **FileNotFoundException** rather than a more general **IOException**.

- Arrange **catch** blocks from specific to general.

  Arrange your **catch** blocks from the most specific exception to the most general exception, as shown:

  ```
  catch (SyntaxException caught) { ... } // Do this
  catch (Exception caught) { ... }
  ```

- Do not let exceptions drop off **Main**.

  Put a general **catch** clause in **Main** to ensure that exceptions never drop off the end of the program.

  ```
  static void Main( )
  {
      try {
          ...
      }
      catch (Exception caught) {
          ...
      }
  }
  ```

Lab 4.2: Using Exceptions

Objectives

After completing this lab, you will be able to:

- Throw and catch exceptions.
- Display error messages.

Prerequisites

Before working on this lab, you should be familiar with the following:

- Creating variables in C#
- Using common operators in C#
- Creating **enum** types in C#

Estimated time to complete this lab: 30 minutes

Exercise 1
Validating the Day Number

In this exercise, you will add functionality to the program that you created in Exercise 1. The program will examine the initial day number that is entered by the user. If it is less than 1 or greater than 365, the program will throw an **InvalidArgument** exception ("Day out of range"). The program will trap this exception in a **catch** clause and display a diagnostic message on the console.

▶ **To validate the day number**

1. Open the project WhatDay2.sln in the
    install folder\Labs\Lab04\Starter\WhatDay2 folder.

2. Enclose the entire contents of **WhatDay.Main** in a **try** block.

3. After the **try** block, add a **catch** clause that catches exceptions of type **System.Exception** and name them **caught**. In the **catch** block, add a **WriteLine** statement to write the exception caught to the console.

4. Add an **if** statement after the declaration of the *dayNum* variable. The **if** statement will throw a **new** exception object of type **System.ArgumentOutOfRangeException** if *dayNum* is less than 1 or greater than 365. Use the **string** literal "Day out of range" to create the exception object.

5. The completed program should be as follows:

```
using System;

enum MonthName { ... }

class WhatDay
{
    static void Main( )
    {
        try {
            Console.Write("Please enter a day number
➥between 1 and 365: ");
            string line = Console.ReadLine( );
            int dayNum = int.Parse(line);

            if (dayNum < 1 || dayNum > 365) {
                throw new ArgumentOutOfRangeException("Day
➥out of range");
            }

            int monthNum = 0;

            foreach (int daysInMonth in DaysInMonths) {
                if (dayNum <= daysInMonth) {
                    break;
                } else {
                    dayNum -= daysInMonth;
                    monthNum++;
                }
            }
            MonthName temp = (MonthName)monthNum;
            string monthName = temp.ToString( );

            Console.WriteLine("{0} {1}", dayNum,
➥monthName);
        }
        catch (Exception caught) {
            Console.WriteLine(caught);
        }
    }
    ...
}
```

6. Save your work.

7. Compile the WhatDay2.cs program and correct any errors. Run the program. Use the table of data provided in Lab4.1 (Exercise 1) to verify that the program is still working correctly.

8. Run the program, entering day numbers less than 1 and greater than 365. Verify that invalid input is safely trapped and that the exception object is thrown, caught, and displayed.

Exercise 2
Handling Leap Years

In this exercise, you will add functionality to the program that you worked on in Exercise 1. After you complete this exercise, the program will prompt the user for a year in addition to a day number. The program will detect whether the specified year is a leap year. It will validate whether the day number is between 1 and 366 if the year is a leap year, or whether it is between 1 and 365 if the year is not a leap year. Finally, it will use a new **foreach** statement to correctly calculate the month and day pair for leap years.

▶ **To enter the year from the console**

1. Open the WhatDay3.sln project in the
   install folder\Labs\Lab04\Starter\WhatDay3 folder.

2. Add to the beginning of **WhatDay.Main** a **System.Console.Write** statement that writes a prompt to the console asking the user to enter a year.

3. Change the declaration and initialization of the **string** *line* to an assignment. Change `string line = Console.ReadLine( );` to
   `line = Console.ReadLine( );`.

4. Add a statement to **Main** that declares a **string** variable called *line* and initializes it with a line read from the console by the **System.Console.ReadLine** method.

5. Add a statement to **Main** that declares an **int** variable called *yearNum* and initializes it with the integer returned by the **int.Parse** method.

6. The completed program should be as follows:

```
using System;

enum MonthName { ... }

class WhatDay
{
    static void Main( )
    {
        try {
            Console.Write("Please enter the year: ");
            string line = Console.ReadLine( );
            int yearNum = int.Parse(line);

            Console.Write("Please enter a day number
↪between 1 and 365: ");
            line = Console.ReadLine( );
            int dayNum = int.Parse(line);

            // As before....
        }
        catch (Exception caught) {
            Console.WriteLine(caught);
        }
    }
    ...
}
```

7. Save your work.

8. Compile the WhatDay3.cs program and correct any errors.

▶ **To determine whether the year is a leap year**

1. Add a statement immediately after the declaration of *yearNum* that declares a **bool** variable called *isLeapYear*. Initialize this variable with a Boolean expression that determines whether *yearNum* is a leap year. A year is a leap year if the following two statements are both true:

    -   It is divisible by 4.

    -   It is either *not* divisible by 100, *or* it is divisible by 400.

2. Add an **if** statement immediately after the declaration of *isLeapYear*. In the **if** statement, write the string " IS a leap year" or " is NOT a leap year" to the console, depending on the value of *isLeapyear*. You will use this **if** statement to verify that the Boolean leap year determination is correct.

3. The completed program should be as follows:

```
using System;

enum MonthName { ... }

class WhatDay
{
    static void Main( )
    {
        try
        {
            Console.Write("Please enter the year: ");
            string line = Console.ReadLine( );
            int yearNum = int.Parse(line);

            bool isLeapYear = (yearNum % 4 == 0)
                && (yearNum % 100 != 0
                    || yearNum % 400 == 0);

            if (isLeapYear)
            {
                Console.WriteLine(" IS a leap year");
            } else
            {
                Console.WriteLine(" is NOT a leap year");
            }

            Console.Write("Please enter a day number
↪between 1 and 365: ");
            line = Console.ReadLine( );
            int dayNum = int.Parse(line);

            // As before...
        }
        catch (Exception caught)
        {
            Console.WriteLine(caught);
        }
    }
    ...
}
```

4. Save your work.

5. Compile the WhatDay3.cs program and correct any errors. Use the following table to verify that the Boolean leap year determination is correct.

A leap year	Not a leap year
1996	1999
2000	1900
2004	2001

6. Comment out the **if** statement that you added in step 2.

▶ **To validate the day number against 365 or 366**

1. Immediately after the declaration of *isLeapYear*, add a declaration of an **int** variable called *maxDayNum*. Initialize *maxDayNum* with either 366 or 365, depending on whether *isLeapYear* is **true** or **false**, respectively.

2. Change the **WriteLine** statement that prompts the user for the day number. It should display the range 1 to 366 if a leap year was entered and 1 to 365 if a non–leap year was entered.

3. Compile the WhatDay3.cs program and correct any errors. Run the program and verify that you have implemented the previous step correctly.

4. Change the **if** statement that validates the value of *dayNum* to use the variable *maxDayNum* instead of the literal 365.

5. The completed program should be as follows:

```
using System;

enum MonthName { ... }

class WhatDay
{
    static void Main( )
    {
        try
        {
            Console.Write("Please enter the year: ");
            string line = Console.ReadLine( );
            int yearNum = int.Parse(line);

            bool isLeapYear = (yearNum % 4 == 0)
                && (yearNum % 100 != 0
                    || yearNum % 400 == 0);

            int maxDayNum = isLeapYear ? 366 : 365;

            Console.Write("Please enter a day number
between 1 and {0}: ", maxDayNum);
            line = Console.ReadLine( );
            int dayNum = int.Parse(line);

            if (dayNum < 1 || dayNum > maxDayNum) {
                throw new ArgumentOutOfRangeException("Day
out of range");
            }
            // As before....
        }
        catch (Exception caught)
        {
            Console.WriteLine(caught);
        }
    }
    ...
}
```

6. Save your work.

7. Compile the WhatDay3.cs program and correct any errors. Run the program and verify that you have implemented the previous step correctly.

▶ **To correctly calculate the month and day pair for leap years**

1. After the **if** statement that validates the day number and the declaration of the *monthNum* integer, add an **if-else** statement. The Boolean expression used in this **if-else** statement will be the variable *isLeapYear*.

2. Move the **foreach** statement so it becomes the embedded statement in the **if-else** statement in *both* the **true** *and* the **false** cases. After this step, your code should be as follows:

```
if (isLeapYear)
{
    foreach (int daysInMonth in DaysInMonths) {
        ...
    }
} else
{
    foreach (int daysInMonth in DaysInMonths) {
        ...
    }
}
```

3. Save your work.

4. Compile the WhatDay3.cs program and correct any errors. Run the program and verify that day numbers in non–leap years are still handled correctly.

5. The next step will use the **DaysInLeapMonths** collection that has been provided. This is a collection of **int** values like **DaysInMonths**, except that the second value in the collection (the number of days in February) is 29 rather than 28.

6. Use **DaysInLeapMonths** instead of **DaysInMonth** in the **true** part of the **if-else** statement.

7. The completed program should be as follows:

```csharp
using System;

enum MonthName { ... }

class WhatDay
{
    static void Main( )
    {
        try {
            Console.Write("Please enter the year: ");
            string line = Console.ReadLine( );
            int yearNum = int.Parse(line);

            bool isLeapYear = (yearNum % 4 == 0)
                && (yearNum % 100 != 0
                    || yearNum % 400 == 0);

            int maxDayNum = isLeapYear ? 366 : 365;

            Console.Write("Please enter a day number
between 1 and {0}: ", maxDayNum);
            line = Console.ReadLine( );
            int dayNum = int.Parse(line);

            if (dayNum < 1 || dayNum > maxDayNum) {
                throw new ArgumentOutOfRangeException("Day
out of range");
            }

            int monthNum = 0;

            if (isLeapYear) {
                foreach (int daysInMonth in
DaysInLeapMonths) {
                    if (dayNum <= daysInMonth) {
                        break;
                    } else {
                        dayNum -= daysInMonth;
                        monthNum++;
                    }
                }
            } else {
                foreach (int daysInMonth in DaysInMonths) {
                    if (dayNum <= daysInMonth) {
                        break;
                    } else {
                        dayNum -= daysInMonth;
                        monthNum++;
                    }
                }
            }
        }
```

Code continued on following page.

```
                    MonthName temp = (MonthName)monthNum;
                    string monthName = temp.ToString( );
                    Console.WriteLine("{0} {1}", dayNum,
   ↪monthName);
            }
            catch (Exception caught) {
                Console.WriteLine(caught);
            }
        }
        ...
}
```

8. Save your work.

9. Compile the WhatDay3.cs program and correct any errors. Run the program, using the data in the following table to verify that the program is working correctly.

Year	Day Number	Month-Day Pair
1999	32	February 1
2000	32	February 1
1999	60	March 1
2000	60	February 29
1999	91	April 1
2000	91	March 31
1999	186	July 5
2000	186	July 4
1999	304	October 31
2000	304	October 30
1999	309	November 5
2000	309	November 4
1999	327	November 23
2000	327	November 22
1999	359	December 25
2000	359	December 24

Review

■ **Introduction to Statements**

■ **Using Selection Statements**

■ **Using Iteration Statements**

■ **Using Jump Statements**

■ **Handling Basic Exceptions**

■ **Raising Exceptions**

1. Write an **if** statement that tests whether an **int** variable called *hour* is greater than or equal to zero and less than 24. If it is not, reset *hour* to zero.

2. Write a **do-while** statement, the body of which reads an integer from the console and stores it in an **int** called *hour*. Write the loop so that the loop will exit only when *hour* has a value between 1 and 23 (inclusive).

3. Write a **for** statement that meets all of the conditions of the preceding question and only allows five attempts to input a valid value for *hour*. Do not use **break** or **continue** statements.

4. Rewrite the code that you wrote for question 3, but this time use a **break** statement.

5. Write a statement that throws an exception of type **ArgumentOutOfRangeException** if the variable *percent* is less than zero or greater than 100.

6. The following code is meant to handle exceptions. Explain why this code is not correct. Fix the problem.

```
try
{
...
}
catch (Exception) {...}
catch (IOException) {...}
```

msdn training

Module 5: Methods and Parameters

Contents

Overview	1
Using Methods	2
Using Parameters	16
Using Overloaded Methods	29
Lab 5.1: Creating and Using Methods	37
Review	48

Microsoft

Overview

- **Using Methods**
- **Using Parameters**
- **Using Overloaded Methods**

In designing most applications, you divide the application into functional units. This is a central principle of application design because small sections of code are easier to understand, design, develop, and debug. Dividing the application into functional units also allows you to reuse functional components throughout the application.

In C#, you structure your application into classes that contain named blocks of code; these are called methods. A *method* is a member of a class that performs an action or computes a value.

After completing this module, you will be able to:

- Create static methods that accept parameters and return values.

- Pass parameters to methods in different ways.

- Declare and use overloaded methods.

◆ Using Methods

- **Defining Methods**
- **Calling Methods**
- **Using the return Statement**
- **Using Local Variables**
- **Returning Values**

In this section, you will learn how to use methods in C#. Methods are important mechanisms for structuring program code. You will learn how to create methods and how to call them from within a single class and from one class to another.

You will learn how to use local variables, as well as how to allocate and destroy them.

You will also learn how to return a value from a method, and how to use parameters to transfer data into and out of a method.

Defining Methods

- **Main is a method**
  - Use the same syntax for defining your own methods

```
using System;
class ExampleClass              — static does not need
{                                 objects.
    static void ExampleMethod( )
    {
        Console.WriteLine("Example method");
    }
    static void Main( )
    {
        // ...
    }
}
```

A method is group of C# statements that have been brought together and given a name. Most modern programming languages have a similar concept; you can think of a method as being like a function, a subroutine, a procedure or a subprogram.

Examples of Methods

The code on the slide contains three methods:

- The **Main** method
- The **WriteLine** method
- The **ExampleMethod** method

The **Main** method is the entry point of the application. The **WriteLine** method is part of the Microsoft® .NET Framework. It can be called from within your program. The **WriteLine** method is a static method of the class **System.Console**. The **ExampleMethod** method belongs to **ExampleClass**. This method calls the **WriteLine** method.

In C#, all methods belong to a class. This is unlike programming languages such as C, C++, and Microsoft Visual Basic®, which allow global subroutines and functions.

Creating Methods

When creating a method, you must specify the following:

- Name

  You cannot give a method the same name as a variable, a constant, or any other non-method item declared in the class. The method name can be any allowable C# identifier, and it is case sensitive.

- Parameter list

  The method name is followed by a parameter list for the method. This is enclosed between parentheses. The parentheses must be supplied even if there are no parameters, as is shown in the examples on the slide.

- Body of the method

  Following the parentheses is the body of the method. You must enclose the method body within braces ({ and }), even if there is only one statement.

Syntax for Defining Methods

To create a method, use the following syntax:

```
static void MethodName( )
{
  method body
}
```

The following example shows how to create a method named **ExampleMethod** in the **ExampleClass** class:

```
using System;
class ExampleClass
{
    static void ExampleMethod( )
    {
        Console.WriteLine("Example method");
    }

    static void Main( )
    {
        Console.WriteLine("Main method");
    }
}
```

Note Method names in C# are case-sensitive. Therefore, you can declare and use methods with names that differ only in case. For example, you can declare methods called **print** and **PRINT** in the same class. However, the common language runtime requires that method names within a class differ in ways other than case alone, to ensure compatibility with languages in which method names are case-insensitive. This is important if you want your application to interact with applications written in languages other than C#.

Calling Methods

■ **After you define a method, you can:**

- Call a method from within the same class
  Use method's name followed by a parameter list in parentheses

- Call a method that is in a different class
  You must indicate to the compiler which class contains the method to call
  The called method must be declared with the **public** keyword

- Use nested calls
  Methods can call methods, which can call other methods, and so on

---

After you define a method, you can call it from within the same class and from other classes.

Calling Methods

To call a method, use the name of the method followed by a parameter list in parentheses. The parentheses are required even if the method that you call has no parameters, as shown in the following example.

```
MethodName( );
```

Note to Visual Basic Developers   There is no **Call** statement. Parentheses are required for all method calls.

In the following example, the program begins at the start of the **Main** method of **ExampleClass**. The first statement displays "The program is starting." The second statement in **Main** is the call to **ExampleMethod**. Control flow passes to the first statement within **ExampleMethod**, and "Hello, world" appears. At the end of the method, control passes to the statement immediately following the method call, which is the statement that displays "The program is ending."

```
using System;

class ExampleClass
{
    static void ExampleMethod( )
    {
        Console.WriteLine("Hello, world");
    }

    static void Main( )
    {
        Console.WriteLine("The program is starting");
        ExampleMethod( );
        Console.WriteLine("The program is ending");
    }
}
```

Calling Methods from Other Classes

To allow methods in one class to call methods in another class, you must:

- Specify which class contains the method you want to call.

  To specify which class contains the method, use the following syntax:

  ```
  ClassName.MethodName( );
  ```

- Declare the method that is called with the **public** keyword.

The following example shows how to call the method **TestMethod**, which is defined in class **A**, from **Main** in class **B**:

```
using System;

class A
{
    public static void TestMethod( )
    {
        Console.WriteLine("This is TestMethod in class A");
    }
}

class B
{
    static void Main( )
    {
        A.TestMethod( );
    }
}
```

If, in the example above, the class name were removed, the compiler would search for a method called **TestMethod** in class **B**. Since there is no method of that name in that class, the compiler will display the following error: "The name 'TestMethod' does not exist in the class or namespace 'B.'"

If you do not declare a method as public, it becomes private to the class by default. For example, if you omit the **public** keyword from the definition of **TestMethod**, the compiler will display the following error: "'A.TestMethod()' is inaccessible due to its protection level."

You can also use the **private** keyword to specify that the method can only be called from inside the class. The following two lines of code have exactly the same effect because methods are private by default:

```
private static void MyMethod( );
static void MyMethod( );
```

The **public** and **private** keywords shown above specify the *accessibility* of the method. These keywords control whether a method can be called from outside of the class in which it is defined.

Nesting Method Calls

You can also call methods from within methods. The following example shows how to nest method calls:

```
using System;
class NestExample
{
    static void Method1( )
    {
        Console.WriteLine("Method1");
    }
    static void Method2( )
    {
        Method1( );
        Console.WriteLine("Method2");
        Method1( );
    }
    static void Main( )
    {
        Method2( );
        Method1( );
    }
}
```

The output from this program is as follows:

```
Method1
Method2
Method1
Method1
```

You can call an unlimited number of methods by nesting. There is no predefined limit to the nesting level. However, the run-time environment might impose limits, usually because of the amount of RAM available to perform the process. Each method call needs memory to store return addresses and other information.

As a general rule, if you are running out of memory for nested method calls, you probably have a class design problem.

Using the return Statement

- **Immediate return**

- **Return with a conditional statement**

```
static void ExampleMethod( )
{
    int numBeans;
    //...

    Console.WriteLine("Hello");
    if (numBeans < 10)
        return;
    Console.WriteLine("World");
}
```

You can use the **return** statement to make a method return immediately to the caller. Without a **return** statement, execution usually returns to the caller when the last statement in the method is reached.

Immediate Return

By default, a method returns to its caller when the end of the last statement in the code block is reached. If you want a method to return immediately to the caller, use the **return** statement.

In the following example, the method will display "Hello," and then immediately return to its caller:

```
static void ExampleMethod( )
{
    Console.WriteLine("Hello");
    return;
    Console.WriteLine("World");
}
```

Using the **return** statement like this is not very useful because the final call to **Console.WriteLine** is never executed. If you have enabled the C# compiler warnings at level 2 or higher, the compiler will display the following message: "Unreachable code detected."

Return with a Conditional Statement

It is more common, and much more useful, to use the **return** statement as part of a conditional statement such as **if** or **switch**. This allows a method to return to the caller if a given condition is met.

In the following example, the method will return if the variable *numBeans* is less than 10; otherwise, execution will continue within this method.

```
static void ExampleMethod( )
{
   int numBeans;
   //...
   Console.WriteLine("Hello");
   if (numBeans < 10)
      return;
   Console.WriteLine("World");
}
```

Tip   It is generally regarded as good programming style for a method to have one entry point and one exit point. The design of C# ensures that all methods begin execution at the first statement. A method with no **return** statements has one exit point, at the end of the code block. A method with multiple **return** statements has multiple exit points, which can make the method difficult to understand and maintain in some cases.

Return with a Value

If a method is defined with a data type rather than **void**, the return mechanism is used to assign a value to the function. This will be discussed later in this module.

Using Local Variables

- **Local variables**
  - Created when method begins
  - Private to the method
  - Destroyed on exit
- **Shared variables**
  - Class variables are used for sharing
- **Scope conflicts**
  - Compiler will not warn if local and class names clash

Each method has its own set of local variables. You can use these variables only inside the method in which they are declared. Local variables are not accessible from elsewhere in the application.

Local Variables

You can include local variables in the body of a method, as shown in the following example:

```
static void MethodWithLocals( )
{
    int x = 1; // Variable with initial value
    ulong y;
    string z;
        ...
}
```

You can assign local variables an initial value. (For an example, see variable x in the preceding code.) If you do not assign a value or provide an initial expression to determine a value, the variable will not be initialized.

The variables that are declared in one method are completely separate from variables that are declared in other methods, even if they have the same names.

Memory for local variables is allocated each time the method is called and released when the method terminates. Therefore, any values stored in these variables will not be retained from one method call to the next.

Shared Variables

Consider the following code, which attempts to count the number of times a method has been called:

```
class CallCounter_Bad
{
    static void Init( )
    {
        int nCount = 0;
    }
    static void CountCalls( )
    {
        int nCount;
        ++nCount;
        Console.WriteLine("Method called {0} time(s)", nCount);
    }
    static void Main( )
    {
        Init( );
        CountCalls( );
        CountCalls( );
    }
}
```

This program cannot be compiled because of two important problems. The variable *nCount* in **Init** is not the same as the variable *nCount* in **CountCalls**. No matter how many times you call the method **CountCalls**, the value *nCount* is lost each time **CountCalls** finishes.

The correct way to write this code is to use a class variable, as shown in the following example:

```
class CallCounter_Good
{
    static int nCount;
    static void Init( )
    {
        nCount = 0;
    }
    static void CountCalls( )
    {
        ++nCount;
        Console.Write("Method called " + nCount + " time(s).");
    }
    static void Main( )
    {
        Init( );
        CountCalls( );
        CountCalls( );
    }
}
```

In this example, *nCount* is declared at the class level rather than at the method level. Therefore, *nCount* is shared between all of the methods in the class.

Scope Conflicts

In C#, you can declare a local variable that has the same name as a class variable, but this can produce unexpected results. In the following example, *NumItems* is declared as a variable of class **ScopeDemo**, and also declared as a local variable in **Method1**. The two variables are completely different. In **Method1**, *numItems* refers to the local variable. In **Method2**, *numItems* refers to the class variable.

```
class ScopeDemo
{
    static int numItems = 0;
    static void Method1( )
    {
        int numItems = 42;
            ...
    }
    static void Method2( )
    {
        numItems = 61;
    }
}
```

Tip   Because the C# compiler will not warn you when local variables and class variables have the same names, you can use a naming convention to distinguish local variables from class variables.

Returning Values

- Declare the method with non-void type
- Add a return statement with an expression
  - Sets the return value
  - Returns to caller
- Non-void methods must return a value

```
static int TwoPlusTwo( ) {
    int a,b;
    a = 2;
    b = 2;
    return a + b;
}
```

```
int x;
x = TwoPlusTwo( );
Console.WriteLine(x);
```

You have learned how to use the **return** statement to immediately terminate a method. You can also use the **return** statement to return a value from a method. To return a value, you must:

1. Declare the method with the value type that you want to return.

2. Add a **return** statement inside the method.

3. Include the value that you want to return to the caller.

Declaring Methods with Non-Void Type

To declare a method so that it will return a value to the caller, replace the **void** keyword with the type of the value that you want to return.

Adding return Statements

The **return** keyword followed by an expression terminates the method immediately and returns the expression as the return value of the method.

The following example shows how to declare a method named **TwoPlusTwo** that will return a value of 4 to **Main** when **TwoPlusTwo** is called:

```
class ExampleReturningValue
{
    static int TwoPlusTwo( )
    {
        int a,b;
        a = 2;
        b = 2;
        return a + b;
    }

    static void Main( )
    {
        int x;
        x = TwoPlusTwo( );
        Console.WriteLine(x);
    }
}
```

Note that the returned value is an **int**. This is because **int** is the return type of the method. When the method is called, the value 4 is returned. In this example, the value is stored in the local variable *x* in **Main**.

Non-Void Methods Must Return Values

If you declare a method with a non-void type, you must add at least one **return** statement. The compiler attempts to check that each non-void method returns a value to the calling method in all circumstances. If the compiler detects that a non-void method has no **return** statement, it will display the following error message: "Not all code paths return a value." You will also see this error message if the compiler detects that it is possible to execute a non-void method without returning a value.

Tip   You can only use the **return** statement to return one value from each method call. If you need to return more than one value from a method call, you can use the **ref** or **out** parameters, which are discussed later in this module. Alternatively, you can return a reference to an array or class or struct, which can contain multiple values. The general guideline that says to avoid using multiple **return** statements in a single method applies equally to non-void methods.

◆ Using Parameters

- ■ **Declaring and Calling Parameters**
- ■ **Mechanisms for Passing Parameters**
- ■ **Pass by Value**
- ■ **Pass by Reference**
- ■ **Output Parameters**
- ■ **Using Variable-Length Parameter Lists**
- ■ **Guidelines for Passing Parameters**
- ■ **Using Recursive Methods**

In this section, you will learn how to declare parameters and how to call methods with parameters. You will also learn how to pass parameters. Finally, you will learn how C# supports recursive method calls.

In this section you will learn how to:

- ■ Declare and call parameters.
- ■ Pass parameters by using the following mechanisms:
  - Pass by value
  - Pass by reference
  - Output parameters
- ■ Use recursive method calls.

Declaring and Calling Parameters

- **Declaring parameters**
  - Place between parentheses after method name
  - Define type and name for each parameter
- **Calling methods with parameters**
  - Supply a value for each parameter

```
static void MethodWithParameters(int n, string y)
{ ... }

MethodWithParameters(2, "Hello, world");
```

Parameters allow information to be passed into and out of a method. When you define a method, you can include a list of parameters in parentheses following the method name. In the examples so far in this module, the parameter lists have been empty.

Declaring Parameters

Each parameter has a type and a name. You declare parameters by placing the parameter declarations inside the parentheses that follow the name of the method. The syntax that is used to declare parameters is similar to the syntax that is used to declare local variables, except that you separate each parameter declaration with a comma instead of with a semicolon.

The following example shows how to declare a method with parameters:

```
static void MethodWithParameters(int n, string y)
{
    // ...
}
```

This example declares the **MethodWithParameters** method with two parameters: *n* and *y*. The first parameter is of type **int**, and the second is of type **string**. Note that commas separate each parameter in the parameter list.

Calling Methods with Parameters

The calling code must supply the parameter values when the method is called.

The following code shows two examples of how to call a method with parameters. In each case, the values of the parameters are found and placed into the parameters *n* and *y* at the start of the execution of **MethodWithParameters**.

```
MethodWithParameters(2, "Hello, world");

int p = 7;
string s = "Test message";

MethodWithParameters(p, s);
```

Mechanisms for Passing Parameters

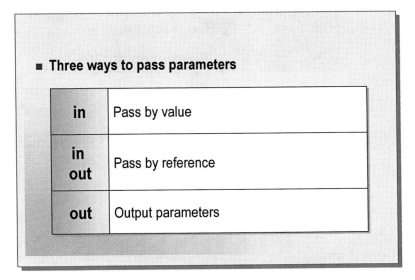

Parameters can be passed in three different ways:

- By value

  Value parameters are sometimes called *in parameters* because data can be transferred into the method but cannot be transferred out.

- By reference

  Reference parameters are sometimes called *in/out parameters* because data can be transferred into the method and out again.

- By output

  Output parameters are sometimes called *out parameters* because data can be transferred out of the method but cannot be transferred in.

Pass by Value

■ **Default mechanism for passing parameters:**

- Parameter value is copied

- Variable can be changed inside the method

- Has no effect on value outside the method

- Parameter must be of the same type or compatible type

```
static void AddOne(int x)
{
    x++; // Increment x
}
static void Main( )
{
    int k = 6;
    AddOne(k);
    Console.WriteLine(k); // Display the value 6, not 7
}
```

In applications, most parameters are used for passing information into a method but not out. Therefore, pass by value is the default mechanism for passing parameters in C#.

Defining Value Parameters

The simplest definition of a parameter is a type name followed by a variable name. This is known as a *value parameter*. When the method is called, a new storage location is created for each value parameter, and the values of the corresponding expressions are copied into them.

The expression supplied for each value parameter must be the same type as the declaration of the value parameter, or a type that can be implicitly converted to that type. Within the method, you can write code that changes the value of the parameter. It will have no effect on any variables outside the method call.

In the following example, the variable *x* inside **AddOne** is completely separate from the variable *k* in **Main**. The variable *x* can be changed in **AddOne**, but this has no effect on *k*.

```
static void AddOne(int x)
{
    x++;
}
static void Main( )
{
    int k = 6;
    AddOne(k);
    Console.WriteLine(k); // Display the value 6, not 7
}
```

Pass by Reference

- ■ **What are reference parameters?**
  - A reference to memory location
- ■ **Using reference parameters**
  - Use the **ref** keyword in method declaration and call
  - Match types and variable values
  - Changes made in the method affect the caller
  - Assign parameter value before calling the method

What Are Reference Parameters?

A reference parameter is a reference to a memory location. Unlike a value parameter, a reference parameter does not create a new storage location. Instead, a reference parameter represents the same location in memory as the variable that is supplied in the method call.

Declaring Reference Parameters

You can declare a reference parameter by using the **ref** keyword before the type name, as shown in the following example:

```
static void ShowReference(ref int nId, ref long nCount)
{
    // ...
}
```

Using Multiple Parameter Types

The **ref** keyword only applies to the parameter following it, not to the whole parameter list. Consider the following method, in which *nId* is passed by reference but *longVar* is passed by value:

```
static void OneRefOneVal(ref int nId, long longVar)
{
    // ...
}
```

Matching Parameter Types and Values

When calling the method, you supply reference parameters by using the **ref** keyword followed by a variable. The value supplied in the call to the method must exactly match the type in the method definition, and it must be a variable, not a constant or calculated expression.

```
int x;
long q;
ShowReference(ref x, ref q);
```

If you omit the **ref** keyword, or if you supply a constant or calculated expression, the compiler will reject the call, and you will receive an error message similar to the following: "Cannot convert from 'int' to 'ref int.'"

Changing Reference Parameter Values

If you change the value of a reference parameter, the variable supplied by the caller is also changed, because they are both references to the same location in memory. The following example shows how changing the reference parameter also changes the variable:

```
static void AddOne(ref int x)
{
    x++;
}
static void Main( )
{
    int k = 6;
    AddOne(ref k);
    Console.WriteLine(k); // Display the value 7
}
```

This works because when **AddOne** is called, its parameter x is set up to refer to the same memory location as the variable k in **Main**. Therefore, incrementing x will increment k.

Assigning Parameters Before Calling the Method

A **ref** parameter must be definitively assigned at the point of call; that is, the compiler must ensure that a value is assigned before the call is made. The following example shows how you can initialize reference parameters before calling the method:

```
static void AddOne(ref int x)
{
    x++;
}

static void Main( )
{
    int k = 6;
    AddOne(ref k);
    Console.WriteLine(k); // 7
}
```

The following example shows what happens if a reference parameter *k* is not initialized before its method **AddOne** is called:

```
int k;
AddOne(ref k);
Console.WriteLine(k);
```

The C# compiler will reject this code and display the following error message: "Use of unassigned local variable '*k*.'"

Output Parameters

- **What are output parameters?**
    - Values are passed out but not in
- **Using output parameters**
    - Like **ref**, but values are not passed into the method
    - Use **out** keyword in method declaration and call

```
static void OutDemo(out int p)
{
     // ...
}
int n;
OutDemo(out n);
```

What Are Output Parameters?

Output parameters are like reference parameters, except that they transfer data out of the method rather than into it. Like a reference parameter, an output parameter is a reference to a storage location supplied by the caller. However, the variable that is supplied for the **out** parameter does not need to be assigned a value before the call is made, and the method will assume that the parameter has not been initialized on entry.

Output parameters are useful when you want to be able to return values from a method by means of a parameter without assigning an initial value to the parameter.

Using Output Parameters

To declare an output parameter, use the keyword **out** before the type and name, as shown in the following example:

```
static void OutDemo(out int p)
{
     // ...
}
```

As with the **ref** keyword, the **out** keyword only affects one parameter, and each **out** parameter must be marked separately.

When calling a method with an **out** parameter, place the **out** keyword before the variable to be passed, as in the following example.

```
int n;
OutDemo(out n);
```

In the body of the method being called, no initial assumptions are made about the contents of the output parameter. It is treated just like an unassigned local variable. The out parameter must be assigned a value inside the method.

Using Variable-Length Parameter Lists

- **Use the params keyword**
- **Declare as an array at the end of the parameter list**
- **Always pass by value**

type of array (handwritten)

```
static long AddList(params long[ ] v)
{
    long total, i;
    for (i = 0, total = 0; i < v.Length; i++)
        total += v[i];
    return total;
}
static void Main( )
{
    long x = AddList(63,21,84);
}
```

name of array (handwritten)

C# provides a mechanism for passing variable-length parameter lists.

Declaring Variable-Length Parameters

It is sometimes useful to have a method that can accept a varying number of parameters. In C#, you can use the **params** keyword to specify a variable-length parameter list. When you declare a variable-length parameter, you must:

- Declare only one **params** parameter per method.

- Place the parameter at the end of the parameter list.

- Declare the parameter as a single-dimension array type.

The following example shows how to declare a variable-length parameter list:

```
static long AddList(params long[ ] v)
{
    long total;
    long i;
    for (i = 0, total = 0; i < v. Length; i++)
        total += v[i];
    return total;
}
```

Because a **params** parameter is always an array, all values must be the same type.

Passing Values

When you call a method with a variable-length parameter, you can pass values to the **params** parameter in one of two ways:

- As a comma separated list of elements (the list can be empty)

- As an array

The following code shows both techniques. The two techniques are treated in exactly the same way by the compiler.

```
static void Main( )
{
    long x;
    x = AddList(63, 21, 84); // List
    x = AddList(new long[ ]{ 63, 21, 84 }); // Array
}
```

Regardless of which method you use to call the method, the **params** parameter is treated like an array. You can use the **Length** property of the array to determine how many parameters were passed to each call.

In a **params** parameter, a copy of the data is made, and although you can modify the values inside the method, the values outside the method are unchanged.

Guidelines for Passing Parameters

- **Mechanisms**
  - Pass by value is most common
  - Method return value is useful for single values
  - Use **ref** and/or **out** for multiple return values
  - Only use **ref** if data is transferred both ways
- **Efficiency**
  - Pass by value is generally the most efficient

With so many options available for parameter passing, the most appropriate choice might not be obvious. Two factors for you to consider when you choose a way to pass parameters are the mechanism and its efficiency.

Mechanisms

Value parameters offer a limited form of protection against unintended modification of parameter values, because any changes that are made inside the method have no effect outside it. This suggests that you should use value parameters unless you need to pass information out of a method.

If you need to pass data out of a method, you can use the **return** statement, reference parameters, or output parameters. The **return** statement is easy to use, but it can only return one result. If you need multiple values returned, you must use the reference and output parameter types. Use **ref** if you need to transfer data in both directions, and use **out** if you only need to transfer data out of the method.

Efficiency

Generally, simple types such as **int** and **long** are most efficiently passed by value.

These efficiency concerns are not built into the language, and you should not rely on them. Although efficiency is sometimes a consideration in large, resource-intensive applications, it is usually better to consider program correctness, stability, and robustness before efficiency. Make good programming practices a higher priority than efficiency.

Using Recursive Methods

- **A method can call itself**
  - Directly
  - Indirectly
- **Useful for solving certain problems**

A method can call itself. This technique is known as *recursion*. You can address some types of problems with recursive solutions. Recursive methods are often useful when manipulating more complex data structures such as lists and trees.

Methods in C# can be mutually recursive. For example, a situation in which method A can call method B, and method B can call method A, is allowable.

Example of a Recursive Method

The Fibonacci sequence occurs in several situations in mathematics and biology (for example, the reproductive rate and population of rabbits). The nth member of this sequence has the value 1 if n is 1 or 2; otherwise, it is equal to the sum of the preceding two numbers in the sequence. Notice that when n is greater than two the value of the nth member of the sequence is derived from the values of two previous values of the sequence. When the definition of a method refers to the method itself, recursion might be involved.

You can implement the **Fibonacci** method as follows:

```
static ulong Fibonacci(ulong n)
{
    if (n <= 2)
        return 1;
    else
        return Fibonacci(n-1) + Fibonacci(n-2);
}
```

Notice that two calls are made to the method from within the method itself.

A recursive method must have a terminating condition that ensures that it will return without making further calls. In the case of the **Fibonacci** method, the test for n <= 2 is the terminating condition.

◆ Using Overloaded Methods

- ■ **Declaring overloaded methods**
- ■ **Method signatures**
- ■ **Using overloaded methods**

Methods cannot not have the same name as other non-method items in a class. However, it is possible for two or more methods in a class to share the same name. Name sharing among methods is called overloading.

In this section, you will learn:

- ■ How to declare overloaded methods.

- ■ How C# uses signatures to distinguish methods that have the same name.

- ■ When to use overloaded methods.

Declaring Overloaded Methods

- **Methods that share a name in a class**
  - Distinguished by examining parameter lists

```
class OverloadingExample
{
    static int Add(int a, int b)
    {
        return a + b;
    }
    static int Add(int a, int b, int c)
    {
        return a + b + c;
    }
    static void Main( )
    {
        Console.WriteLine(Add(1,2) + Add(1,2,3));
    }
}
```

Overloaded methods are methods in a single class that have the same name. The C# compiler distinguishes overloaded methods by comparing the parameter lists.

Examples of Overloaded Methods

The following code shows how you can use different methods with the same name in one class:

```
class OverloadingExample
{
    static int Add(int a, int b)
    {
        return a + b;
    }
    static int Add(int a, int b, int c)
    {
        return a + b + c;
    }
    static void Main( )
    {
        Console.WriteLine(Add(1,2) + Add(1,2,3));
    }
}
```

The C# compiler finds two methods called **Add** in the class, and two method calls to methods called **Add** within **Main**. Although the method names are the same, the compiler can distinguish between the two **Add** methods by comparing the parameter lists.

The first **Add** method takes two parameters, both of type **int**. The second **Add** method takes three parameters, also of type **int**. Because the parameter lists are different, the compiler allows both methods to be defined within the same class.

The first statement within **Main** includes a call to **Add** with two **int** parameters, so the compiler translates this as a call to the first **Add** method. The second call to **Add** takes three **int** parameters, so the compiler translates this as a call to the second **Add** method.

You cannot share names among methods and variables, constants, or enumerated types in the same class. The following code will not compile because the name *k* has been used for both a method and a class variable:

```
class BadMethodNames
{
  static int k;
  static void k( ) {
    // ...
  }
}
```

Method Signatures

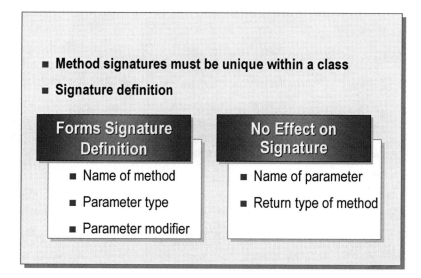

The C# compiler uses signatures to distinguish between methods in a class. In each class, the signature of each method must differ from the signatures of all other methods that are declared in that class.

Signature Definition

The signature of a method consists of the name of the method, the number of parameters that the method takes, and the type and modifier (such as **out** or **ref**) of each parameter.

The following three methods have different signatures, so they can be declared in the same class.

```
static int LastErrorCode( )
{

}
static int LastErrorCode(int n)
{

}

static int LastErrorCode(int n, int p)
{

}
```

Elements That Do Not Affect the Signature

The method signature does *not* include the return type. The following two methods have the same signatures, so they cannot be declared in the same class.

```
static int LastErrorCode(int n)
{
}
static string LastErrorCode(int n)
{
}
```

The method signature does *not* include the names of the parameters. The following two methods have the same signature, even though the parameter names are different.

```
static int LastErrorCode(int n)
{
}
static int LastErrorCode(int x)
{
}
```

Using Overloaded Methods

- **Consider using overloaded methods when:**
  - You have similar methods that require different parameters
  - You want to add new functionality to existing code
- **Do not overuse because:**
  - Hard to debug
  - Hard to maintain

Overloaded methods are useful when you have two similar methods that require different numbers or types of parameters.

Similar Methods That Require Different Parameters

Imagine that you have a class containing a method that sends a greeting message to the user. Sometimes the user name is known, and sometimes it is not. You could define two different methods called **Greet** and **GreetUser**, as shown in the following code:

```
class GreetDemo
{
    static void Greet( )
    {
        Console.WriteLine("Hello");
    }
    static void GreetUser(string Name)
    {
        Console.WriteLine("Hello " + Name);
    }
    static void Main( )
    {
        Greet( );
        GreetUser("Alex");
    }
}
```

This will work, but now the class has two methods that perform almost exactly the same task but that have different names. You can rewrite this class with method overloading as shown in the following code:

```
class GreetDemo
{
    static void Greet( )
    {
        Console.WriteLine("Hello");
    }
    static void Greet(string Name)
    {
        Console.WriteLine("Hello " + Name);
    }
    static void Main( )
    {
        Greet( );
        Greet("Alex");
    }
}
```

Adding New Functionality to Existing Code

Method overloading is also useful when you want to add new features to an existing application without making extensive changes to existing code. For example, the previous code could be expanded by adding another method that greets a user with a particular greeting, depending on the time of day, as shown in the following code:

```
class GreetDemo
{
    enum TimeOfDay { Morning, Afternoon, Evening }

    static void Greet( )
    {
        Console.WriteLine("Hello");
    }
    static void Greet(string Name)
    {
        Console.WriteLine("Hello " + Name);
    }
    static void Greet(string Name, TimeOfDay td)
    {
        string Message = "";

        switch(td)
        {
        case TimeOfDay.Morning:
            Message="Good morning";
            break;
        case TimeOfDay.Afternoon:
            Message="Good afternoon";
            break;
        case TimeOfDay.Evening:
            Message="Good evening";
            break;
        }
        Console.WriteLine(Message + " " + Name);
    }
    static void Main( )
    {
        Greet( );
        Greet("Alex");
        Greet("Sandra", TimeOfDay.Morning);
    }
}
```

Determining When to Use Overloading

Overuse of method overloading can make classes hard to maintain and debug. In general, only overload methods that have very closely related functions but differ in the amount or type of data that they need.

Lab 5.1: Creating and Using Methods

Objectives

After completing this lab, you will be able to:

- Create and call methods with and without parameters.
- Use various mechanisms for passing parameters.

Prerequisites

Before working on this lab, you should be familiar with the following:

- Creating and using variables
- C# statements

Estimated time to complete this lab: 60 minutes

Exercise 1
Using Parameters in Methods That Return Values

In this exercise, you will define and use input parameters in a method that returns a value. You will also write a test framework to read two values from the console and display the results.

You will create a class called **Utils**. In this class, you will create a method called **Greater**. This method will take two integer parameters as input and will return the value of the greater of the two.

To test the class, you will create another class called **Test** that prompts the user for two numbers, then calls **Utils.Greater** to determine which number is the greater of the two, and then prints the result.

▶ **To create the Greater method**

1. Open the Utils.sln project in the *install folder*\Labs\Lab05\Starter\Utility folder.

   This contains a namespace called **Utils** that contains a class also called **Utils**. You will write the **Greater** method in this class.

2. Create the **Greater** method as follows:

   a. Open the **Utils** class.

   b. Add a public static method called **Greater** to the **Utils** class.

   c. The method will take two **int** parameters, called *a* and *b*, which will be passed by value. The method will return an **int** value representing the greater of the two numbers.

   The code for the **Utils** class should be as follows:

```
namespace Utils
{
    using System;

    class Utils
    {

      //
      // Return the greater of two integer values
      //

      public static int Greater(int a, int b)
      {
        if (a > b)
            return a;
        else
            return b;
      }
    }
}
```

▶ **To test the Greater method**

1. Open the **Test** class.

2. Within the **Main** method, write the following code.

    a. Define two integer variables called *x* and *y*.

    b. Add statements that read two integers from keyboard input and use them to populate *x* and *y*. Use the **Console.ReadLine** and **int.Parse** methods that were presented in earlier modules.

    c. Define another integer called *greater*.

    d. Test the **Greater** method by calling it, and assign the returned value to the variable *greater*.

3. Write code to display the greater of the two integers by using **Console.WriteLine**.

The code for the **Test** class should be as follows:

```
namespace Utils
{
    using System;

    /// <summary>
    ///    This the test harness
    /// </summary>

    public class Test
    {
        public static void Main( )
        {
            int x;        // Input value 1
            int y;        // Input value 2
            int greater;  // Result from Greater( )

            // Get input numbers
            Console.WriteLine("Enter first number:");
            x = int.Parse(Console.ReadLine( ));
            Console.WriteLine("Enter second number:");
            y = int.Parse(Console.ReadLine( ));

            // Test the Greater( ) method
            greater = Utils.Greater(x,y);
            Console.WriteLine("The greater value is "+
 greater);

        }
    }
}
```

4. Save your work.

5. Compile the project and correct any errors. Run and test the program.

Exercise 2
Using Methods with Reference Parameters

In this exercise, you will write a method called **Swap** that will exchange the values of its parameters. You will use parameters that are passed by reference.

▶ **To create the Swap method**

1. Open the Utils.sln project in the *install folder*\Labs\Lab05\Starter\Utility folder, if it is not already open.

2. Add the **Swap** method to the **Utils** class as follows:

   a. Add a public static void method called **Swap**.

   b. **Swap** will take two **int** parameters called *a* and *b*, which will be passed by reference.

   c. Write statements inside the body of **Swap** that exchange the values of *a* and *b*. You will need to create a local **int** variable in **Swap** to temporarily hold one of the values during the exchange. Name this variable *temp*.

The code for the **Utils** class should be as follows:

```
namespace Utils
{
    using System;

    public class Utils
    {

    ... existing code omitted for clarity ...

    //
    // Exchange two integers, passed by reference
    //

    public static void Swap(ref int a, ref int b)
    {
        int temp = a;
        a = b;
        b = temp;
    }

    }
}
```

▶ **To test the Swap method**

1. Edit the **Main** method in the **Test** class by performing the following steps:

   a. Populate integer variables *x* and *y*.

   b. Call the **Swap** method, passing these values as parameters.

   Display the new values of the two integers before and after exchanging them. The code for the **Test** class should be as follows:

```
namespace Utils
{
    using System;

    public class Test
    {

    public static void Main( )
    {
        ... existing code omitted for clarity ...

        // Test the Swap method
        Console.WriteLine("Before swap: " + x + "," + y);
        Utils.Swap(ref x,ref y);
        Console.WriteLine("After swap: " + x + "," + y);

    }

    }
}
```

2. Save your work.

3. Compile the project, correcting any errors you find. Run and test the program.

Tip If the parameters were not exchanged as you expected, check to ensure that you passed them as **ref** parameters.

Exercise 3
Using Methods with Output Parameters

In this exercise, you will define and use a static method with an output parameter.

You will write a new method called **Factorial** that takes an **int** value and calculates its factorial. The factorial of a number is the product of all the numbers between 1 and that number. The factorial of zero is defined to be 1. The following are examples of factorials:

- Factorial(0) = 1
- Factorial(1) = 1
- Factorial(2) = 1 * 2 = 2
- Factorial(3) = 1 * 2 * 3 = 6
- Factorial(4) = 1 * 2 * 3 * 4 = 24

▶ **To create the Factorial method**

1. Open the Utils.sln project in the *install folder*\Labs\Lab05\Starter\Utility folder, if it is not already open.

2. Add the **Factorial** method to the **Utils** class, as follows:

   a. Add a new public static method called **Factorial**.

   b. This method will take two parameters called *n* and *answer*. The first, passed by value, is an **int** value for which the factorial is to be calculated. The second parameter is an **out int** parameter that will be used to return the result.

   c. The **Factorial** method should return a **bool** value that indicates whether the method succeeded. (It could overflow and raise an exception.)

3. Add functionality to the **Factorial** method.

   The easiest way to calculate a factorial is by using a loop. Perform the following steps to add functionality to the method:

   a. Create an **int** variable called *k* in the **Factorial** method. This will be used as a loop counter.

   b. Create another **int** variable called *f*, which will be used as a working value inside the loop. Initialize the working variable *f* with the value 1.

   c. Use a **for** loop to perform the iteration. Start with a value of 2 for *k*, and finish when *k* reaches the value of parameter *n*. Increment *k* each time the loop is performed.

   d. In the body of the loop, multiply *f* successively by each value of *k*, storing the result in *f*.

   e. Factorial results can be very large even for small input values, so ensure that all the integer calculations are in a checked block, and that you have caught exceptions such as arithmetic overflow.

   f. Assign the result value in *f* to the out parameter *answer*.

   g. Return **true** from the method if the calculation is successful, and **false** if the calculation is not successful (that is, if an exception occurs).

The code for the **Utils** class should be as follows:

```
namespace Utils
{
    using System;

    public class Utils
    {

    ... existing code omitted for clarity ...

    //
    // Calculate factorial
    // and return the result as an out parameter
    //

    public static bool Factorial(int n, out int answer)
    {
        int k;        // Loop counter
        int f;        // Working value
        bool ok=true; // True if okay, false if not

        // Check the input value

        if (n<0)
            ok = false;

        // Calculate the factorial value as the
        // product of all of the numbers from 2 to n

        try
        {
            checked
            {
                f = 1;
                for (k=2; k<=n; ++k)
                {
                    f = f * k;
                }
            }
        }
        catch(Exception)
        {
            // If something goes wrong in the calculation,
            // catch it here. All exceptions
            // are handled the same way: set the result
            // to zero and return false.
```

Code continued on following page.

```
                f = 0;
                ok = false;
            }


            // Assign result value
            answer = f;
            // Return to caller
            return ok;
        }



    }
}
```

▶ **To test the Factorial method**

1. Edit the **Test** class as follows:

    a. Declare a **bool** variable called *ok* to hold the **true** or **false** result.

    b. Declare an **int** variable called *f* to hold the factorial result.

    c. Request an integer from the user. Assign the input value to the **int** variable *x*.

    d. Call the **Factorial** method, passing *x* as the first parameter and *f* as the second parameter. Return the result in *ok*.

    e. If *ok* is **true**, display the values of *x* and *f*; otherwise, display a message indicating that an error has occurred.

The code for the **Test** class should be as follows:

```
namespace Utils
{
    public class Test
    {

    static void Main( )
    {
        int f;        // Factorial result
        bool ok;      // Factorial success or failure

        ... existing code omitted for clarity ...

        // Get input for factorial

        Console.WriteLine("Number for factorial:");
        x = int.Parse(Console.ReadLine( ));

        // Test the factorial function
        ok = Utils.Factorial(x, out f);
        // Output factorial results
        if (ok)
            Console.WriteLine("Factorial(" + x + ") = " +
f);
        else
            Console.WriteLine("Cannot compute this
↪factorial");
    }
    }
}
```

2. Save your work.

3. Compile the program, correct any errors, and then run and test the program.

If Time Permits
Implementing a Method by Using Recursion

In this exercise, you will re-implement the **Factorial** method that you created in Exercise 3 by using recursion rather than a loop.

The factorial of a number can be defined recursively as follows: the factorial of zero is 1, and you can find the factorial of any larger integer by multiplying that integer with the factorial of the previous number. In summary:

If n=0, then Factorial(n) = 1; otherwise it is n * Factorial(n-1)

▶ To modify the existing Factorial method

1. Edit the **Utils** class and modify the existing **Factorial** method so that it uses recursion rather than iteration.

   The parameters and return types will be the same, but the internal functionality of the method will be different. If you want to keep your existing solution to Exercise 3, you will need to use another name for this method.

2. Use the pseudo code shown above to implement the body of the **Factorial** method. (You will need to convert it into C# syntax.)

3. Add code to the **Test** class to test your new method.

4. Save your work.

5. Compile the program, correct any errors, and then run and test the program.

The recursive version of the **Factorial** method (**RecursiveFactorial**) is shown below:

```
//
// Another way to solve the factorial problem,
// this time as a recursive function
//

public static bool RecursiveFactorial(int n, out int f)
{
    bool ok=true;

    // Trap negative inputs
    if (n<0)
    {
        f=0;
        ok = false;
    }

    if (n<=1)
        f=1;
    else
    {
        try
        {
            int pf;
            checked
            {
                ok = RecursiveFactorial(n-1,out pf);
                f = n * pf;
            }
        }
        catch(Exception)
        {
            // Something went wrong. Set error
            // flag and return zero.
            f=0;
            ok=false;
        }

    }

    return ok;
}
```

Review

- Using Methods
- Using Parameters
- Using Overloaded Methods

1. Explain what methods are and why they are important.

2. List the three ways in which data can be passed in parameters, and the associated C# keywords.

3. When are local variables created and destroyed?

4. What keyword should be added to a method definition if the method needs to be called from another class?

5. What parts of a method are used to form the signature?

6. Define the signature of a static method called **Rotate** that does not return a value but that must "right rotate" its three integer parameters.

msdn training

Module 6: Arrays

Contents

Overview	1
Overview of Arrays	2
Creating Arrays	10
Using Arrays	17
Lab 6.1: Creating and Using Arrays	29
Review	40

Overview

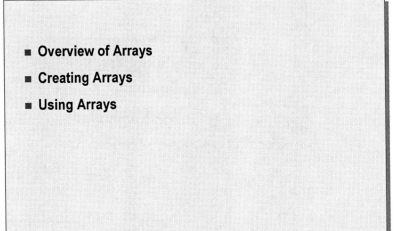

- **Overview of Arrays**
- **Creating Arrays**
- **Using Arrays**

Arrays provide an important means for grouping data. To make the most of C#, it is important to understand how to use and create arrays effectively.

After completing this module, you will be able to:

- Create, initialize, and use arrays of varying rank.
- Use command-line arguments in a C# program.
- Understand the relationship between an array variable and an array instance.
- Use arrays as parameters for methods.
- Return arrays from methods.

◆ Overview of Arrays

- **What Is an Array?**
- **Array Notation in C#**
- **Array Rank**
- **Accessing Array Elements**
- **Checking Array Bounds**
- **Comparing Arrays to Collections**

This section provides an overview of general array concepts, introduces the key syntax used to declare arrays in C#, and describes basic array features such as rank and elements. In the next section, you will learn how to define and use arrays.

What Is an Array?

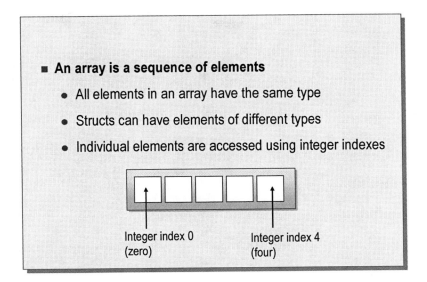

There are two fundamental ways to group related data: structures (**structs**) and arrays.

■ Structures are groups of related data that have different types.

For example, a name (**string**), age (**int**), and gender (**enum**) naturally group together in a **struct** that describes a person. You can access the individual members of a struct by using their field names.

■ Arrays are sequences of data of the same type.

For example, a sequence of houses naturally group together to form a street. You can access an individual element of an array by using its integer position, which is called an index.

Arrays allow random access. The elements of an array are located in contiguous memory. This means a program can access all array elements equally quickly.

Array Notation in C#

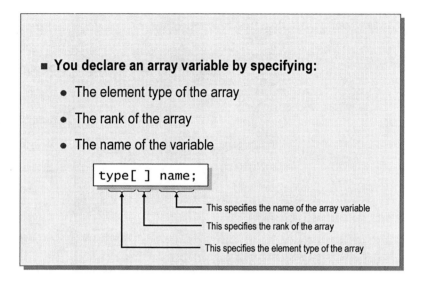

■ **You declare an array variable by specifying:**

- The element type of the array

- The rank of the array

- The name of the variable

```
type[ ] name;
```

This specifies the name of the array variable

This specifies the rank of the array

This specifies the element type of the array

You use the same notation to declare an array that you would use to declare a simple variable. First, specify the type, and then specify the name of the variable followed by a semicolon. You declare the variable type as an array by using square brackets. Many other programming languages, such as C and C++, also use square brackets to declare an array. Other languages, like Microsoft® Visual Basic®, use parentheses.

In C#, array notation is very similar to the notation used by C and C++, although it differs in two subtle-but-important ways:

- You cannot write square brackets to the right of the name of the variable.

- You do not specify the size of the array when declaring an array variable.

The following are examples of allowed and disallowed notation in C#:

```
type[ ]name;     // Allowed
type name[ ];    // Disallowed in C#
type[4] name;    // Also disallowed in C#
```

Array Rank

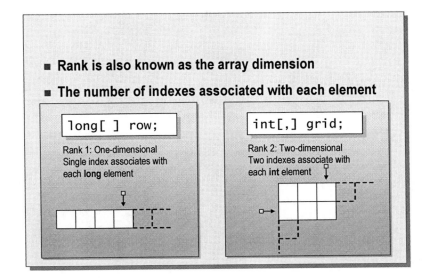

To declare a one-dimensional array variable, you use unadorned square brackets as shown on the slide. Such an array is also called an array of rank 1 because one integer index associates with each element of the array.

To declare a two-dimensional array, you use a single comma inside the square brackets, as shown on the slide. Such an array is called an array of rank 2 because two integer indexes associate with each element of the array. This notation extends in the obvious way: each additional comma between the square brackets increases the rank of the array by one.

You do not include the length of the dimensions in the declaration for an array variable.

Accessing Array Elements

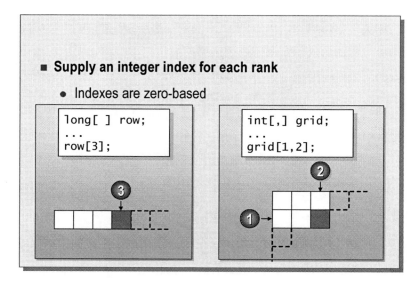

To access array elements, you use a syntax that is similar to the syntax you use to declare array variables—both use square brackets. This visual similarity (which is deliberate and follows a trend popularized by C and C++) can be confusing if you are not familiar with it. Therefore, it is important for you to be able to distinguish between an array variable declaration and an array element access expression.

To access an element inside an array of rank 1, use one integer index. To access an element inside an array of rank 2, use two integer indexes separated by a comma. This notation extends in the same way as the notation for declaring variables. To access an element inside an array of rank n, use n integer indexes separated by commas. Notice again that the syntax used in an array element access expression mirrors the syntax that is used to declare variables.

Array indexes (for all ranks) start from zero. To access the first element inside a row, use the expression:

```
row[0]
```

rather than the expression:

```
row[1]
```

Some programmers use the phrase "initial element" rather than "first element" to try to avoid any potential confusion. Indexing from 0 means that the last element of an array instance containing *size* elements is found at [*size-1*] and not at [*size*]. Accidentally using [*size*] is a common off-by-one error, especially for programmers used to a language that indexes from one, such as Visual Basic.

Note   Although the technique is rarely used, it is possible to create arrays that have user-defined integer index lower bounds. For more information, search for "Array.CreateInstance" in the Microsoft .NET Framework SDK Help documents.

Checking Array Bounds

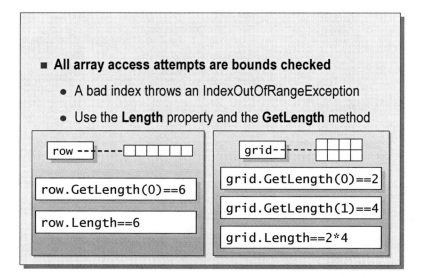

In C#, an array element access expression is automatically checked to ensure that the index is valid. This implicit bounds check cannot be turned off. Bounds checking is one of the ways of ensuring that C# is a type-safe language.

Even though array bounds are automatically checked, you should still make sure that integer indexes are always in bounds. To do this, you should manually check the index bounds, often using a **for** statement termination condition, as follows:

```
for (int i = 0; i < row.Length; i++) {
    Console.WriteLine(row[i]);
}
```

The **Length** property is the total length of the array, regardless of the rank of the array. To determine the length of a specific dimension, you can use the **GetLength** method, as follows:

```
for (int r = 0; r < grid.GetLength(0); r++) {
    for (int c = 0; c < grid.GetLength(1); c++) {
        Console.WriteLine(grid[r,c]);
    }
}
```

Comparing Arrays to Collections

- **An array cannot resize itself when full**
  - A collection class, such as ArrayList, can resize
- **An array is intended to store elements of one type**
  - A collection is designed to store elements of different types
- **Elements of an array cannot have read-only access**
  - A collection can have read-only access
- **In general, arrays are faster but less flexible**
  - Collections are slightly slower but more flexible

The size of an array instance and the type of its elements are permanently fixed when the array is created. To create an array that always contains exactly 42 elements of type **int**, use the following syntax:

```
int[ ] rigid = new int [ 42 ];
```

The array will never shrink or expand, and it will never contain anything other than **ints**. Collections are more flexible; they can expand or contract as elements are removed and added. Arrays are intended to hold elements of a single type, but collections were designed to contain elements of many different types. You can achieve this flexibility by using boxing, as follows:

```
ArrayList flexible = new ArrayList( );
flexible.Add("one"); // Add a string here
...
flexible.Add(99);    // And an int here!
```

You cannot create an array instance with read-only elements. The following code will not compile:

```
const int[ ] array = {0, 1, 2, 3};
readonly int[ ] array = {4,2};
```

However, you can create a read-only collection as follows:

```
ArrayList flexible = new ArrayList( );
...
ArrayList noWrite = ArrayList.ReadOnly(flexible);
noWrite[0] = 42;   // Causes run-time exception
```

◆ Creating Arrays

- **Creating Array Instances**
- **Initializing Array Elements**
- **Initializing Multidimensional Array Elements**
- **Creating a Computed Size Array**
- **Copying Array Variables**

In this section, you will learn how to create array instances, how to explicitly initialize array instance elements, and how to copy array variables.

Creating Array Instances

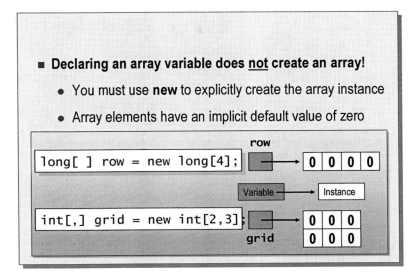

Declaring an array variable does not actually create an array instance. This is because arrays are reference types and not value types. You use the **new** keyword to create an array instance, also referred to as an array creation expression. You must specify the size of all rank lengths when creating an array instance. The following code will result in a compile-time error:

```
long[ ] row = new long[ ];    // Not allowed
int[,] grid = new int[,];     // Not allowed
```

The C# compiler implicitly initializes each array element to a default value dependent on the array element type: integer array elements are implicitly initialized to 0, floating-point array elements are implicitly initialized to 0.0, and Boolean array are implicitly initialized to **false**. In other words, the C# code:

```
long[ ] row = new long[4];
```

will execute the following code at run-time:

```
long[ ] row = new long[4];
row[0] = 0L;
row[1] = 0L;
row[2] = 0L;
row[3] = 0L;
```

The compiler always allocates arrays in contiguous memory, regardless of the base type of the array and the number of dimensions. If you create an array with an expression such as new int[2,3,4], it is conceptually 2 x 3 x 4, but the underlying memory allocation is a single block of memory large enough to contain 2*3*4 elements.

Initializing Array Elements

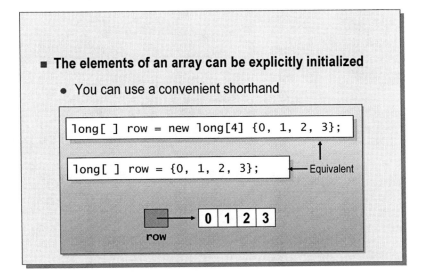

- ■ **The elements of an array can be explicitly initialized**
  - • You can use a convenient shorthand

```
long[ ] row = new long[4] {0, 1, 2, 3};
```

```
long[ ] row = {0, 1, 2, 3};
```
← Equivalent

```
      0  1  2  3
row
```

You can use an array initializer to initialize the values of the array instance elements. An array initializer is a sequence of expressions enclosed by curly braces and separated by commas. Array initializers are executed from left to right and can include method calls and complex expressions, as in the following example:

```
int[ ] data = new int[4]{a, b( ), c*d, e( )+f( )};
```

You can also use array initializers to initialize arrays of structs:

```
struct Date { ... }
Date[ ] dates = new Date[2];
```

You can only use this convenient shorthand notation when you initialize an array instance as part of an array variable declaration and not as part of an ordinary assignment statement.

```
int[ ] data1 = new int[4]{0, 1, 2, 3};  // Allowed
int[ ] data2 =           {0, 1, 2, 3};  // Allowed
data2 = new int[4]{0, 1, 2, 3};         // Allowed
data2 =           {0, 1, 2, 4};         // Not allowed
```

When initializing arrays, you must explicitly initialize all array elements. It is not possible to let trailing array elements revert back to their default value of zero:

```
int[ ] data3 = new int[2]{};      // Not allowed
int[ ] data4 = new int[2]{42};    // Still not allowed
int[ ] data5 = new int[2]{42,42}; // Allowed
```

Initializing Multidimensional Array Elements

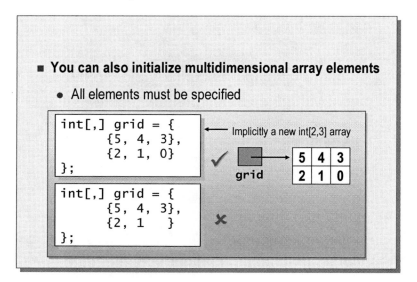

You must explicitly initialize all array elements regardless of the array dimension:

```
int[,] data = new int[2,3] {        // Allowed
        {42, 42, 42},
        {42, 42, 42},
};

int[,] data = new int[2,3] {        // Not allowed
        {42, 42},
        {42, 42, 42},
};

int[,] data = new int[2,3] {        // Not allowed
        {42},
        {42, 42, 42},
};
```

Creating a Computed Size Array

- **The array size does not need to be a compile-time constant**
  - Any valid integer expression will work
  - Accessing elements is equally fast in all cases

    Array size specified by compile-time integer constant:

```
long[ ] row = new long[4];
```

Array size specified by run-time integer value:

```
string s = Console.ReadLine();
int size = int.Parse(s);
long[ ] row = new long[size];
```

You can create multidimensional arrays by using run-time expressions for the length of each dimension, as shown in the following code:

```
System.Console.WriteLine("Enter number of rows : ");
string s1 = System.Console.ReadLine( );
int rows = int.Parse(s1);
System.Console.WriteLine("Enter number of columns: ");
string s2 = System.Console.ReadLine( );
int cols = int.Parse(s2);
...
int[,] matrix = new int[rows,cols];
```

Alternatively, you can use a mixture of compile-time constants and run-time expressions:

```
System.Console.WriteLine("Enter number of rows: ");
string s1 = System.Console.ReadLine( );
int rows = int.Parse(s1);
...
int[,] matrix = new int[rows,4];
```

There is one minor restriction. You cannot use a run-time expression to specify the size of an array in combination with array-initializers:

```
string s = System.Console.ReadLine( );
int size = int.Parse(s);
int[ ] data = new int[size]{0,1,2,3}; // Not allowed
```

Copying Array Variables

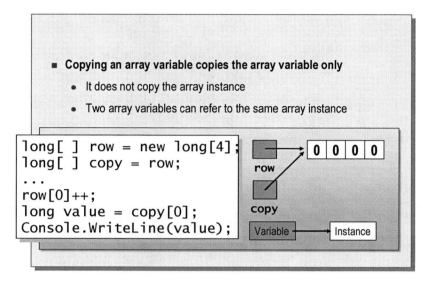

When you copy an array variable, you do not get a full copy of the array instance. Analyzing the code shown in the slide reveals what happens when an array variable is copied.

The following statements declare array variables called *copy* and *row* that both refer to the same array instance (of four **long** integers).

```
long[ ] row = new long[4];
long[ ] copy = row;
```

The following statement increments the initial element of this array instance from 0 to 1. Both array variables still refer to the same array instance, whose initial element is now 1.

```
row[0]++;
```

The next statement initializes a **long** integer called *value* from copy[0], which is the initial array element of the array instance referred to by *copy*.

```
long value = copy[0];
```

Since *copy* and *row* both refer to the same array instance, initializing the value from row[0] has exactly the same effect.

The final statement writes out *value* (which is 1) to the console:

```
Console.WriteLine(value);
```

◆ Using Arrays

- **Array Properties**
- **Array Methods**
- **Returning Arrays from Methods**
- **Passing Arrays as Parameters**
- **Command-Line Arguments**
- **Demonstration: Arguments for Main**
- **Using Arrays with foreach**
- **Quiz: Spot the Bugs**

In this section, you will learn how to use arrays and how to pass arrays as parameters to methods.

You will learn about the rules that govern the default values of array instance elements. Arrays implicitly inherit from the **System.Array** class, which provides many properties and methods. You will learn about some of the commonly used properties and methods. You will also learn how to use the **foreach** statement to iterate through arrays. Finally, you will learn how to avoid some common pitfalls.

Array Properties

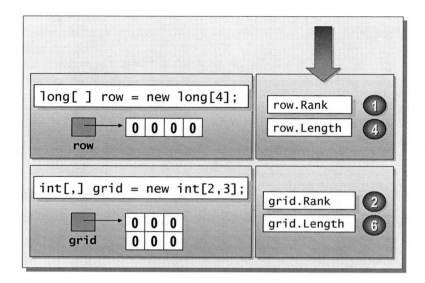

The **Rank** property is a read-only integer value that specifies the dimension of the array instance. For example, given the code

```
int[ ] one = new int[a];
int[,] two = new int[a,b];
int[,,] three = new int[a,b,c];
```

the resulting rank values are as follows:

```
one.Rank == 1
two.Rank == 2
three.Rank == 3
```

The **Length** property is a read-only integer value that specifies the total length of the array instance. For example, given the same three array declarations above, the resulting length values are:

```
one.Length == a
two.Length == a * b
three.Length == a * b * c
```

Array Methods

> - **Commonly used methods**
>   - **Sort** – sorts the elements in an array of rank 1
>   - **Clear** – sets a range of elements to zero or **null**
>   - **Clone** – creates a copy of the array
>   - **GetLength** – returns the length of a given dimension
>   - **IndexOf** – returns the index of the first occurrence of a value

The **System.Array** class (a class that all arrays implicitly support) provides many methods that you can use when working with arrays. This topic describes some of the most commonly used methods.

- **Sort** method

  This method performs an in-place sort on an array provided as an argument. You can use this method to sort arrays of structures and classes as long as they support the **IComparable** interface.

  ```
  int[ ] data = {4,6,3,8,9,3};  // Unsorted
  System.Array.Sort(data);      // Now sorted
  ```

- **Clear** method

  This method resets a range of array elements to zero (for value types) or **null** (for reference types), as shown:

  ```
  int[ ] data = {4,6,3,8,9,3};
  System.Array.Clear(data, 0, data.Length);
  ```

- **Clone** method

  This method creates a new array instance whose elements are copies of the elements of the cloned array. You can use this method to clone arrays of user-defined structs and classes. Following is an example:

  ```
  int[ ] data = {4,6,3,8,9,3};
  int[ ] clone = (int [ ])data.Clone( );
  ```

  ***

  Caution The **Clone** method performs a shallow copy. If the array being copied contains references to objects, the references will be copied and not the objects; both arrays will refer to the same objects.

  ***

- **GetLength** method

  This method returns the length of a dimension provided as an integer argument. You can use this method for bounds-checking multidimensional arrays. Following is an example:

  ```
  int[,] data = { {0, 1, 2, 3}, {4, 5, 6, 7} };
  int dim0 = data.GetLength(0); // == 2
  int dim1 = data.GetLength(1); // == 4
  ```

- **IndexOf** method

  This method returns the integer index of the first occurrence of a value provided as an argument, or −1 if the value is not present. You can only use this method on one-dimensional arrays. Following is an example:

  ```
  int[ ] data = {4,6,3,8,9,3};
  int where = System.Array.IndexOf(data, 9); // == 4
  ```

Note Depending on the type of the elements in the array, the **IndexOf** method may require that you override the **Equals** method for the element type. You will learn more about this in a later module.

Returning Arrays from Methods

- **You can declare methods to return arrays**

```
class Example {
    static void Main( ) {
        int[ ] array = CreateArray(42);
        ...
    }
    static int[ ] CreateArray(int size) {
        int[ ] created = new int[size];
        return created;
    }
}
```

In the slide, the **CreateArray** method is implemented by using two statements. You can combine these two statements into one **return** statement as follows:

```
static int[ ] CreateArray(int size) {
  return new int[size];
}
```

C++ programmers should note that in both cases the size of the array that is returned is not specified. If you specify the array size, you will get a compile-time error, as in this example:

```
static int[4] CreateArray( ) // Compiler error

{
  return new int[4];
}
```

You can also return arrays of rank greater than one, as shown in the following example:

```
static int[,] CreateArray( ) {
  string s1 = System.Console.ReadLine( );
  int rows = int.Parse(s1);
  string s2 = System.Console.ReadLine( );
  int cols = int.Parse(s2);
  return new int[rows,cols];
}
```

Passing Arrays as Parameters

■ **An array parameter is a copy of the array variable**

- Not a copy of the array instance

```
class Example2 {
    static void Main( ) {
        int[ ] arg = {10, 9, 8, 7};
        Method(arg);
        System.Console.WriteLine(arg[0]);
    }
    static void Method(int[ ] parameter) {
        parameter[0]++;
    }
}
```

This method will modify the original array instance created in Main

*copies only the address of memory not the instance.

∴ changes in 2nd variable will change values of 1st variable since they have same memory location.

When you pass an array variable as an argument to a method, the method parameter becomes a copy of the array variable argument. In other words, the array parameter is initialized from the argument. You use the same syntax to initialize the array parameter that you used to initialize an array variable, as described earlier in the Copying Array Variables topic. The array argument and the array parameter both refer to the same array instance.

In the code shown on the slide, **arg** is initialized with an array instance of length 4 that contains the integers 10, 9, 8, and 7. Then **arg** is passed as the argument to **Method**. **Method** accepts **arg** as a parameter, meaning that **arg** and parameter both refer to the same array instance (the one used to initialize **arg**). The expression `parameter[0]++` inside **Method** then increments the initial element in the same array instance from 10 to 11. (Since the initial element of an array is accessed by specifying the index value 0 and not 1, it is also referred to as the "zeroth" element.) **Method** then returns and **Main** writes out the value of `arg[0]` to the console. The **arg** parameter still refers to the same array instance, the zeroth element of which has just been incremented, so 11 is written to the console.

Because passing an array variable does not create a deep copy of the array instance, passing an array as a parameter is very fast. If you want a method to have write access to the argument's array instance, this shallow copy behavior is entirely appropriate.

The **Array.Copy** method is useful when you need to ensure that the called method will not alter the array instance and you are willing to trade a longer running time for this guarantee. You can also pass a newly created array as an array parameter as follows:

```
Method(new int[4]{10, 9, 8, 7});
```

Command-Line Arguments

- **The runtime passes command line arguments to Main**
  - **Main** can take an array of strings as a parameter
  - The name of the program is not a member of the array

```
class Example3 {
    static void Main(string[ ] args) {
        for (int i = 0; i < args.Length; i++) {
            System.Console.WriteLine(args[i]);
        }
    }
}
```

When you run console-based programs, you often pass extra arguments on the command line. For example, if you run the **pkzip** program from a command prompt, you can add extra arguments to control the creation of .zip files. The following command recursively adds all *.cs code files into code.zip:

```
C:\> pkzip –add –rec –path=relative c:\code *.cs
```

If you had written the **pkzip** program using C#, you would capture these command-line arguments as an array of strings that the runtime would pass to **Main**:

```
class PKZip {
  static void Main(string[ ] args) {
      ...
  }
}
```

In this example, when you run the **pkzip** program, the runtime would effectively execute the following code:

```
string[ ] args = {
  "-add",
  "-rec",
  "-path=relative",
  "c:\\code",
  "*.cs"
};
PKZip.Main(args);
```

Note   Unlike in C and C++, the name of the program itself is not passed as args[0] in C#.

Demonstration: Arguments for Main

In this demonstration, you will see how to pass command-line arguments to a C# program.

Using Arrays with foreach

■ **The foreach statement abstracts away many details of array handling**

```
class Example4 {
    static void Main(string[ ] args) {
        foreach (string arg in args) {
            System.Console.WriteLine(arg);
        }
    }
}
```

When it is applicable, the **foreach** statement is useful because it abstracts the mechanics of iterating through every element of an array. Without **foreach**, you might write:

```
for (int i = 0; i < args.Length; i++) {
  System.Console.WriteLine(args[i]);
}
```

With **foreach**, you can write:

```
foreach (string arg in args) {
  System.Console.WriteLine(arg);
}
```

Notice that when you use the **foreach** statement, you do not need or use:

■ An integer index (int i)

■ An array bounds check (i < args.Length)

■ An array access expression (args[i])

You can also use the **foreach** statement to iterate through the elements in an array of rank 2 or higher. For example, the following **foreach** statement will write out the values 0, 1, 2, 3, 4, and 5:

```
int[,] numbers = { {0,1,2}, {3,4,5} };
foreach (int number in numbers) {
  System.Console.WriteLine(number);
}
```

Quiz: Spot the Bugs

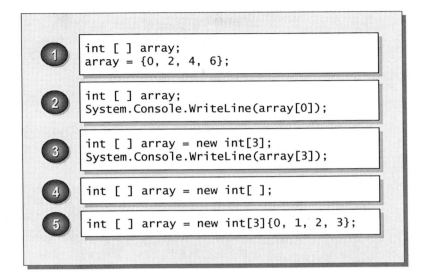

In this quiz, you can work with a partner to spot the bugs in the code on the slide. To see the answers to this quiz, turn the page.

Answers

These are the bugs that you should have found:

1. An array initializer is used in an assignment without an array creation expression. The shortcut int[ ] array = { … }; is only possible in an array declaration. This bug will result in a compile-time error.

2. The array variable has been declared, but there is no array creation expression, and hence there is no array instance. This bug will also result in a compile-time error.

3. A classic off-by-one out-of-bounds error. The array has length three, making valid index values 0, 1, and 2. Remember, arrays are indexed from zero in C#. This bug will cause a **System.IndexOutOfRange** run-time exception.

4. The length of the array is not specified in the array creation expression. The length of an array must be specified when an array instance is created.

5. The number of array elements is specified as 3 in new int[3] however, there are four integer literals in the array initializer.

Lab 6.1: Creating and Using Arrays

Objectives

After completing this lab, you will be able to:

- Create and use arrays of value types.
- Pass arguments to **Main**.
- Create and use computed size arrays.
- Use arrays of multiple rank.

Prerequisites

Before working on this lab, you should be familiar with the following:

- Using C# programming statements.
- Writing and using methods in C#.

Estimated time to complete this lab: 60 minutes

Exercise 1
Working with an Array of Value Types

In this exercise, you will write a program that expects the name of a text file as an argument to **Main**. The program will summarize the contents of the text file. It will read the contents of the text file into an array of characters and then iterate through the array, counting the number of vowels and consonants. Finally, it will print the total number of characters, vowels, consonants, and new lines to the console.

▶ **To capture the name of the text file as a parameter to the Main method**

1. Open the project FileDetails.sln. This project is in the *install folder*\Labs\Lab06\Starter\FileDetails folder.

2. Add an array of strings called **args** as a parameter to the **Main** method of the **FileDetails** class. This array will contain all of the command-line arguments supplied when the program is run. This is how the runtime passes command-line arguments to **Main**. In this exercise, the command-line argument passed to **Main** will be the name of the text file.

3. Add a statement to **Main** that writes the length of **args** to the console. This statement will verify that the length of **args** is zero when no command-line arguments are passed to **Main** by the runtime.

4. Add a **foreach** statement to **Main** that writes each string in **args** to the console. This statement will verify that **Main** receives the command-line arguments from the runtime.

   Your completed code should look as follows:

   ```
   static void Main(string[ ] args)
   {
       Console.WriteLine(args.Length);
       foreach (string arg in args) {
           Console.WriteLine(arg);
       }
   }
   ```

5. Compile the FileDetails.cs program and correct any errors. Run the program from the command line, supplying no command-line arguments. Verify that the length of **args** is zero.

   Tip   To run the program from the command line, open the Command window and go to the *install folder*\Labs\Lab06\Starter\FileDetails\bin\Debug folder. The executable file will be located in this folder.
   ---

6. Run the program from the command line, supplying the name of the *install folder*\Labs\Lab06\Solution\FileDetails\FileDetails.cs file. Verify that the runtime passes the file name to **Main**.

7. Test the program by supplying a variety of other command-line arguments, and verify that each command-line argument is written to the console as expected. Comment out the statements that write to the console.

8. Add a statement to **Main** that declares a **string** variable called *fileName* and initialize it with args[0].

▶ **To read from the text file into an array**

1. Remove the comment from the FileStream and StreamReader declaration and initialization code.

2. Determine the length of the text file.

Tip   To locate an appropriate property of the **Stream** class, search for "Stream class" in the .NET Framework SDK Help documents.

---

3. Add a statement to **Main** that declares a character array variable called *contents*. Initialize *contents* with a new array instance whose length is equal to the length of the text file, which you have just determined.

4. Add a **for** statement to **Main**. The body of the **for** statement will read a single character from *reader* and add it to *contents*.

Tip   Use the **Read** method, which takes no parameters and returns an **int**. Cast the result to a **char** before storing it in the array.

---

5. Add a **foreach** statement to **Main** that writes the whole character array to the console character by character. This statement will verify that the text file has been successfully read into the *contents* array.

   Your completed code should look as follows:

```
static void Main(string[ ] args)
{
    string fileName = args[0];
    FileStream stream = new FileStream(fileName,
                               FileMode.Open);
    StreamReader reader = new StreamReader(stream);
    int size = (int)stream.Length;
    char[ ] contents = new char[size];
    for (int i = 0; i < size; i++) {
        contents[i] = (char)reader.Read( );
    }
    foreach(char ch in contents) {
        Console.Write(ch);

    }
}
```

6. Compile the program and correct any errors. Run the program, supplying the name of the *install folder*\Labs\Lab06\Solution\FileDetails\ FileDetails.cs file as a command-line argument. Verify that the contents of the file are correctly written to the console.

7. Comment out the **foreach** statement.

8. Close the **Reader** object by calling the appropriate **StreamReader** method.

▶ **To classify and summarize the contents of the file**

1. Declare a new static method called **Summarize** in the **FileDetails** class. This method will not return anything and will expect a character array parameter. Add a statement to **Main** that calls the **Summarize** method, passing *contents* as the argument.

2. Add a **foreach** statement to **Summarize** that inspects each character in the array argument. Count the number of vowel, consonant, and new line characters that occur, storing the results in separate variables.

Tip To determine whether a character is a vowel, create a string containing all possible vowels and use the **IndexOf** method on that string to determine whether the character exists in that string, as follows:

```
if ("AEIOUaeiou".IndexOf(myCharacter) != -1) {
    // myCharacter is a vowel
} else {
    // myCharacter is not a vowel
}
```

---

3. Write four lines to the console that display:

   - The total number of characters in the file.

   - The total number of vowels in the file.

   - The total number of consonants in the file.

   - The total number of lines in the file.

   Your completed code should look as follows:

```
static void Summarize(char[ ] contents)
{
    int vowels = 0, consonants = 0, lines = 0;
    foreach (char current in contents) {
        if (Char.IsLetter(current)) {
            if ("AEIOUaeiou".IndexOf(current) != -1) {
                vowels++;
            } else {
                consonants++;
            }
        }
        else if (current == '\n') {
            lines++;
        }
    }
    Console.WriteLine("Total no of characters: {0}",
➥contents.Length);
    Console.WriteLine("Total no of vowels    : {0}",
➥vowels);
    Console.WriteLine("Total no of consonants: {0}",
➥consonants);
    Console.WriteLine("Total no of lines     : {0}",
➥lines);
}
```

4. Compile the program and correct any errors. Run the program from the command line to summarize the contents of the solution file: *install folder*\Labs\Lab06\Solution\FileDetails\FileDetails.cs. The correct totals should be as follows:

- 1,353 characters
- 247 vowels
- 394 consonants
- 41 lines

Exercise 2
Multiplying Matrices

In this exercise, you will write a program that uses arrays to multiply matrices together. The program will read four integer values from the console and store them in a 2 x 2 integer matrix. It will then read another four integer values from the console and store them in a second 2 x 2 integer matrix. The program will then multiply the two matrices together, storing the result in a third 2 x 2 integer matrix. Finally, it will print the resulting matrix to the console.

The formula for multiplying two matrices—A and B—together is as follows:

$$
\begin{array}{cc} A1 & A2 \\ A3 & A4 \end{array} \times \begin{array}{cc} B1 & B2 \\ B3 & B4 \end{array} = \begin{array}{cc} A1.B1 + A2.B3 & A1.B2 + A2.B4 \\ A3.B1 + A4.B3 & A3.B2 + A4.B4 \end{array}
$$

▶ **To multiply two matrices together**

1. Open the project MatrixMultiply.sln in the
   install folder\Labs\Lab06\Starter\MatrixMultiply folder.

2. In the **MatrixMultiply** class, add a statement to **Main** that declares a 2 x 2 array of **ints** and names the array **a**. The final solution for the program will read the values of **a** from the console. For now, initialize **a** with the integer values in the following table. (This is to help verify that the multiplication is performed correctly and that the subsequent refactoring retains the intended behavior.)

$$
\begin{pmatrix} 1 & 2 \\ 3 & 4 \end{pmatrix}
$$

3. Add a statement to **Main** that declares a 2 x 2 array of **ints** and names the array **b**. The final solution for the program will read the values of **b** from the console. For now, initialize **b** with the integer values shown in the following table:

$$
\begin{pmatrix} 5 & 6 \\ 7 & 8 \end{pmatrix}
$$

4. Add a statement to **Main** that declares a 2 x 2 array of **ints** and names the array **result**. Initialize **result** by using the following cell formulae:

a[0,0] * b[0,0] + a[0,1] * b[1,0]   a[0,0] * b[0,1] + a[0,1] * b[1,1]

a[1,0] * b[0,0] + a[1,1] * b[1,0]   a[1,0] * b[0,1] + a[1,1] * b[1,1]

5. Add four statements to **Main** that write the four **int** values in **result** to the console. These statements will help you to check that you have copied the formulae correctly.

Your completed code should look as follows:

```
static void Main( )
{
        int[,] a = new int[2,2];
        a[0,0] = 1; a[0,1] = 2;
        a[1,0] = 3; a[1,1] = 4;

        int[,] b = new int[2,2];
        b[0,0] = 5; b[0,1] = 6;
        b[1,0] = 7; b[1,1] = 8;

        int[,] result = new int[2,2];
        result[0,0]=a[0,0]*b[0,0] + a[0,1]*b[1,0];
        result[0,1]=a[0,0]*b[0,1] + a[0,1]*b[1,1];
        result[1,0]=a[1,0]*b[0,0] + a[1,1]*b[1,0];
        result[1,1]=a[1,0]*b[0,1] + a[1,1]*b[1,1];

        Console.WriteLine(result[0,0]);
        Console.WriteLine(result[0,1]);
        Console.WriteLine(result[1,0]);
        Console.WriteLine(result[1,1]);
}
```

6. Compile the program and correct any errors. Run the program. Verify that the four values in **result** are as follows:

$$\begin{pmatrix} 19 & 22 \\ 43 & 50 \end{pmatrix}$$

▶ **To output the result by using a method with an array parameter**

1. Declare a new static method called **Output** in the **MatrixMultiply** class. This method will not return anything and will expect an **int** array of rank 2 as a parameter called **result**.

2. Cut from **Main** the four statements that write the four values of **result** to the console and paste them into **Output**.

3. Add a statement to **Main** that calls the **Output** method, passing **result** as the argument. (This should replace the code that was cut in the previous step.)

Your completed code should look as follows:

```
static void Output(int[,] result)
{
        Console.WriteLine(result[0,0]);
        Console.WriteLine(result[0,1]);
        Console.WriteLine(result[1,0]);
        Console.WriteLine(result[1,1]);
}
```

4. Compile the program and correct any errors. Run the program. Verify that the four values written to the console are still as follows:

$$\begin{pmatrix} 19 & 22 \\ 43 & 50 \end{pmatrix}$$

5. Refactor the **Output** method to use two nested **for** statements instead of four **WriteLine** statements. Use the literal value 2 in both array bounds checks.

Your completed code should look as follows:

```
static void Output(int[,] result)
{
    for (int r = 0; r < 2; r++) {
        for (int c = 0; c < 2; c++) {
            Console.Write("{0} ", result[r,c]);
        }
        Console.WriteLine( );
    }
}
```

6. Compile the program and correct any errors. Run the program. Verify that the four values written to the console are still as follows:

$$\begin{pmatrix} 19 & 22 \\ 43 & 50 \end{pmatrix}$$

7. Modify the **Output** method again, to make it more generic. Replace the literal value 2 in the array bounds checks with calls to the **GetLength** method of each.

Your completed code should look as follows:

```
static void Output(int[,] result)
{
    for (int r = 0; r < result.GetLength(0); r++) {
        for (int c = 0; c < result.GetLength(1); c++) {
            Console.Write("{0} ", result[r,c]);
        }
        Console.WriteLine( );
    }
}
```

8. Compile the program and correct any errors. Run the program. Verify that the four values written to the console are still as follows:

$$\begin{pmatrix} 19 & 22 \\ 43 & 50 \end{pmatrix}$$

▶ **To calculate result in a method and return it**

1. Declare a new static method called **Multiply** inside the **MatrixMultiply** class. This method will return an **int** array of rank 2 and will expect two **int** arrays of rank 2, named **a** and **b**, as parameters.

2. Copy (but do not cut) the declaration and initialization of **result** from **Main** into **Multiply**.

3. Add a **return** statement to **Multiply** that returns **result**.

4. Replace the initialization of **result** in **Main** with a call to **Multiply**, passing **a** and **b** as arguments.

   Your completed code should look as follows:

```
static int[,] Multiply(int[,] a, int [,] b)
{
    int[,] result = new int[2,2];
    result[0,0]=a[0,0]*b[0,0] + a[0,1]*b[1,0];
    result[0,1]=a[0,0]*b[0,1] + a[0,1]*b[1,1];
    result[1,0]=a[1,0]*b[0,0] + a[1,1]*b[1,0];
    result[1,1]=a[1,0]*b[0,1] + a[1,1]*b[1,1];
    return result;
}
```

5. Compile the program, and correct any errors. Run the program. Verify that the four values written to the console are still as follows:

$$\begin{pmatrix} 19 & 22 \\ 43 & 50 \end{pmatrix}$$

▶ **To calculate result in a method by using for statements**

1. Replace the initialization of **result** in **Multiply** with a newly created 2 x 2 array of **ints**.

2. Add two nested **for** statements to **Multiply**. Use an integer called *r* in the outer **for** statement to iterate through each index of the first dimension of **result**. Use an integer called *c* in the inner **for** statement to iterate through each index of the second dimension of **result**. Use the literal value 2 for both array bounds. The body of the inner **for** statement will need to calculate and set the value of result[r,c] by using the following formula:

```
result[r,c] = a[r,0] * b[0,c]
                + a[r,1] * b[1,c]
```

Your completed code should look like this:

```
static int[,] Multiply(int[,] a, int [,] b)
{
    int[,] result = new int[2,2];
    for (int r = 0; r < 2; r++) {
        for (int c = 0; c < 2; c++) {
            result[r,c] += a[r,0] * b[0,c] + a[r,1] * b[1,c];
        }
    }
    return result;
}
```

3. Compile the program and correct any errors. Run the program. Verify that the four values written to the console are still as follows:

$$\begin{pmatrix} 19 & 22 \\ 43 & 50 \end{pmatrix}$$

▶ **To input the first matrix from the console**

1. Replace the initialization of **a** in **Main** with a newly created 2 x 2 array of **ints**.

2. Add statements to **Main** that prompt the user and read four values into **a** from the console. These statements should be placed before invoking the **Multiply** method. The statements to read *one* value from the console are:

```
string s = Console.ReadLine( );
a[0,0] = int.Parse(s);
```

3. Compile the program and correct any errors. Run the program, entering the same four values for **a** from the console (that is, 1, 2, 3, and 4). Verify that the four values written to the console are still as follows:

$$\begin{pmatrix} 19 & 22 \\ 43 & 50 \end{pmatrix}$$

4. Declare a new static method called **Input** inside the **MatrixMultiply** class. This method will not return anything and will expect an **int** array of rank 2 as a parameter called **dst**.

5. Cut the statements that read four values into **a** from **Main** and paste them into **Input**. Add a statement to **Main** that calls **Input**, passing in **a** as the parameter. This should be placed before the call to **Multiply**.

6. Compile the program and correct any errors. Run the program, entering the same four values for **a** from the console (that is, 1, 2, 3, and 4). Verify that the four values written to the console are still as follows:

$$\begin{pmatrix} 19 & 22 \\ 43 & 50 \end{pmatrix}$$

7. Change the **Input** method to use two nested **for** statements. Use the literal value 2 for both array bounds. Include a **Write** statement inside the **Input** method that prompts the user for each input.

   Your completed code should look as follows:

```
static void Input(int[,] dst)
{
    for (int r = 0; r < 2; r++) {
        for (int c = 0; c < 2; c++) {
            Console.Write(
↳"Enter value for [{0},{1}] : ", r, c);
            string s = Console.ReadLine( );
            dst[r,c] = int.Parse(s);
        }
    }
    Console.WriteLine( );
}
```

8. Compile the program and correct any errors. Run the program, entering the same four values for **a** from the console (that is, 1, 2, 3, and 4). Verify that the four values written to the console are still as follows:

$$\begin{pmatrix} 19 & 22 \\ 43 & 50 \end{pmatrix}$$

▶ **To input the second matrix from the console**

1. Replace the initialization of **b** in **Main** with a newly created 2 x 2 array of **ints** whose four values all default to zero.

2. Add a statement to **Main** that reads values into **b** from the console by calling the **Input** method and passing **b** as the argument.

3. Compile the program and correct any errors. Run the program, entering the same four values for **a** (1, 2, 3, and 4) and the same four values for **b** (5, 6, 7, and 8). Verify that the four values written to the console are still as follows:

$$\begin{pmatrix} 19 & 22 \\ 43 & 50 \end{pmatrix}$$

4. Run the program with different data. Collaborate with a fellow student to see whether you get the same answer for the same input.

Review

■ Overview of Arrays

■ Creating Arrays

■ Using Arrays

1. Declare an array of **ints** of rank 1 called *evens*, and initialize it with the first five even numbers, starting with zero.

2. Write a statement that declares variable called *crowd* of type **int**, and initialize it with the second element of *evens*. Remember, the second element does not reside at index 2 because array indexes do not start at 1.

3. Write two statements. The first will declare an array of **ints** of rank 1 called *copy*; the second will assign to *copy* from *evens*.

4. Write a static method called **Method** that returns an array of **ints** of rank 2 and expects no arguments. The body of **Method** will contain a single **return** statement. This statement returns a newly created array of rank 2 with dimensions 3 and 5 whose 15 elements are all initialized to 42.

5. Write a static method called **Parameter** that returns nothing and expects a two-dimensional array as its single argument. The body of the method will contain two **WriteLine** statements that write the length of each dimension to the console.

6. Write a **foreach** statement that iterates over a one-dimensional array of strings called *names*, writing each name to the console.

msdn® training

Module 7: Essentials of Object-Oriented Programming

Contents

Overview	1
Classes and Objects	2
Using Encapsulation	10
C# and Object Orientation	21
Lab 7.1: Creating and Using Classes	39
Defining Object-Oriented Systems	52
Review	61

Microsoft®

Overview

- **Classes and Objects**
- **Using Encapsulation**
- **C# and Object Orientation**
- **Defining Object-Oriented Systems**

C# is an object-oriented programming language. In this lesson, you will learn the terminology and concepts required to create and use classes in C#.

After completing this module, you will be able to:

- Define the terms *object* and *class* in the context of object-oriented programming.
- Define the three core aspects of an object: identity, state, and behavior.
- Describe abstraction and how it helps you to create reusable classes that are easy to maintain.
- Use encapsulation to combine methods and data in a single class and enforce abstraction.
- Explain the concepts of inheritance and polymorphism.
- Create and use classes in C#.

◆ Classes and Objects

- ■ **What Is a Class?**
- ■ **What Is an Object?**
- ■ **Comparing Classes to Structs**
- ■ **Abstraction**

The whole structure of C# is based on the object-oriented programming model. To make the most effective use of C# as a language, you need to understand the nature of object-oriented programming.

After completing this lesson, you will be able to:

- Define the terms *object* and *class* in the context of object-oriented programming.

- Apply the concept of abstraction.

What Is a Class?

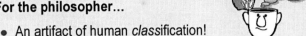

- **For the philosopher...**
  - An artifact of human *class*ification!
  - *Class*ify based on common behavior or attributes
  - Agree on descriptions and names of useful *classes*
  - Create vocabulary; we communicate; we think!
- **For the object-oriented programmer...**
  - A named syntactic construct that describes common behavior and attributes
  - A data structure that includes both data and functions

The root word of classification is *class*. Forming classes is an act of classification, and it is something that all human beings (not just programmers) do. For example, all cars share common behavior (they can be steered, stopped, and so on) and common attributes (they have four wheels, an engine, and so on). You use the word *car* to refer to all of these common behaviors and properties. Imagine what it would be like if you were not able to classify common behaviors and properties into named concepts! Instead of saying *car*, you would have to say all the things that *car* means. Sentences would be long and cumbersome. In fact, communication would probably not be possible at all. As long as everyone agrees what a word means, that is, as long as we all speak the same language, communication works well—we can express complex but precise ideas in a compact form. We then use these named concepts to form higher-level concepts and to increase the expressive power of communication.

All programming languages can describe common data and common functions. This ability to describe common features helps to avoid duplication. A key motto in programming is "Don't repeat yourself." Duplicate code is troublesome because it is more difficult to maintain. Code that does not repeat itself is easier to maintain, partly because there is just less of it! Object-oriented languages take this concept to the next level by allowing descriptions of classes (sets of objects) that share structure and behavior. If done properly, this paradigm works extremely well and fits naturally into the way people think and communicate.

Classes are not restricted to classifying concrete objects (such as cars); they can also be used to classify abstract concepts (such as time). However, when you are classifying abstract concepts, the boundaries are less clear, and good design becomes more important.

The only real requirement for a class is that it helps people communicate.

What Is an Object?

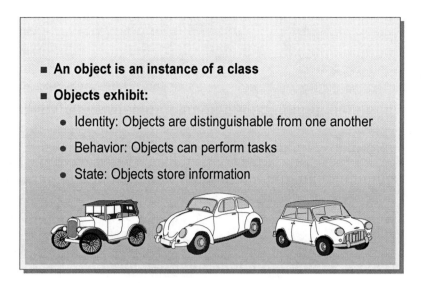

- **An object is an instance of a class**
- **Objects exhibit:**
  - Identity: Objects are distinguishable from one another
  - Behavior: Objects can perform tasks
  - State: Objects store information

The word *car* means different things in different contexts. Sometimes we use the word car to refer to the general concept of a car: we speak of car as a *class*, meaning the set of all cars, and do not have a specific car in mind. At other times we use the word car to mean a specific car. Programmers use the term *object* or *instance* to refer to a specific car. It is important to understand this difference.

The three characteristics of identity, behavior, and state form a useful way to think about and understand objects.

Identity

Identity is the characteristic that distinguishes one object from all other objects of the same class. For example, imagine that two neighbors own a car of exactly the same make, model, and color. Despite the obvious similarities, the registration numbers are guaranteed to be unique and are an outward reflection that cars exhibit identity. The law determines that it is necessary to distinguish one car object from another. (How would car insurance work without car identity?)

Behavior

Behavior is the characteristic that makes objects useful. Objects exist in order to provide behavior. Most of the time you ignore the workings of the car and think about its high-level behavior. Cars are useful because you can drive them. The workings exist but are mostly inaccessible. It is the behavior of an object that is accessible. The behavior of an object also most powerfully determines its classification. Objects of the same class share the same behavior. A car is a car because you can drive it; a pen is a pen because you can write with it.

State

State refers to the inner workings of an object that enable it to provide its defining behavior. A well-designed object keeps its state inaccessible. This is closely linked to the concepts of abstraction and encapsulation. You do not care how an object does what it does; you just care that it does it. Two objects may coincidentally contain the same state but nevertheless be two different objects. For example, two identical twins contain exactly the same state (their DNA) but are two distinct people.

Comparing Classes to Structs

- **A struct is a blueprint for a value**
  - No identity, accessible state, no added behavior
- **A class is a blueprint for an object**
  - Identity, inaccessible state, added behavior

```
struct Time                    class BankAccount
{                              {
    public int hour;               ...
    public int minute;             ...
}                              }
```

Structs

A struct, such as *Time* in the preceding code, has no identity. If you have two *Time* variables both representing the time 12:30, the program will behave exactly the same regardless of which one you use. Software entities with no identity are called *values*. The built-in types described in Module 3, "Using Value-Type Variables," in Course 2124C, *Programming with C#*, such as **int**, **bool**, **decimal**, and all **struct** types, are called *value types* in C#.

Variables of the struct type are allowed to contain methods, but it is recommended that they do not. They should contain only data. However, it is perfectly reasonable to define operators in structs. Operators are stylized methods that do not add new behavior; they only provide a more concise syntax for existing behavior.

Classes

A class, such as **BankAccount** in the preceding code, has identity. If you have two **BankAccount** objects, the program will behave differently depending on which one you use. Software entities that have identity are called *objects*. (Variables of the struct type are also sometimes loosely called objects, but strictly speaking they are *values*.) Types represented by classes are called *reference types* in C#. In contrast to structs, nothing but methods should be visible in a well-designed class. These methods add extra high-level behavior beyond the primitive behavior present in the lower-level inaccessible data.

Value Types and Reference Types

Value types are the types found at the lowest level of a program. They are the elements used to build larger software entities. Value type instances can be freely copied and exist on the stack as local variables or as attributes inside the objects they describe.

Reference types are the types found at the higher levels of a program. They are built from smaller software entities. Reference type instances generally cannot be copied, and they exist on the heap.

Abstraction

> ■ **Abstraction is selective ignorance**
>
> - Decide what is important and what is not
>
> - Focus and depend on what is important
>
> - Ignore and do not depend on what is unimportant
>
> - Use encapsulation to enforce an abstraction
>
> ---
>
> **The purpose of abstraction is not to be vague,**
> **but to create a new semantic level in which one can be absolutely precise.**
> **Edsger Dijkstra**

Abstraction is the tactic of stripping an idea or object of its unnecessary accompaniments until you are left with its essential, minimal form. A good abstraction clears away unimportant details and allows you to focus and concentrate on the important details.

Abstraction is an important software principle. A well-designed class exposes a minimal set of carefully considered methods that provide the essential behavior of the class in an easy-to-use manner. Unfortunately, creating good software abstractions is not easy. Finding good abstractions usually requires a deep understanding of the problem and its context, great clarity of thought, and plenty of experience.

Minimal Dependency

The best software abstractions make complex things simple. They do this by ruthlessly hiding away unessential aspects of a class. These unessential aspects, once truly hidden away, cannot then be seen, used, or depended upon in any way.

It is this principle of minimal dependency that makes abstraction so important. One of the few things guaranteed in software development is that the code will need to be changed. Perfect understanding only comes at the end of the development process, if it comes at all; early decisions will be made with an incomplete understanding of the problem and will need to be revisited. Specifications will also change when a clearer understanding of the problem is reached. Future versions will require extra functionality. Change is normal in software development. The best you can do is to minimize the impact of change when it happens. And the less you depend on something, the less you are affected when it changes.

Related Quotes

To illustrate the principle of minimal dependency that makes abstraction so important, here are some related quotes:

The more perfect a machine becomes, the more they are invisible behind their function. It seems that perfection is achieved not when there is nothing more to add, but when there is nothing more to take away. At the climax of its evolution, the machine conceals itself entirely.

—Antoine de Saint-Exupéry, *Wind, Sand and Stars*

The minimum could be defined as the perfection that an artifact achieves when it is no longer possible to improve it by subtraction. This is the quality that an object has when every component, every detail, and every junction has been reduced or condensed to the essentials. It is the result of the omission of the inessentials.

—John Pawson, *Minimum*

The main aim of communication is clarity and simplicity. Simplicity means focused effort.

—Edward de Bono, *Simplicity*

◆ Using Encapsulation

- **Combining Data and Methods**
- **Controlling Access Visibility**
- **Why Encapsulate?**
- **Object Data**
- **Using Static Data**
- **Using Static Methods**

After completing this lesson, you will be able to:

- Combine data and methods in a single capsule.
- Use encapsulation within a class.
- Use static data methods in a class.

Combining Data and Methods

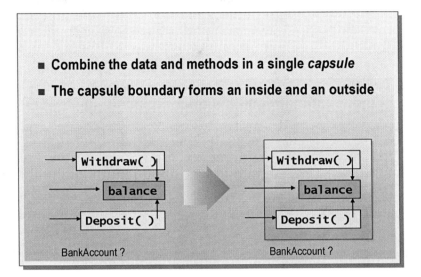

There are two important aspects to encapsulation:

- Combining data and functions in a single entity (covered in the slide)
- Controlling the accessibility of the entity members (covered in the next slide)

Procedural Programming

Traditional procedural programs written in languages such as C essentially contain a lot of data and many functions. Every function can access every piece of data. For a small program this highly coupled approach can work, but as the program grows larger it becomes less feasible. Changing the data representation causes havoc. All functions that use (and hence depend upon) the changed data fail. As the program becomes larger, making any change becomes more difficult. The program becomes more brittle and less stable. The separate data-function approach does not scale. It does not facilitate change, and as all software developers know, change is the only constant.

There is another serious problem with keeping the data separated from the functions. This technique does not correspond to the way people naturally think, in terms of high-level behavioral abstractions. Because people (the ones who are programmers) write programs, it is much better to use a programming model that approximates the way people think rather than the way computers are currently built.

Object-Oriented Programming

Object-oriented programming arose to alleviate these problems. Object-oriented programming, if understood and used wisely, is really person-oriented programming because people naturally think and work in terms of the high-level behavior of objects.

The first and most important step away from procedural programming and towards object-oriented programming is to combine the data and the functions into a single entity.

Controlling Access Visibility

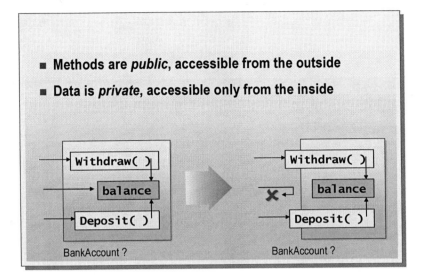

In the graphic on the left, **Withdraw**, **Deposit**, and **balance** have been grouped together inside a "capsule." The slide suggests that the name of the capsule is **BankAccount**. However, there is something wrong with this model of a bank account: the **balance** data is accessible. (Imagine if real bank account balances were directly accessible like this; you could increase your balance without making any deposits!) This is not how bank accounts work: the problem and its model have poor correspondence.

You can solve this problem by using encapsulation. Once data and functions are combined into a single entity, the entity itself forms a closed boundary, naturally creating an inside and an outside. You can use this boundary to selectively control the accessibility of the entities: some will be accessible only from the inside; others will be accessible from both the inside and the outside. Those members that are always accessible are *public*, and those that are only accessible from the inside are *private*.

To make the model of a bank account closer to a real bank account, you can make the **Withdraw** and **Deposit** methods public, and the **balance** private. Now the only way to increase the account balance from the outside is to deposit some money into the account. Note that **Deposit** can access the **balance** because **Deposit** is on the inside.

C#, like many other object-oriented programming languages, gives you complete freedom when choosing whether to make members accessible. You can, if you want, create public data. However, it is recommended that data always be marked private. (Some programming languages enforce this guideline.)

Types whose data representation is completely private are called abstract data types (ADTs). They are abstract in the sense that you cannot access (and rely on) the private data representation; you can only use the behavioral methods.

The built-in types such as **int** are, in their own way, ADTs. When you want to add two integer variables together, you do not need to know the internal binary representation of each integer value; you only need to know the name of the method that performs addition: the addition operator (+).

When you make members accessible (public), you can create different views of the same entity. The view from the outside is a subset of the view from the inside. A restricted view relates closely to the idea of abstraction: stripping an idea down to its essence.

A lot of design is related to the decision of whether to place a feature on the inside or on the outside. The more features you can place on the inside (and still retain usability) the better.

Why Encapsulate?

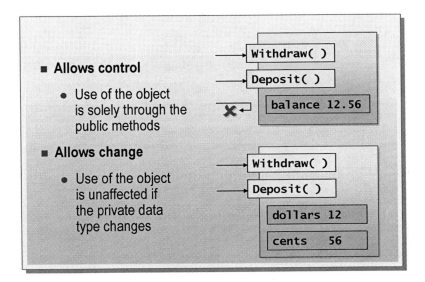

Two reasons to encapsulate are:

- To control use.
- To minimize the impact of change.

Encapsulation Allows Control

The first reason to encapsulate is to control use. When you drive a car, you think only about the act of driving, not about the internals of the car. When you withdraw money from an account, you do not think about how the account is represented. You can use encapsulation and behavioral methods to design software objects so that they can only be used in the way you intend.

Encapsulation Allows Change

The second reason to encapsulate follows from the first. If an object's implementation detail is private, it can be changed and the changes will not directly affect users of the object (who can only access the public methods). In practice, this can be tremendously useful. The names of the methods typically stabilize well before the implementation of the methods.

The ability to make internal changes links closely to abstraction. Given two designs for a class, as a rule of thumb, use the one with fewer public methods.

In other words, if you have a choice about whether to make a method public or private, make it private. A private method can be freely changed and perhaps later promoted into a public method. But a public method cannot be demoted into a private method without breaking the client code.

Object Data

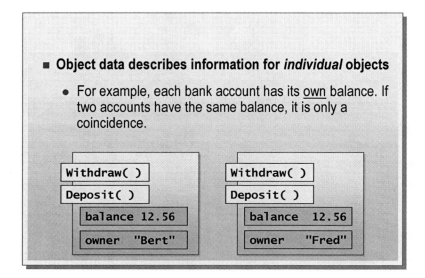

Most items of data inside an object describe information about that individual object. For example, each bank account has its own balance. It is, of course, perfectly possible for many bank accounts to have the same balance. However, this would only be a coincidence.

The data inside an object is held privately, and is accessible only to the object methods. This encapsulation and separation means that an object is effectively self-contained.

Using Static Data

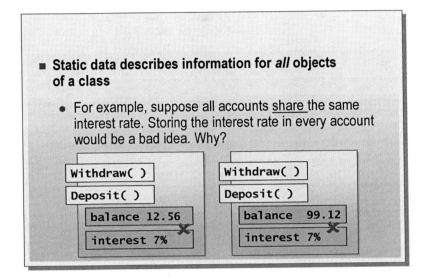

■ **Static data describes information for *all* objects of a class**

● For example, suppose all accounts share the same interest rate. Storing the interest rate in every account would be a bad idea. Why?

| Withdraw( ) |
| Deposit( ) |
| balance 12.56 |
| interest 7% |

| Withdraw( ) |
| Deposit( ) |
| balance 99.12 |
| interest 7% |

Sometimes it does not make sense to store information inside every object. For example, if all bank accounts always share the same interest rate, then storing the rate inside every account object would be a bad idea for the following reasons:

■ It is a poor implementation of the problem as described: "All bank accounts share the same interest rate."

■ It needlessly increases the size of each object, using extra memory resources when the program is running and extra disk space when it is saved to disk.

■ It makes it difficult to change the interest rate. You would need to change the interest rate in every account object. If you needed to make the interest rate change in each individual object, an interest rate change might make all accounts inaccessible while the change took place.

■ It increases the size of the class. The private interest rate data would require public methods. The account class is starting to lose its cohesiveness. It is no longer doing one thing and one thing well.

To solve this problem, do not share information that is common between objects at the object level. Instead of describing the interest rate many times at the object level, describe the interest rate once at the class level. When you define the interest rate at the class level, it effectively becomes global data.

However, global data, by definition, is not stored inside a class, and therefore cannot be encapsulated. Because of this, many object-oriented programming languages (including C#) do not allow global data. Instead, they allow data to be described as static.

Declaring Static Data

Static data is physically declared inside a class (which is a static, compile-time entity) and benefits from the encapsulation the class affords, but it is logically associated with the class itself and not with each object. In other words, static data is declared inside a class as a syntactic convenience and exists even if the program never creates any objects of that class.

Using Static Methods

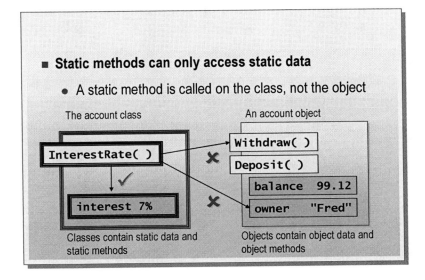

- **Static methods can only access static data**
  - A static method is called on the class, not the object

You use static methods to encapsulate static data. In the example in the slide, the interest rate belongs to the account class and not to an individual account object. It therefore makes sense to provide methods at the class level that can be used to access or modify the interest rate.

You can declare methods as static in the same way that you would declare data as static. Static methods exist at the class level. You can control accessibility for both static methods and static data by using access modifiers such as public and private. By choosing public static methods and private static data, you can encapsulate static data in the same way that you can encapsulate object data.

A static method exists at the class level and is called against the class and not against an object. This means that a static method cannot use **this**, the operator that implicitly refers to the object making an object method call. In other words, a static method cannot access non-static data or non-static methods. The only members of a class that a static method can access are static data and other static methods.

Static methods retain access to all private members of a class and can access private non-static data by means of an object reference. The following code provides an example:

```
class Time
{
    ...
    public static void Reset(Time t)
    {
        t.hour = 0;     // Okay
        t.minute = 0;   // Okay
        hour = 0;          // compile-time error
        minute = 0;        // compile-time  error
    }
    private int hour, minute;
}
```

◆ C# and Object Orientation

- Hello, World Revisited
- Defining Simple Classes
- Instantiating New Objects
- Using the this Operator
- Creating Nested Classes
- Accessing Nested Classes

In this lesson, you will re-examine the original Hello, World program. The structure of the program will be explained from an object-oriented perspective.

After completing this lesson, you will be able to:

- Use the mechanisms that enable one object to create another in C#.
- Define nested classes.

Hello, World Revisited

```
using System;

class Hello
{
        public static int Main( )
        {
                Console.WriteLine("Hello, World");
                return 0;
        }
}
```

The code for Hello, World is shown in the slide. There are some questions that can be asked and answered:

- How does the runtime invoke a class?

- Why is **Main** static?

How Does the Runtime Invoke a Class?

If there is a single **Main** method, the compiler will automatically make it the program entry point. The following code provides an example:

```
// OneEntrance.cs
class OneEntrance
{
    static void Main( )
    {
        ...
    }
}
// end of file

c:\> csc OneEntrance.cs
```

Warning   The entry point of a C# program must be **Main** with a capital "M." The signature of **Main** is also important.

However, if there are several methods called **Main**, one of them must explicitly be designated as the program entry point (and that **Main** must also be explicitly public). The following code provides an example:

```
// TwoEntries.cs
using System;
class EntranceOne
{
    public static void Main( )
    {
        Console.Write("EntranceOne.Main( )");
    }
}
class EntranceTwo
{
    public static void Main( )
    {
        Console.Write("EntranceTwo.Main( )");
    }
}
// End of file
```

```
c:\> csc /main:EntranceOne TwoEntries.cs
c:\> twoentries.exe
EntranceOne.Main( )
c:\> csc /main:EntranceTwo TwoEntries.cs
c:\> twoentries.exe
EntranceTwo.Main( )
c:\>
```

Note that the command-line option is case sensitive. If the name of the class containing **Main** is **EntranceOne** (with a capital E and a capital O) then the following will not work:

```
c:\> csc /main:entranceone TwoEntries.cs
```

If there is no **Main** method in the project, you cannot create an executable program. However, you can create a dynamic-link library (DLL) as follows:

```
// NoEntrance.cs
using System;
class NoEntrance
{
    public static void NotMain( )
    {
        Console.Write("NoEntrance.NotMain( )");
    }
}
// End of file

c:\> csc /target:library NoEntrance.cs
c:\> dir
...
NoEntrance.dll
...
```

Why Is Main Static?

Making **Main** static allows it to be invoked without the runtime needing to create an instance of the class.

Non-static methods can only be called on an object, as shown in the following code:

```
class Example
{
    void NonStatic( ) { ... }
    static void Main( )
    {
        Example eg = new Example( );
        eg.NonStatic( );  // Compiles
        NonStatic( );     // compile-time error
    }
    ...
}
```

This means that if **Main** is non-static, as in the following code, the runtime needs to create an object in order to call **Main**.

```
class Example
{
    void Main( )
    {
        ...
    }
}
```

In other words, the runtime would effectively need to execute the following code:

```
Example run = new Example( );
run.Main( );
```

Defining Simple Classes

- **Data and methods together inside a class**
- **Methods are public, data is private**

```
class BankAccount
{
    public void Withdraw(decimal amount)
    { ... }
    public void Deposit(decimal amount)
    { ... }
    private decimal balance;
    private string name;
}
```

Public methods describe accessible behaviour

Private fields describe inaccessible state

Although classes and structs are semantically different, they do have syntactic similarity. To define a class rather than a struct:

- Use the keyword **class** instead of **struct**.
- Declare your data inside the class exactly as you would for a struct.
- Declare your methods inside the class.
- Add access modifiers to the declarations of your data and methods. The simplest two access modifiers are **public** and **private**. (The other three will be covered later in this course.)

Note It is up to you to use **public** and **private** wisely to enforce encapsulation. C# does not prevent you from creating public data.

The meaning of *public* is "access not limited." The meaning of *private* is "access limited to the containing type." The following example clarifies this:

```
class BankAccount
{
    public void Deposit(decimal amount)
    {
        balance += amount;
    }
    private decimal balance;
}
```

In this example, the **Deposit** method can access the private **balance** because **Deposit** is a method of **BankAccount** (the type that contains **balance**). In other words, **Deposit** is on the inside. From the outside, private members are always inaccessible. In the following example, the expression `underAttack.balance` will fail to compile.

```
class BankRobber
{
    public void StealFrom(BankAccount underAttack)
    {
        underAttack.balance -= 999999M;
    }
}
```

The expression `underAttack.balance` will fail to compile because the expression is inside the **StealFrom** method of the **BankRobber** class. Only methods of the **BankAccount** class can access private members of **BankAccount** objects.

To declare static data, follow the pattern used by static methods (such as **Main**), and prefix the field declaration with the keyword **static**. The following code provides an example:

```
class BankAccount
{
    public void Deposit(decimal amount) { ... }
    public static void Main( ) { ... }
    ...
    private decimal balance;
    private static decimal interestRate;
}
```

If you do not specify an access modifier when declaring a class member, it will default to private. In other words, the following two methods are semantically identical:

```
class BankAccount
{
    ...
    decimal balance;
}

class BankAccount
{
    ...
    private decimal balance;
}
```

Tips   It is considered good style to explicitly write **private** even though it is not strictly necessary.

The order in which members of a class are declared is not significant to the C# compiler. However, it is considered good style to declare the public members (methods) before the private members (data). This is because a class user only has access to the public members anyway, and declaring public members before private members naturally reflects this priority.

Accessor – gather

Mutator – send

Instantiating New Objects

- **Declaring a class variable does not create an object**
  - Use the **new** operator to create an object

```
class Program
{
    static void Main( )
    {
        Time now;
        now.hour = 11;
        BankAccount yours = new BankAccount( );
        yours.Deposit(999999M);
    }
}
```

now `hour / minute`

yours ──────→ new BankAccount object

Consider the following code examples:

```
struct Time
{
    public int hour, minute;
}
class Program
{
    static void Main( )
    {
        Time now;
        now.hour = 11;
        now.minute = 59;
        ...
    }
}
```

Variables of the struct type are *value types*. This means that when you declare a struct variable (such as *now* in **Main**), you create a value on the stack. In this case, the *Time* struct contains two ints, so the declaration of *now* creates two **int**s on the stack, one called *now.hour* and one called *now.minute*. These two ints are not, repeat not, default initialized to zero. Hence the value of *now.hour* or *now.minute* cannot be read until they have been assigned a definite value. Values are scoped to the block in which they are declared. In this example, *now* is scoped to **Main**. This means that when the control flow exits **Main** (either through a normal return or because an exception has been thrown), *now* will go out of scope; it will cease to exist.

Classes are completely different as shown in the following code:

```
class Time // NOTE: Time is now a class
{
    public int hour, minute;
}
class Program
{
    static void Main( )
    {
        Time now;
        now.hour = 11;
        now.minute = 59;
        ...
    }
}
```

When you declare a class variable, you do not create an instance or object of that class. In this case, the declaration of *now* does not create an object of the **Time** class. Declaring a class variable creates a reference that is capable of referring to an object of that class. This is why classes are called *reference types*. This means that if the runtime were allowed to run the preceding code, it would be trying to access the integers inside a non-existent *Time* object. Fortunately, the compiler will warn you about this error. If you compile the preceding code, you will get the following error message:

```
error CS0165: Use of unassigned local variable 'now'
```

To fix this error, you must create a *Time* object (using the **new** keyword) and make the reference variable *now* actually refer to the newly created object, as in the following code:

```
class Program
{
    static void Main( )
    {
        Time now = new Time( );
        now.hour = 11;
        now.minute = 59;
        ...
    }
}
```

Recall that when you create a local struct value on the stack, the fields are not, repeat not, default initialized to zero. Classes are different: when you create an object as an instance of a class, as above, the fields of the object are default initialized to zero. Hence the following code compiles cleanly:

```
class Program
{
    static void Main( )
    {
        Time now = new Time( );
        Console.WriteLine(now.hour);    // writes 0
        Console.WriteLine(now.minute); // writes 0
        ...
    }
}
```

Using the this Keyword

- ■ **The this keyword refers to the object used to call the method**
  - Useful when identifiers from different scopes clash

```
class BankAccount
{
    ...
    public void SetName(string name)
    {
        this.name = name;
    }
    private string name;
}
```

If this statement were
name = name;
What would happen?

The **this** keyword implicitly refers to the object that is making an object method call.

In the following code, the statement name = name would have no effect at all. This is because the identifier *name* on the left side of the assignment does not resolve to the private **BankAccount** field called *name*. Both identifiers resolve to the method parameter, which is also called *name*.

```
class BankAccount
{
    public void SetName(string name)
    {
        name = name;
    }
    private string name;
}
```

Warning   The C# compiler does *not* emit a warning for this bug.

Using the this Keyword

You can solve this reference problem by using the **this** keyword, as illustrated on the slide. The **this** keyword refers to the current object for which the method is called.

Note   Static methods cannot use **this** as they are not called by using an object.

Changing the Parameter Name

You can also solve the reference problem by changing the name of the parameter, as in the following example:

```
class BankAccount
{
    public void SetName(string newName)
    {
        name = newName;
    }
    private string name;
}
```

Tip Using **this** when writing constructors is a common C# idiom. The following code provides an example:

```
struct Time
{
    public Time(int hour, int minute)
    {
        this.hour = hour;
        this.minute = minute;
    }
    private int hour, minute;
}
```

Tip   The **this** keyword is also used to implement call chaining. Notice in the following class that both methods return the calling object:

```
class Book
{
    public Book SetAuthor(string author)
    {
        this.author = author;
        return this;
    }
    public Book SetTitle(string title)
    {
        this.title = title;
        return this;
    }
    private string author, title;
}
```

Returning **this** allows method calls to be chained together, as follows:

```
class Usage
{
    static void Chained(Book good)
    {
        good.SetAuthor(" Fowler").SetTitle(" Refactoring");
    }
    static void NotChained(Book good)
    {
        good.SetAuthor("Fowler");
        good.SetTitle(" Refactoring");
    }
}
```

Note   A static method exists at the class level and is called against the class and not against an object. This means that a static method cannot use the **this** operator.

Creating Nested Classes

■ **Classes can be nested inside other classes**

```
class Program
{
    static void Main( )
    {
        Bank.Account yours = new Bank.Account( );
    }
}
class Bank
{
    ... class Account { ... }
}
```

what are we creating

The full name of the nested class includes the name of the outer class

---

There are five different kinds of types in C#:

■ class

■ struct

■ interface

■ enum

■ delegate

You can nest all five of these inside a class or a struct.

Note You cannot nest a type inside an interface, an enum, or a delegate.

In the code above, the **Account** class is nested inside the **Bank** class. The full name of the nested class is **Account.Bank**, and this name must be used when naming the nested type outside the scope of **Bank**. The following code provides an example:

```
// Program.cs
class Program
{
    static void Main( )
    {
        Account yours = new Account( ); // compile-time error
    }
}
// end of file
c:\> csc Program.cs
error CS0246: The type...'Account' could not be found...
```

In contrast, just the name **Account** can be used from inside of **Bank,** as in the following example:

```
class Bank
{
    class Account { ... }

    Account OpenAccount( )
    {
        return new Account( );
    }
}
```

Note See the next topic for a more thorough examination of the example.

Nested classes offer several useful features:

- Nested classes can be declared with specific accessibility. This is covered in the next topic.

- Using nested classes removes more names from the global scope or the containing namespace.

- Nested classes allow extra structure to be expressed in the grammar of the language. For example, the name of the class is **Bank.Account** (three tokens) rather than **BankAccount** (one token).

Accessing Nested Classes

■ **Nested classes can also be declared as public or private**

```
class Bank
{
    public  class Account { ... }
    private class AccountNumberGenerator { ... }
}
class Program
{
    static void Main( )
    {
        Bank.Account                    accessible;   ✔
        Bank.AccountNumberGenerator inaccessible;  ✘
    }
}
```

You control the accessibility of data and methods by declaring them as public or private. You control the accessibility of a nested class in exactly the same way.

Public Nested Class

A public nested class has no access restrictions. It is declared to be publicly accessible. The full name of a nested class must still be used when outside the containing class.

Private Nested Class

A private nested class has exactly the same access restrictions as private data or methods. A private nested class is inaccessible from outside the containing class, as the following example shows:

```
class Bank
{
    private class AccountNumberGenerator
    {
        ...
    }
}
class Program
{
    static void Main( )
    {
        // Compile time error
        Bank.AccountNumberGenerator variable;
    }
}
```

In this example, **Main** cannot use **Bank.AccountNumberGenerator** because **Main** is a method of **Program** and **AccountNumberGenerator** is private and hence only accessible to its outer class, **Bank**.

A private nested class is accessible only to members of the containing class as the following examples shows:

```
class Bank
{
    public class Account
    {
        public void Setup( )
        {
            NumberSetter.Set(this);
            balance = 0M;
        }

        private class NumberSetter
        {
            public static void Set(Account a)
            {
                a.number = nextNumber++;
            }
            private static int nextNumber = 2311;
        }

        private int number;
        private decimal balance;
    }
}
```

In this code, note that the **Account.Setup** method can access the **NumberSetter** class because, although **NumberSetter** is a private class, it is private to **Account**, and **Setup** is a method of **Account**.

Notice also that the **Account.NumberSetter.Set** method can access the private *balance* field of the **Account** object *a*. This is because **Set** is a method of class **NumberSetter**, which is nested inside **Account**. Hence **NumberSetter** (and its methods) have access to the private members of **Account**.

The default accessibility of a nested class is private (as it is for data and methods). In the following example, the **Account** class defaults to private:

```
class Bank
{
    class Account { ... }

    public Account OpenPublicAccount( )
    {
        Account opened = new Account( );
        opened.Setup( );
        return opened;
    }

    private Account OpenPrivateAccount( )
    {
        Account opened = new Account( );
        opened.Setup( );
        return opened;
    }
}
```

The **Account** class is accessible to **OpenPublicAccount** and **OpenPrivateAccount** because both methods are nested inside **Bank**. However, the **OpenPublicAccount** method will not compile. The problem is that **OpenPublicAccount** is a public method, usable as in the following code:

```
class Program
{
    static void Main( )
    {
        Bank b = new Bank( );
        Bank.Account opened = b.OpenPublicAccount( );
        ...
    }
}
```

This code will not compile because **Bank.Account** is not accessible to **Program.Main, Bank.Account** is private to **Bank**, and **Main** is not a method of **Bank**. The following error message appears:

```
error CS0050: Inconsistent accessibility: return type
'Bank.Account' is less accessible than method
'Bank.OpenPublicAccount()'
```

The accessibility rules for a top-level class (that is, a class that is not nested inside another class) are not the same as those for a nested class. A top-level class cannot be declared private and defaults to internal accessibility. (Internal access is covered fully in a later module.)

Lab 7.1: Creating and Using Classes

Objectives

After completing this lab, you will be able to:

- Create classes and instantiate objects.
- Use non-static data and methods.
- Use static data and methods.

Prerequisites

Before working on this lab, you must be familiar with the following:

- Creating methods in C#
- Passing arguments as method parameters in C#

Estimated time to complete this lab: 45 minutes

Exercise 1
Creating and Using a Class

In this exercise, you will take the bank account struct that you developed in a previous module and convert it into a class. You will declare its data members as private but provide non-static public methods for accessing the data. You will build a test harness that creates an account object and populates it with an account number and balance that is specified by the user. Finally, you will print the data in the account.

▶ **To change BankAccount from a struct to a class**

1. Open the CreateAccount.sln project in the
   install folder\Labs\Lab07\Starter\CreateAccount folder.

2. Study the code in the BankAccount.cs file. Notice that *BankAccount* is a struct type.

3. Compile and run the program. You will be prompted to enter an account number and an initial balance. Repeat this process to create another account.

4. Modify *BankAccount* in BankAccount.cs to make it a class rather than a struct.

5. Compile the program. It will fail to compile. Open the CreateAccount.cs file and view the **CreateAccount** class. The class will look as follows:

```
class CreateAccount
{
    ...
    static BankAccount NewBankAccount( )
    {
        BankAccount created;
        ...
        created.accNo = number; // Error here
        ...
    }
    ...
}
```

6. The assignment to *created.accNo* compiled without error when **BankAccount** was a struct. Now that it is a class, it does not compile! This is because when **BankAccount** was a struct, the declaration of the *created* variable created a **BankAccount** *value* (on the stack). Now that **BankAccount** is a class, the declaration of the *created* variable does not create a **BankAccount** value; it creates a **BankAccount** *reference* that does not yet refer to a **BankAccount** *object*.

7. Change the declaration of *created* so that it is initialized with a newly created **BankAccount** object, as shown:

```
class CreateAccount
{
    ...
    static BankAccount NewBankAccount( )
    {
        BankAccount created = new BankAccount( );
        ...
        created.accNo = number;
        ...
    }
    ...
}
```

8. Save your work.

9. Compile and run the program. Verify that the data entered at the console is correctly read back and displayed in the **CreateAccount.Write** method.

▶ **To encapsulate the BankAccount class**

1. All the data members of the **BankAccount** class are currently public. Modify them to make them private, as shown:

```
class BankAccount
{
    private long accNo;
    private decimal accBal;
    private AccountType accType;
}
```

2. Compile the program. It will fail to compile. The error occurs in the **CreateAccount** class as shown:

```
class CreateAccount
{
    ...
    static BankAccount NewBankAccount( )
    {
        BankAccount created = new BankAccount( );
        ...
        created.accNo = number; // Error here again
        ...

    }
    ...
}
```

3. The **BankAccount** data member assignments now fail to compile because the data members are private. Only **BankAccount** methods can access the private **BankAccount** data members. You need to write a public **BankAccount** method to do the assignments for you. Perform the following steps:

   Add a non-static public method called **Populate** to **BankAccount**. This method will return **void** and expect two parameters: a long (the bank account number) and a decimal (the bank account balance). The body of this method will assign the long parameter to the *accNo* field and the decimal parameter to the *accBal* field. It will also set the *accType* field to **AccountType.Checking** as shown:

   ```
   class BankAccount
   {
       public void Populate(long number, decimal balance)
       {
           accNo = number;
           accBal = balance;
           accType = AccountType.Checking;
       }

       private long accNo;
       private decimal accBal;
       private AccountType accType;
   }
   ```

4. Comment out the three assignments to the *created* variable in the **CreateAccount.NewbankAccount** method. In their place, add a statement that calls the **Populate** method on the *created* variable, passing **number** and **balance** as arguments. This will look as follows:

   ```
   class CreateAccount
   {
       ...
       static BankAccount NewBankAccount( )
       {
           BankAccount created = new BankAccount( );
           ...
           // created.accNo = number;
           // created.accBal = balance;
           // created.accType = AccountType.Checking;

           created.Populate(number, balance);
           ...
       }
       ...
   }
   ```

5. Save your work.

6. Compile the program. It will fail to compile. There are still three statements in the **CreateAccount.Write** method that attempt to directly access the private **BankAccount** fields. You need to write three public **BankAccount** methods that return the values of these three fields. Perform the following steps:

   a. Add a non-static public method to **BankAccount** called **Number**. This method will return a long and expect no parameters. It will return the value of the *accNo* field as shown:

```
class BankAccount
{
    public void Populate(...) ...

    public long Number( )
    {
        return accNo;
    }
    ...
}
```

   b. Add a non-static public method to **BankAccount** called **Balance**, as shown in the following code. This method will return a decimal and expect no parameters. It will return the value of the *accBal* field.

```
class BankAccount
{
    public void Populate(...) ...

    ...
    public decimal Balance( )
    {
        return accBal;
    }
    ...
}
```

   c. Add a non-static public method called **Type** to **BankAccount**, as shown in the following code. This method will return an **AccountType** and expect no parameters. It will return the value of the *accType* field.

```
class BankAccount
{
    public void Populate(...) ...

    ...
    public AccountType Type( )
    {
        return accType;
    }
    ...
}
```

   d. Finally, replace the three statements in the **CreateAccount.Write**
      method that attempt to directly access the private **BankAccount** fields
      with calls to the three public methods you have just created, as shown:

```
class CreateAccount
{
    ...
    static void Write(BankAccount toWrite)
    {
        Console.WriteLine("Account number is {0}",
➥toWrite.Number( ));
        Console.WriteLine("Account balance is {0}",
➥toWrite.Balance( ));
        Console.WriteLine("Account type is {0}",
➥toWrite.Type( ));
    }
}
```

7. Save your work.

8. Compile the program and correct any other errors. Run the program. Verify
   that the data entered at the console and passed to the
   BankAccount.Populate method is correctly read back and displayed in the
   CreateAccount.Write method.

▶ **To further encapsulate the BankAccount class**

1. Change the **BankAccount.Type** method so that it returns the type of the
   account as a string rather than as an **AccountType** enum, as shown:

```
class BankAccount
{
    ...
    public string Type( )
    {
        return accType.ToString( );
    }
    ...
    private AccountType accType;
}
```

2. Save your work.

3. Compile the program and correct any errors. Run the program. Verify that
   the data entered at the console and passed to the **BankAccount.Populate**
   method is correctly read back and displayed in the **CreateAccount.Write**
   method.

Exercise 2
Generating Account Numbers

In this exercise, you will modify the **BankAccount** class from Exercise 1 so that it will generate unique account numbers. You will accomplish this by using a static variable in the **BankAccount** class and a method that increments and returns the value of this variable. When the test harness creates a new account, it will call this method to generate the account number. It will then call the method of the **BankAccount** class that sets the number for the account, passing in this value as a parameter.

▶ **To ensure that each BankAccount number is unique**

1. Open the project UniqueNumbers.sln in the *install folder*\Labs\Lab07\Starter\UniqueNumbers folder.

   Note   This project is the same as the completed CreateAccount project from Exercise 1.

2. Add a private static long called *nextAccNo* to the **BankAccount** class, as shown:

   ```
   class BankAccount
   {
       ...
       private long accNo;
       private decimal accBal;
       private AccountType accType;

       private static long nextAccNo;
   }
   ```

3. Add a public static method called **NextNumber** to the **BankAccount** class, as shown in the following code. This method will return a long and expect no parameters. It will return the value of the *nextAccNo* field in addition to incrementing this field.

   ```
   class BankAccount
   {
       ...
       public static long NextNumber( )
       {
           return nextAccNo++;
       }

       private long accNo;
       private decimal accBal;
       private AccountType accType;

       private static long nextAccNo;
   }
   ```

4. Comment out the statement in the **CreateAccount.NewBankAccount** method that writes a prompt to the console asking for the bank account number, as shown:

```
//Console.Write("Enter the account number: ");
```

5. Replace the initialization of *number* in the **CreateAccount.NewBankAccount** method with a call to the **BankAccount.NextNumber** method you have just created, as shown:

```
//long number = long.Parse(Console.ReadLine( ));
long number = BankAccount.NextNumber( );
```

6. Save your work.

7. Compile the program and correct any errors. Run the program. Verify that the two accounts have account numbers 0 and 1.

8. Currently, the **BankAccount.nextAccNo** static field has a default initialization to zero. Explicitly initialize this field to 123.

9. Compile and run the program. Verify that the two accounts created have account numbers 123 and 124.

▶ **To further encapsulate the BankAccount class**

1. Change the **BankAccount.Populate** method so that it expects only one parameter—the decimal *balance*. Inside the method, assign the *accNo* field by using the **BankAccount.NextNumber** static method, as shown:

```
class BankAccount
{
    public void Populate(decimal balance)
    {
        accNo = NextNumber( );
        accBal = balance;
        accType = AccountType.Checking;
    }
    ...
}
```

2. Change **BankAccount.NextNumber** into a private method, as shown:

```
class BankAccount
{
    ...
    private static long NextNumber( ) ...
}
```

3. Comment out the declaration and initialization of *number* in the
   CreateAccount.NewBankAccount method. Change the **created.Populate**
   method call so that it only passes a single parameter, as shown:

```
class CreateAccount
{
    ...
    static BankAccount NewBankAccount( )
    {
        BankAccount created = new BankAccount( );

        //long number = BankAccount.NextNumber( );
        ...
        created.Populate(balance);
        ...
    }
    ...
}
```

4. Save your work.

5. Compile the program and correct any errors. Run the program. Verify that
   the two accounts still have account numbers 123 and 124.

Exercise 3
Adding More Public Methods

In this exercise, you will add two methods to the **Account** class: **Withdraw** and **Deposit**.

Withdraw will take a decimal parameter and will deduct the given amount from the balance. However, it will check first to ensure that sufficient funds are available, since accounts are not allowed to become overdrawn. It will return a bool value indicating whether the withdrawal was successful.

Deposit will also take a decimal parameter whose value it will add to the balance in the account. It will return the new value of the balance.

▶ **To add a Deposit method to the BankAccount class**

1. Open the project MoreMethods.sln in the *install folder*\Labs\Lab07\Starter\MoreMethods folder.

Note   This project is the same as the completed UniqueNumbers project from Exercise 2.

---

2. Add a public non-static method called **Deposit** to the **BankAccount** class, as shown in the following code. This method will also take a decimal parameter whose value it will add to the balance in the account. It will return the new value of the balance.

```
class BankAccount
{
    ...
    public decimal Deposit(decimal amount)
    {
        accBal += amount;
        return accBal;
    }
    ...
}
```

3. Add a public static method called **TestDeposit** to the **CreateAccount** class, as shown in the following code. This method will return **void** and expect a **BankAccount** parameter. The method will write a prompt to the console prompting the user for the amount to deposit, capture the entered amount as a decimal, and then call the **Deposit** method on the **BankAccount** parameter, passing the amount as an argument.

```
class CreateAccount
{
    ...
    public static void TestDeposit(BankAccount acc)
    {
        Console.Write("Enter amount to deposit: ");
        decimal amount = decimal.Parse(Console.ReadLine());
        acc.Deposit(amount);
    }
    ...
}
```

4. Add to **CreateAccount.Main** statements that call the **TestDeposit** method you have just created, as shown in the following code. Ensure that you call **TestDeposit** for both account objects. Use the **CreateAccount.Write** method to display the account after the deposit takes place.

```
class CreateAccount
{
    static void Main( )
    {
        BankAccount berts = NewBankAccount( );
        Write(berts);
        TestDeposit(berts);
        Write(berts);

        BankAccount freds = NewBankAccount( );
        Write(freds);
        TestDeposit(freds);
        Write(freds);
    }
}
```

5. Save your work.

6. Compile the program and correct any errors. Run the program. Verify that deposits work as expected.

Note   If you have time, you might want to add a further check to **Deposit** to ensure that the decimal parameter passed in is not negative.

▶ **To add a Withdraw method to the BankAccount class**

1. Add a public non-static method called **Withdraw** to **BankAccount**, as shown in the following code. This method will expect a decimal parameter specifying the amount to withdraw. It will deduct the amount from the balance only if sufficient funds are available, since accounts are not allowed to become overdrawn. It will return a bool indicating whether the withdrawal was successful.

```
class BankAccount
{
    ...
    public bool Withdraw(decimal amount)
    {
        bool sufficientFunds = accBal >= amount;
        if (sufficientFunds) {
            accBal -= amount;
        }
        return sufficientFunds;
    }
    ...
}
```

2. Add a public static method called **TestWithdraw** to the **CreateAccount** class, as shown in the following code. This method will return **void** and will expect a **BankAccount** parameter. The method will write a prompt to the console prompting the user for the amount to withdraw, capture the entered amount as a decimal, and then call the **Withdraw** method on the **BankAccount** parameter, passing the amount as an argument. The method will capture the bool result returned by **Withdraw** and write a message to the console if the withdrawal failed.

```
class CreateAccount
{
    ...
    public static void TestWithdraw(BankAccount acc)
    {
        Console.Write("Enter amount to withdraw: ");
        decimal amount = decimal.Parse(Console.ReadLine());
        if (!acc.Withdraw(amount)) {
            Console.WriteLine("Insufficient funds.");
        }
    }
    ...
}
```

3. Add to **CreateAccount.Main** statements that call the **TestWithdraw** method you have just created, as shown in the following code. Ensure that you call **TestWithdraw** for both account objects. Use the **CreateAccount.Write** method to display the account after the withdrawal takes place.

```
class CreateAccount
{
    static void Main( )
    {
        BankAccount berts = NewBankAccount( );
        Write(berts);
        TestDeposit(berts);
        Write(berts);
        TestWithdraw(berts);
        Write(berts);

        BankAccount freds = NewBankAccount( );
        Write(freds);
        TestDeposit(freds);
        Write(freds);
        TestWithdraw(freds);
        Write(freds);
    }
}
```

4. Save your work.

5. Compile the program and correct any errors. Run the program. Verify that withdrawals work as expected. Test successful and unsuccessful withdrawals.

◆ Defining Object-Oriented Systems

- **Inheritance**
- **Class Hierarchies**
- **Single and Multiple Inheritance**
- **Polymorphism**
- **Abstract Base Classes**
- **Interfaces**
- **Early and Late Binding**

In this lesson, you will learn about inheritance and polymorphism. You will learn how to implement these concepts in C# in later modules.

Inheritance

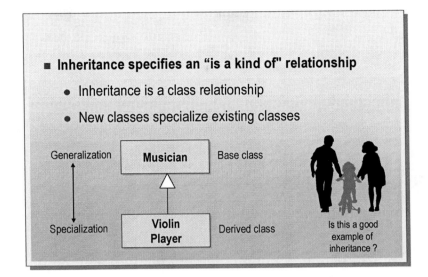

Inheritance is a relationship that is specified at the class level. A new class can be derived from an existing class. In the slide above, the **ViolinPlayer** class is derived from the **Musician** class. The **Musician** class is called the *base* class (or, less frequently, the parent class, or the superclass); the **ViolinPlayer** class is called the *derived* class (or, less frequently, the child class, or subclass). The inheritance is shown by using the Unified Modeling Language (UML) notation. More UML notation will be covered in later slides.

Inheritance is a powerful relationship because a derived class inherits everything from its base class. For example, if the base class **Musician** contains a method called **TuneYourInstrument**, this method is automatically a member of the derived **ViolinPlayer** class.

A base class can have any number of derived classes. For example, new classes (such as **FlutePlayer**, or **PianoPlayer**) could all be derived from the **Musician** class. These new derived classes would again automatically inherit the **TuneYourInstrument** method from the **Musician** base class.

Note   A change to a base class is automatically a change to all derived classes. For example, if a field of type **MusicalIntrument** was added to the **Musician** base class, then every derived class (**ViolinPlayer**, **FlutePlayer**, **PianoPlayer**, and so on) would automatically acquire a field of type **MusicalInstrument**. If a bug is introduced into a base class, it will automatically become a bug in every derived class. (This is known as the *fragile base class problem*.)

Understanding Inheritance in Object-Oriented Programming

The graphic on the slide shows a man, a woman, and a small girl riding a bicycle. If the man and the woman are the biological parents of the girl, then she will inherit half of her genes from the man and half of her genes from the woman.

But this is not an example of class inheritance. It is implementation mechanism!

The classes are **Man** and **Woman**. There are two instances of the **Woman** class (one with an **age** attribute of less than 16) and one instance of the **Man** class. There is no class inheritance. The only possible way there could be class inheritance in this example is if the **Man** class and the **Woman** class share a base class **Person**.

Class Hierarchies

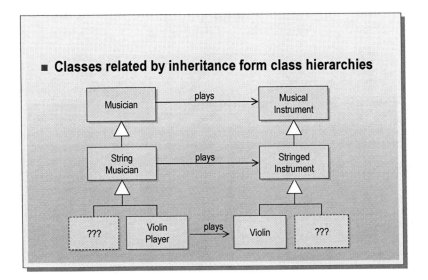

Classes that derive from base classes can themselves be derived from. For example, in the slide the **StringMusician** class is derived from the **Musician** class but is itself a base class for the further derived **ViolinPlayer** class. A group of classes related by inheritance forms a structure known as a *class hierarchy*. As you move up a hierarchy, the classes represent more general concepts (generalization); as you move down a hierarchy the classes represent more specialized concepts (specialization).

The depth of a class hierarchy is the number of levels of inheritance in the hierarchy. Deeper class hierarchies are harder to use and harder to implement than shallow class hierarchies. Most programming guidelines recommend that the depth be limited to between five and seven classes.

The slide depicts two parallel class hierarchies: one for musicians and another for musical instruments. Creating class hierarchies is not easy: classes need to be designed as base classes from the start. Inheritance hierarchies are also the dominant feature of frameworks—models of work that can be built on and extended.

Single and Multiple Inheritance

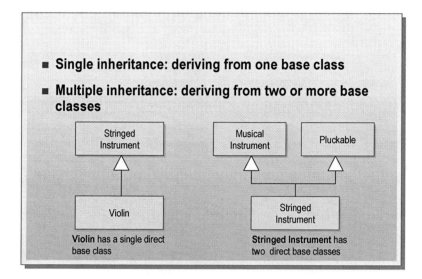

Single inheritance occurs when a class has a single direct base class. In the example in the slide, the **Violin** class inherits from one class, **StringedInstrument**, and is an example of single inheritance. **StringedInstrument** derives from two classes, but that is not relevant to the **Violin** class. Single inheritance can still be difficult to use wisely. It is well known that inheritance is one of the most powerful software modeling tools, and at the same time one of the most misunderstood and misused.

Multiple inheritance occurs when a class has two or more direct base classes. In the example in the slide, the **StringedInstrument** class derives directly from two classes, **MusicalInstrument** and **Pluckable**, and provides an example of multiple inheritance. Multiple inheritance offers multiple opportunities to misuse inheritance! C#, like most modern programming languages (but not C++), restricts the use of multiple inheritance: you can inherit from as many interfaces as you want, but you can only inherit from one non-interface (that is, at most one abstract or concrete class). The terms interface, abstract class, and concrete class are covered later in this module.

Notice that all forms of inheritance, but multiple inheritance in particular, offer many views of the same object. For example, a **Violin** object could be used at the **Violin** class level, but it could also be used at the **StringedInstrument** class level.

Polymorphism

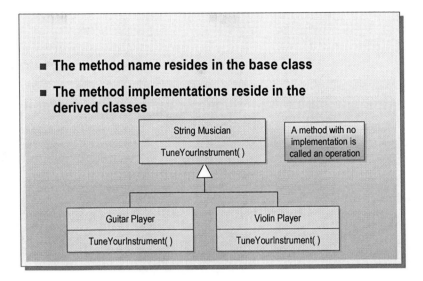

Polymorphism literally means *many forms* or *many shapes*. It is the concept that a method declared in a base class can be implemented in many different ways in the different derived classes.

Consider the scenario of an orchestra of musicians all tuning their instruments as they get ready for a concert. Without polymorphism, the conductor needs to visit each musician in turn, seeing what kind of instrument the musician plays, and giving detailed instructions about how to tune that particular kind of instrument. With polymorphism, the conductor just tells each musician, "tune your instrument." The conductor does not need to know which particular instrument each musician plays, just that each musician will respond to the same request for behavior in a manner appropriate to their particular instrument. Rather than the conductor being responsible for the knowledge of how to tune all of the different kinds of instruments, the knowledge is partitioned across the different kinds of musicians as appropriate: a guitar player knows how to tune a guitar, a violin player knows how to tune a violin. In fact, the conductor does not know how to tune *any* of the instruments. This decentralized allocation of responsibilities also means that new derived classes (such as **DrumPlayer**) can be added to the hierarchy without necessarily needing to modify existing classes (such as the conductor).

There is one problem though. What is the body of the method at the base-class level? Without knowing which particular kind of instrument a musician plays, it is impossible to know how to tune the instrument. To manage this, only the name of the method (and no body) can be declared in the base class. A method name with no method body is called an *operation*. One of the ways of denoting an operation in UML is to use italics, as is shown in the slide.

Abstract Base Classes

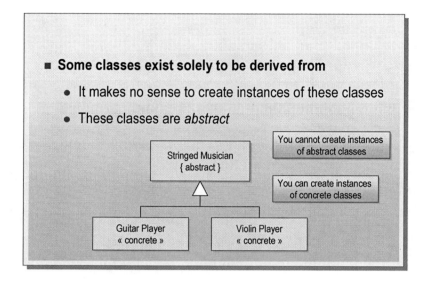

In a typical class hierarchy, the operation (the name of a method) is declared in the base class, and the method is implemented in different ways in the different derived classes. The base class exists solely to introduce the name of the method into the hierarchy. In particular, the base class operation does not require an implementation. This makes it vital that the base class not be used as a regular class. Most importantly, you must not be allowed to create instances of the base class: if you could, what would happen if you called the operation that had no implementation? A mechanism is required that makes it impossible to create instances of these base classes: the base class needs to be marked abstract.

In a UML design, you can constrain a class as abstract by writing the name of the class in italics or by placing the word *abstract* within braces ({ and }). In contrast, you can use the word *concrete* or *class* between guillemets (<< and >>) as a stereotype to denote in UML a class that is not abstract, a class that can be used to create instances. This is shown in the slide. All object-oriented programming languages have grammatical constructs that implement an abstract constraint. (Even C++ can use protected constructors.)

Sometimes the creation of an abstract base class is more retrospective: duplicate common features in the derived classes are factored into a new base class. However, once again, the base class should be marked abstract because its purpose is to be derived from, and not to create instances.

Interfaces — *only abstract classes*

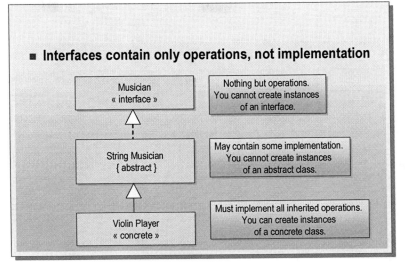

Abstract classes and interfaces are alike in that neither can be used to instantiate objects. However, they differ in that an abstract class may contain some implementation whereas an interface contains no implementation of any kind; an interface contains only operations (the names of methods). You could say that an interface is even more abstract than an abstract class.

In UML, you can depict an interface by using the word *interface* between guillemets (<< and >>). All object-oriented programming languages have grammatical constructs that implement an interface.

Interfaces are important constructs in object-oriented programs. In UML, interfaces have specific notation and terminology. When you derive from an interface, it is said that you *implement* that interface. UML depicts this with a dashed line called *realization*. When you derive from a non-interface (an abstract class or a concrete class) it is said that you *extend* that class. UML depicts this with a solid line called *generalization/specialization*.

Place your interfaces at the top of a class hierarchy. The idea is simple: if you can program to an interface—that is, if you use only those features of an object that are declared in its interface—your program loses all dependence on the specific object and its concrete class. In other words, when you program to an interface, many different objects of many different classes can be used interchangeably. It is this ability to make changes with no impact that leads to the object-oriented maxim, "Program to an interface and not to an implementation."

Early and Late Binding

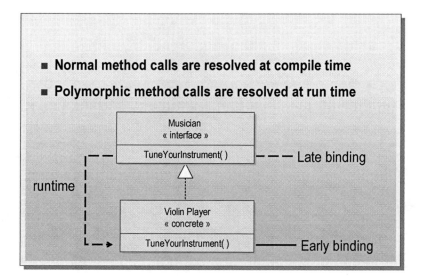

- **Normal method calls are resolved at compile time**

- **Polymorphic method calls are resolved at run time**

When you make a method call directly on an object, that is, not through a base class operation, the method call is resolved at compile time. This is also known as *early binding* or *static binding*.

When you make a method call indirectly on an object—that is, through a base class operation—the method call is resolved at run time. This is also known as *late binding* or *dynamic binding*.

An example of late binding occurs when a conductor tells all of the musicians in an orchestra to tune their instruments. By working at the interface level, the conductor does not need to know (and hence be dependent on) the specific different kinds of concrete musicians (such as **ViolinPlayer**). The conductor is also freed from needing to know when a new class is added to the hierarchy for a new kind of musician (for example, **HarpPlayer**).

The flexibility of late binding comes with a physical price and a logical price:

- Physical price

  Late bound calls are slightly slower than early bound calls. In effect, the extra work that must be performed as a result of a late bound call is to discover the class of the calling object. This is done in an efficient manner (you would not be able to do it faster yourself), but it is extra work.

- Logical price

  With late binding, derived classes can be substituted for their base classes. An operation call can be made through an interface, and at run time the derived class object will correctly have its method called. In other words, all derived classes that implement an interface can act as substitutes for the interface type. Newcomers to object-oriented programming often fail to fully appreciate the substitutability aspect of inheritance.

Review

- Classes and Objects
- Using Encapsulation
- C# and Object Orientation
- Defining Object-Oriented Systems

1. Explain the concept of abstraction and why it is important in software engineering.

2. What are the two principles of encapsulation?

3. Describe inheritance in the context of object-oriented programming.

4. What is polymorphism? How is it related to early and late binding?

5. Describe the differences between interfaces, abstract classes, and concrete classes.

msdn® training

Module 8: Using Reference-Type Variables

Contents

Overview	1
Using Reference-Type Variables	2
Using Common Reference Types	15
The Object Hierarchy	23
Namespaces in the .NET Framework	29
Lab 8.1: Defining And Using Reference-Type Variables	35
Data Conversions	44
Multimedia: Type-Safe Casting	57
Lab 8.2: Converting Data	58
Review	63

Overview

- **Using Reference-Type Variables**
- **Using Common Reference Types**
- **The Object Hierarchy**
- **Namespaces in the .NET Framework**
- **Data Conversions**

In this module, you will learn how to use reference types in C#. You will learn about a number of reference types, such as **string**, that are built into the C# language and run-time environment. These are discussed as examples of reference types.

You will also learn about the **System.Object** class hierarchy and the **object** type in particular, so you can understand how the various reference types are related to each other and to the value types. You will learn how to convert data between reference types by using explicit and implicit conversions. You will also learn how boxing and unboxing conversions convert data between reference types and value types.

After completing this module, you will be able to:

- Describe the important differences between reference types and value types.
- Use common reference types, such as string.
- Explain how the **object** type works and become familiar with the methods it supplies.
- Describe common namespaces in the Microsoft® .NET Framework.
- Determine whether different types and objects are compatible.
- Explicitly and implicitly convert data types between reference types.
- Perform boxing and unboxing conversions between reference and value data.

◆ Using Reference-Type Variables

- **Comparing Value Types to Reference Types**
- **Declaring and Releasing Reference Variables**
- **Invalid References**
- **Comparing Values and Comparing References**
- **Multiple References to the Same Object**
- **Using References as Method Parameters**

Reference types are important features of the C# language. They enable you to write complex and powerful applications and effectively use the run-time framework.

After completing this lesson, you will be able to:

- Describe the important differences between reference types and value types.
- Use and discard reference variables.
- Pass reference types as method parameters.

Comparing Value Types to Reference Types

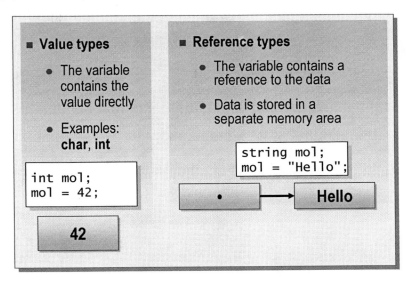

C# supports basic data types such as **int**, **long** and **bool**. These types are also referred to as *value types*. C# also supports more complex and powerful data types known as *reference types*.

Value Types

Value-type variables are the basic built-in data types such as char and int. Value types are the simplest types in C#. Variables of value type directly contain their data in the variable.

Reference Types

Reference-type variables contain a reference to the data, not the data itself. The data itself is stored in a separate memory area.

You have already used several reference types in this course so far, perhaps without realizing it. Arrays, strings, and exceptions are all reference types that are built into the C# compiler and the .NET Framework. Classes, both built-in and user-defined, are also a kind of reference type.

Declaring and Releasing Reference Variables

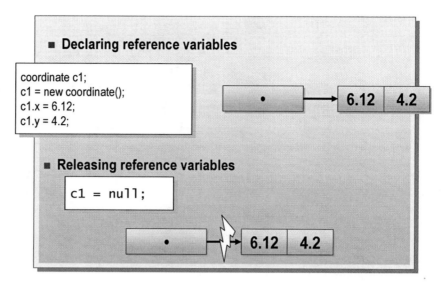

To use reference-type variables, you need to know how to declare and initialize them and how to release them.

Declaring Reference Variables

You declare reference-type variables by using the same syntax that you use when declaring value-type variables:

```
coordinate c1;
```

The preceding example declares a variable *c1* that can hold a reference to an object of type **coordinate**. However, this variable is not initialized to reference any **coordinate** objects.

To initialize a **coordinate** object, use the **new** operator. This creates a new object and returns an object reference that can be stored in the reference variable.

```
coordinate c1;
c1 = new coordinate( );
```

If you prefer, you can combine the **new** operator with the variable declaration so that the variable is declared and initialized in one statement, as follows:

```
coordinate c1 = new coordinate( );
```

After you have created an object in memory to which *c1* refers, you can then reference member variables of that object by using the **dot** operator as shown in the following example:

```
c1.x = 6.12;
c1.y = 4.2;
```

Example of Declaring Reference Variables

Classes are reference types. The following example shows how to declare a user-defined class called **coordinate**. For simplicity, this class has only two public member variables: x and y.

```
class coordinate
{
    public double x = 0.0;
    public double y = 0.0;
}
```

This simple class will be used in later examples to demonstrate how reference variables can be created, used, and destroyed.

Releasing Reference Variables

After you assign a reference to a new object, the reference variable will continue to reference the object until it is assigned to refer to a different object.

C# defines a special value called **null**. A reference variable contains **null** when it does not refer to any valid object. To release a reference, you can explicitly assign the value **null** to a reference variable (or simply allow the reference to go out of scope).

Invalid References

> ■ **If you have invalid references**
>
>   • You cannot access members or variables
>
> ■ **Invalid references at compile time**
>
>   • Compiler detects use of uninitialized references
>
> ■ **Invalid references at run time**
>
>   • System will generate an exception error

You can only access the members of an object through a reference variable if the reference variable has been initialized to point to a valid reference. If a reference is not valid, you cannot access member variables or methods.

The compiler can detect this problem in some cases. In other cases, the problem must be detected and handled at run time.

Invalid References at Compile Time

The compiler is able to detect situations in which a reference variable is not initialized prior to use.

For example, if a **coordinate** variable is declared but not assigned, you will receive an error message similar to the following: "Use of unassigned local variable c1." The following code provides an example:

```
coordinate c1;
c1.x = 6.12; // Will fail: variable not assigned
```

Invalid References at Run Time

In general, it is not possible to determine at compile time when a variable reference is not valid. Therefore, C# will check the value of a reference variable before it is used, to ensure that it is not **null**.

If you try to use a reference variable that has the value **null**, the run-time system will throw a **NullReferenceException** exception. If you want, you can check for this condition by using **try** and **catch**. The following is an example:

```
try {
    c1.x = 45;
}
catch (NullReferenceException) {
    Console.WriteLine("c1 has a null value");
}
```

Alternatively, you can check for **null** explicitly, thereby avoiding exceptions. The following example shows how to check that a reference variable contains a non-null reference before trying to access its members:

```
if (c1 != null)
    c1.x = 45;
else
    Console.WriteLine("c1 has a null value");
```

Comparing Values and Comparing References

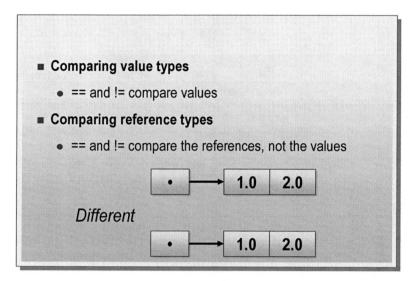

The equality (==) and inequality (!=) operators might not work in the way you expect for reference variables.

Comparing Value Types

For value types, you can use the == and != operators to compare values.

Comparing Reference Types

For reference types other than **string**, the == and != operators determine whether the two reference variables are referring to the same object. You are *not* comparing the contents of the objects to which the variables refer. For string type, == compares the value of the strings.

Consider the following example, in which two coordinate variables are created and initialized to the same values:

```
coordinate c1= new coordinate( );
coordinate c2= new coordinate( );
c1.x = 1.0;
c1.y = 2.0;
c2.x = 1.0;
c2.y = 2.0;
if (c1 == c2)
    Console.WriteLine("Same");
else
    Console.WriteLine("Different");
```

The output from this code is "Different." Even though the objects that *c1* and *c2* are referring to have the same values, they are references to different objects, so == returns **false**.

For reference types, you cannot use the other relational operators (<, >, <=, and >=) to compare whether two variables are referring to the object.

Multiple References to the Same Object

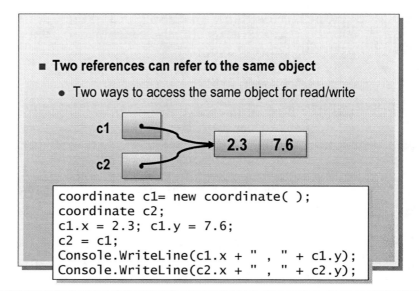

Two reference variables can refer to the same object because reference variables hold a reference to the data. This means that you can write data through one reference and read the same data through another reference.

Multiple References to the Same Object

In the following example, the variable $c1$ is initialized to point to a new instance of the class, and its member variables x and y are initialized. Then $c1$ is copied to $c2$. Finally, the values in the objects that $c1$ and $c2$ reference are displayed.

```
coordinate c1 = new coordinate( );
coordinate c2;
c1.x = 2.3;
c1.y = 7.6;
c2 = c1;
Console.WriteLine(c1.x + " , " + c1.y);
Console.WriteLine(c2.x + " , " + c2.y);
```

The output of this program is as follows:

```
2.3 , 7.6
2.3 , 7.6
```

Assigning $c2$ to $c1$ copies the reference so that both variables are referencing the same instance. Therefore, the values printed for the member variables of $c1$ and $c2$ are the same.

Writing and Reading the Same Data Through Different References

In the following example, an assignment has been added immediately before the calls to **Console.WriteLine**.

```
coordinate c1 = new coordinate( );
coordinate c2;
c1.x = 2.3;
c1.y = 7.6;
c2 = c1;
c1.x = 99; // This is the extra statement
Console.WriteLine(c1.x + " , " + c1.y);
Console.WriteLine(c2.x + " , " + c2.y);
```

The output of this program is as follows:

```
99 , 7.6
99 , 7.6
```

This shows that the assignment of 99 to $c1.x$ has also changed $c2.x$. Because the reference in $c1$ was previously assigned to $c2$, a program can write data through one reference and read the same data through another reference.

Using References as Method Parameters

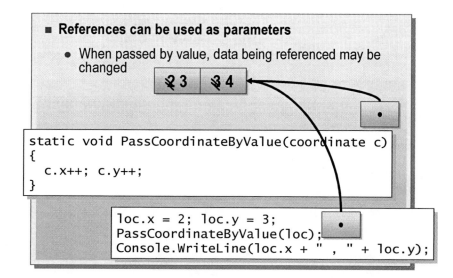

- **References can be used as parameters**
  - When passed by value, data being referenced may be changed

```
static void PassCoordinateByValue(coordinate c)
{
    c.x++; c.y++;
}
```

```
loc.x = 2; loc.y = 3;
PassCoordinateByValue(loc);
Console.WriteLine(loc.x + " , " + loc.y);
```

You can pass reference variables in and out of a method.

References and Methods

You can pass reference variables into methods as parameters by using any of the three calling mechanisms:

- By value
- By reference
- Output parameters

The following example shows a method that passes three coordinate references. The first is passed by value, the second is passed by reference, and the third is an output parameter. The return value of the method is a coordinate reference.

```
static coordinate Example(
    coordinate ca,
    ref coordinate cb,
    out coordinate cc)
{
    // ...
}
```

Passing References by Value

When you use a reference variable as a value parameter, the method receives a copy of the reference. This means that for the duration of the call there are two references referencing the same object. For example, the following code displays the values 3, 4:

```
static void PassCoordinateByValue(coordinate c)
{
    c.x++; c.y++; //c referencing loc
}
coordinate loc = new coordinate( );
loc.x = 2; loc.y = 3;
PassCoordinateByValue(loc);
Console.WriteLine(loc.x + " , " + loc.y);
```

It also means that any changes to the method parameter cannot affect the calling reference. For example, the following code displays the values 0 , 0:

```
static void PassCoordinateByValue(coordinate c)
{
    c = new coordinate( ); //c no longer referencing loc
    c.x = c.y  = 22.22;
}
coordinate loc = new coordinate( );
PassCoordinateByValue(loc);
Console.WriteLine(loc.x + " , " + loc.y);
```

Passing References by Reference

When you use a reference variable as a **ref** parameter, the method receives the actual reference variable. In contrast to passing by value, in this case there is only one reference. The method does *not* make its own copy. This means that any changes to the method parameter will affect the calling reference. For example, the following code displays the values 33.33 , 33.33:

```
static void PassCoordinateByRef(ref coordinate c)
{
    c = new coordinate( );
    c.x = c.y  = 33.33;
}
coordinate loc = new coordinate( );
PassCoordinateByRef(ref loc);
Console.WriteLine(loc.x + " , " + loc.y);
```

Passing References by Output

When you use a reference variable as an **out** parameter, the method receives the actual reference variable. In contrast to passing by value, in this case there is only one reference. The method does *not* make its own copy. Passing by **out** is similar to passing by **ref** except that the method *must* assign to the **out** parameter. For example, the following code displays the values 44.44 , 44.44:

```
static void PassCoordinateByOut(out coordinate c)
{
    c = new coordinate( );
    c.x = c.y  = 44.44;
}
coordinate loc = new coordinate( );
PassCoordinateByOut(out loc);
Console.WriteLine(loc.x + " , " + loc.y);
```

Passing References into Methods

Variables of reference types do not hold the value directly, but hold a reference to the value instead. This also applies to method parameters, and this means that the pass-by-value mechanism can produce unexpected results.

Using the **coordinate** class as an example, consider the following method:

```
static void PassCoordinateByValue(coordinate c)
{
    c.x++;
    c.y++;
}
```

The **coordinate** parameter *c* is passed by value. In the method, both the *x* and *y* member variables are incremented. Now consider the following code that calls the **PassCoordinateByValue** method:

```
coordinate loc = new coordinate( );
loc.x = 2;
loc.y = 3;
PassCoordinateByValue(loc);
Console.WriteLine(loc.x + " , " + loc.y);
```

The output of this code is the following:

```
3 , 4
```

This shows that the values referenced by **loc** have been changed by the method. This might seem to be in conflict with the explanation of pass by value given previously in the course, but in fact it is consistent. The reference variable *loc* is copied into the parameter *c* and cannot be changed by the method, but the memory to which it refers is not copied and is under no such restriction. The variable *loc* still refers to the same area of memory, but that area of memory now contains different data.

◆ Using Common Reference Types

- **Exception Class**
- **String Class**
- **Common String Methods, Operators, and Properties**
- **String Comparisons**
- **String Comparison Operators**

A number of reference-type classes are built in to the C# language.

After completing this lesson, you will be able to:

- Describe how built-in classes work.
- Use built-in classes as models when creating your own classes.

Exception Class

- **Exception is a class**
- **Exception objects are used to raise exceptions**
  - Create an **Exception** object by using **new**
  - Throw the object by using **throw**
- **Exception types are subclasses of Exception**

You create and throw **Exception** objects to raise exceptions.

Exception Class.

Exception is the name of a class provided in the .NET Framework.

Exception Objects

Only objects of **Exception** type can be thrown with **throw** and caught with **catch**. In other respects, the **Exception** class is like other reference types.

Exception Types

Exception represents a generic fault in an application. There are also specific exception types (such as **InvalidCastException**). There are classes that inherit from **Exception** that represent each of these specific exceptions.

String Class

- **Multiple character Unicode data**
- **Shorthand for System.String**
- **Immutable** ⟶ *can change the value but not the location/ref. If you change string value it also change loc/ref.*

```
string s = "Hello";
s[0] = 'c'; // Compile-time error
```

In C#, the string type is used for processing multiple character Unicode character data. (The char type, by comparison, is a value type that handles single characters.)

The type name **string** is a shortened name for the **System.String** class. The compiler can process this shortened form; therefore **string** and **System.String** can be used interchangeably.

The **String** class represents an immutable string of characters. An instance of **String** is immutable: the text of a string cannot be modified after it has been created. Methods that might appear at first sight to modify a string value actually return a new instance of string that contains the modification.

Tip   The **StringBuilder** class is often used in partnership with the **String** class. A **StringBuilder** builds an internally modifiable string that can be converted into an immutable **String** when complete. **StringBuilder** removes the need to repeatedly create temporary immutable **String**s and can provide improved performance.

The **System.String** class has many methods. This course will not provide a full tutorial for string processing, but it will list some of the more useful methods. For further details, consult the .NET Framework software development kit (SDK) Help documents.

Common String Methods, Operators, and Properties

- ■ **Brackets**
- ■ **Insert method**
- ■ **Length property**
- ■ **Copy method**
- ■ **Concat method**
- ■ **Trim method**
- ■ **ToUpper and ToLower methods**

Brackets [ ]

You can extract a single character at a given position in a string by using the string name followed by the index in brackets ([and]). This process is similar to using an array. The first character in the string has an index of zero.

The following code provides an example:

```
string s = "Alphabet";
char firstchar = s[2]; // 'p'
```

Strings are immutable, so assigning a character by using brackets is not permitted. Any attempt to assign a character to a string in this way will generate a compile-time error, as shown:

```
s[2] = '*'; // Not valid
```

Insert Method

If you want to insert characters into a string variable, use the **Insert** instance method to return a new string with a specified value inserted at a specified position in this string. This method takes two parameters: the position of the start of the insertion and the string to insert.

The following code provides an example:

```
string s = "C is great!";
s = s.Insert(2, "Sharp ");
Console.WriteLine(s); // C Sharp is great!
```

Length Property

The **Length** property returns the length of a string as an integer, as shown:

```
string msg = "Hello";
int slen = msg.Length; // 5
```

Copy Method

The **Copy** class method creates a new string by copying another string. The **Copy** method makes a duplicate of a specified string.

The following code provides an example:

```
string s1 = "Hello";
string s2 = String.Copy(s1);
```

Concat Method

The **Concat** class method creates a new string from one or more strings or objects represented as strings.

The following code provides an example:

```
string s3 = String.Concat("a", "b", "c", "d", "e", "f", "g");
```

The + operator is overloaded for strings, so the example above can be re-written as follows:

```
string s = "a" + "b" + "c" + "d" + "e" + "f" + "g";
Console.WriteLine(s);
```

Trim Method

The **Trim** instance method removes all of the specified characters or white space from the beginning and end of a string.

The following code provides an example:

```
string s = "    Hello   ";
s = s.Trim( );
Console.WriteLine(s); // "Hello"
```

ToUpper and ToLower Methods

The **ToUpper** and **ToLower** instance methods return a string with all characters converted to uppercase and lowercase, respectively, as shown:

```
string sText = "How to Succeed ";
Console.WriteLine(sText.ToUpper( )); // HOW TO SUCCEED
Console.WriteLine(sText.ToLower( )); // how to succeed
```

String Comparisons

- **Equals method**
  - Value comparison
- **Compare method**
  - More comparisons
  - Case-insensitive option
  - Dictionary ordering
- **Locale-specific compare options**

You can use the == and != operators on string variables to compare string contents.

Equals Method

The **System.String** class contains an instance method called **Equals**, which can be used to compare two strings for equality. The method returns a **bool** value that is **true** if the strings are the same and **false** otherwise. This method is overloaded and can be used as an instance method or a static method. The following example shows both forms.

```
string s1 = "Welcome";
string s2 = "Welcome";

if (s1.Equals(s2))
    Console.WriteLine("The strings are the same");

if (String.Equals(s1,s2))
    Console.WriteLine("The strings are the same");
```

Compare Method

The **Compare** method compares two strings lexically; that is, it compares the strings according to their sort order. The return value from **Compare** is as follows:

- A negative integer if the first string comes before the second
- 0 if the strings are the same
- A positive integer if the first string comes after the second

```
string s1 = "Tintinnabulation";
string s2 = "Velocipede";
int comp = String.Compare(s1,s2);  // Negative return
```

By definition, any string, including an empty string, compares greater than a **null** reference, and two **null** references compare equal to each other.

Compare is overloaded. There is a version with three parameters, the third of which is a **bool** value that specifies whether the case should be ignored in the comparison. The following example shows a case-insensitive comparison:

```
s1 = "cabbage";
s2 = "Cabbage";
comp = String.Compare(s1, s2, true); // Ignore case
```

Locale-Specific Compare Options

The **Compare** method has overloaded versions that allow string comparisons based on language-specific sort orders. This can be useful when writing applications for an international market. Further discussion of this feature is beyond the scope of the course. For more information, search for "System.Globalization namespace" and "CultureInfo class" in the .NET Framework SDK Help documents.

String Comparison Operators

- **The == and != operators are overloaded for strings**
- **They are equivalent to String.Equals and !String.Equals**

```
string a = "Test";
string b = "Test";
if (a == b) ...   // Returns true
```

The == and != operators are overloaded for the **String** class. You can use these operators to examine the contents of strings.

```
string a = "Test";
string b = "Test";
if (a == b) ...  // Returns true
```

The following operators and methods are equivalent:

- The == operator is equivalent to the **String.Equals** method.
- The != operator is equivalent to the **!String.Equals** method.

The other relational operators (<, >, <=, and >=) are not overloaded for the **String** class.

◆ The Object Hierarchy

- **The object Type**
- **Common Methods**
- **Reflection**

All classes in the .NET Framework derive from the **System.Object** class. The **object** type is an alias for System.Object class in C# language.

After completing this lesson, you will be able to:

- Describe how the object hierarchy works.

- Use the **object** type.

The object Type

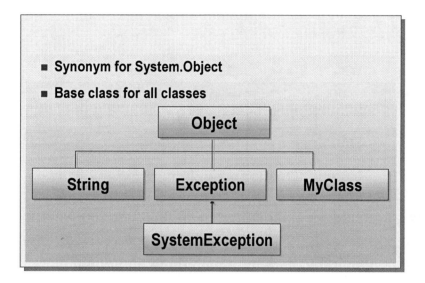

The **object** type is the base class for all types in C#.

System.Object

The **object** keyword is a synonym for the **System.Object** class in the .NET Framework. Anywhere the keyword **object** appears, the class name **System.Object** can be substituted. Because of its convenience, the shorter form is more common.

Base Class

All classes inherit from **object** either directly or indirectly. This includes the classes you write in your application and those classes that are part of the system framework. When you declare a class with no explicit parent, you are actually inheriting from **object**.

Common Methods

> - **Common methods for all reference types**
>   - **ToString** method
>   - **Equals** method
>   - **GetType** method
>   - **Finalize** method

The **object** type has a number of common methods that are inherited by all other reference types.

Common Methods for All Reference Types

The **object** type provides a number of common methods. Because every type inherits from **object**, the derived types have these methods too. These common methods include the following:

- **ToString**
- **Equals**
- **GetType**
- **Finalize**

ToString Method

The **ToString** method returns a string that represents the current object.

The default implementation, as found in the **Object** class, returns the type name of the class. The following example uses the **coordinate** example class defined earlier:

```
coordinate c = new coordinate( );
Console.WriteLine(c.ToString( ));
```

This example will display "coordinate" on the console.

However, you can override the **ToString** method in class **coordinate** to render objects of that type into something more meaningful, such as a string containing the values held in the object.

Equals Method

The **Equals** method determines whether the specified object is the same instance as the current object. The default implementation of **Equals** supports reference equality only, as you have already seen.

Subclasses can override this method to support value equality instead.

GetType Method

This method allows extraction of run-time type information from an object. It is discussed in more detail in the Data Conversions section later in this module.

Finalize Method

This method is called by the run-time system when an object becomes inaccessible.

Reflection

- **You can query the type of an object**
- **System.Reflection namespace**
- **The typeof operator returns a type object**
  - Compile-time classes only
- **GetType method in System.Object**
  - Run-time class information

You can obtain information about the type of an object by using a mechanism called reflection.

The reflection mechanism in C# is handled by the **System.Reflection** namespace in the .NET Framework. This namespace contains classes and interfaces that provide a view of types, methods, and fields.

The **System.Type** class provides methods for obtaining information about a type declaration, such as the constructors, methods, fields, properties, and events of a class. A **Type** object that represents a type is unique; that is, two **Type** object references refer to the same object only if they represent the same type. This allows comparison of **Type** objects through reference comparisons (the == and != operators).

The typeof Operator

At compile time, you can use the **typeof** operator to return the type information from a given type name.

The following example retrieves run-time type information for the type byte, and displays the type name to the console.

```
using System;
using System.Reflection;
Type t = typeof(byte);
Console.WriteLine("Type: {0}", t);
```

The following example displays more detailed information about a class. Specifically, it lists the methods for that class.

```
using System;
using System.Reflection;
Type t = typeof(string); // Get type information
MethodInfo[ ] mi = t.GetMethods( );
foreach (MethodInfo m in mi)  {
    Console.WriteLine("Method: {0}", m);
}
```

GetType Method

The **typeof** operator only works on classes that exist at compile time. If you need type information at run time, you can use the **GetType** method of the **Object** class.

For more information about reflection, search for "System.Reflection" in the .NET Framework SDK Help documents.

◆ Namespaces in the .NET Framework

- **System.IO Namespace**
- **System.Xml Namespace**
- **System.Data Namespace**
- **Other Useful Namespaces**

The .NET Framework provides common language services to a variety of application development tools. The classes in the framework provide an interface to the common language runtime, the operating system, and the network.

The .NET Framework is large and powerful, and full coverage of every feature is beyond the scope of this course. For more detailed information, please consult the Microsoft Visual Studio® .NET and .NET Framework SDK Help documents.

After completing this lesson, you will be able to:

- Identify common namespaces within the framework.
- Use some of the common namespaces in the framework.

System.IO Namespace

■ **Access to file system input/output**

- File, Directory
- StreamReader, StreamWriter   *— string reader/writer*
- FileStream   *— lower level than Stream*
- BinaryReader, BinaryWriter

The **System.IO** namespace is important because it contains many classes that allow an application to perform input and output (I/O) operations in various ways through the file system.

The **System.IO** namespace also provides classes that allow an application to perform input and output operations on files and directories.

The **System.IO** namespace is large and cannot be explained in detail here. However, the following list gives an indication of the facilities available:

■ The **File** and **Directory** classes allow an application to create, delete, and manipulate directories and files.

■ The **StreamReader** and **StreamWriter** classes enable a program to access file contents as a stream of bytes or characters.

■ The **FileStream** class can be used to provide random access to files.

■ The **BinaryReader** and **BinaryWriter** classes provide a way to read and write primitive data types as binary values.

System.IO Example

A brief example follows, to show how a file can be opened and read as a stream. The example is not meant to illustrate all of the possible ways in which the **System.IO** namespace can be used, but does show how you can perform a simple file copy operation.

```
using System;
using System.IO; // Use IO namespace
// ...
StreamReader reader = new StreamReader("infile.txt");
    // Text in from file
StreamWriter writer = new StreamWriter("outfile.txt");
    // Text out to file
string line;
while ((line = reader.ReadLine( )) != null)
{
    writer.WriteLine(line);
}

reader.Close( );
writer.Close( );
```

To open a file for reading, the code in the example creates a new **StreamReader** object and passes the name of the file that needs to be opened in the constructor. Similarly, to open a file for writing, the example creates a new **StreamWriter** object and passes the output file name in its constructor. In the example, the file names are hard-coded, but they could also be string variables.

The example program copies a file by reading one line at a time from the input stream and writing that line to the output stream.

ReadLine and **WriteLine** might look familiar. The **Console** class has two static methods of that name. In the example, the methods are instance methods of the **StreamReader** and **StreamWriter** classes, respectively.

For more information about the **System.IO** namespace, search for "System.IO namespace" in the .NET Framework SDK Help documents.

System.Xml Namespace

- **XML support**
- **Various XML-related standards**

Applications that need to interact with Extensible Markup Language (XML) can use the **System.Xml** namespace, which provides standards-based support for processing XML.

The **System.Xml** namespace supports a number of XML-related standards, including the following:

- XML 1.0 with document type definition (DTD) support
- XML namespaces
- XSD schemas
- XPath expressions
- XSL/T transformations
- DOM Level 1 core
- DOM Level 2 core

The **XmlDocument** class is used to represent an entire XML document. Elements and attributes in an XML document are represented in the **XmlElement** and **XmlAttribute** classes.

A detailed discussion of XML namespaces is beyond the scope of this course. For further information, search for "System.Xml namespace" in the .NET Framework SDK Help documents.

System.Data Namespace

- **System.Data.SqlClient**
  - SQL Server .NET Data Provider
- **System.Data**
  - Consists mostly of the classes that constitute the ADO.NET architecture

The **System.Data** namespace contains classes that constitute the ADO.NET architecture. The ADO.NET architecture enables you to build components that efficiently manage data from multiple data sources. ADO.NET provides the tools to request, update, and reconcile data in *n*-tier systems.

Within ADO.NET, you can use the **DataSet** class. In each **DataSet**, there are **DataTable** objects, and each **DataTable** contains data from a single data source, such as Microsoft SQL Server™.

The **System.Data.SqlClient** namespace provides direct access to SQL Server. Note that this namespace is specific to SQL Server.

For access to other relational databases and sources of structured data, there is the **System.Data.OleDb** namespace, which provides high-level access to the OLEDB database drivers.

A detailed discussion of the **System** namespaces is not within the scope of this course. For further information, search for "System.Data namespace" in the .NET Framework SDK Help documents.

Other Useful Namespaces

- **System namespace**
- **System.Net namespace**
- **System.Net.Sockets namespace**
- **System.Windows.Forms namespace**

There are many other useful namespaces and classes in the .NET Framework. This course does not discuss them all at length, but the following information might be helpful when you search the reference files and documentation:

- The **System** namespace contains classes that define commonly used value and reference data types, events and event handlers, interfaces, attributes, and processing exceptions. Other classes provide services that support data type conversion, method parameter manipulation, mathematics, remote and local program invocation, and application management.

- The **System.Net** namespace provides a simple programming interface to many of the protocols found on the network today. The **System.Net.Sockets** namespace provides an implementation of the Microsoft Windows® Sockets interface for developers who need to low-level access to Transmission Control Protocol/Internet Protocol (TCP/IP) network facilities.

- **System.Windows.Forms** is the graphical user interface (GUI) framework for Windows applications, and provides support for forms, controls, and event handlers.

For more information about **System** namespaces, search for "System namespace" in the .NET Framework SDK Help documents.

Lab 8.1: Defining And Using Reference-Type Variables

Objectives

After completing this lab, you will be able to:

- Create reference variables and pass them as method parameters.
- Use the system frameworks.

Prerequisites

Before working on this lab, you should be familiar with the following:

- Creating and using classes
- Calling methods and passing parameters
- Using arrays

Estimated time to complete this lab: 45 minutes

Exercise 1
Adding an Instance Method with Two Parameters

In Lab 7, you developed a **BankAccount** class. In this exercise, you will reuse this class and add a new instance method, called **TransferFrom**, which transfers money from a specified account into this one. If you did not complete Lab 7, you can obtain a copy of the **BankAccount** class in the *install folder*\Labs\Lab08\Starter\Bank folder.

▶ **To create the TransferFrom method**

1. Open the Bank.sln project in the *install folder*\Labs\Lab08\Starter\Bank folder.

2. Edit the **BankAccount** class as follows:

   a. Create a public instance method called **TransferFrom** in the **BankAccount** class.

   b. The first parameter is a reference to another **BankAccount** object, called **accFrom**, from which the money is to be transferred.

   c. The second parameter is a **decimal** value, called *amount*, passed by value and indicating the amount to transfer.

   d. The method has no return value.

3. In the body of **TransferFrom**, add two statements that perform the following tasks:

   a. Debit *amount* from the balance of **accFrom** (by using **Withdraw**).

   b. Test to ensure that the withdrawal was successful. If it was, credit *amount* to the balance of the current account (by using **Deposit**).

The **BankAccount** class should be as follows:

```
class BankAccount
{

    ... additional code omitted for clarity ...

    public void TransferFrom(BankAccount accFrom, decimal
↵amount)
    {
        if (accFrom.Withdraw(amount))
            this.Deposit(amount);
    }

}
```

▶ **To test the TransferFrom method**

1. Add Test.cs file to the current project.

2. Add the following class to this file. This is the test harness.

```
using System;

public class Test
{
    public static void Main()
    {

    }
}
```

3. In the **Main** method, add code to create two **BankAccount** objects, each having an initial balance of $100. (Use the **Populate** method.)

4. Add code to display the type, account number, and current balance of each account.

5. Add code to call **TransferFrom** and move $10 from one account to the other.

6. Add code to display the current balances after the transfer.

   The **Test** class could be as follows:

```
public static void Main( )
{
    BankAccount b1 = new BankAccount( );
    b1.Populate(100);

    BankAccount b2 = new BankAccount( );
    b2.Populate(100);

    Console.WriteLine("Before transfer");
    Console.WriteLine("{0} {1} {2}",
        ➥b1.Type( ), b1.Number( ), b1.Balance( ));
    Console.WriteLine("{0} {1} {2}",
        ➥b2.Type( ), b2.Number( ), b2.Balance( ));

    b1.TransferFrom(b2, 10);

    Console.WriteLine("After transfer");
    Console.WriteLine("{0} {1} {2}",
        ➥b1.Type( ), b1.Number( ), b1.Balance( ));
    Console.WriteLine("{0} {1} {2}",
        ➥b2.Type( ), b2.Number( ), b2.Balance( ));
}
```

7. Save your work.

8. Compile the project and correct any errors. Run and test the program.

Exercise 2
Reversing a String

In Module 5, you developed a **Utils** class that contained a variety of utility methods.

In this exercise, you will add a new static method called **Reverse** to the **Utils** class. This method takes a string and returns a new string with the characters in reverse order.

▶ **To create the Reverse method**

1. Open the Utils.sln project in the *install folder*\Labs\Lab08\Starter\Utils folder.

2. Add a public static method called **Reverse** to the **Utils** class, as follows:

    a. It has a single parameter called *s* that is a reference to a **string**.

    b. The method has a **void** return type.

3. In the **Reverse** method, create a **string** variable called *sRev* to hold the returned string result. Initialize this string to "".

4. To create a reversed string:

   a. Write a loop extracting one character at a time from *s*. Start at the end (use the **Length** property), and work backwards to the start of the string. You can use array notation ([ ]) to examine an individual character in a string.

   Tip The last character in a string is at position **Length** − 1. The first character is at position 0.

   ---

   b. Append this character to the end of *sRev*.

   The **Utils** class might contain the following:

```
class Utils
{

... additional methods omitted for clarity ...

    //
    // Reverse a string
    //

    public static void Reverse(ref string s)
    {

        string sRev = "";

        for (int k = s.Length - 1; k >= 0 ; k--)
                sRev = sRev + s[k];

        // Return result to caller
        s = sRev;
    }
}
```

▶ **To test the Reverse method**

1. Add Test.cs file to the current project.

2. Add the following class to this file. This is the test harness.

```
namespace Utils
{
    using System;

    public class Test
    {
        public static void Main()
        {

        }
    }
}
```

3. In the **Main** method, create a **string** variable.

4. Read a value into the **string** variable by using **Console.ReadLine**.

5. Pass the string into **Reverse**. Do not forget the **ref** keyword.

6. Display the value returned by **Reverse**.

   The **Test** class might contain the following:

```
static void Main( )
{
    string message;

    // Get an input string
    Console.WriteLine("Enter string to reverse:");
    message = Console.ReadLine( );

    // Reverse the string
    Utils.Reverse(ref message);

    // Display the result
    Console.WriteLine(message);
}
```

7. Save your work.

8. Compile the project and correct any errors. Run and test the program.

Exercise 3
Making an Uppercase Copy of a File

In this exercise, you will write a program that prompts the user for the name of a text file. The program will check that the file exists, displaying a message and quitting if it does not. The file will be opened and copied to another file (prompting the user for the file name), but with every character converted to uppercase.

Before you start, you might want to look briefly at the documentation for **System.IO** in the .NET Framework SDK Help documents. In particular, look at the documentation for the **StreamReader** and **StreamWriter** classes.

▶ **To create the file-copying application**

1. Open the CopyFileUpper.sln project in the *install folder*\Labs\Lab08\Starter\CopyFileUpper folder.

2. Edit the **CopyFileUpper** class and add a **using** statement for the **System.IO** namespace.

3. In the **Main** method, declare two **string** variables called *sFrom* and *sTo* to hold the input and output file names.

4. Declare a variable of type **StreamReader** called *srFrom*. This variable will hold the reference to the input file.

5. Declare a variable of type **StreamWriter** called *swTo*. This variable will hold the reference to the output stream.

6. Prompt for the name of the input file, read the name, and store it in the **string** variable *sFrom*.

7. Prompt for the name of the output file, read the name, and store it in the **string** variable *sTo*.

8. The I/O operations that you will use can raise exceptions, so begin a **try-catch** block that can catch **FileNotFoundException** (for non-existent files) and **Exception** (for any other exceptions). Print out a meaningful message for each exception.

9. In the **try** block, create a new **StreamReader** object using the input file name in *sFrom*, and store it in the **StreamReader** reference variable *srFrom*.

10. Similarly, create a new **StreamWriter** object using the input file name in *sTo*, and store it in the **StreamWriter** reference variable *swTo*.

11. Add a **while** loop that loops if the **Peek** method of the input stream does not return -1. Within the loop:

    a. Use the **ReadLine** method on the input stream to read the next line of input into a **string** variable called *sBuffer*.

    b. Perform the **ToUpper** method on *sBuffer*.

    c. Use the **WriteLine** method to send *sBuffer* to the output stream.

12. After the loop has finished, close the input and output streams.

13. The CopyFileUpper.cs file should be as follows:

```csharp
using System;
using System.IO;

class CopyFileUpper
{
    static void Main( )
    {
        string      sFrom, sTo;
        StreamReader srFrom;
        StreamWriter swTo;

        // Prompt for input file name
        Console.Write("Copy from:");
        sFrom = Console.ReadLine( );

        // Prompt for output file name
        Console.Write("Copy to:");
        sTo = Console.ReadLine( );

        Console.WriteLine("Copy from {0} to {1}", sFrom,
        ↪sTo);

        try
        {
            srFrom = new StreamReader(sFrom);
            swTo   = new StreamWriter(sTo);

            while (srFrom.Peek( )!=-1)
            {
                string sBuffer = srFrom.ReadLine( );
                sBuffer = sBuffer.ToUpper( );
                swTo.WriteLine(sBuffer);
            }
            swTo.Close( );
            srFrom.Close( );

        }
        catch (FileNotFoundException)
        {
            Console.WriteLine("Input file not found");
        }
        catch (Exception e)
        {
            Console.WriteLine("Unexpected exception");
            Console.WriteLine(e.ToString( ));
        }
    }
}
```

14. Save your work. Compile the project and correct any errors.

▶ **To test the program**

1. Open a Command window and go to the
   install folder\Labs\Lab08\Starter\CopyFileUpper\bin\debug folder.

2. Execute CopyFileUpper.

3. When prompted, specify a source file name of
   drive:\path**CopyFileUpper.cs**

   (This is the source file you have just created.)

4. Specify a destination file of **Test.cs**.

5. When the program is finished, use a text editor to examine the Test.cs file. It
   should contain a copy of your source code in all uppercase letters.

◆ Data Conversions

- ■ Converting Value Types
- ■ Parent/Child Conversions
- ■ The is Operator
- ■ The as Operator
- ■ Conversions and the object Type
- ■ Conversions and Interfaces
- ■ Boxing and Unboxing

This section explains how to perform data conversions between reference types in C#. You can convert references from one type to another, but the reference types must be related.

After completing this lesson, you will be able to:

- Identify permitted and prohibited conversions between reference types.
- Use conversion mechanisms (casts, **is**, and **as**).
- Identify special considerations for conversion to and from the **object** type.
- Use the reflection mechanism, which allows examination of run-time type information.
- Perform automatic conversions (boxing and unboxing) between value types and reference types.

Converting Value Types

- **Implicit conversions**
- **Explicit conversions**
  - Cast operator
- **Exceptions**
- **System.Convert class**
  - Handles the conversions internally

C# supports implicit and explicit data conversions.

Implicit Conversions

For value types, you have learned about two ways to convert data: implicit conversion and explicit conversion using the cast operator.

Implicit conversion occurs when a value of one type is assigned to another type. C# only allows implicit conversion for certain combinations of types, typically when the first value can be converted to the second without any data loss. The following example shows how data is converted implicitly from **int** to **long**:

```
int a = 4;
long b;
b = a; // Implicit conversion of int to long
```

Explicit Conversions

You can explicitly convert value types by using the cast operator, as shown:

```
int a;
long b = 7;
a = (int) b;
```

Exceptions

When you use the cast operator, you should be aware that problems might occur if the value cannot be held in the target variable. If a problem is detected during an explicit conversion (such as trying to fit the value 9,999,999,999 into an **int** variable), C# might raise an exception (in this case, the **OverflowException**). If you want, you can catch this exception by using **try** and **catch**, as shown:

```
try {
    a = checked((int) b);
}
catch (Exception) {
    Console.WriteLine("Problem in cast");
}
```

For operations that involve integers, use the **checked** keyword or compile with the appropriate compiler settings, otherwise checking will not be performed.

System.Convert Class

Conversions between the different base types (such as int, long, and bool) are handled within the .NET Framework by the **System.Convert** class.

You do not usually need to make calls to methods of **System.Convert**. The compiler handles these calls automatically.

Parent/Child Conversions

- **Conversion to parent class reference**
  - Implicit or explicit
  - Always succeeds
  - Can always assign to object
- **Conversion to child class reference**
  - Explicit casting required
  - Will check that the reference is of the correct type
  - Will raise **InvalidCastException** if not

You can convert a reference to an object of a child class to an object of its parent class, and vice versa, under certain conditions.

Conversion to Parent Class Reference

References to objects of one class type can be converted into references to another type if one class inherits from the other, either directly or indirectly.

A reference to an object can always be converted to a reference to a parent class object. This conversion can be performed implicitly (by assignment or as part of an expression) or explicitly (by using the cast operator).

The following examples will use two classes: **Animal** and **Bird**. **Animal** is the parent class of **Bird**, or, to put it another way, **Bird** inherits from **Animal**.

The following example declares a variable of type **Animal** and a variable of type **Bird**:

```
Animal a;
Bird b = new Bird(...);
```

Now consider the following assignment, in which the reference in *b* is copied to *a*:

```
a = b;
```

The **Bird** class inherits from the **Animal** class. Therefore, a method that is found in **Animal** is also found in **Bird**. (The **Bird** class might have overridden some of the methods of **Animal** to create its own version of them, but an implementation of the method will exist nonetheless.) Therefore, it is possible for references to **Bird** objects to be assigned to variables containing references to objects of type **Animal**.

In this case, C# performs a type conversion from **Bird** to **Animal**. You can explicitly convert **Bird** to **Animal** by using a cast operator, as shown:

```
a = (Animal) b;
```

The preceding code will produce exactly the same result.

Conversion to Child Class Reference

You can convert a reference to a child type, but you must explicitly specify the conversion by using a cast. An explicit conversion is subject to run-time checking to ensure that the types are compatible, as shown in the following example:

```
Bird b = (Bird) a; // Okay
```

This code will compile successfully. At run time, the cast operator performs a check to determine whether the object referred to is really of type **Bird**. If it is not, the run-time **InvalidCastException** is raised.

If you attempt to assign to a child type without a conversion operator, as in the following code, the compiler will display an error message stating, "Cannot implicitly convert type 'Animal' to 'Bird.'"

```
b = a; // Will not compile
```

You can trap a type conversion error by using **try** and **catch**, just like any other exception, as shown in the following code:

```
try {
    b = (Bird) a;
}
catch (InvalidCastException) {
    Console.WriteLine("Not a bird");
}
```

The is Operator

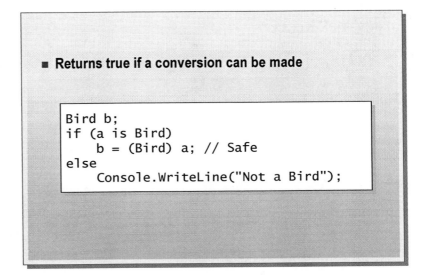

- **Returns true if a conversion can be made**

```
Bird b;
if (a is Bird)
    b = (Bird) a; // Safe
else
    Console.WriteLine("Not a Bird");
```

You can handle incompatible types by catching **InvalidCastException**, but there are other ways of handling this problem, such as the **is** operator.

You can use the **is** operator to test the type of the object without performing a conversion. The **is** operator returns **true** if the value on the left is not **null** and a cast to the class on the right, if performed, would complete without throwing an exception. Otherwise, **is** returns **false**.

```
if (a is Bird)
    b = (Bird) a; // Safe, because "a is Bird" returns true
else
    Console.WriteLine("Not a Bird");
```

You can think of the relationship between inherited classes as an "is a kind of" relationship, as in "A bird is a kind of animal." References in the variable *a* must be references to **Animal** objects, and *b* is a kind of animal. Of course, *b* is a bird as well, but a bird is just a special case of an animal. The converse is not true. An animal is not a type of bird. Some animals are birds, but it is not true that all animals are birds.

So the following expression can be read as "If *a* is a kind of bird," or "If *a* is a bird or a type derived from bird."

```
if (a is Bird)
```

The as Operator

practically checks for reference.

- **Converts between reference types, like cast**
- **On error**
  - Returns null
  - Does not raise an exception

```
Bird b = a as Bird; // Convert

if (b == null)
        Console.WriteLine("Not a bird");
```

You can use the **as** operator to perform conversions between types.

Example

The following statement performs a conversion of the reference in *a* to a value that references a class of type **Bird**, and the runtime automatically checks to ensure that the conversion is acceptable.

```
b = a as Bird;
```

Error Handling

The **as** operator differs from the cast operator in the way it handles errors. If, in the preceding example, the reference in variable *a* cannot be converted in a reference to an object of class **Bird**, the value **null** is stored in *b*, and the program continues. The **as** operator never raises an exception.

You can rewrite the previous code as follows to display an error message if the conversion cannot be performed:

```
Bird b = a as Bird;
if (b == null)
    Console.WriteLine("Not a bird");
```

Although **as** never raises an exception, any attempt to access through the converted value will raise a **NullReferenceException** if it is **null**. Therefore, you should always check the return value from **as**.

Conversions and the object Type

- **The object type is the base for all classes**
- **Any reference can be assigned to object**
- **Any object variable can be assigned to any reference**
  - With appropriate type conversion and checks
- **The object type and is operator**

```
object ox;
ox = a;
ox = (object) a;
ox = a as object;
```

```
b = (Bird) ox;
b = ox as Bird;
```

All reference types are based on the **object** type. This means that any reference can be stored in a variable of type **object**.

The object Type Is the Base for All Classes

The **object** type is the base for all reference types.

Any Reference Can Be Assigned to object

Because all classes are based directly or indirectly on the **object** type, you can assign any reference to a variable of type **object**, either with an implicit conversion or with a cast. The following code provides an example:

```
object ox;
ox = a;
ox = (object) a;
ox = a as object;
```

Any object Variable Can Be Assigned to Any Reference

You can assign a value of type **object** to any other object reference, if you cast it correctly. Remember that the run-time system will perform a check to ensure that the value being assigned is of the correct type. The following code provides an example:

```
b = (Bird) ox;
b = ox as Bird;
```

The preceding examples can be written with full error checking as follows:

```
try {
    b = (Bird) ox;
}
catch (InvalidCastException) {
    Console.WriteLine("Cannot convert to Bird");
}
b = ox as Bird;
if (b == null)
    Console.WriteLine("Cannot convert to Bird");
```

The object Type and is operator

Because every value is derived ultimately from **object**, checking a value with the **is** operator to see if it is an **object** will always return **true**.

```
if (a is object) // Always returns true
```

Conversion and Interfaces

- ■ **An interface can only be used to access its own members**
- ■ **Other methods and variables of the class are not accessible through the interface**

You can perform conversions by using the casting operators, **as** and **is**, when working with interfaces.

For example, you can declare a variable of an interface type, as shown:

```
IHashCodeProvider hcp;
```

Converting a Reference to an Interface

You can use the cast operator to convert the object reference into a reference to a given interface, as shown:

```
IHashCodeProvider hcp;
hcp = (IHashCodeProvider) x;
```

As with conversion between class references, the cast operator will raise an **InvalidCastException** if the object provided does not implement the interface. You should determine whether an object supports an interface before casting the object, or use **try** and **catch** to trap the exception.

Determining Whether an Interface Is Implemented

You can use the **is** operator to determine whether an object supports an interface. The syntax is the same as the syntax used for classes:

```
if (x is IHashCodeProvider) ...
```

Using the as Operator

You can also use the **as** operator as an alternative to casting, as shown:

```
IHashCodeProvider hcp;
hcp = x as IHashCodeProvider;
```

As with conversion between classes, if the reference that is being converted does not support the interface, the **as** operator returns **null**.

After you have converted a reference to a class into a reference to an interface, the new reference can only access members of that interface, and cannot access the other public members of the class.

Example

Consider the following example to learn how converting references to interfaces works. Suppose you have created an interface called **IVisual** that specifies a method called **Paint**, as follows:

```
interface IVisual
{
    void Paint( );
}
```

Suppose that you also have a **Rectangle** class that implements the **IVisual** interface. It implements the **Paint** method, but it can also define its own methods. In this example, **Rectangle** has defined an additional method called **Move** that is not part of **IVisual**.

You can create a **Rectangle**, *r*, and use its **Move** and **Paint** methods, as you would expect. You can even reference it through an **IVisual** variable, *v*. However, despite the fact that *v* and *r* both refer to the same object in memory, you cannot call the **Move** method by using *v* because it is not part of the **IVisual** interface. The following code provides examples:

```
Rectangle r = new Rectangle( );
r.Move( );       // Okay
r.Paint( );      // Okay
IVisual v = (IVisual) r;
v.Move( );       // Not valid
v.Paint( );      // Okay
```

Boxing and Unboxing

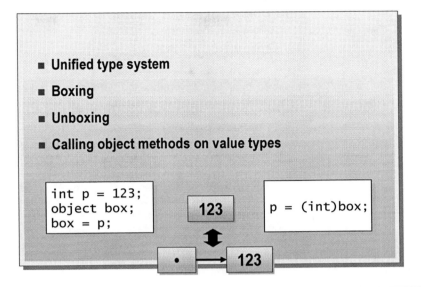

C# can convert value types into object references and object references into value types.

Unified Type System

C# has a unified type system that allows value types to be converted to references of type **object** and object references to be converted into value types. Value types can be converted into references of type **object**, and vice versa.

Values of types like **int** and **bool** can therefore be handled as simple values most of the time. This is normally the most efficient technique because there is none of the overhead that is associated with references. However, when you want to use these values as if they were references, they can be temporarily *boxed* for you to do so.

Boxing

Expressions of value types can also be converted to values of type **object**, and back again. When a variable of value type needs to be converted to **object** type, an object *box* is allocated to hold the value and the value is copied into the box. This process is known as *boxing*.

```
int p = 123;
object box;
box = p;            // Boxing (implicit)
box = (object) p; // Boxing (explicit)
```

The boxing operation can be done implicitly, or explicitly with a cast to an object. Boxing occurs most typically when a value type is passed to a parameter of type **object**.

Unboxing

When a value in an object is converted back into a value type, the value is copied out of the box and into the appropriate storage location. This process is known as *unboxing*.

```
p = (int) box;     // Unboxing
```

You must perform unboxing with an explicit cast operator.

If the value in the reference is not the exact type of the cast, the cast will raise an **InvalidCastException**.

Calling Object Methods on Value Types

Because boxing can take place implicitly, you can call methods of the object type on any variable or expression, even those having value types. The following code provides an example:

```
static void Show(object o)
{
    Console.WriteLine(o.ToString( ));
}
Show(42);
```

This works because the value 42 is implicitly boxed into an **object** parameter, and the **ToString** method of this parameter is then called.

It produces the same result as the following code:

```
object o = (object) 42; // Box
Console.WriteLine(o.ToString( ));
```

Note   Boxing does *not* occur when you call **Object** methods *directly* on a value. For example, the expression `42.ToString( )` does not box 42 into an **object**. This is because the compiler can statically determine the type and discerns which method to call.

Multimedia: Type-Safe Casting

Lab 8.2: Converting Data

Objectives

After completing this lab, you will be able to:

- Convert values of one reference type to another.
- Test whether a reference variable supports a given interface.

Prerequisites

Before working on this lab, you should be familiar with the following:

- Concepts of object-oriented programming
- Creating classes
- Defining methods

Estimated time to complete this lab: 30 minutes

Exercise 1
Testing for the Implementation of an Interface

In this exercise, you will add a static method called **IsItFormattable** to the **Utils** class that you created in Lab 5. If you did not complete that lab, you can obtain a copy of the class in the *install folder*\Labs\Lab08\Starter folder.

The **IsItFormattable** method takes one parameter of type **object** and tests whether that parameter implements the **System.IFormattable** interface. If the object does have this interface, the method will return **true**. Otherwise, it will return **false**.

A class implements the **System.IFormattable** interface to return a string representation of an instance of that class. Base types such as **int** and **ulong** implement this interface (after the value has been boxed). Many reference types, for example **string**, do not. User-defined types can implement the interface if the developer requires it. For more information about this interface, consult the .NET Framework SDK Help documentation.

You will write test code that will call the **Utils.IsItFormattable** method with arguments of different types and display the results on the screen.

▶ **To create the IsItFormattable method**

1. Open the InterfaceTest.sln project in the *install folder*\Labs\Lab08\Starter\InterfaceTest folder.

2. Edit the **Utils** class as follows:

   a. Create a public static method called **IsItFormattable** in the **Utils** class.

   b. This method takes one parameter called *x* of type **object** that is passed by value. The method returns a **bool**.

   c. Use the **is** operator to determine whether the passed object supports the **System.IFormattable** interface. If it does, return **true**; otherwise return **false**.

The completed method should be as follows:

```
using System;

...

class Utils
{
        public static bool IsItFormattable(object x)
        {
                // Use the is operator to test whether the
                // object has the IFormattable interface

                if (x is IFormattable)
                        return true;
                else
                        return false;

        }
}
```

► **To test the IsItFormattable method**

1. Edit the file **Test** class.

2. In the **Main** method, declare and initialize variables of types **int**, **ulong**, and **string**.

3. Pass each variable to **Utils.IsItFormattable()**, and print the result from each call.

4. The class **Test** might be as follows:

```
using System;
public class Test
{
    static void Main( )
    {
        int   i = 0;
        ulong ul = 0;
        string s = "Test";

        Console.WriteLine("int: {0}",
            Utils.IsItFormattable(i));
        Console.WriteLine("ulong: {0}",
            Utils.IsItFormattable(ul));
        Console.WriteLine("String: {0}",
            Utils.IsItFormattable(s));
    }
}
```

5. Compile and test the code. You should see **true** for the **int** and **ulong** values, and **false** for the **string** value.

Exercise 2
Working with Interfaces

In this exercise, you will write a **Display** method that will use the **as** operator to determine whether the object passed as a parameter supports a user-defined interface called **IPrintable** and call a method of that interface if it is supported.

▶ **To create the Display method**

1. Open the TestDisplay.sln project in the
   install folder\Labs\Lab08\Starter\TestDisplay folder.

   The starter code includes the definition for an interface called **IPrintable**, which contains a method called **Print**. A class that implements this interface should use the **Print** method to display to the console the values held inside the object. Also defined in the starter code files is a class called **Coordinate** that implements the **IPrintable** interface.

   A **Coordinate** object holds a pair of numbers that can define a position in two-dimensional space. You do not need to understand how the **Coordinate** class works (although you might want to look at it). All you need to know is that it implements the **IPrintable** interface and that you can use the **Print** method to display its contents.

2. Edit the **Utils** class as follows:

   a. Add a public static **void** method called **Display** in the **Utils** class. This method should take one parameter, an **object** passed by value, called *item*.

   b. In **Display**, declare an interface variable called *ip* of type **IPrintable**.

   c. Convert the reference in the parameter *item* into a reference to the **IPrintable** interface that uses the **as** operator. Store the result in *ip*.

   d. If the value of *ip* is not **null**, use the **IPrintable** interface to call **Print**. If it is **null**, the object does not support the interface. In this case, use **Console.WriteLine** to display to results of the **ToString** method on the parameter instead.

   The completed method should be as follows:

```
public static void Display(object item)
{
    IPrintable ip;

    ip = (item as IPrintable);

    if (ip != null)
            ip.Print( );
    else
            Console.WriteLine(item.ToString( ));
}
```

▶ **To test the Display method**

1. Within the **Main** method in the **Test** class, create a variable of type **int**, a variable of type **string**, and a variable of type **Coordinate**. To initialize the **Coordinate** variable, you can use the two-parameter constructor:

```
Coordinate c = new Coordinate(21.0, 68.0);
```

2. Pass these three variables, in turn, to **Utils.Display** to print them out.

3. The code should be as follows:

```
public class Test
{
    static void Main( )
    {
        int    num = 65;
        string msg = "A String";
        Coordinate c = new Coordinate(21.0,68.0);

        Utils.Display(num);
        Utils.Display(msg);
        Utils.Display(c);
    }
}
```

4. Compile and test your application.

Review

- Using Reference-Type Variables
- Using Common Reference Types
- The Object Hierarchy
- Namespaces in the .NET Framework
- Data Conversions

1. Explain how a memory is allocated and de-allocated for a variable of reference type.

2. What special value indicates that a reference variable does not contain a reference to an object? What happens if you try to access a reference variable with this value?

3. List the key features of the **String** class.

4. What type is the base type for all classes?

5. Explain the difference between the cast operator and the **as** operator when used to convert between class references.

6. List ways in which you can determine the type of an **object**.

msdn training

Module 9: Creating and Destroying Objects

Contents

Overview	1
Using Constructors	2
Initializing Data	13
Lab 9.1: Creating Objects	32
Objects and Memory	40
Resource Management	46
Lab 9.2: Managing Resources	55
Review	58

Microsoft®

Overview

- **Using Constructors**
- **Initializing Data**
- **Objects and Memory**
- **Resource Management**

In this module, you will learn what happens when an object is created, how to use constructors to initialize objects, and how to use destructors to destroy objects. You will also learn what happens when an object is destroyed and how garbage collection reclaims memory.

After completing this module, you will be able to:

- Use constructors to initialize objects.
- Create overloaded constructors that can accept varying parameters.
- Describe the lifetime of an object and what happens when it is destroyed.
- Create destructors.
- Implement the **Dispose** method.

◆ Using Constructors

- ■ **Creating Objects**
- ■ **Using the Default Constructor**
- ■ **Overriding the Default Constructor**
- ■ **Overloading Constructors**

Constructors are special methods that you use to initialize objects when you create them. Even if you do not write a constructor yourself, a default constructor is provided for you whenever you create an object from a reference type.

After completing this lesson, you will be able to:

- ■ Use default constructors.
- ■ Use constructors to control what happens when an object is created.

Creating Objects

> ■ **Step 1: Allocating memory**
>   ● Use **new** keyword to allocate memory from the heap
> ■ **Step 2: Initializing the object by using a constructor**
>   ● Use the name of the class followed by parentheses
>
> ```
> Date when = new Date( );
> ```

The process of creating an object in C# involves two steps:

1. Use the **new** keyword to acquire and allocate memory for the object.
2. Write a constructor to turn the memory acquired by **new** into an object.

Even though there are two steps in this process, you must perform both steps in one expression. For example, if **Date** is the name of a class, use the following syntax to allocate memory and initialize the object **when**:

```
Date when = new Date( );
```

Step 1: Allocating Memory

The first step in creating an object is to allocate memory for the object. All objects are created by using the **new** operator. There are no exceptions to this rule. You can do this explicitly in your code, or the compiler will do it for you.

In the following table, you can see examples of code and what they represent.

Code example	Represents
string s = "Hello";	string s = **new** string(new char[]{'H','e','l','l','o'});
int[ ] array = {1,2,3,4};	int[ ] array = **new** int[4]{1,2,3,4};

Step 2: Initializing the Object by Using a Constructor

The second step in creating an object is to call a constructor. A constructor turns the memory allocated by **new** into an object. There are two types of constructors: instance constructors and static constructors. Instance constructors are constructors that initialize objects. Static constructors are constructors that initialize classes.

How new and Instance Constructors Collaborate

It is important to realize how closely **new** and instance constructors collaborate to create objects. The only purpose of **new** is to acquire raw uninitialized memory. The only purpose of an instance constructor is to initialize the memory and convert it into an object that is ready to use. Specifically, **new** is not involved with initialization in any way, and instance constructors are not involved in acquiring memory in any way.

Although **new** and instance constructors perform separate tasks, as a programmer you cannot use them separately. This is one way for C# to help guarantee that memory is always definitely set to a valid value before it is read. (This is called *definite assignment*.)

Note to C++ Programmers   In C++, you can allocate memory and not initialize it (by directly calling operator **new**). You can also initialize memory allocated previously (by using placement **new**). This separation is not possible in C#.

Using the Default Constructor

- **Features of a default constructor**
  - Public accessibility
  - Same name as the class
  - No return type—not even **void**
  - Expects no arguments
  - Initializes all fields to **zero**, **false** or **null**
- **Constructor syntax**

```
class Date { public Date( ) { ... } }
```

When you create an object, the C# compiler provides a default constructor if you do not write one yourself. Consider the following example:

```
class Date
{
    private int ccyy, mm, dd;
}

class Test
{
    static void Main( )
    {
        Date when = new Date( );
        ...
    }
}
```

The statement inside **Test.Main** creates a **Date** object called **when** by using **new** (which allocates memory from the heap) and by calling a special method that has the same name as the class (the instance constructor). However, the **Date** class does not declare an instance constructor. (It does not declare any methods at all.) By default, the compiler automatically generates a default instance constructor.

Features of a Default Constructor

Conceptually, the instance constructor that the compiler generates for the **Date** class looks like the following example:

```
class Date
{
    public Date( )
    {
        ccyy = 0;
        mm = 0;
        dd = 0;
    }
    private int ccyy, mm, dd;
}
```

The constructor has the following features:

- Same name as the class name

  By definition, an instance constructor is a method that has the same name as its class. This is a natural and intuitive definition and matches the syntax that you have already seen. Following is an example:

  ```
  Date when = new Date( );
  ```

- No return type

  This is the second defining characteristic of a constructor. A constructor never has a return type—not even **void**.

- No arguments required

  It is possible to declare constructors that take arguments. However, the default constructor generated by the compiler expects no arguments.

- All fields initialized to zero

  This is important. The compiler-generated default constructor implicitly initializes all non-static fields as follows:

  - Numeric fields (such as **int**, **double**, and **decimal**) are initialized to zero.

  - Fields of type **bool** are initialized to **false**.

  - Reference types (covered in an earlier module) are initialized to **null**.

  - Fields of type **struct** are initialized to contain zero values in all their elements.

- Public accessibility

  This allows new instances of the object to be created.

Note   Module 10, "Inheritance in C#," in Course 2124C, *Programming with C#*, covers abstract classes. The compiler-generated default constructor for an abstract class has protected access.

Overriding the Default Constructor

■ **The default constructor might be inappropriate**

  ● If so, do not use it; write your own!

```
class Date
{
    public Date( )
    {
        ccyy = 1970;
        mm = 1;
        dd = 1;
    }
    private int ccyy, mm, dd;
}
```

Sometimes it is not appropriate for you to use the compiler-generated default constructor. In these cases, you can write your own constructor that contains only the code to initialize fields to non-zero values. Any fields that you do not initialize in your constructor will retain their default initialization of zero.

What If the Default Constructor Is Inappropriate?

There are several cases in which the compiler-generated default constructor may be inappropriate:

■ Public access is sometimes inappropriate.

  The Factory Method pattern uses a non-public constructor. (The Factory Method pattern is discussed in *Design Patterns: Elements of Reusable Object-Oriented Software*, by E. Gamma, R. Helm, R. Johnson, and J. Vlissides. It is covered in a later module.)

  Procedural functions (such as **Cos** and **Sin**) often use private constructors.

  The Singleton pattern typically uses a private constructor. (The Singleton pattern is also covered in *Design Patterns: Elements of Reusable Object-Oriented Software* and in a later topic in this section.)

■ Zero initialization is sometimes inappropriate.

  Consider the compiler-generated default constructor for the following **Date** class:

```
class Date
{
    private int ccyy, mm, dd;
}
```

The default constructor will initialize the year field (*ccyy*) to zero, the month field (*mm*) to zero, and the day field (*dd*) to zero. This might not be appropriate if you want the date to default to a different value.

- Invisible code is hard to maintain.

  You cannot see the default constructor code. This can occasionally be a problem. For example, you cannot single-step through invisible code when debugging. Additionally, if you choose to use the default initialization to zero, how will developers who need to maintain the code know that this choice was deliberate?

Writing Your Own Default Constructor

If the compiler-generated default constructor is inappropriate, you must write your own default constructor. The C# language helps you to do this.

You can write a constructor that only contains the code to initialize fields to non-zero values. All fields that are not initialized in your constructor retain their default initialization to zero. The following code provides an example:

```
class DefaultInit
{
    public int a, b;
    public DefaultInit( )
    {
        a = 42;
        // b retains default initialization to zero
    }
}
class Test
{
    static void Main( )
    {
        DefaultInit di = new DefaultInit( );
        Console.WriteLine(di.a); // Writes 42
        Console.WriteLine(di.b); // Writes zero
    }
}
```

You should be wary of doing more than simple initializations in your own constructors. You must consider potential failure: the only sensible way you can signal an initialization failure in a constructor is by throwing an exception.

Note   The same is also true for operators. Operators are discussed in Module 12, "Operators, Delegates, and Events," in Course 2124C, *Programming with C#.*

When initialization succeeds, you have an object that you can use. If initialization fails, you do not have an object.

Overloading Constructors

- **Constructors are methods and can be overloaded**
  - Same scope, same name, different parameters
  - Allows objects to be initialized in different ways
- **WARNING**
  - If you write a constructor for a class, the compiler does not create a default constructor

```
class Date
{
    public Date( ) { ... }
    public Date(int year, int month, int day) { ... }
    ...
}
```

Constructors are special kinds of methods. Just as you can overload methods, you can overload constructors.

What Is Overloading?

Overloading is the technical term for declaring two or more methods in the same scope with the same name. The following code provides an example:

```
class Overload
{
    public void Method( ) { ... }
    public void Method(int x) { ... }
}
class Use
{
    static void Main( )
    {
        Overload o = new Overload( );
        o.Method( );
        o.Method(42);
    }
}
```

In this code example, two methods called **Method** are declared in the scope of the **Overload** class, and both are called in **Use.Main**. There is no ambiguity, because the number and types of the arguments determine which method is called.

Initializing an Object in More Than One Way

The ability to initialize an object in different ways was one of the primary motivations for allowing overloading. Constructors are special kinds of methods, and they can be overloaded exactly like methods. This means you can define different ways to initialize an object. The following code provides an example:

```
class Overload
{
    public Overload( ) { this.data = -1; }
    public Overload(int x) { this.data = x; }
    private int data;

}

class Use
{
    static void Main( )
    {
        Overload o1 = new Overload( );
        Overload o2 = new Overload(42);
        ...
    }
}
```

Object **o1** is created by using the constructor that takes no arguments, and the private instance variable *data* is set to –1. Object **o2** is created by using the constructor that takes a single integer, and the instance variable *data* is set to 42.

Initializing Fields to Non-Default Values

You will find many cases in which fields cannot be sensibly initialized to zero. In these cases, you can write your own constructor that requires one or more parameters that are then used to initialize the fields. For example, consider the following **Date** class:

```
class Date
{
    public Date(int year, int month, int day)
    {
        ccyy = year;
        mm = month;
        dd = day;
    }
    private int ccyy, mm, dd;
}
```

One problem with this constructor is that it is easy to get the order of the arguments wrong. For example:

```
Date birthday = new Date(23, 11, 1968); // Error
```

The code should read new `Date(1968,11,23)`. This error will not be detected as a compile-time error because all three arguments are integers. One way you could fix this would be to use the Whole Value pattern. You could turn *Year*, *Month*, and *Day* into **struct**s rather than **int** values, as follows:

```
struct Year
{
    public readonly int value;
    public Year(int value) { this.value = value; }
}

struct Month // Or as an enum
{
    public readonly int value;
    public Month(int value) { this.value = value; }
}
struct Day
{
    public readonly int value;
    public Day(int value) { this.value = value; }
}
class Date
{
    public Date(Year y, Month m, Day d)
    {
        ccyy = y.value;
        mm = m.value;
        dd = d.value;
    }
    private int ccyy, mm, dd;
}
```

Tip Using **struct**s or **enum**s rather than classes for *Day*, *Month*, and *Year* reduces the overhead when creating a **Date** object. This will be explained later in this module.

The following code shows a simple change that would not only catch argument-order errors but would also allow you to create overloaded **Date** constructors for U.K. format, U.S. format, and ISO format:

```
class Date
{
    public Date(Year y, Month m, Day d) { ... } // ISO
    public Date(Month m, Day d, Year y) { ... } // US
    public Date(Day d, Month m, Year y) { ... } // UK
    ...
    private int ccyy, mm, dd;
}
```

Overloading and the Default Constructor

If you declare a class with a constructor, the compiler does not generate the default constructor. In the following example, the **Date** class is declared with a constructor, so the expression new Date( ) will not compile:

```
class Date
{
    public Date(Year y, Month m, Day d) { ... }
    // No other constructor
    private int ccyy, mm, dd;
}
class Fails
{
    static void Main( )
    {
        Date defaulted = new Date( ); // Compile-time error
    }
}
```

This means that if you want to be able to create **Date** objects without supplying any constructor arguments, you will need to explicitly declare an overloaded default constructor, as in the following example:

```
class Date
{
    public Date( ) { ... }
    public Date(Year y, Month m, Day d) { ... }
    ...
    private int ccyy, mm, dd;
}
class Succeeds
{
    static void Main( )
    {
        Date defaulted = new Date( ); // Okay
    }
}
```

◆ Initializing Data

- Using Initializer Lists
- Declaring Readonly Variables and Constants
- Initializing Readonly Fields
- Declaring a Constructor for a Struct
- Using Private Constructors
- Using Static Constructors

You have seen the basic elements of constructors. Constructors also have a number of additional features and uses.

After completing this lesson, you will be able to:

- Initialize the data in objects by using constructors.
- Use private constructors.
- Use static constructors.

Using Initializer Lists

■ **Overloaded constructors might contain duplicate code**

- Refactor by making constructors call each other
- Use the **this** keyword in an initializer list

```
class Date
{
    ...
    public Date( ) : this(1970, 1, 1) { }
    public Date(int year, int month, int day) { ... }
}
```

You can use special syntax called an initializer list to implement one constructor by calling an overloaded constructor.

Avoiding Duplicate Initializations

The following code shows an example of overloaded constructors with duplicated initialization code:

```
class Date
{
    public Date( )
    {
        ccyy = 1970;
        mm = 1;
        dd = 1;
    }
    public Date(int year, int month, int day)
    {
        ccyy = year;
        mm = month;
        dd = day;
    }
    private int ccyy, mm, dd;
}
```

Notice the duplication of *dd*, *mm*, and *ccyy* on the left side of the three initializations. This is not extensive duplication, but it is duplication nonetheless, and you should avoid it if possible. For example, suppose you decided to change the representation of a **Date** to one **long** field. You would need to rewrite every **Date** constructor.

Refactoring Duplicate Initializations

A standard way to refactor duplicate code is to extract the common code into its own method. The following code provides an example:

```
class Date
{
    public Date( )
    {
        Init(1970, 1, 1);
    }
    public Date(int year, int month, int day)
    {
        Init(day, month, year);
    }
    private void Init(int year, int month, int day)
    {
        ccyy = year;
        mm = month;
        dd = day;
    }
    private int ccyy, mm, dd;
}
```

This is better than the previous solution. Now if you changed the representation of a **Date** to one **long** field, you would only need to modify **Init**. Unfortunately, refactoring constructors in this way works some of the time but not all of the time. For example, it will not work if you try to refactor the initialization of a **readonly** field. (This is covered later in this module.) Object-oriented programming languages provide mechanisms to help solve this known problem. For example, in C++ you can use default values. In C# you use initializer lists.

Using an Initializer List

An initializer list allows you to write a constructor that calls another constructor in the same class. You write the initializer list between the closing parenthesis mark and the opening left brace of the constructor. An initializer list starts with a colon and is followed by the keyword **this** and then any arguments between parentheses. For example, in the following code, the default **Date** constructor (the one with no arguments) uses an initializer list to call the second **Date** constructor with three arguments: 1970, 1, and 1.

```
class Date
{
    public Date( ) : this(1970, 1, 1)
    {
    }
    public Date(int year, int month, int day)
    {
        ccyy = year;
        mm = month;
        dd = day;
    }
    private int ccyy, mm, dd;
}
```

This syntax is efficient, it always works, and if you use it you do not need to create an extra **Init** method.

Initializer List Restrictions

There are three restrictions you must observe when initializing constructors:

- You can only use initializer lists in constructors as shown in the following example:

```
class Point
{
    public Point(int x, int y) { ... }
    // Compile-time error
    public void Init( ) : this(0, 0) { }
}
```

- You cannot write an initializer list that calls itself. The following code provides an example:

```
class Point
{
    // Compile-time error
    public Point(int x, int y) : this(x, y) { }
}
```

■ You cannot use the **this** keyword in an expression to create a constructor argument. The following code provides an example:

```
class Point
{
    // Compile-time error
    public Point( ) : this(X(this), Y(this)) { }
    public Point(int x, int y) { ... }
    private static int X(Point p) { ... }
    private static int Y(Point p) { ... }
}
```

Declaring Readonly Variables and Constants

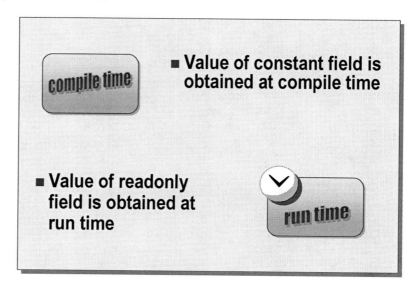

When using constructors, you need to know how to declare **readonly** variables and constants.

Using Readonly Variables

You can qualify a field as **readonly** in its declaration, as follows:

```
readonly int nLoopCount = 10;
```

You will get a compile-time error if you attempt to change the value.

Using Constant Variables

A constant variable represents a constant value that is computed at compile time. Using constant variables, you can define variables whose values never change, as shown in the following example:

```
const int speedLimit = 55;
```

Constants can depend on other constants within the same program as long as the dependencies are not of a circular nature. The compiler automatically evaluates the constant declarations in the appropriate order.

Initializing Readonly Fields

- **Readonly fields must be initialized**
  - Implicitly to zero, **false** or **null**
  - Explicitly at their declaration in a variable initializer
  - Explicitly inside an instance constructor

```
class SourceFile
{
    private readonly ArrayList lines;
}
```

Fields that cannot be reassigned and that must be initialized are called **readonly** fields. There are three ways to initialize a **readonly** field:

- Use the default initialization of a **readonly** field.
- Initialize a **readonly** field in a constructor.
- Initialize **readonly** fields by using a variable initializer.

Using the Default Initialization of a Readonly Field

The compiler-generated default constructor will initialize all fields (whether they are **readonly** or not) to their default value of zero, **false**, or **null**. The following code provides an example:

```
class SourceFile
{
    public readonly ArrayList lines;
}
class Test
{
    static void Main( )
    {
        SourceFile src = new SourceFile( );
        Console.WriteLine(src.lines == null); // True
    }
}
```

There is no **SourceFile** constructor, so the compiler writes a default constructor for you, which will initialize *lines* to **null**. Hence the **WriteLine** statement in the preceding example writes "*True.*"

If you declare your own constructor in a class and do not explicitly initialize a **readonly** field, the compiler will still automatically initialize the field. Following is an example:

```
class SourceFile
{
    public SourceFile( ) { }
    public readonly ArrayList lines;
}
class Test
{
    static void Main( )
    {
        SourceFile src = new SourceFile( );
        Console.WriteLine(src.lines == null); // Still true
    }
}
```

This is not very useful. In this case, the **readonly** field is initialized to **null**, and it will remain **null** because you cannot reassign a **readonly** field.

Initializing a Readonly Field in a Constructor

You can explicitly initialize a **readonly** field in the body of a constructor. Following is an example:

```
class SourceFile
{
    public SourceFile( )
    {
        lines = new ArrayList( );
    }
    private readonly ArrayList lines;
}
```

The statement inside the constructor looks syntactically like an assignment to *lines*, which would not normally be allowed because *lines* is a **readonly** field. However, the statement compiles because the compiler recognizes that the assignment occurs inside a constructor body and so treats it as an initialization.

An advantage of initializing **readonly** fields like this is that you can use constructor parameters in the **new** expression. Following is an example:

```
class SourceFile
{
    public SourceFile(int suggestedSize)
    {
        lines = new ArrayList(suggestedSize);
    }
    private readonly ArrayList lines;
}
```

Initializing Readonly Fields Using a Variable Initializer

You can initialize a **readonly** field directly at its declaration by using a variable initializer. Following is an example:

```
class SourceFile
{
    public SourceFile( )
    {
        ...
    }
    private readonly ArrayList lines = new ArrayList( );
}
```

This is really just convenient shorthand. The compiler conceptually rewrites a variable initialization (whether it is **readonly** or not) into an assignment inside all constructors. For example, the preceding class will conceptually be converted into the following class:

```
class SourceFile
{
    public SourceFile( )
    {
        lines = new ArrayList( );
        ...
    }
    private readonly ArrayList lines;
}
```

Declaring a Constructor for a Struct

- **The compiler**
  - Always generates a default constructor. Default constructors automatically initialize all fields to zero.
- **The programmer**
  - Can declare constructors with one or more arguments. Declared constructors do not automatically initialize fields to zero.
  - Can never declare a default constructor.
  - Can never declare a protected constructor.

The syntax you use to declare a constructor is the same for a struct as it is for a class. For example, the following is a **struct** called **Point** that has a constructor:

```
struct Point
{
    public Point(int x, int y) { ... }
    ...
}
```

Struct Constructor Restrictions

Although the syntax for struct and class constructors is the same, there are some additional restrictions that apply to **struct** constructors:

- The compiler always creates a default **struct** constructor.
- You cannot declare a default constructor in a **struct**.
- You cannot declare a protected constructor in a **struct**.
- You must initialize all fields.

The Compiler Always Creates a Default Struct Constructor

The compiler always generates a default constructor, regardless of whether you declare constructors yourself. (This is unlike the situation with classes, in which the compiler-generated default constructor is only generated if you do not declare any constructors yourself.) The compiler generated **struct** constructor initializes all fields to zero, **false**, or **null**.

```
struct SPoint
{
    public SPoint(int x, int y) { ... }
    ...
    static void Main( )
    {
        // Okay
        SPoint p = new SPoint( );
    }
}
class CPoint
{
    public CPoint(int x, int y) { ... }
    ...
    static void Main( )
    {
        // Compile-time error
        CPoint p = new CPoint( );
    }
}
```

This means that a struct value created with

```
SPoint p = new SPoint( );
```

creates a new struct value on the stack (using **new** to create a struct does not acquire memory from the heap) and initializes the fields to zero. There is no way to change this behavior.

However, a struct value created with

```
SPoint p;
```

still creates a struct value on the stack but does not initialize any of the fields (so any field must be definitely assigned before it can be referenced). Following is an example:

```
struct SPoint
{
    public int x, y;
    ...
    static void Main( )
    {
        SPoint p1;
        Console.WriteLine(p1.x); // Compile-time error
        SPoint p2;
        p2.x = 0;
        Console.WriteLine(p2.x); // Okay
    }
}
```

Tip Ensure that any **struct** type that you define is valid with all fields set to zero.

You Cannot Declare a Default Constructor in a Struct

The reason for this restriction is that the compiler always creates a default constructor in a struct (as just described), so you would end up with a duplicate definition.

```
class CPoint
{
    // Okay because CPoint is a class
    public CPoint( ) { ... }
    ...
}
struct SPoint
{
    // Compile-time error because SPoint is a struct
    public SPoint( ) { ... }
    ...
}
```

You can declare a struct constructor as long as it expects at least one argument. If you declare a struct constructor, it will not automatically initialize any field to a default value (unlike the compiler-generated struct default constructor which will).

```
struct SPoint
{
    public SPoint(int x, int y) { ... }
    ...
}
```

You Cannot Declare a Protected Constructor in a Struct

The reason for this restriction is that you can never derive other classes or structs from a struct, and so protected access would not make sense, as shown in the following example:

```
class CPoint
{
    // Okay
    protected CPoint(int x, int y) { ... }
}
struct SPoint
{
    // Compile-time error
    protected SPoint(int x, int y) { ... }
}
```

You Must Initialize All Fields

If you declare a class constructor that fails to initialize a field, the compiler will ensure that the field nevertheless retains its default zero initialization. The following code provides an example:

```
class CPoint
{
    private int x, y;
    public CPoint(int x, int y) { /*nothing*/ }
    // Okay. Compiler ensures that x and y are initialized to
    // zero.
}
```

However, if you declare a struct constructor that fails to initialize a field, the compiler will generate a compile-time error:

```
struct SPoint1 // Okay: initialized when declared
{
    private int x,y;
    public SPoint1(int a, int b) { }
}
struct SPoint2 // Okay: initialized in constructor
{
    private int x, y;
    public SPoint2(int x, int y)
    {
        this.x = x;
        this.y = y;
    }
}
```

Using Private Constructors

■ **A private constructor prevents unwanted objects from being created**

- Instance methods cannot be called

- Static methods can be called

- A useful way of implementing procedural functions

```
public class Math
{
    public static double Cos(double x) { ... }
    public static double Sin(double x) { ... }
    private Math( ) { }
}
```

So far, you have learned how to use public constructors. C# also provides private constructors, which are useful in some applications.

Using Private Constructors for Procedural Functions

Object-oriented programming offers a powerful paradigm for structuring software in many diverse domains. However, it is not a universally applicable paradigm. For example, there is nothing object oriented about calculating the sine or cosine of a double-precision floating-point number.

Declaring Functions

The most intuitive way to calculate a sine or cosine is to use global functions defined outside an object, as follows:

```
double Cos(double x) { ... }
double Sin(double x) { ... }
```

The preceding code is not allowable in C#. Global functions are possible in procedural languages such as C and in hybrid languages such as C++, but they are not allowed in C#. In C#, functions must be declared inside a class or struct, as follows:

```
class Math
{
    public double Cos(double x) { ... }
    public double Sin(double x) { ... }
}
```

Declaring Static vs. Instance Methods

The problem with the technique in the preceding example is that, because **Cos** and **Sin** are instance methods, you are forced to create a **Math** object from which to invoke **Sin** or **Cos**, as shown in the following code:

```
class Cumbersome
{
    static void Main( )
    {
      Math m = new Math( );
      double answer;
      answer = m.Cos(42.0);
      // Or
      answer = new Math( ).Cos(42.0);
  }
}
```

However, you can easily solve this by declaring **Cos** and **Sin** as static methods, as follows:

```
class Math
{
    public static double Cos(double x) { ... }
    public static double Sin(double x) { ... }
    private Math( ) { ... }
}
class LessCumbersome
{
    static void Main( )
    {
      double answer = Math.Cos(42.0);
  }
}
```

Benefits of Static Methods

If you declare **Cos** as a static method, the syntax for using **Cos** becomes:

- Simpler

  You have only one way to call **Cos** (by means of **Math**), whereas in the previous example you had two ways (by means of **m** and by means of new Math( )).

- Faster

  You no longer need to create a new **Math** object.

One slight problem remains. The compiler will generate a default constructor with public access, allowing you to create **Math** objects. Such objects can serve no purpose because the **Math** class contains static methods only. There are two ways you can prevent **Math** objects from being created:

- Declare **Math** as an abstract class.

  This is not a good idea. The purpose of abstract classes is to be derived from.

- Declare a private **Math** constructor.

  This is a better solution. When you declare a constructor in the **Math** class, you prevent the compiler from generating the default constructor, and if you also declare the constructor as private, you stop **Math** objects from being created. The private constructor also prevents **Math** from being used as a base class.

The Singleton Pattern

The intent of the Singleton pattern (which is discussed in *Design Patterns: Elements of Reusable Object-Oriented Software*) is to "ensure a class only has one instance, and provide a global point of access to it." The technique of declaring a class by using a private constructor and static methods is sometimes suggested as a way to implement the Singleton pattern.

Note A key aspect of the Singleton pattern is that a class has a single instance. With a private constructor and static methods, there is no instance at all. The canonical implementation of the Singleton pattern is to create a static method that gives access to the single instance, and this instance is then used to call instance methods.

Using Static Constructors

- **Purpose**
  - Called by the class loader at run time
  - Can be used to initialize static fields
  - Guaranteed to be called before instance constructor
- **Restrictions**
  - Cannot be called
  - Cannot have an access modifier
  - Must be parameterless

Just as an instance constructor guarantees that an object is in a well-defined initial state before it is used, a static constructor guarantees that a class is in a well-defined initial state before it is used.

Loading Classes at Run Time

C# is a dynamic language. When the common language runtime is running a Microsoft® .NET-based program, it often encounters code that uses a class that has not yet been loaded. In these situations, execution is momentarily suspended, the class is dynamically loaded, and then execution continues.

Initializing Classes at Load Time

C# ensures that a class is always initialized before it is used in code in any way. This guarantee is achieved by using static constructors.

You can declare a static constructor as you would an instance constructor, but prefix it with the keyword **static**, as follows:

```
class Example
{
    static Example( ) { ... }
}
```

After the class loader loads a class that will soon be used, but before it continues normal execution, it executes the static constructor for that class. Because of this process, you are guaranteed that classes are always initialized before they are used. The exact timing of static constructor execution is implementation-dependent, but is subject to the following rules:

- The static constructor for a class is executed before any instance of the class is created.

- The static constructor for a class is executed before any static members of the class are referenced.

- The static constructor for a class executes at most one time during a single program instantiation.

Static Field Initializations and Static Constructors

The most common use for a static constructor is to initialize the static fields of a class. This is because when you initialize a static field directly at its point of declaration, the compiler conceptually converts the initialization into an assignment inside the static constructor. In other words:

```
class Example
{
    private static Wibble w = new Wibble( );
}
```

is effectively converted by the compiler into

```
class Example
{
    static Example( )
    {
        w = new Wibble( );
    }
    private static Wibble w;
}
```

Static Constructor Restrictions

Understanding the following four restrictions on the syntax of static constructors will help you understand how the common language runtime uses static constructors:

- You cannot call a static constructor.

- You cannot declare a static constructor with an access modifier.

- You cannot declare a static constructor with parameters.

- You cannot use the **this** keyword in a static constructor.

You Cannot Call a Static Constructor

A static constructor must be called before any instances of the class are referenced in code. If the responsibility for enforcing this rule were given to programmers rather than the Microsoft .NET Framework runtime, eventually programmers would fail to meet the responsibility. They would forget to make the call, or, perhaps worse, they would call the static constructor more than once. The .NET runtime avoids these potential problems by disallowing calls to static constructors in code. Only the .NET runtime can call a static constructor.

```
class Point
{
    static Point( ) { ... }
    static void Main( )
    {
        Point.Point( ); // Compile-time error
    }
}
```

You Cannot Declare a Static Constructor with an Access Modifier

Because you cannot call a static constructor, declaring a static constructor with an access modifier does not make sense and causes a compile-time error:

```
class Point
{
    public static Point( ) { ... } // Compile-time error
}
```

You Cannot Declare a Static Constructor with Parameters

Because you cannot call a static constructor, declaring a static constructor with parameters does not make sense and causes a compile-time error. This also means that you cannot declare overloaded static constructors. Following is an example:

```
class Point
{
    static Point(int x) { ... } // Compile-time error
}
```

You Cannot Use the this Keyword in a Static Constructor

Because a static constructor initializes the class and not object instances, it does not have an implicit **this** reference, so any attempt to use the **this** keyword results in a compile-time error:

```
class Point
{
    private int x, y;
    static Point( ) : this(0,0)   // Compile-time error
    {
        this.x = 0; // Compile-time error
        this.y = 0; // Compile-time error
    }
    ...
}
```

Lab 9.1: Creating Objects

Objectives

In this lab, you will modify the **BankAccount** class that you created in the previous labs so that it uses constructors. You will also create a new class, **BankTransaction**, and use it to store information about the transactions (deposits and withdrawals) performed on an account.

After completing this lab, you will be able to:

- Override the default constructor.
- Create overloaded constructors.
- Initialize **readonly** data.

Prerequisites

Before working on this lab, you must be able to:

- Create classes and instantiate objects.
- Define and call methods.

You should also have completed Lab 8.1. If you did not complete Lab 8.1, you can use the solution code provided.

Estimated time to complete this lab: 60 minutes

Exercise 1
Implementing Constructors

In this exercise, you will modify the **BankAccount** class that you created in the previous labs. You will remove the methods that populate the account number and account type instance variables and replace them with a series of constructors that can be used when a **BankAccount** is instantiated.

You will override the default constructor to generate an account number (by using the technique that you used earlier), set the account type to **Checking**, and set the balance to zero.

You will also create three more constructors that take different combinations of parameters:

- The first will take an **AccountType**. The constructor will generate an account number, set the balance to zero, and set the account type to the value passed in.

- The second will take a **decimal**. The constructor will generate an account number, set the account type to **Checking**, and set the balance to the value passed in.

- The third will take an **AccountType** and a **decimal**. The constructor will generate an account number, set the account type to the value of the **AccountType** parameter, and set the balance to the value of the **decimal** parameter.

▶ **To create the default constructor**

1. Open the Constructors.sln project in the *Lab Files*\Lab09\Starter\Constructors folder.

2. In the **BankAccount** class, delete the **Populate** method.

3. Create a default constructor, as follows:

   a. The name is **BankAccount**.

   b. It is public.

   c. It takes no parameters.

   d. It has no return type.

   e. The body of the constructor should generate an account number by using the **NextNumber** method, set the account type to **AccountType.Checking**, and initialize the account balance to zero.

The completed constructor is as follows:

```
public BankAccount( )
{
  accNo = NextNumber( );
  accType = AccountType.Checking;
  accBal = 0;
}
```

▶ **To create the remaining constructors**

1. Add another constructor that takes a single **AccountType** parameter called **aType**. The constructor should:

   a. Generate an account number as before.

   b. Set *accType* to **aType**.

   c. Set *accBal* to zero.

2. Define another constructor that takes a single **decimal** parameter called **aBal**. The constructor should:

   a. Generate an account number.

   b. Set *accType* to **AccountType.Checking**.

   c. Set *accBal* to **aBal**.

3. Define a final constructor that takes two parameters: an **AccountType** called **aType** and a **decimal** called **aBal**. The constructor should:

   a. Generate an account number.

   b. Set *accType* to **aType**.

   c. Set *accBal* to **aBal**.

   The completed code for all three constructors is as follows:

```
public BankAccount(AccountType aType)
{
   accNo = NextNumber( );
   accType = aType;
   accBal = 0;
}

public BankAccount(decimal aBal)
{
   accNo = NextNumber( );
   accType = AccountType.Checking;
   accBal = aBal;
}

public BankAccount(AccountType aType, decimal aBal)
{
   accNo = NextNumber( );
   accType = aType;
   accBal = aBal;
}
```

▶ **To test the constructors**

1. In the **Main** method of the **CreateAccount** class, define four **BankAccount** variables called *acc1*, *acc2*, *acc3*, and *acc4*.

2. Instantiate *acc1* by using the default constructor.

3. Instantiate *acc2* by using the constructor that takes only an **AccountType**. Set the type of *acc2* to **AccountType.Deposit**.

4. Instantiate *acc3* by using the constructor that takes only a **decimal** balance. Set the balance of *acc3* to 100.

5. Instantiate *acc4* by using the constructor that takes an **AccountType** and a **decimal** balance. Set the type of *acc4* to **AccountType.Deposit**, and set the balance to 500.

6. Use the **Write** method (supplied with the **CreateAccount** class) to display the contents of each account one by one. The completed code is as follows:

```
static void Main( )
{
    BankAccount acc1, acc2, acc3, acc4;

    acc1 = new BankAccount( );
    acc2 = new BankAccount(AccountType.Deposit);
    acc3 = new BankAccount(100);
    acc4 = new BankAccount(AccountType.Deposit, 500);

    Write(acc1);
    Write(acc2);
    Write(acc3);
    Write(acc4);
}
```

7. Compile the project and correct any errors. Execute it, and check that the output is as expected.

Exercise 2
Initializing readonly Data

In this exercise, you will create a new class called **BankTransaction**. It will hold information about a deposit or withdrawal transaction that is performed on an account.

Whenever the balance of an account is changed by means of the **Deposit** or **Withdraw** method, a new **BankTransaction** object will be created. The **BankTransaction** object will contain the current date and time (generated from **System.DateTime**) and the amount added (positive) or deducted (negative) from the account. Because transaction data cannot be changed once it is created, this information will be stored in two **readonly** instance variables in the **BankTransaction** object.

The constructor for **BankTransaction** will take a single decimal parameter, which it will use to populate the transaction amount instance variable. The date and time instance variable will be populated by **DateTime.Now**, a property of **System.DateTime** that returns the current date and time.

You will modify the **BankAccount** class to create transactions in the **Deposit** and **Withdraw** methods. You will store the transactions in an instance variable in the **BankAccount** class of type **System.Collections.Queue**. A queue is a data structure that holds an ordered list of objects. It provides methods for adding elements to the queue and for iterating through the queue. (Using a queue is better than using an array because a queue does not have a fixed size: it will grow automatically as more transactions are added.)

▶ **To create the BankTransaction class**

1. Open the Constructors.sln project in the *Lab Files*\Lab09\Starter\Constructors folder, if it is not already open.

2. Add a new class called **BankTransaction**.

3. In the **BankTransaction** class, remove the **namespace** directive together with the first opening brace ({), and the final closing brace (}). (You will learn more about namespaces in a later module.)

4. In the summary comment, add a brief description of the **BankTransaction** class. Use the description above to help you.

5. Delete the default constructor created by Microsoft Visual Studio®.

6. Add the following two private **readonly** instance variables:

   a. A **decimal** called *amount*.

   b. A **DateTime** variable called *when*. The **System.DateTime** structure is useful for holding dates and times, and contains a number of methods for manipulating these values.

7. Add two accessor methods, called **Amount** and **When**, that return the values of the two instance variables:

```
private readonly decimal amount;
private readonly DateTime when;
...
public decimal Amount( )
{
  return amount;
}

public DateTime When( )
{
  return when;
}
```

▶ **To create the constructor**

1. Define a public constructor for the **BankTransaction** class. It will take a decimal parameter called *tranAmount* that will be used to populate the *amount* instance variable.

2. In the constructor, initialize *when* with **DateTime.Now**.

Tip   **DateTime.Now** is a property and not a method, so you do not need to use parentheses.

The completed constructor is as follows:

```
public BankTransaction(decimal tranAmount)
{
     amount = tranAmount;
     when = DateTime.Now;
}
```

3. Compile the project and correct any errors.

▶ **To create transactions**

1. As described above, transactions will be created by the **BankAccount** class and stored in a queue whenever the **Deposit** or **Withdraw** method is invoked. Return to the **BankAccount** class.

2. Before the start of the **BankAccount** class, add the following **using** directive:

```
using System.Collections;
```

3. Add a private instance variable call *tranQueue* to the **BankAccount** class. Its data type should be **Queue** and it should be initialized with a new empty queue:

```
private Queue tranQueue = new Queue( );
```

4. In the **Deposit** method, before returning, create a new transaction using the deposit amount as the parameter, and append it to the queue by using the **Enqueue** method, as follows:

```
public decimal Deposit(decimal amount)
{
  accBal += amount;
  BankTransaction tran = new BankTransaction(amount);
  tranQueue.Enqueue(tran);
  return accBal;
}
```

5. In the **Withdraw** method, if there are sufficient funds, create a transaction and append it to *tranQueue* as in the **Deposit** method, as follows:

```
public bool Withdraw(decimal amount)
{
  bool sufficientFunds = accBal >= amount;
  if (sufficientFunds) {
    accBal -= amount;
    BankTransaction tran = new BankTransaction(-amount);
    tranQueue.Enqueue(tran);
  }
  return sufficientFunds;
}
```

Note For the **Withdraw** method, the value passed to the constructor of the **BankTransaction** should be the amount being withdrawn preceded by the negative sign.

▶ **To test transactions**

1. For testing purposes, add a public method called **Transactions** to the **BankAccount** class. Its return type should be **Queue**, and the method should return *tranQueue*. You will use this method for displaying transactions in the next step. The method will be as follows:

```
public Queue Transactions( )
{
  return tranQueue;
}
```

2. In the **CreateAccount** class, modify the **Write** method to display the details of transactions for each account. Queues implement the **IEnumerable** interface, which means that you can use the **foreach** construct to iterate through them.

3. In the body of the **foreach** loop, print out the date and time and the amount for each transaction, by using the **When** and **Amount** methods, as follows:

```
static void Write(BankAccount acc)
{
  Console.WriteLine("Account number is {0}",
↪acc.Number( ));
  Console.WriteLine("Account balance is {0}",
↪acc.Balance( ));
  Console.WriteLine("Account type is {0}", acc.Type( ));
  Console.WriteLine("Transactions:");
  foreach (BankTransaction tran in acc.Transactions( ))
  {
    Console.WriteLine("Date/Time: {0}\tAmount: {1}",
↪tran.When( ), tran.Amount( ));
  }
  Console.WriteLine( );
}
```

4. In the **Main** method, add statements to deposit and withdraw money from each of the four accounts (*acc1*, *acc2*, *acc3*, and *acc4*).

5. Compile the project and correct any errors.

6. Execute the project. Examine the output and check whether transactions are displayed as expected.

◆ Objects and Memory

- **Object Lifetime**
- **Objects and Scope**
- **Garbage Collection**

In your applications, you will need to know what happens when an object, as opposed to a value, goes out of scope or is destroyed.

After completing this lesson, you will be able to:

- Identify the role of garbage collection when an object goes out of scope or is destroyed.

Object Lifetime

- **Creating objects**
  - You allocate memory by using **new**
  - You initialize an object in that memory by using a constructor
- **Using objects**
  - You call methods
- **Destroying objects**
  - The object is converted back into memory
  - The memory is de-allocated

In C#, destroying an object is a two-step process that corresponds to and reverses the two-step object creation process.

Creating Objects

In the first section, you learned that creating a C# object for a reference type is a two-step process, as follows:

1. Use the **new** keyword to acquire and allocate memory.

2. Call a constructor to turn the raw memory acquired by **new** into an object.

Destroying Objects

Destroying a C# object is also a two-step process:

1. De-initialize the object.

   This converts the object back into raw memory. In C# this is done by the destructor. This is the reverse of the initialization performed by the constructor. You can control what happens in this step by writing your own destructor or finalize method.

2. The raw memory is de-allocated; that is, it is given back to the memory heap.

   This is the reverse of the allocation performed by **new**. You cannot change the behavior of this step in any way.

Objects and Scope

- **The lifetime of a local value is tied to the scope in which it is declared**
  - Short lifetime (typically)
  - Deterministic creation and destruction
- **The lifetime of a dynamic object is not tied to its scope**
  - A longer lifetime
  - A non-deterministic destruction

Unlike values such as **int** and **struct** values, which are allocated on the stack and are destroyed at the end of their scope, objects are allocated on the managed heap and are not destroyed at the end of their scope.

Values

The lifetime of a local value is tied to the scope in which it is declared. Local values are variables that are allocated on the stack and not on the managed heap. This means that if you declare a variable whose type is one of the primitives (such as **int**), **enum**, or **struct**, you cannot use it outside the scope in which you declare it. For example, in the following code fragment, three values are declared inside a **for** statement, and so go out of scope at the end of the **for** statement:

```
struct Point { public int x, y; }
enum Season { Spring, Summer, Fall, Winter }
class Example
{
    void Method(int limit)
    {
        for (int i = 0; i < limit; i++) {
            int x = 42;
            Point p = new Point( );
            Season s = Season.Winter;
            ...
        }
        x = 42;              // Compile-time error
        p = new Point( );  // Compile-time error
        s = Season.Winter; // Compile-time error
    }
}
```

> **Note** In the previous example, it appears as though a **new Point** is created. However, because **Point** is a **struct**, **new** does not allocate memory from the managed heap. The "new" **Point** *is* created on the stack.

This means that local values have the following characteristics:

- Deterministic creation and destruction

  A local variable is created when you declare it, and is destroyed at the end of the scope in which it is declared. The start point and the end point of the value's life are deterministic; that is, they occur at known, fixed times.

- Usually very short lifetimes

  You declare a value somewhere in a method, and the value cannot exist beyond the method call. When you return a value from a method, you return a copy of the value.

Objects

The lifetime of an object is not tied to the scope in which it is created. Objects are initialized in heap memory allocated through the **new** operator. For example, in the following code, the reference variable *eg* is declared inside a **for** statement. This means that *eg* goes out of scope at the end of the **for** statement and is a local variable. However, *eg* is initialized with a **new Example( )** object, and this object does not go out of scope with *eg*. Remember, a reference variable and the object it references are different things.

```
class Example
{
    void Method(int limit)
    {
        for (int i = 0; i < limit; i++) {
            Example eg = new Example( );
            ...
        }
        // eg is out of scope
        // Does eg still exist?
        // Does the object still exist?
    }
}
```

This means that objects typically have the following characteristics:

- Non-deterministic destruction

  An object is created when you create it, but, unlike a value, it is it not destroyed at the end of the scope in which it is created. The creation of an object is deterministic, but the destruction of an object is not. You cannot control exactly when an object will be destroyed.

- Longer lifetimes

  Because the life of an object is not tied to the method that creates it, an object can exist well beyond a single method call.

Garbage Collection

- **You cannot explicitly destroy objects**
  - C# does not have an opposite of **new** (such as **delete**)
  - This is because an explicit delete function is a prime source of errors in other languages
- **Garbage collection destroys objects for you**
  - It finds unreachable objects and destroys them for you
  - It finalizes them back to raw unused heap memory
  - It typically does this when memory becomes low

So far, you have seen that you create objects in C# in exactly the same way that you create objects in other languages, such as C++. You use the **new** keyword to allocate memory from the heap, and you call a constructor to convert that memory into an object. However, as far as the method for the destruction of objects, there is no similarity between C# and its predecessors.

You Cannot Explicitly Destroy Objects

In many programming languages, you can explicitly control when an object will be destroyed. For example, in C++ you can use a **delete** expression to de-initialize (or finalize) the object (turn it back into raw memory) and then return the memory to the heap. In C#, there is no way to explicitly destroy objects. In many ways, this restriction is a useful one because programmers often misuse the ability to explicitly destroy objects by:

- Forgetting to destroy objects.

    If you had the responsibility for writing the code that destroyed an object, you might sometimes forget to write the code. This can happen in C++ code, and this is a problematic bug that causes the user's computer to get slower as the program uses more memory. This is known as *memory leak*. Often the only way to reclaim the lost memory is to shut down and then restart the offending program.

- Attempting to destroy the same object more than once.

    You might sometimes accidentally attempt to destroy the same object more than once. This can happen in C++ code, and it is a serious bug with undefined consequences. The problem is that when you destroy the object the first time, the memory is reclaimed and can be used to create a new object, probably of a completely different class. When you then attempt to destroy the object the second time, the memory refers to a completely different object.

- Destroying an active object.

  You might sometimes destroy an object that was still being referred to in another part of the program. This is also a serious bug known as the *dangling pointer problem*, and it also has undefined consequences.

Garbage Collection Destroys Objects for You

In C#, you cannot destroy an object explicitly in code. Instead, C# has *garbage collection*, which destroys objects for you. Garbage collection is automatic. It ensures that:

- Objects are destroyed.

  However, garbage collection does not specify exactly when the object will be destroyed.

- Objects are destroyed only once.

  This means that you cannot get the undefined behavior of double deletion that is possible in C++. This is important because it helps to ensure that a C# program always behaves in a well-defined way.

- Only unreachable objects are destroyed.

  Garbage collection ensures that an object is never destroyed if another object holds a reference to it. Garbage collection only destroys an object when no other object holds a reference to it. The ability of one object to reach another object through a reference variable is called *reachability*. Only unreachable objects are destroyed. It is the function of garbage collection to follow all of the object references to determine which objects are reachable and hence, by a process of elimination, to find the remaining unreachable objects. This can be a time-consuming operation, so garbage collection only collects garbage to reclaim unused memory when memory becomes low.

Note You can force garbage collection explicitly in your code, but it is not recommended. Let the .NET runtime manage memory for you.

◆ Resource Management

- **Object Cleanup**
- **Writing Destructors**
- **Warnings About Destructor Timing**
- **IDisposable Interface and Dispose Method**
- **The using Statement in C#**

After completing this section, you will be able to:

- Write destructors.
- Use the Disposal design pattern.

Object Cleanup

■ **The final actions of different objects will be different**

- They cannot be determined by garbage collection.

- Objects in .NET Framework have a **Finalize** method.

- If present, garbage collection will call destructor before reclaiming the raw memory.

- In C#, implement a destructor to write cleanup code. You cannot call or override **Object.Finalize**.

You have already seen that destroying an object is a two-step process. In the first step, the object is converted back into raw memory. In the second step, the raw memory is returned to the heap to be recycled. Garbage collection completely automates the second step of this process for you.

However, the actions required to finalize a specific object back into raw memory to clean it up will depend on the specific object. This means that garbage collection cannot automate the first step for you. If there are any specific statements that you want an object to execute when it is picked up by garbage collection and just before its memory is reclaimed, you need to write these statements yourself in a destructor.

Finalization

When garbage collection is destroying an unreachable object, it will check whether the class of the object has its own destructor or **Finalize** method. If the class has a destructor or **Finalize** method, it will call the method before recycling the memory back to the heap. The statements you write in the destructor or **Finalize** method will be specific to the class.

Writing Destructors

- **A destructor is the mechanism for cleanup**
  - It has its own syntax:
    - No access modifier
    - No return type, not even **void**
    - Same name as name of class with leading ~
    - No parameters

```
class SourceFile
{
    ~SourceFile( ) { ... }
}
```

You can write a destructor to implement object cleanup. In C#, the **Finalize** method is not directly available, and you cannot call or override the **Finalize** method. You must place code to be executed during finalization inside a destructor.

The following example shows the C# destructor syntax for a class named **SourceFile**:

```
~ SourceFile( ) {
// Perform cleanup
}
```

A destructor does not have:

- An access modifier.

  You do not call the destructor; garbage collection does.

- A return type.

  The purpose of the destructor is not to return a value but to perform the required cleanup actions.

- Parameters.

  Again, you do not call the destructor, so you cannot pass it any arguments. Note that this means that the destructor cannot be overloaded.

Note   The C# compiler automatically converts a destructor into a **Finalize** method.

Warnings About Destructor Timing

- **The order and timing of destruction is undefined**
  - Not necessarily the reverse of construction
- **Destructors are guaranteed to be called**
  - Cannot rely on timing
- **Avoid destructors if possible**
  - Performance costs
  - Complexity
  - Delay of memory resource release

You have seen that in C# garbage collection is responsible for destroying objects when they are unreachable. This is unlike other languages such as C++, in which the programmer is responsible for explicitly destroying objects. Shifting the responsibility for destroying objects away from the programmer is a good thing, but it you cannot control exactly when a C# object is destroyed. This is sometimes referred to as *non-deterministic finalization*.

The Order and Timing of Destructor is Undefined

In languages like C++, you can explicitly control when objects are created and when objects are destroyed. In C#, you can control the order in which you create objects but you cannot control the order in which they are destroyed. This is because you do not destroy the objects at all—garbage collection does.

In C#, the order of the creation of objects does not determine the order of the destruction of those objects. They can be destroyed in any order, and many other objects might be destroyed in between. However, in practice this is rarely a problem because garbage collection guarantees that an object will never be destroyed if it is reachable. If one object holds a reference to a second object, the second object is reachable from the first object. This means that the second object will never be destroyed before the first object.

Avoid Destructors If Possible

Avoid destructors or finalizers if possible. Finalization adds overhead and complexity, and delays the reclamation of an object's memory resources. You should only implement finalization, or implement a destructor in C#, on classes that require finalization. If your class has only managed resources and it does not manage non-memory resources, you should not implement finalize code. Heap memory for managed objects is only released through garbage collection.

IDisposable Interface and Dispose Method

- **To reclaim a resource:**
  - Inherit from **IDisposable** Interface and implement **Dispose** method that releases resources
  - Call **GC.SuppressFinalize** method
  - Ensure that calling **Dispose** more than once is benign
  - Ensure that you do not try to use a reclaimed resource

Memory is the most common resource that your programs use, and you can rely on garbage collection to reclaim unreachable memory when the heap becomes low. However, memory is not the only resource. Other fairly common resources that your program might use include file handles and mutex locks. Often these other kinds of resources are in much more limited supply than memory or need to be released quickly.

In these situations, you cannot rely on garbage collection to perform the release by means of a destructor because, as you have seen, you cannot know when garbage collection will run. Instead, you should write a public **Dispose** method that releases the resource, and then make sure to call this method at the right point in the code. These methods are called Disposal Methods.

In C#, when implementing a **Dispose** Method:

- Inherit from the **IDisposable** interface
- Implement the **Dispose** method
- Ensure that the **Dispose** Method can be called repeatedly
- Call **SuppressFinalize**

A type's **Dispose** method should release all of the resources that it owns. It should also release all resources owned by its base types by calling its parent type's **Dispose** method. The parent type's **Dispose** method should release all resources that it owns and in turn call its parent type's **Dispose** method, propagating this pattern through the hierarchy of base types. To ensure that resources are always cleaned up appropriately, a **Dispose** method should be safely callable multiple times without throwing an exception.

The following code example illustrates one possible design pattern for implementing a **Dispose** method for classes that encapsulate unmanaged resources. You might find this pattern convenient to use because it is implemented throughout the .NET Framework. However, this is not the only possible implementation of a **Dispose** method. The base class implements a public **Dispose** method that can be called by users of the class. It in turn calls the appropriate virtual **Dispose** method, depending upon the intent of the caller. The appropriate cleanup code for the object is executed in the virtual **Dispose** method. The base class provides a **Finalize** method or destructor as a safeguard in the event that **Dispose** is not called.

```
public class BaseResource: IDisposable
{
    // Pointer to an external resource
    private IntPtr handle;
    // Other resource this class uses
    private Component Components;
    // To track whether Dispose has been called
    private bool disposed = false;

    // Constructor for the BaseResource object
    public BaseResource( )
    {
        handle = // Insert code here to allocate on the
        // unmanaged side
        Components = new Component (...);
    }

    // Implement IDisposable.
    // Do not make this method virtual.
    // A derived class should not be able to override
    // this method.
    public void Dispose( )
    {
        Dispose(true);
        // Take yourself off of the Finalization queue
        GC.SuppressFinalize(this);
    }
```

`Code continued on following page.`

```
protected virtual void Dispose(bool disposing)
{
    // Check to see if Dispose has already been
    // called
    if(!this.disposed)
    {
        // If this is a call to Dispose, dispose all
        // managed resources
        if(disposing)
        {
            Components.Dispose( );
        }
        // Release unmanaged resources.
        // Note that this is not thread-safe.
        // Another thread could start disposing the
        // object after the managed resources are
        // disposed, but before the disposed flag is
        // set to true.
        this.disposed = true;
        Release(handle);
        handle = IntPtr.Zero;
    }
}

// Use C# destructor syntax for finalization code.
// This destructor will run only if the Dispose
// method does not get called. It gives your base
// class the opportunity to finalize. Do not
// provide destructors in types derived from
// this class.
~BaseResource( )
{
    Dispose(false);
}

// Allow your Dispose method to be called multiple
// times, but throw an exception if the object has
// been disposed. Whenever you do something with
// this class, check to see if it has been disposed.
public void DoSomething( )
{
    if(this.disposed)
    {
        throw new ObjectDisposedException(...);
    }
}
}

// Design pattern for a derived class.
// Note that this derived class inherently implements
// the IDisposable interface because it is implemented
// in the base class.
public class MyResourceWrapper: BaseResource
{
    private bool disposed = false;
```

Code continued on following page.

```csharp
public MyResourceWrapper( )
{
    // Constructor for this object
}

protected override void Dispose(bool disposing)
{
    if(!this.disposed)
    {
        try
        {
            if(disposing)
            {
                // Release any managed resources here
            }
            // Release any unmanaged resources here
            this.disposed = true;
        }
        finally
        {
            // Call Dispose on your base class
            base.Dispose(disposing);
        }
    }
}
}

// This derived class does not have a Finalize method
// or a Dispose method with parameters because it
// inherits them from the base class
```

The using Statement in C#

■ **Syntax**

```
using (Resource r1 = new Resource( ))
{
        r1.Method( );
}
```

■ **Dispose is automatically called at the end of the using block**

The **using** statement in C# defines a scope at the end of which an object will be disposed.

You create an instance in a **using** statement to ensure that **Dispose** is called on the object when the **using** statement is exited. In the following example, **Resource** is a reference type that implements **IDisposable**:

```
using (Resource r1 = new Resource( )) {
  r1.Test( );
}
```

This statement is semantically equivalent to the following statement:

```
Resource r1 = new Resource( );
try {
  r1.Test( );
}
finally {
  if (r1 != null) ((IDisposable)r1).Dispose( );
}
```

Lab 9.2: Managing Resources

Objectives

In this lab, you will learn how to use finalizers to perform processing before garbage collection destroys an object.

After completing this lab, you will be able to:

- Create a destructor.
- Make requests of garbage collection.
- Use the Disposal design pattern.

Prerequisites

Before working on this lab, you must be able to:

- Create classes and instantiate objects.
- Define and call methods.
- Define and use constructors.
- Use the **StreamWriter** class to write text to a file.

You should also have completed Lab 9.1. If you did not complete Lab 9.1, you can use the solution code provided.

Estimated time to complete this lab: 15 minutes

Exercise 1
Using the Disposal Design Pattern

In this exercise, you will add a **Dispose** method to the **BankAccount** class to persist data in Transaction.dat file. The **Dispose** method in **BankAccount** will iterate through all of the transactions in its transaction queue, save the transaction log in a file.

▶ **To create a Dispose method for the BankAccount class**

1. Open the Finalizers.sln project in the *Lab Files*\Lab09\Starter\Finalizers folder.

2. Add the **sealed** modifier to the **BankAccount** class and inherit from **IDisposable** interface. A sealed class cannot be inherited. The sealed modifier is added to keep the dispose method's implementation simple.

3. Add a private **bool** instance variable called disposed. Initialize it to **false**.

4. In the **BankAccount** class, add a public **void** method called **Dispose**:

```
public void Dispose( )
{

}
```

5. In the **Dispose** method, add statements to:

   a. Examine the value of *disposed*. If it is **true**, return from the method and do nothing else.

   b. If *disposed* is **false**, create a new **StreamWriter** variable that opens the Transactions.dat file in the current directory in append mode (that is, it writes data to the end of the file if it already exists). You can achieve this by using the File.AppendText method.

```
StreamWriter swFile =
⮕File.AppendText("Transactions.Dat");
```

   c. Use the WriteLine method and write account number, type, and balance.

```
swFile.WriteLine("Account number is {0}",  accNo);
swFile.WriteLine("Account balance is {0}", accBal);
swFile.WriteLine("Account type is {0}", accType);
```

   d. Iterate through all of the **BankTransaction** objects in *tranQueue* and using WriteLine write the amount and time of the transaction. Use a **foreach** statement, as you did in Lab 9.1.

   e. Close the **StreamWriter**.

   f. Set *disposed* to **true**.

   g. Call **GC.SuppressFinalize** method.

The completed code should be as follows:

```
public void Dispose( )
{
    if (!disposed)
    {
        StreamWriter swFile =
➥File.AppendText("Transactions.Dat");
        swFile.WriteLine("Account number is {0}", accNo);
        swFile.WriteLine("Account balance is {0}", accBal);
        swFile.WriteLine("Account type is {0}", accType);
        swFile.WriteLine("Transactions:");
        foreach(BankTransaction tran in tranQueue)
        {
            swFile.WriteLine("Date/Time: {0}\tAmount:{1}",
➥tran.When( ), tran.Amount( ));
        }
        swFile.Close( );
        disposed = true;
        GC.SuppressFinalize(this);
    }
}
```

6. Add a destructor to the **BankAccount** class that calls the **Dispose** method.

7. Compile the project and correct any errors.

▶ **To test the destructor**

1. Open the CreateAccount.cs test harness.

2. Modify the code in **Main** to use the **using** statement., as follows:

```
using (BankAccount acc1 = new BankAccount( ))
    {
        acc1.Deposit(100);
        acc1.Withdraw(50);
        acc1.Deposit(75);
        acc1.Withdraw(50);
        acc1.Withdraw(30);
        acc1.Deposit(40);
        acc1.Deposit(200);
        acc1.Withdraw(250);
        acc1.Deposit(25);
        Write(acc1);

    }
```

3. Compile the project and correct any errors.

4. Run the program.

5. Open a text editor and examine the Transactions.Dat file in the *Lab Files*\Lab09\Starter\Finalizers\bin\Debug folder.

Review

- **Using Constructors**
- **Initializing Data**
- **Objects and Memory**
- **Resource Management**

1. Declare a class called **Date** with a public constructor that expects three **int** parameters called *year*, *month*, and *day*.

2. Will the compiler generate a default constructor for the **Date** class that you declared in question 1? What if **Date** were a **struct** with the same three-**int** constructor?

3. Which method does garbage collection call on the object just before it recycles the object's memory back to the heap?

4. What is the purpose of the **using** statement?

msdn training

Module 10:
Inheritance in C#

Contents

Overview	1
Deriving Classes	2
Implementing Methods	10
Using Sealed Classes	27
Using Interfaces	29
Using Abstract Classes	42
Lab 10.1: Using Inheritance to Implement an Interface	52
Review	70

Microsoft

Overview

- **Deriving Classes**
- **Implementing Methods**
- **Using Sealed Classes**
- **Using Interfaces**
- **Using Abstract Classes**

Inheritance, in an object-oriented system, is the ability of an object to inherit data and functionality from its parent object. Therefore, a child object can substitute for the parent object. Also, by using inheritance, you can create new classes from existing classes instead of starting at the beginning and creating them new. You can then write new code to add the features required in the new class. The parent class on which the new class is based is known as a *base class*, and the child class is known as a *derived class*.

When you create a derived class, it is important to remember that a derived class can substitute for the base class type. Therefore, inheritance is a type-classification mechanism in addition to a code-reuse mechanism, and the former is more important than the latter.

In this module, you will learn how to derive a class from a base class. You will also learn how to implement methods in a derived class by defining them as virtual methods in the base class and overriding or hiding them in the derived class, as required. You will learn how to seal a class so that it cannot be derived from. You will also learn how to implement interfaces and abstract classes, which define the terms of a contract to which derived classes must adhere.

After completing this module, you will be able to:

- Derive a new class from a base class, and call members and constructors of the base class from the derived class.
- Declare methods as **virtual** and **override** or hide them as required.
- Seal a class so that it cannot be derived from.
- Implement interfaces by using both the implicit as well as the explicit methods.
- Describe the use of abstract classes and their implementation of interfaces.

◆ Deriving Classes

- **Extending Base Classes**
- **Accessing Base Class Members**
- **Calling Base Class Constructors**

You can only derive a class from a base class if the base class was designed to enable inheritance. This is because objects must have the proper structure or inheritance cannot work effectively. A base class that is designed for inheritance should make this fact clear. If a new class is derived from a base class that is not designed appropriately, then the base class might change at some later time, and this would make the derived class inoperable.

After completing this lesson, you will be able to:

- Derive a new class from a base class.
- Access the members and constructors of the base class from the derived class.

Extending Base Classes

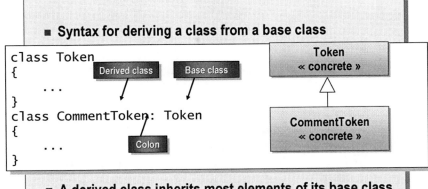

- Syntax for deriving a class from a base class

```
class Token
{
    ...
}
class CommentToken: Token
{
    ...
}
```

Derived class   Base class   Colon

Token
« concrete »

CommentToken
« concrete »

- A derived class inherits most elements of its base class
- A derived class cannot be more accessible than its base class

Deriving a class from a base class is also known as *extending* the base class. A C# class can extend at most one class.

Syntax for Deriving a Class

To specify that one class is derived from another, you use the following syntax:

```
class Derived: Base
{
    ...
}
```

The elements of this syntax are labeled on the slide. When you declare a derived class, the base class is specified after a colon. The white space around the colon is not significant. The recommended style for using this syntax is to include no spaces before the colon and a single space after it.

Derived Class Inheritance

A derived class inherits everything from its base class except for the base class constructors and destructors. Public members of the base class are implicitly public members of the derived class. Private members of the base class, though inherited by the derived class, are accessible only to the members of the base class.

Accessibility of a Derived Class

A derived class cannot be more accessible than its base class. For example, it is not possible to derive a public class from a private class, as is shown in the following code:

```
class Example
{
    private class NestedBase { }
    public class NestedDerived: NestedBase { } // Error
}
```

The C# syntax for deriving one class from another is also allowed in C++, where it implicitly specifies a private inheritance relationship between the derived and base classes. C# has no private inheritance; all inheritance is public.

Accessing Base Class Members

```
class Token
{    ...
     protected string name;
}
class CommentToken: Token
{    ...
     public string Name( )
     {
          return name; ✓
     }
}
```

```
class Outside
{
     void Fails(Token t)
     {
          ...
          t.name ✗
          ...
     }
}
```

- Inherited protected members are implicitly protected in the derived class
- Methods of a derived class can access only their inherited protected members
- Protected access modifiers cannot be used in a struct

The meaning of the **protected** access modifier depends on the relationship between the class that has the modifier and the class that seeks to access the members that use the modifier.

Members of a derived class can access all of the protected members of their base class. To a derived class, the **protected** keyword behaves like the **public** keyword. Hence, in the code fragment shown on the slide, the **Name** method of **CommentToken** can access the string *name*, which is protected inside **Token**. It is protected inside **Token** because **CommentToken** has specified **Token** as its base class.

However, between two classes that are not related by a derived-class and base-class relationship, protected members of one class act like private members for the other class. Hence, in the other code fragment shown on the slide, the **Fails** method of **Outside** cannot access the string *name*, which is protected inside **Token** because **Outside** does not specify **Token** as its base class.

Inherited Protected Members

When a derived class inherits a protected member, that member is also implicitly a protected member of the derived class. This means that protected members are accessible to all directly and indirectly derived classes of the base class. This is shown in the following example:

```
class Base
{
    protected string name;
}

class Derived: Base
{
}

class FurtherDerived: Derived
{
    void Compiles( )
    {
        Console.WriteLine(name); // Okay
    }
}
```

Protected Members and Methods

Methods of a derived class can only access their own inherited protected members. They cannot access the protected members of the base class through references to the base class. For example, the following code will generate an error:

```
class CommentToken: Token
{
    void Fails(Token t)
    {
        Console.WriteLine(t.name); // Compile-time error
    }
}
```

Tip   Many coding guidelines recommend keeping all data private and using protected access only for methods.

Protected Members and structs

A **struct** does not support inheritance. Consequently, you cannot derive from a **struct**, and, therefore, the **protected** access modifier cannot be used in a **struct**. For example, the following code will generate an error:

```
struct Base
{
    protected string name; // Compile-time error
}
```

Calling Base Class Constructors

■ **Constructor declarations must use the base keyword**

```
class Token
{
    protected Token(string name) { ... }
    ...
}
class CommentToken: Token
{
    public CommentToken(string name) : base(name) { }
    ...
}
```

■ **A private base class constructor cannot be accessed by a derived class**

■ **Use the base keyword to qualify identifier scope**

To call a base class constructor from the derived class constructor, use the keyword **base**. The syntax for this keyword is as follows:

```
C(...): base( ) {...}
```

The colon and the accompanying base class constructor call are together known as the *constructor initializer*.

Constructor Declarations

If the derived class does not explicitly call a base class constructor, the C# compiler will implicitly use a constructor initializer of the form :base( ). This implies that a constructor declaration of the form

```
C(...) {...}
```

is equivalent to

```
C(...): base( ) {...}
```

Often this implicit behavior is perfectly adequate because:

■ A class with no explicit base classes implicitly extends the **System.Object** class, which contains a public parameterless constructor.

■ If a class does not contain a constructor, the compiler will automatically provide a public parameterless constructor called the default constructor.

If a class provides an explicit constructor of its own, the compiler will not create a default constructor. However, if the specified constructor does not match any constructor in the base class, the compiler will generate an error as shown in the following code:

```
class Token
{
    protected Token(string name) { ... }
}

class CommentToken: Token
{
    public CommentToken(string name) { ... } // Error here
}
```

The error occurs because the **CommentToken** constructor implicitly contains a :base( ) constructor initializer, but the base class **Token** does not contain a parameterless constructor. You can fix this error by using the code shown on the slide.

Constructor Access Rules

The access rules for a derived constructor to call a base class constructor are exactly the same as those for regular methods. For example, if the base class constructor is private, then the derived class cannot access it:

```
class NonDerivable
{
    private NonDerivable( ) { ... }
}

class Impossible: NonDerivable
{
    public Impossible( ) { ... } // Compile-time error
}
```

In this case, there is no way for a derived class to call the base class constructor.

Scoping an Identifier

You can use the keyword **base** to also qualify the scope of an identifier. This can be useful, since a derived class is permitted to declare members that have the same names as base class members. The following code provides an example:

```
class Token
{
    protected string name;
}
class CommentToken: Token
{
    public void Method(string name)
    {
        base.name = name;
    }
}
```

Note Unlike in C++, the name of the base class, such as **Token** in the example in the slide, is not used. The keyword **base** unambiguously refers to the base class because in C# a class can extend one base class at most.

◆ Implementing Methods

- **Defining Virtual Methods**
- **Working with Virtual Methods**
- **Overriding Methods**
- **Working with Override Methods**
- **Using new to Hide Methods**
- **Working with the new Keyword**
- **Practice: Implementing Methods**
- **Quiz: Spot the Bugs**

You can redefine the methods of a base class in a derived class when the methods of the base class have been designed for overriding.

After completing this lesson, you will be able to:

- Use the **virtual** method type.
- Use the **override** method type.
- Use the **hide** method type.

Defining Virtual Methods

■ **Syntax: Declare as virtual**

```
class Token
{
    ...
    public int LineNumber( )
    { ...
    }
    public virtual string Name( )
    { ...
    }
}
```

■ **Virtual methods are polymorphic**

A virtual method specifies *an* implementation of a method that can be polymorphically overridden in a derived class. Conversely, a non-virtual method specifies *the only* implementation of a method. You cannot polymorphically override a non-virtual method in a derived class.

Note   In C#, whether a class contains a virtual method or not is a good indication of whether the author designed it to be used as a base class.

Keyword Syntax

To declare a virtual method, you use the **virtual** keyword. The syntax for this keyword is shown on the slide.

When you declare a virtual method, it must contain a method body. If it does not contain a body, the compiler will generate an error, as shown:

```
class Token
{
    public virtual string Name( ); // Compile-time error
}
```

Working with Virtual Methods

■ **To use virtual methods:**

- • You cannot declare virtual methods as static
- • You cannot declare virtual methods as private

To use virtual methods effectively, you need to understand the following:

■   You cannot declare virtual methods as static.

You cannot qualify virtual methods as static because static methods are class methods and polymorphism works on objects, not on classes.

■   You cannot declare virtual methods as private.

You cannot declare virtual methods as private because they cannot be polymorphically overridden in a derived class. Following is an example:

```
class Token
{
    private virtual string Name( ) { ... }
    // Compile-time error
}
```

Overriding Methods

■ **Syntax: Use the override keyword**

```
class Token
{   ...
    public virtual string Name( ) { ... }
}
class CommentToken: Token
{   ...
    public override string Name( ) { ... }
}
```

An override method specifies *another* implementation of a virtual method. You define virtual methods in a base class, and they can be polymorphically overridden in a derived class.

Keyword Syntax

You declare an override method by using the keyword **override**, as shown in the following code:

```
class Token
{   ...
    public virtual string Name( ) { ... }
}
class CommentToken: Token
{   ...
    public override string Name( ) { ... }
}
```

As with a virtual method, you must include a method body in an override method or the compiler generates an error. Following is an example:

```
class Token
{
    public virtual string Name( ) { ... }
}
class CommentToken: Token
{
    public override string Name( ); // Compile-time error
}
```

Working with Override Methods

- **You can only override identical inherited virtual methods**

```
class Token
{   ...
    public int LineNumber( )  { ... }
    public virtual string Name( ) { ... }
}
class CommentToken: Token
{   ...
    public override int LineNumber( ) { ... }   ✗
    public override string Name( ) { ... }      ✓
}
```

- **You must match an override method with its associated virtual method**
- **You can override an override method**
- **You cannot explicitly declare an override method as virtual**
- **You cannot declare an override method as static or private**

To use override methods effectively, you must understand a few important restrictions:

- You can only override identical inherited virtual methods.
- You must match an override method with its associated virtual method.
- You can override an override method.
- You cannot implicitly declare an override method as virtual.
- You cannot declare an override method as static or private.

Each of these restrictions is described in more detail as in the following topics.

You Can Only Override Identical Inherited Virtual Methods

You can use an override method to override only an identical inherited virtual method. In the code on the slide, the **LineNumber** method in the derived class **CommentToken** causes a compile-time error because the inherited method **Token.LineNumber** is not marked virtual.

You Must Match an Override Method with Its Associated Virtual Method

An override declaration must be identical in every way to the virtual method it overrides. They must have the same access level, the same return type, the same name, and the same parameters.

For example, the override in the following example fails because the access-levels are different (protected as opposed to public), the return types are different (**string** as opposed to **void**), and the parameters are different (**none** as opposed to **int**):

```
class Token
{
    protected virtual string Name( ) { ... }
}
class CommentToken: Token
{
    public override void Name(int i) { ... } // Errors
}
```

You Can Override an Override Method

An override method is implicitly virtual, so you can override it. Following is an example:

```
class Token
{
    public virtual string Name( ) { ... }
}
class CommentToken: Token
{
    public override string Name( ) { ... }
}
class OneLineCommentToken: CommentToken
{
    public override string Name( ) { ... }    // Okay
}
```

You Cannot Explicitly Declare an Override Method As Virtual

An override method is implicitly virtual but cannot be explicitly qualified as virtual. Following is an example:

```
class Token
{
    public virtual string Name( ) { ... }
}
class CommentToken: Token
{
    public virtual override string Name( ) { ... } // Error
}
```

You Cannot Declare an Override Method As Static or Private

An override method can never be qualified as static because static methods are class methods and polymorphism works on objects rather than classes.

Also, an override method can never be private. This is because an override method must override a virtual method, and a virtual method cannot be private.

Using new to Hide Methods

- **Syntax: Use the new keyword to hide a method**

```
class Token
{   ...
    public int LineNumber( )  { ... }
}
class CommentToken: Token
{   ...
    new public int LineNumber( )  { ... }

}
```

You can hide an identical inherited method by introducing a new method into the class hierarchy. The old method that was inherited by the derived class from the base class is then replaced by a completely different method.

Keyword Syntax

You use the **new** keyword to hide a method. The syntax for this keyword is as follows:

```
class Token
{   ...
    public int LineNumber( )  { ... }

}
class CommentToken: Token
{   ...
    new public int LineNumber( ) { ... }

}
```

Working with the new Keyword

- **Hide both virtual and non-virtual methods**

```
class Token
{   ...
    public int LineNumber( )  { ... }
    public virtual string Name( ) { ... }
}
class CommentToken: Token
{   ...
    new public int LineNumber( )  { ... }
    public override string Name( ) { ... }
}
```

- **Resolve name clashes in code**

- **Hide methods that have identical signatures**

By using the **new** keyword, you can do the following:

- Hide both virtual and non-virtual methods.

- Resolve name clashes in code.

- Hide methods that have identical signatures.

Each of these tasks is described in detail in the following subtopics.

Hide Both Virtual and Non-Virtual Methods

Using the **new** keyword to hide a method has implications if you use polymorphism. For example, in the code on the slide, **CommentToken.LineNumber** is a **new** method. It is not related to the **Token.LineNumber** method at all. Even if **Token.LineNumber** was a virtual method, **CommentToken.LineNumber** would still be a **new** unrelated method.

In this example, **CommentToken.LineNumber** is not virtual. This means that a further derived class cannot override **CommentToken.LineNumber**. However, the **new CommentLineToken.LineNumber** method could be declared virtual, in which case further derived classes could override it, as follows:

```
class CommentToken: Token
{
    ...
    new public virtual int LineNumber( ) { ... }
}
class OneLineCommentToken: CommentToken
{
    public override int LineNumber( ) { ... }
}
```

Tip The recommended layout style for new virtual methods is

```
new public virtual int LineNumber( ) { ... }
```
rather than
```
public new virtual int LineNumber( ) { ... }
```

Resolve Name Clashes in Code

Name clashes often generate warnings during compilation. For example, consider the following code:

```
class Token
{
    public virtual int LineNumber( ) { ... }
}
class CommentToken: Token
{
    public int LineNumber( ) { ... }
}
```

When you compile this code, you will receive a warning stating that **CommentToken.LineNumber** hides **Token.LineNumber**. This warning highlights the name clash. You then have three options to choose from:

1. Add an **override** qualifier to **CommentToken.LineNumber**.

2. Add a **new** qualifier to **CommentToken.LineNumber**. In this case, the method still hides the identical method in the base class, but the explicit **new** tells the compiler and the code maintenance personnel that the name clash is not accidental.

3. Change the name of the method.

Hide Methods That Have Identical Signatures

The **new** modifier is necessary only when a derived class method hides a visible base class method that has an identical signature. In the following example, the compiler warns that **new** is unnecessary because the methods take different parameters and so do not have identical signatures:

```
class Token
{
    public int LineNumber(short s) { ... }
}
class CommentToken: Token
{
    new public int LineNumber(int i) { ... } // Warning
}
```

Conversely, if two methods have identical signatures, then the compiler will warn that **new** should be considered because the base class method is hidden. In the following example, the two methods have identical signatures because return types are not a part of a method's signature:

```
class Token
{
    public virtual int LineNumber( ) { ... }
}
class CommentToken: Token
{
    public void LineNumber( ) { ... } // Warning
}
```

Note   You can also use the **new** keyword to hide fields and nested classes.

Practice: Implementing Methods

```
class A {
    public virtual void M() { Console.Write("A"); }
}
class B: A {
    public override void M() { Console.Write("B"); }
}
class C: B {
    new public virtual void M() { Console.Write("C"); }
}
class D: C {
    public override void M() { Console.Write("D"); }
    static void Main() {
        D d = new D(); C c = d; B b = c; A a = b;
        d.M(); c.M(); b.M(); a.M();
    }
}
```

To practice the use of the **virtual**, **override** and **new** keywords, work through the code displayed on this slide to figure out what the output of the code will be.

The Solution

After the program executes, it will display the result DDBB to the console.

Program Logic

There is only one object created by the program. This is the object of type **D** created in the following declaration:

```
D d = new D( );
```

The remaining declaration statements in **Main** declare variables of different types that all refer to this one object:

- c is a **C** reference to d.

- b is a **B** reference to c, which is reference to d.

- a is an **A** reference to b, which is reference to c, which is reference to d.

Then come the four expression statements. The following text explains each one individually.

The first statement is

```
d.M( )
```

This is a call to **D.M**, which is declared override and hence is implicitly virtual. This means that at run time the compiler calls the most derived implementation of **D.M** in the object of type **D**. This implementation is **D.M**, which writes D to the console.

The second statement is

```
c.M( )
```

This is a call to **C.M**, which is declared virtual. This means that at run time the compiler calls the most derived implementation of **C.M** in the object of type **D**. Since **D.M** overrides **C.M**, **D.M** is the most derived implementation, in this case. Hence **D.M** is called, and it writes D to the console again.

The third statement is

```
b.M( )
```

This is a call to **B.M**, which is declared override and hence is implicitly virtual. This means that at run time the compiler calls the most derived implementation of **B.M** in the object of type **D**. Since **C.M** does not override **B.M** but introduces a **new** method that *hides* **C.M**, the most derived implementation of **B.M** in the object of type **D** is **B.M**. Hence **B.M** is called, and it writes B to the console.

The last statement is

```
a.M( )
```

This is a call to **A.M**, which is declared virtual. This means that at run time the compiler calls the most derived implementation of **A.M** in the object of type **D**. **B.M** overrides **A.M**, but as before **C.M** does not override **B.M**. Hence the most derived implementation of **A.M** in the object of type **D** is **B.M**. Hence **B.M** is called, which writes B to the console again.

This is how the program generates the output DDBB and writes it to the console.

In this example, the **C** and **D** classes contain two **virtual** methods that have the same signature: the one introduced by **A** and the one introduced by **C**. The method introduced by **C** hides the method introduced by **A**. Thus, the **override** declaration in **D** overrides the method introduced by **C**, and it is not possible for **D** to override the method introduced by **A**.

Quiz: Spot the Bugs

```
class Base
{
    public void Alpha( ) { ... }
    public virtual void Beta( ) { ... }
    public virtual void Gamma(int i) { ... }
    public virtual void Delta( ) { ... }
    private virtual void Epsilon( ) { ... }
}
class Derived: Base
{
    public override void Alpha( ) { ... }
    protected override void Beta( ) { ... }
    public override void Gamma(double d) { ... }
    public override int Delta( ) { ... }
}
```

[handwritten annotations: "s/b identical", "shld have a method to override when virtual", "s/b identical", "s/b identical"]

In this quiz, you can work with a partner to spot the bugs in the code on the slide. To see the answers to this quiz, turn the page.

Answers

The following errors occur in this code:

1. The **Base** class declares a private virtual method called **Epsilon**. Private methods cannot be virtual. The C# compiler traps this bug as a compile-time error. You can correct the code as follows:

```
class Base
{
    ...
    public virtual void Epsilon( ) { ... }
}
```

You can also correct the code in this manner:

```
class Base
{
    ...
    private void Epsilon( ) { ... } // Not virtual
}
```

2. The **Derived** class declares the **Alpha** method with the **override** modifier. However, the **Alpha** method in the base class is not marked virtual. You can only override a virtual method. The C# compiler traps this bug as a compile-time error. You can correct the code as follows:

```
class Base
{
    public virtual void Alpha( ) { ... }
    ...
}
```

You can also correct the code in this manner:

```
class Derived: Base
{
    /*any*/ new void Alpha( ) { ... }
    ...
}
```

3. The **Derived** class declares a protected method called **Beta** with the **override** modifier. However, the base class method **Beta** is public. When overriding a method, you cannot change its access. The C# compiler traps this bug as a compile-time error. You can correct the code as follows:

```
class Derived: Base
{
    ...
    public override void Beta( ) { ... }
    ...
}
```

You can also correct the code in this manner:

```
class Derived: Base
{
    ...
    /* any access */ new void Beta( ) { ... }
    ...
}
```

4. The **Derived** class declares a public method called **Gamma** with the **override** modifier. However, the base class method called **Gamma** and the **Derived** class method called **Gamma** take different parameters. When overriding a method, you cannot change the parameter types. The C# compiler traps this bug as a compile-time error. You can correct the code as follows:

```
class Derived: Base
{
    ...
    public override void Gamma(int i) { ... }
}
```

You can also correct the code in this manner:

```
class Derived: Base
{
    ...
    /* any access */ void Gamma(double d) { ... }
    ...
}
```

5. The **Derived** class declares a public method called **Delta** with the **override** modifier. However, the base class method called **Delta** and the derived class method called **Delta** return different types. When overriding a method, you cannot change the return type. The C# compiler traps this bug as a compile-time error. You can correct the code as follows:

```
class Derived: Base
{
    ...
    public override void Delta( ) { ... }
}
```

You can also correct the code in this manner:

```
class Derived: Base
{
    ...
    /* any access */ new int Delta( ) { ... }
    ...
}
```

Using Sealed Classes

- **You cannot derive from a sealed class**
- **You can use sealed classes for optimizing operations at run time**
- **Many .NET Framework classes are sealed: String, StringBuilder, and so on**
- **Syntax: Use the sealed keyword**

```
namespace System
{
    public sealed class String
    {
        ...
    }
}
namespace Mine
{
    class FancyString: String { ... } ✖
}
```

Creating a flexible inheritance hierarchy is not easy. Most classes are stand-alone classes and are not designed to have other classes derived from them. However, in terms of the syntax, deriving from a class is very easy and the procedure involves only a few keystrokes. This ease of derivation creates a dangerous opportunity for programmers to derive from a class that is not designed to act as a base class.

To alleviate this problem and to better express the programmers' intentions to the compiler and to fellow programmers, C# allows a class to be declared *sealed*. You cannot derive from a sealed class.

Keyword Syntax

You can seal a class by using the **sealed** keyword. The syntax for this keyword is as shown:

```
namespace System
{
    public sealed class String
    {
        ...
    }
}
```

There are many examples of sealed classes in the Microsoft® .NET Framework. The slide shows the **System.String** class, where the keyword **string** is an alias for this class. This class is sealed, and so you cannot derive from it.

Optimizing Operations at Run Time

The **sealed** modifier enables certain run-time optimizations. In particular, because a sealed class is known to never have any derived classes, it is possible to transform virtual function member calls on sealed class instances into non-virtual function member calls.

◆ Using Interfaces

- ■ Declaring Interfaces
- ■ Implementing Multiple Interfaces
- ■ Implementing Interface Methods
- ■ Implementing Interface Methods Explicitly
- ■ Quiz: Spot the Bugs

An interface specifies a syntactic and semantic contract that all derived classes must adhere to. Specifically, an interface describes the *what* part of the contract and the classes that implement the interface describe the *how* part of the contract.

After completing this lesson, you will be able to:

- ■ Use the syntax for declaring interfaces.
- ■ Use the two techniques for implementing interface methods in derived classes.

Declaring Interfaces

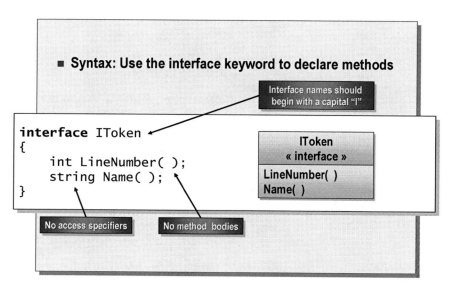

An interface resembles a class without any code. You declare an interface in a similar manner to the way in which you declare a class. To declare an interface in C#, you use the keyword **interface** instead of **class**. The syntax for this keyword is explained on the slide.

Note It is recommended that all interface names be prefixed with a capital "I." For example, use **IToken** rather than **Token**.

Features of Interfaces

The following are two important features of interfaces.

Interface Methods Are Implicitly Public

The methods declared in an interface are implicitly public. Therefore, explicit **public** access modifiers are not allowed, as shown in the following example:

```
interface IToken
{
    public int LineNumber( ); // Compile-time error
}
```

Interface Methods Do Not Contain Method Bodies

The methods declared in an interface are not allowed to contain method bodies. For example, the following code is not allowed:

```
interface IToken
{
    int LineNumber( ) { ... } // Compile-time error
}
```

Strictly speaking, interfaces can contain interface property declarations, which are declarations of properties with no body, interface event declarations, which are declarations of events with no body, and interface indexer declarations, which are declarations of indexers with no body.

Implementing Multiple Interfaces

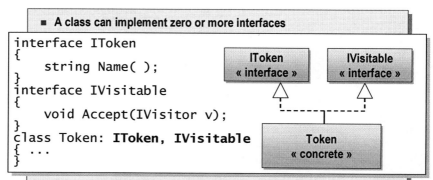

- A class can implement zero or more interfaces

```
interface IToken
{
    string Name( );
}
interface IVisitable
{
    void Accept(IVisitor v);
}
class Token: IToken, IVisitable
{ ...
}
```

IToken « interface »

IVisitable « interface »

Token « concrete »

- An interface can extend zero or more interfaces
- A class can be more accessible than its base interfaces
- An interface cannot be more accessible than its base interfaces
- A class must implement all inherited interface methods

Although C# permits only single inheritance, it allows you to implement multiple interfaces in a single class. This topic discusses the differences between a class and an interface with respect to implementation and extension of interfaces, respectively, in addition to their accessibility in comparison to their base interfaces.

Interface Implementation

A class can implement zero or more interfaces but can explicitly extend no more than one class. An example of this feature is displayed on the slide.

Note Strictly speaking, a class always extends one class. If you do not specify a base class, your class will implicitly inherit from **object**.

In contrast, an interface can extend zero or more interfaces. For example, you can rewrite the code on the slide as follows:

```
interface IToken { ... }
interface IVisitable { ... }
interface IVisitableToken: IVisitable, IToken { ... }
class Token: IVisitableToken { ... }
```

Accessibility

A class can be more accessible than its base interfaces. For example, you can declare a public class that implements a private interface, as follows:

```
class Example
{
    private interface INested { }
    public class Nested: INested { } // Okay
}
```

However, an interface cannot be more accessible than any of its base interfaces. It is an error to declare a public interface that extends a private interface, as shown in the following example:

```
class Example
{
    private interface INested { }

    public interface IAlsoNested: INested { }
    // Compile-time error
}
```

Interface Methods

A class must implement all methods of any interfaces it extends, regardless of whether the interfaces are inherited directly or indirectly.

Implementing Interface Methods

- **The implementing method must be the same as the interface method**

- **The implementing method can be virtual or non-virtual**

```
class Token: IToken, IVisitable
{
    public virtual string Name( )
    { ...
    }
    public void Accept(IVisitor v)
    { ...
    }
}
```

Same access
Same return type
Same name
Same parameters

When a class implements an interface, it must implement every method declared in that interface. This requirement is practical because interfaces cannot define their own method bodies.

The method that the class implements must be identical to the interface method in every way. It must have the same:

- Access

    Since an interface method is implicitly public, this means that the implementing method must be explicitly declared public. If the access modifier is omitted, then the method defaults to being private.

- Return type

    If the return type in the interface is declared as **T**, then the return type in the implementing class cannot be declared as a type derived from **T**; it must be **T**. In other words, return type covariance is not supported in C#.

- Name

    Remember that names in C# are case sensitive.

- Parameter-type list

The following code meets all of these requirements:

```
interface IToken
{
    string Name( );
}
interface IVisitable
{
    void Accept(IVisitor v);
}
class Token: IToken, IVisitable
{
    public virtual string Name( )
    { ...
    }
    public void Accept(IVisitor v)
    { ...
    }
}
```

The implementing method can be virtual, such as **Name** in the preceding code. In this case, the method can be overridden in further derived classes. The implementing method can also be non-virtual, such as **Accept** in the preceding code. In the latter case, the method cannot be overridden in further derived classes.

Implementing Interface Methods Explicitly

- **Use the fully qualified interface method name**

```
class Token: IToken, IVisitable
{
    string IToken.Name( )
    { ...
    }
    void IVisitable.Accept(IVisitor v)
    { ...
    }
}
```

- **Restrictions of explicit interface method implementation**
  - You can only access methods through the interface
  - You cannot declare methods as virtual
  - You cannot specify an access modifier

An alternative way for a class to implement a method inherited from an interface is to use an explicit interface method implementation.

Use the Fully Qualified Interface Method Name

When using the explicit interface method implementation, you must use the fully qualified name of the implementing method. This implies that the name of the method must include the name of the interface as well, such as **IToken** in **IToken.Name**.

An example of two interface methods implemented explicitly by the **Token** class is displayed on the slide. Notice the differences between this implementation and the earlier implementation.

Restrictions of Explicit Interface Method Implementation

When implementing explicit interfaces, you need to be aware of certain restrictions.

You Can Only Access Methods Through the Interface

You cannot access an explicit interface method implementation from anywhere except through the interface. This is shown in the following example:

```
class Token: IToken, IVisitable
{
    string IToken.Name( )
    {
        ...
    }
    private void Example( )
    {
        Name( );                 // Compile-time error

        ((IToken)this).Name( ); // Okay
    }
    ...
}
```

You Cannot Declare Methods As Virtual

In particular, a further derived class cannot access an explicit interface method implementation, and, as a result, no method can override it. This implies that an explicit interface method implementation is not virtual and cannot be declared virtual.

You Cannot Specify an Access Modifier

When defining an explicit interface method implementation, you cannot specify an access modifier. This is because explicit interface member implementations have different accessibility characteristics than other methods.

No Direct Access

An explicit interface method implementation is not directly accessible to clients and in this sense is private. This is shown in the following code:

```
class InOneSensePrivate
{
    void Method(Token t)
    {
        t.Name( ); // Compile-time error
    }
}
```

Indirect Access Through Interface Variable

An explicit interface method implementation is indirectly accessible to clients by means of an interface variable and polymorphism. In this sense, it is public. This is shown in the following code:

```
class InAnotherSensePublic
{
    void Method(Token t)
    {
        ((IToken)t).Name( ); // Okay
    }
}
```

Advantages of an Explicit Implementation

Explicit interface member implementations serve two primary purposes:

1. They allow interface implementations to be excluded from the public interface of a class or **struct**. This is useful when a class or **struct** implements an internal interface that is of no interest to the class or **struct** user.

2. They allow a class or **struct** to provide different implementations for interface methods that have the same signature. Following is an example:

```
interface IArtist
{
    void Draw( );
}
interface ICowboy
{
    void Draw( );
}
class ArtisticCowboy: IArtist, ICowboy
{
    void IArtist.Draw( )
    {
        ...
    }
    void ICowboy.Draw( )
    {
        ...
    }
}
```

Quiz: Spot the Bugs

```
interface IToken
{
    string Name( );
    int LineNumber( ) { return 42; }
    string name;
}

class Token
{
    string IToken.Name( ) { ... }
    static void Main( )
    {
        IToken t = new IToken( );
    }
}
```

In this quiz, you can work with a partner to spot the bugs in the code on the slide. To see the answers to this quiz, turn the page.

Answers

The following bugs occur in the code on the slide:

1. The **IToken** interface declares a method called **LineNumber** that has a body. An interface cannot contain any implementation. The C# compiler traps this bug as a compile-time error. The corrected code is as follows:

```
interface IToken
{
    ...
    int LineNumber( );
    ...
}
```

2. The **IToken** interface declares a field called name. An interface cannot contain any implementation. The C# compiler traps this bug as a compile-time error. The corrected code is as follows:

```
interface IToken
{
    string Name( );
    int LineNumber( );
    //string name; // Field now commented out
}
```

3. The **Token** class contains the explicit interface method implementation IToken.Name( ) but the class does not specify **IToken** as a base interface. The C# compiler traps this bug as a compile-time error. The corrected code is as follows:

```
class Token: IToken
{
    ...
}
```

4. Now that **Token** specifies **IToken** as a base interface, it must implement both methods declared in that interface. The C# compiler traps this bug as a compile-time error. The corrected code is as follows:

```
class Token: IToken
{
    string IToken.Name( ) { ... }
    public int LineNumber( ) { ... }
    ...
}
```

5. The **Token.Main** method attempts to create an instance of the interface **IToken**. However, you cannot create an instance of an interface. The C# compiler traps this bug as a compile-time error. The corrected code is as follows:

```
class Token: IToken
{
    ...
    static void Main( )
    {
        IToken t = new Token( );
        ...
    }
}
```

◆ Using Abstract Classes

- **Declaring Abstract Classes**
- **Using Abstract Classes in a Class Hierarchy**
- **Comparing Abstract Classes to Interfaces**
- **Implementing Abstract Methods**
- **Working with Abstract Methods**
- **Quiz: Spot the Bugs**

Abstract classes are used to provide partial class implementations that can be completed by derived concrete classes. Abstract classes are particularly useful for providing a partial implementation of an interface that can be reused by multiple derived classes.

After completing this lesson, you will be able to:

- Use the syntax for declaring an abstract class.
- Explain how to use abstract classes in a class hierarchy.

Declaring Abstract Classes

- **Use the abstract keyword**

```
abstract class Token
{
    ...
}
class Test
{
    static void Main( )
    {
        new Token( ); ✖
    }
}
```

> **Token**
> **{ abstract }**

An abstract class cannot be instantiated

You declare an abstract class by using the keyword **abstract**, as is shown on the slide.

The rules governing the use of an abstract class are almost exactly the same as those governing a non-abstract class. The only differences between using abstract and non-abstract classes are:

- You cannot create an instance of an abstract class.

  In this sense, abstract classes are like interfaces.

- You can create an abstract method in an abstract class.

  An abstract class can declare an abstract method, but a non-abstract class cannot.

Common features of abstract classes and non-abstract classes are:

- Limited extensibility

  An abstract class can extend at most one other class or abstract class. Note that an abstract class can extend a non-abstract class

- Multiple interfaces

  An abstract class can implement multiple interfaces

- Inherited interface methods

  An abstract class must implement all inherited interface methods

Using Abstract Classes in a Class Hierarchy

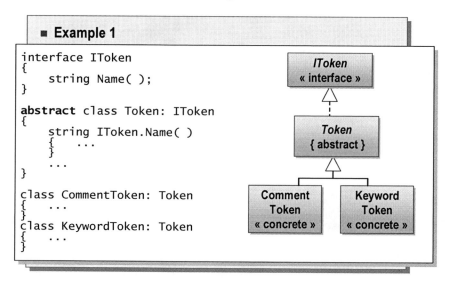

```
■ Example 1

interface IToken
{
    string Name( );
}

abstract class Token: IToken
{
    string IToken.Name( )
    {   ...
    }
    ...
}

class CommentToken: Token
{
    ...
}
class KeywordToken: Token
{
    ...
}
```

The role of abstract classes in a classic three-tier hierarchy, consisting of an interface, an abstract class, and a concrete class, is to provide a complete or partial implementation of an interface.

An Abstract Class Implementing an Interface

Consider Example 1, which appears on the slide. In this example, the abstract class implements an interface. It is an explicit implementation of the interface method. The explicit implementation is not virtual and therefore cannot be overridden in the further derived classes, such as **CommentToken**.

However, it is possible for **CommentToken** to re-implement the **IToken** interface as follows:

```
interface IToken
{
    string Name( );
}

abstract class Token: IToken
{
    string IToken.Name( ) { ... }
}

class CommentToken: Token, IToken
{
    public virtual string Name( ) { ... }
}
```

Note that in this case it is not necessary to mark **CommentToken.Name** as a **new** method. This is because a derived class method can hide only a visible base class method, but the explicit implementation of **Name** in **Token** is not directly visible in **CommentToken**.

Using Abstract Classes in a Class Hierarchy *(continued)*

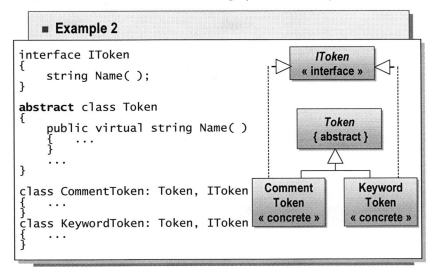

To continue the discussion of the role played by abstract classes in a classic three-tier hierarchy, another example is presented in the slide.

An Abstract Class That Does Not Implement an Interface

Consider Example 2, which appears on the slide. In this example, the abstract class does not implement the interface. This means that the only way it can supply an interface implementation to a further derived concrete class is by providing a public method. The method definition in the abstract class is optionally virtual, so it can be overridden in the classes as shown in the following code:

```
interface IToken
{
    string Name( );
}
abstract class Token
{
    public virtual string Name( ) { ... }
}
class CommentToken: Token, IToken
{
    public override string Name( ) { ... } // Okay
}
```

This shows that a class can inherit its interface and its implementation of that interface from separate branches of the inheritance.

Comparing Abstract Classes to Interfaces

- **Similarities**
  - Neither can be instantiated
  - Neither can be sealed
- **Differences**
  - Interfaces cannot contain any implementation
  - Interfaces cannot declare non-public members
  - Interfaces cannot extend non-interfaces

Both abstract classes and interfaces exist to be derived from (or implemented). However, a class can extend at most one abstract class, so you need to be more careful when deriving from an abstract class than you need to be when deriving from an interface. Reserve the use of abstract classes for implementing true "is a" relationships.

The similarities between abstract classes and interfaces are that they:

- Cannot be instantiated.

  This means that they cannot be used directly to create objects.

- Cannot be sealed.

  This is acceptable because a sealed interface cannot be implemented.

The differences between abstract classes and interfaces are summarized in the following table.

Interfaces	Abstract classes
Cannot contain implementation	Can contain implementation
Cannot declare non-public members	Can declare non-public members
Can extend only other interfaces	Can extend other classes, which can be non-abstract

When comparing the similarities and differences between abstract classes and interfaces, think of abstract classes as unfinished classes that contain plans for what needs to be finished.

Implementing Abstract Methods

- **Syntax: Use the abstract keyword**

```
abstract class Token
{
    public virtual string Name( ) { ... }
    public abstract int Length( );
}
class CommentToken: Token
{
    public override string Name( ) { ... }
    public override int Length( ) { ... }
}
```

- **Only abstract classes can declare abstract methods**
- **Abstract methods cannot contain a method body**

You declare an abstract method by adding the **abstract** modifier to the method declaration. The syntax of the **abstract** modifier is displayed on the slide.

Only abstract classes can declare abstract methods. Following is an example:

```
interface IToken
{
    abstract string Name( ); // Compile-time error
}
class CommentToken
{
    abstract string Name( ); // Compile-time error
}
```

Note   C++ developers can consider abstract methods to be the same as pure virtual methods in C++.

Abstract Methods Cannot Contain a Method Body

Abstract methods cannot contain any implementation. This is highlighted in the following code:

```
abstract class Token
{
    public abstract string Name( ) { ... }
    // Compile-time error
}
```

Working with Abstract Methods

- **Abstract methods are virtual**
- **Override methods can override abstract methods in further derived classes**
- **Abstract methods can override base class methods declared as virtual**
- **Abstract methods can override base class methods declared as override**

When implementing abstract methods, you need to be aware of the following:

- Abstract methods are virtual.
- Override methods can override abstract methods in further derived classes.
- Abstract methods can override base class methods that are declared as virtual.
- Abstract methods can override base class methods that are declared as override.

Each of these is described in detail in the following topics.

Abstract Methods Are Virtual

Abstract methods are considered implicitly virtual but cannot be explicitly marked as virtual, as shown in the following code:

```
abstract class Token
{
    public virtual abstract string Name( ) { ... }
    // Compile-time error
}
```

Override Methods Can Override Abstract Methods in Further Derived Classes

Because they are implicitly virtual, you can override abstract methods in derived classes. Following is an example:

```
class CommentToken: Token
{
    public override string Name( ) {...}
}
```

Abstract Methods Can Override Base Class Methods Declared As Virtual

Overriding a base class method declared as virtual forces a further derived class to provide its own method implementation and makes the original implementation of the method unavailable. Following is an example:

```
class Token
{
    public virtual string Name( ) { ... }
}
abstract class Force: Token
{
    public abstract override string Name( );
}
```

Abstract Methods Can Override Base Class Methods Declared As Override

Overriding a base class method declared as override forces a further derived class to provide its own method implementation and makes the original implementation of the method unavailable. Following is an example:

```
class Token
{
    public virtual string Name( ) { ... }
}
class AnotherToken: Token
{
    public override string Name( ) { ... }
}
abstract class Force: AnotherToken
{
    public abstract override string Name( );
}
```

Quiz: Spot the Bugs

```
class First
{
    public abstract void Method( );
}
```
(1)

```
abstract class Second
{
    public abstract void Method( ) { }
}
```
(2)

```
interface IThird
{
    void Method( );
}
abstract class Third: IThird
{
}
```
(3)

In this quiz, you can work with a partner to spot the bugs in the code on the slide. To see the answers to this quiz, turn the page.

Answers

The following bugs occur in the code on the slide:

1. You can only declare an abstract method in an abstract class. The C#
    compiler traps this bug as a compile-time error. You can fix the code by
    rewriting it as follows:

```
abstract class First
{
    public abstract void Method( );
}
```

2. An abstract method cannot declare a method body. The C# compiler traps
    this bug as a compile-time error. You can fix the code by rewriting it as
    follows:

```
abstract class Second
{
    public abstract void Method( );
}
```

3. The C# compiler traps this as a compile-time error. An abstract class must
    provide for the implementation of all methods in interfaces that it
    implements in much the same way as a concrete class. The main difference
    is that when you use an abstract class this can be achieved directly or
    indirectly. You can fix the code by rewriting it as follows:

```
abstract class Third: IThird
{
    public virtual void Method( ) { ... }
}
```

Alternatively, if you do not want to implement the body of **Method** in an
abstract class, you can declare it abstract and thus ensure that a derived class
will implement it:

```
abstract class Third: IThird
{
    public abstract void Method( );
}
```

Lab 10.1: Using Inheritance to Implement an Interface

Objectives

After completing this lab, you will be able to:

- Define and use interfaces, abstract classes, and concrete classes.
- Implement an interface in a concrete class.
- Know how and when to use the **virtual** and **override** keywords.
- Define an abstract class and use it in a class hierarchy.
- Create sealed classes to prevent inheritance.

Prerequisites

Before working on this lab, you must be able to:

- Create classes in C#.
- Define methods for classes.

Estimated time to complete this lab: 75 minutes

Exercise 1
Converting a C# Source File into a Color Syntax HTML File

Frameworks are extremely useful because they provide an easy-to-use, flexible body of code. Unlike a library, which you use by directly calling a method, you use a framework by creating a new class that implements an interface. The framework code can then polymorphically call the methods of your class by means of the interface operations. Hence, a well-designed framework can be used in many different ways, unlike a library method, which can only be used in one way.

Scenario

This exercise uses a pre-written hierarchy of interfaces and classes that form a miniature framework. The framework tokenizes a C# source file and stores the different kinds of tokens in a collection held in the **SourceFile** class. An **ITokenVisitor** interface with **Visit** operations is also provided, which in combination with the **Accept** method of **SourceFile** allows every token of the source file to be *visited* and processed in sequence. When you visit a token, your class can perform whatever processing it requires by using that token.

An abstract class called **NullTokenVisitor** has been created that implements all the **Visit** methods in **ITokenVisitor** by using empty methods. If you do not want to implement every method in **ITokenVisitor**, you can derive a class from **NullTokenVisitor** instead and override only the **Visit** methods that you want.

In this exercise, you will derive an **HTMLTokenVisitor** class from the **ITokenVisitor** interface. You will implement each overloaded **Visit** method in this derived class to output to the console the token bracketed by Hypertext Markup Language (HTML) <span class=...> and </span> markers. You will run a simple batch file, which will run the created executable and redirect console output to create an HTML page that uses a cascading style sheet. You will then open the HTML page in Microsoft Internet Explorer to see the original source file displayed with color-coded syntax.

► **To familiarize yourself with the interfaces**

1. Open the ColorTokeniser.sln project in the
   install folder\Labs\Lab10\Starter\ColorTokeniser folder.

2. Study the classes and interfaces in the files Itoken.cs, Itoken_visitor.cs and
   source_file.cs. These collaborate in the following hierarchy:

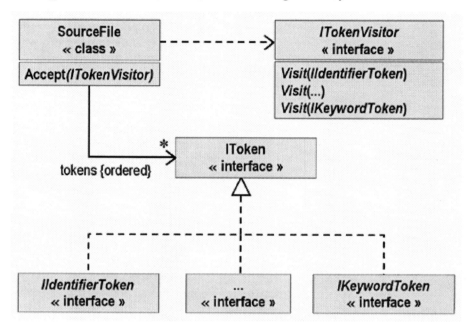

▶ **To create an abstract NullTokenVisitor class**

1. Open the null_token_visitor.cs file.

   Notice that **NullTokenVisitor** is derived from the **ITokenVisitor** interface, yet it does not implement any of the operations specified in the interface. You will implement all of the inherited operations to be empty methods in order to enable **HTMLTokenVisitor** to be built incrementally.

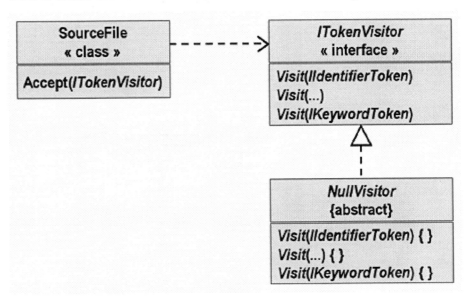

2. Add a public virtual method called **Visit** to the **NullTokenVisitor** class. This method will return **void** and accept a single **ILineStartToken** parameter. The body of the method will be empty. The method will look as follows:

```
public class NullTokenVisitor : ITokenVisitor
{
    public virtual void Visit(ILineStartToken t) { }
    ...
}
```

3. Repeat step 2 for all other overloaded **Visit** methods declared in the **ITokenVisitor** interface.

   Implement all **Visit** methods in **NullTokenVisitor** as empty bodies.

4. Save your work.

5. Compile null_token_visitor.cs.

   If you have implemented all of the **Visit** operations from the **ITokenVisitor** interface, the compilation will be successful. If you have omitted any operations, the compiler will issue an error message.

6. Add a private static void method called **Test** to the **NullTokenVisitor** class.

    This method will expect no parameters. The body of this method should contain a single statement that creates a **new NullTokenVisitor** object. This statement will verify that the **NullTokenVisitor** class has implemented all of the **Visit** operations and that **NullTokenVisitor** instances can be created. The code for this method will be as follows:

    ```
    public class NullTokenVisitor : ITokenVisitor
    {
        ...
        static void Test( )
        {
            new NullTokenVisitor( );
        }
    }
    ```

7. Save your work.

8. Compile null_token_visitor.cs and correct any errors.

9. Change the definition of **NullTokenVisitor**.

    Since the purpose of the **NullTokenVisitor** class is not to be instantiated but to be derived from, you need to change the definition so that it is an abstract class.

10. Compile null_token_visitor.cs again.

    Also, verify that the **new** statement inside the **Test** method now causes an error, as you cannot create instances of an abstract class.

11. Delete the **Test** method.

12. **NullTokenVisitor** should now look like this:

    ```
    public abstract class NullTokenVisitor : ITokenVisitor
    {
        public virtual void Visit(ILineStartToken t) { }
        public virtual void Visit(ILineEndToken   t) { }

        public virtual void Visit(ICommentToken    t) { }
        public virtual void Visit(IDirectiveToken   t) { }
        public virtual void Visit(IIdentifierToken t) { }
        public virtual void Visit(IKeywordToken    t) { }
        public virtual void Visit(IWhiteSpaceToken t) { }

        public virtual void Visit(IOtherToken t) { }
    }
    ```

▶ **To create an HTMLTokenVisitor class**

1. Open the html_token_visitor.cs file.

2. Change the **HTMLTokenVisitor** class so that it derives from the **NullTokenVisitor** abstract class.

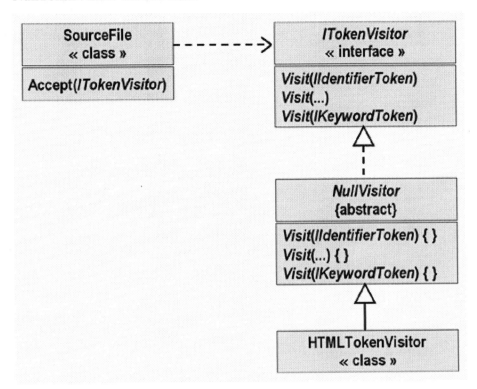

3. Open the main.cs file, and add two statements to the static **InnerMain** method.

   a. The first statement will declare a variable called *visitor* of type **HTMLTokenVisitor** and initialize it with a newly created **HTMLTokenVisitor** object.

   b. The second statement will pass *visitor* as the parameter to the **Accept** method being called on the already declared *source* variable.

4. Save your work.

5. Compile the program and correct any errors.

   Run the program from the command line, passing the name of a .cs source file from the *install folder*\Labs\Lab10\Starter\ColorTokeniser\bin\debug folder as the command-line argument.

   Nothing will happen, because you have not yet defined any methods in **HTMLTokenVisitor** class!

6. Add a public non-static **Visit** method to the **HTMLTokenVisitor** class. This method will return **void** and accept a single **ILineStartToken** parameter called **line**.

   Implement the body of the method as a single statement that calls **Write** (*not* **WriteLine**), displaying the value of **line.Number( )** to the console. Note that **Number** is an operation declared in the **ILineStartToken** interface. Do not qualify the method with a **virtual** or **override** keyword. This is shown in the following code:

```
public class HTMLTokenVisitor : NullTokenVisitor
{
    public void Visit(ILineStartToken line)
    {
        Console.Write(line.Number( )); // Not WriteLine
    }
}
```

7. Save your work.

8. Compile the program.

   Run the program again, as before. Nothing will happen, because the **Visit** method in **HTMLTokenVisitor** is hiding the **Visit** method in the base class **NullTokenVisitor**.

9. Change **HTMLTokenVisitor.Visit(ILineStartToken)** so that it overrides **Visit** from its base class.

   This will make **HTMLTokenVisitor.Visit** polymorphic, as shown in the following code:

```
public class HTMLTokenVisitor : NullTokenVisitor
{
    public override void Visit(ILineStartToken line)
    {
        Console.Write(line.Number( ));
    }
}
```

10. Save your work.

11. Compile the program and correct any errors.

    Run the program as before. Output will be displayed. It will contain ascending numbers with no intervening white space. (The numbers are generated line numbers for the file that you specified.)

12. In **HTMLTokenVisitor,** define an overloaded public non-static **Visit** method that returns **void** and accepts a single **ILineEndToken** parameter.

This revision adds a new line between lines of output tokens. Notice that this operation is declared in the **ITokenVisitor** interface. Implement the body of this method to print a single new line to the console, as shown. (Note that this method uses **WriteLine,** not **Write.)**

```
public class HTMLTokenVisitor : NullTokenVisitor
{
    ...
    public override void Visit(ILineEndToken t)
    {
        Console.WriteLine( );  // Not Write
    }
}
```

13. Save your work.

14. Compile the program and correct any errors.

Run the program as before. This time each line number is terminated with a separate line.

▶ **To use HTMLTokenVisitor to display C# source file tokens**

1. Add a public non-static **Visit** method to the **HTMLTokenVisitor** class. This method will return **void** and accept a single **IIdentifierToken** parameter called **token.** It should override the corresponding method in the **NullTokenVisitor** base class.

2. Implement the body of the method as a single statement that calls **Write,** displaying **token** to the console as a **string.** This is shown in the following code:

```
public class HTMLTokenVisitor : NullTokenVisitor
{
    ...
    public override void Visit(IIdentifierToken token)
    {
        Console.Write(token.ToString( ));
    }
}
```

Note Open the IToken.cs file and note that **IIdentifierToken** is derived from **IToken** and that **IToken** declares a **ToString** method.

---

3. Save your work.

4. Compile the program and correct any errors.

Run the program as before. This time the output includes all of the identifiers.

5. Repeat steps 1 through 4, adding four more overloaded **Visit** methods to **HTMLTokenVisitor.**

Each of these will expect a single parameter of type **ICommentToken, IKeywordToken, IWhiteSpaceToken,** and **IOtherToken,** respectively. The bodies of these methods will all be exactly as described in step 2.

▶ **To convert a C# source file into an HTML filex**

1. In the *install folder*\Labs\Lab10\Starter\ColorTokeniser\bin\debug folder, there is a batch script called generate.bat. This script executes the ColorTokeniser program, using a command-line parameter that you pass to it. It also performs some pre-processing and post-processing of the tokenized file that is produced. It performs this processing by using a cascading style sheet (code_style.css) to convert the output into HTML.

   From the command prompt, run the program by using the generate batch file, passing in token.cs file as a parameter. (This is actually a copy of part of the source code for your program, but it will work as an example .cs file.) Capture the output to another file that has an .html suffix. Following is an example:

   ```
   generate token.cs > token.html
   ```

2. Use Internet Explorer to display the .html file that you just created (token.html in the example in the previous step). You can do this by typing **token.html** at the command prompt.

   The displayed result will show many formatting flaws. Line numbers greater than 9 are all indented differently from the lines with numbers less than 10. This is because numbers less than 10 have a single digit, whereas numbers greater than 9 have two digits. Notice also that the line numbers are in the same color as the source file tokens, which is not helpful.

▶ **To find and fix the line number and indentation problems**

1. Change the definition of the **Visit(ILineStartToken)** method as follows to add some output that fixes both of these problems. This is shown in the following code:

   ```
   public class HTMLTokenVisitor : NullTokenVisitor
   {
       public override void Visit(ILineStartToken line)
       {
           Console.Write("<span class=\"line_number\">");
           Console.Write("{0,3}", line.Number( ));
           Console.Write("</span>");
       }
       ...
   }
   ```

2. Save your work.

3. Compile the program and correct any errors.

4. Re-create the token.html file from the token.cs source file from the command line as before:

```
generate token.cs > token.html
```

5. Open token.html in Internet Explorer.

   There is still a problem. Compare the appearance of token.html in Internet Explorer to the original token.cs file. Notice that the first comment in token.cs (/// <summary>) appears in the browser as "///". The <summary> has been lost. The problem is that in HTML some characters have a special meaning. To display the left angle bracket (<), the HTML source must be **<** and to display the right angle bracket (>) the HTML source must be **>**. To display the ampersand (&), the HTML source must be **&**.

▶ **To make the changes required to correctly display the angle bracket and ampersand characters**

1. Add to **HTMLTokenVisitor** a private non-static method called **FilteredWrite** that returns **void** and expects a single parameter of type **IToken** called **token**.

   This method will create a **string** called **dst** from **token** and iterate through each character in **dst**, applying the transformations described above. The code will look as follows:

```
public class HTMLTokenVisitor : NullTokenVisitor
{
    ...
    private void FilteredWrite(IToken token)
    {
        string src = token.ToString( );
        for (int i = 0; i != src.Length; i++) {
            string dst;
            switch (src[i]) {
            case '<' :
                dst = "&lt;"; break;
            case '>' :
                dst = "&gt;"; break;
            case '&' :
                dst = "&amp;"; break;
            default :
                dst = new string(src[i], 1); break;
            }
            Console.Write(dst);
        }
    }
}
```

2. Change the definition of **HTMLTokenVisitor.Visit(ICommentToken)** to use the new **FilteredWrite** method instead of **Console.Write**, as follows:

```
public class HTMLTokenVisitor : NullTokenVisitor
{
    public override void Visit(ICommentToken token)
    {
        FilteredWrite(token);
    }
    ...
}
```

3. Change the definition of **HTMLTokenVisitor.Visit(IOtherToken)** to use the new **FilteredWrite** method instead of **Console.Write**, as follows:

```
public class HTMLTokenVisitor : NullTokenVisitor
{
    public override void Visit(IOtherToken token)
    {
        FilteredWrite(token);
    }
    ...
}
```

4. Save your work.

5. Compile the program and correct any errors.

6. Re-create the token.html file from the token.cs source file from the command line as before:

```
generate token.cs > token.html
```

7. Open token.html in Internet Explorer and verify that the angle bracket and ampersand characters are now displayed correctly.

▶ **To add color comments to the HTML file**

1. Use Notepad to open the code_style.css style sheet in the *install folder*\Labs\Lab10\Starter\ColorTokeniser\bin\debug folder.

    The cascading style sheet file called code_style.css will be used to add color to the HTML file. This file has already been created for you. The following is an example of its contents:

    ```
    ...
    SPAN.LINE_NUMBER
    {
        background-color: white;
        color: gray;
    }
    ...
    SPAN.COMMENT
    {
        color: green;
        font-style: italic;
    }
    ```

    The **HTMLTokenVisitor.Visit(ILineStartToken)** method already uses this style sheet:

    ```
    public class HTMLTokenVisitor : NullTokenVisitor
    {
        public override void Visit(ILineStartToken line)
        {
            Console.Write("<span class=\"line_number\">");
            Console.Write("{0,3}", line.Number( ));
            Console.Write("</span>");
        }
        ...
    }
    ```

    Notice that this method writes the words "span" and "line_number," and that the style sheet contains an entry for SPAN.LINE_NUMBER.

2. Change the body of **HTMLTokenVisitor.Visit(ICommentToken)** so that it takes the following pattern:

    ```
    public class HTMLTokenVisitor : NullTokenVisitor
    {
        public override void Visit(ICommentToken token)
        {
            Console.Write("<span class=\"comment\">");
            FilteredWrite(token);
            Console.Write("</span>");
        }
        ...
    }
    ```

3. Save your work.

4. Compile the program and correct any errors.

5. Re-create the token.html file from the token.cs source file as before:

```
generate token.cs > token.html
```

6. Open token.html in Internet Explorer.

   Verify that the source file comments are now green and are italicized.

▶ **To add color keywords to the HTML file**

1. Notice that the code_style.css file contains the following entry:

```
...
SPAN.KEYWORD
{
    color: blue;
}
...
```

2. Change the body of **HTMLTokenVisitor.Visit(IKeywordToken)** to use the style specified in the style sheet, as follows:

```
public class HTMLTokenVisitor : NullTokenVisitor
{
    public override void Visit(IKeywordToken token)
    {
        Console.Write("<span class=\"keyword\">");
        FilteredWrite(token);
        Console.Write("</span>");
    }
    ...
}
```

3. Save your work.

4. Compile the program and correct any errors.

5. Re-create the token.html file from the token.cs source file by using the generate batch file as before:

```
generate token.cs > token.html
```

6. Open token.html in Internet Explorer and verify that the keywords are now in blue.

▶ **To refactor the Visit methods to eliminate duplication**

1. Notice the duplication in the two previous **Visit** methods. That is, both methods write span strings to the console.

   You can refactor the **Visit** methods to avoid this duplication. Define a new private non-static method called **SpannedFilteredWrite** that returns **void** and expects two parameters, a **string** called **spanName** and an **IToken** called **token**. The body of this method will contain three statements. The first statement will write the span string to the console by using the **spanName** parameter. The second statement will call the **FilteredWrite** method, passing **token** as the argument. The third statement will write the closing span string to the console. The code will look as follows:

```
public class HTMLTokenVisitor : NullTokenVisitor
{
    ...
    private void SpannedFilteredWrite(string spanName,
↪IToken token)
    {
        Console.Write("<span class=\"{0}\">", spanName);
        FilteredWrite(token);
        Console.Write("</span>");
    }
    ...
}
```

2. Change **HTMLTokenVisitor.Visit(ICommentToken)** to use this new method, as follows:

```
public class HTMLTokenVisitor : NullTokenVisitor
{
    ...
    public override void Visit(ICommentToken token)
    {
        SpannedFilteredWrite("comment", token);
    }
    ...
}
```

3. Change **HTMLTokenVisitor.Visit(IKeywordToken)** to use this new method, as follows:

```
public class HTMLTokenVisitor : NullTokenVisitor
{
    ...
    public override void Visit(IKeywordToken token)
    {
        SpannedFilteredWrite("keyword", token);
    }
    ...
}
```

4. Change the **HTMLTokenVisitor.Visit(IIdentifierToken)** method body so that it calls the **SpannedFilteredWrite** method. You must do this because identifier tokens also have an entry in the code_style.css file:

```
public class HTMLTokenVisitor : NullTokenVisitor
{
    ...
    public override void Visit(IIdentifierToken token)
    {
        SpannedFilteredWrite("identifier", token);
    }
    ...
}
```

5. Save your work.

6. Compile the program and correct any errors.

7. Re-create the token.html file from the token.cs source file by using the generate batch file as before:

```
generate token.cs > token.html
```

8. Open token.html in Internet Explorer.

   Verify that the comments are still green and that the keywords are still blue.

▶ **To implement HTMLTokenVisitor directly from ITokenVisitor**

1. Open the html_token_visitor.cs file.

2. Change the code so that the **HTMLTokenVisitor** class derives from the **ITokenVisitor** interface. Because you have implemented nearly all of the **Visit** methods in **HTMLTokenVisitor**, it no longer needs to inherit from the **NullTokenVisitor** abstract class (which provides a default empty implementation of every method in **ITokenVisitor**). It can be derived directly from the **ITokenVisitor** interface.

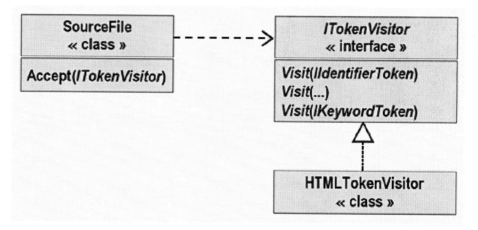

The class should look as follows:

```
public class HTMLTokenVisitor : ITokenVisitor
{
    ...
}
```

3. Save your work.

4. Compile the program.

   There will be many errors. The problem is that the **Visit** methods in **HTMLTokenVisitor** are still qualified as override, but you cannot override an operation in an interface.

5. Remove the keyword **override** from every **Visit** method definition.

6. Compile the program.

   There will still be an error. The problem this time is that **HTMLTokenVisitor** does not implement the **Visit(IDirectiveToken)** operation inherited from its **ITokenVisitor** interface. Previously, **HTMLTokenVisitor** inherited an empty implementation of this operation from **NullTokenVisitor**.

7. In **HTMLTokenVisitor**, define a public non-static method called **Visit** that returns **void** and expects a single parameter of type **IDirectiveToken** called *token*. This will fix the implementation problem.

   The body of this method will call the **SpannedFilteredWrite** method, passing it two parameters: the **string** literal "directive" and the variable *token*.

```
public class HTMLTokenVisitor : ITokenVisitor
{
    ...
    public void Visit(IDirectiveToken token)
    {
        SpannedFilteredWrite("directive", token);
    }
    ...
}
```

8. Save your work.

9. Compile the program and correct any errors.

10. Re-create the token.html file from the token.cs source file by using the generate batch file as before:

```
generate token.cs > token.html
```

11. Open token.html in Internet Explorer.

   Verify that the comments are still green and that the keywords are still blue.

▶ **To prevent the use of HTMLTokenVisitor as a base class**

1. Declare **HTMLTokenVisitor** as a sealed class.

   Given that the methods of **HTMLTokenVisitor** are no longer virtual, it makes sense for **HTMLTokenVisitor** to be declared as a sealed class. This is shown in the following code:

   ```
   public sealed class HTMLTokenVisitor : ITokenVisitor
   {
       ...
   }
   ```

2. Compile the program and correct any errors.

3. Re-create the token.html file from the token.cs source file by using the generate batch file as before:

   ```
   generate token.cs > token.html
   ```

4. Open token.html in Internet Explorer, and verify that the comments are still green and that the keywords are still blue.

Exercise 2
Converting a C# Source File into a Color Syntax HTML File

In this exercise, you will examine a second application that uses the same C# tokenizer framework used in Exercise 1.

Scenario

In this application, the **ColorTokenVisitor** class derives from the **ITokenVisitor** interface. The **Visit** methods of this class write colored tokens to a **RichTextBox** inside a Microsoft Windows® Forms application. The collaborating classes form the following hierarchy:

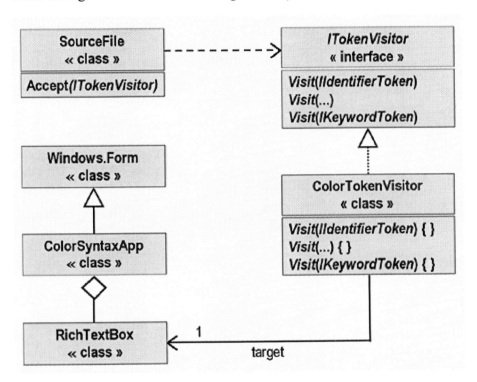

To familiarize yourself with the interfaces:

1. Open the ColorSyntaxApp.sln project in the *install folder*\Labs\Lab10\Solution\ColourSyntaxApp folder.

2. Study the contents of the two .cs files. Notice that the **ColorTokenVisitor** class is very similar to the **HTMLTokenVisitor** class that you created in Exercise 1. The main difference is that **ColorTokenVisitor** writes the color tokens to a **RichTextBox** form component rather than to the console.

3. Build the project.

4. Run the application.

   a. Click **Open File**.

   b. In the dialog box that appears, click a .cs source file.

   c. Click **Open**.

   The contents of the selected .cs source file will appear, in color.

Review

- **Deriving Classes**
- **Implementing Methods**
- **Using Sealed Classes**
- **Using Interfaces**
- **Using Abstract Classes**

1. Create a class called **Widget** that declares two public methods. Create both methods so that they return **void** and so that they do not use parameters. Call the first method **First**, and declare it as virtual. Call the second method **Second**, and do not declare it as virtual. Create a class called **FancyWidget** that extends **Widget**, overriding the inherited **First** method and hiding the inherited **Second** method.

2. Create an interface called **IWidget** that declares two methods. Create both methods so that they return **void** and so that they do not use parameters. Call the first method **First**, and call the second method **Second**. Create a class called **Widget** that implements **IWidget**. Implement **First** as virtual, and implement **Second** explicitly.

3. Create an abstract class called **Widget** that declares a protected abstract method called **First** that returns **void** and does not use parameters. Create a class called **FancyWidget** that extends **Widget**, overriding the inherited **First** method.

4. Create a sealed class called **Widget** that implements the **IWidget** interface that you created in question 2. Create **Widget** so that it implements both inherited methods explicitly.

msdn® training

Module 11: Aggregation, Namespaces, and Advanced Scope

Contents

Overview	1
Using Internal Classes, Methods, and Data	2
Using Aggregation	11
Lab 11.1: Specifying Internal Access	22
Using Namespaces	28
Using Modules and Assemblies	49
Lab 11.2: Using Namespaces and Assemblies	57
Review	63

Microsoft®

Overview

- ■ **Using Internal Classes, Methods, and Data**
- ■ **Using Aggregation**
- ■ **Using Namespaces**
- ■ **Using Modules and Assemblies**

In this module, you will learn how to use the **internal** access modifier to make code accessible at the component or assembly level. Internal access enables you to share access to classes and their members in a way that is similar to the friendship concept in C++ and Microsoft® Visual Basic®. You can specify an access level for a group of collaborating classes rather than for an individual class.

Creating well-designed individual classes is an important part of object-oriented programming, but projects of any size require you to create logical and physical structures that are larger than individual classes. You will learn how to group classes together into larger, higher-level classes. You will also learn how to use namespaces to allow you to logically group classes together inside named spaces and to help you to create logical program structures beyond individual classes.

Finally, you will learn how to use assemblies to physically group collaborating source files together into a reusable, versionable, and deployable unit.

After completing this module, you will be able to:

- ■ Use internal access to allow classes to have privileged access to each other.
- ■ Use aggregation to implement powerful patterns such as Factories.
- ■ Use namespaces to organize classes.
- ■ Create simple modules and assemblies.

◆ Using Internal Classes, Methods, and Data

- ■ **Why Use Internal Access?**
- ■ **Internal Access**
- ■ **Syntax**
- ■ **Internal Access Example**

Access modifiers define the level of access that certain code has to class members such as methods and properties. You need to apply the desired access modifier to each member, otherwise the default access type is implied. You can apply one of four access modifiers, as shown in the following table.

Access modifier	Description
Public	A public member is accessible from anywhere. This is the least restrictive access modifier.
Protected	A protected member is accessible from within the class and all derived classes. No access from the outside is permitted.
Private	A private member is accessible only from within the same class. Not even derived classes can access it.
Internal	An internal member is accessible from within any part of the same Microsoft .NET-based assembly. You can think of it as public at the assembly level and private from outside the assembly.
protected internal	An internal protected member is accessible from within the current assembly or from within types derived from the containing class.

In this section, you will learn how to use internal access to specify accessibility at the assembly level instead of at the class level. You will learn why internal access is necessary, and you will learn how to declare internal classes, internal methods, and internal data. Finally, you will see some examples that use internal access.

Why Use Internal Access?

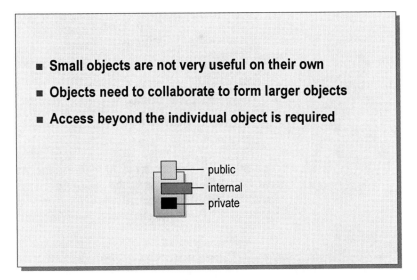

Adding More Objects

Creating well-designed object-oriented programs is not easy. Creating large well-designed object-oriented programs is harder still. The often-repeated advice is to make each entity in the program do and be one thing and one thing only, to make each entity small, focused, and easy to use.

However, if you follow that advice, you will create many classes instead of just a few classes. It is this insight that helps to make sense of the initially confusing advice from Grady Booch: "If your system is too complex, add more objects."

Systems are complex if they are hard to understand. Large classes are harder to understand than smaller classes. Breaking a large class into several smaller classes helps to make the overall functionality easier to discern.

Using Object Relationships to Form Object Collaborations

The power of object orientation is in the relationships between the objects, not in the individual objects. Objects are built from other objects to form object collaborations. Collaborating objects form larger entities.

Limit Access to the Object Collaboration?

There is, however, a potential problem. The **public** and **private** access modifiers do not fit seamlessly into the object collaboration model:

- Public access is unlimited.

  You sometimes need to limit access to just those objects in the collaboration.

- Private access is limited to the individual class.

  You sometimes need to extend access to only those objects in the collaboration.

You often need an access level that is somewhere in between these two extremes to limit access to the various objects in a particular collaboration. Protected access is not a sufficient answer because the **protected** modifier specifies access at the class level in an inheritance hierarchy.

In a well-designed object-oriented project, object relationships should be much more common than class relationship (inheritance). You need a mechanism that restricts access to the objects in a given object collaboration.

Internal Access

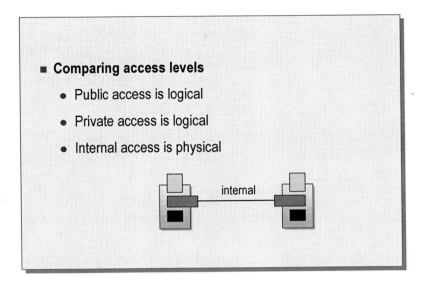

Comparing Access Levels

It is important to realize that internal access is different from public or private access:

- Public access is logical.

  The physical deployment of a public class (or a public class member) does not affect its accessibility. Regardless of how you deploy a public class, it remains public.

- Private access is also logical.

  The physical deployment of a private class (or a private class member) does not affect its accessibility. Regardless of how you deploy a private class, it remains private.

- Internal access is physical.

  The physical deployment of an internal class (or an internal class member) does affect its accessibility. You can deploy an internal class directly in an executable file. In this case, the internal class is visible only to its containing compilation unit. Alternatively, you can deploy an internal class in an assembly, which you will learn about later in this module. You can share this assembly between several executable files, but internal access is still limited to the assembly. If an executable file uses several assemblies, each assembly has its own internal access.

Comparing Internal Access to Friendship

In languages such as C++ and Visual Basic, you can use friendship to grant to the private members of one class access to another class. If class A grants friendship to class B, the methods of class B can access the private members of class A. Such friendship creates a strong dependency from B to A. In some ways, the dependency is even stronger than inheritance. After all, if B were derived from A instead, it would not have access to the private members of A. To counteract this strong dependency, friendship has a few built-in safety restrictions:

- Friendship is closed.

    If X needs to access the private members of Y, it cannot grant itself friendship to Y. In this case, only Y can grant friendship to X.

- Friendship is not reflexive.

    If X is a friend of Y, that does not mean that Y is automatically a friend of X.

Internal access is different from friendship:

- Internal access is open.

    You can compile a C# class (in a source file) into a module and then add the module to an assembly. In this way, a class can grant itself access to the internals of the assembly that other classes have made available.

- Internal access is reflexive.

    If X has access to the internals of Y, then Y has access to the internals of X. Note also that X and Y must be in the same assembly.

Syntax

```
internal class <outername>
{
    internal class <nestedname> { ... }
    internal <type> field;
    internal <type> Method( ) { ... }

    protected internal class <nestedname> { ... }
    protected internal <type> field;
    protected internal <type> Method( ) { ... }
}
```

protected internal means protected *or* internal

When you define a class as internal, you can only access the class from the current assembly. When you define a class as protected internal, you can access the class from the current assembly or from types derived from the containing class.

Non-Nested Types

You can declare types directly in the global scope or in a namespace as public or internal but not as protected or private. The following code provides examples:

```
public class Bank { ... }       // Okay
internal class Bank { ... }     // Okay
protected class Bank { ... }    // Compile-time error
private class Bank { ... }      // Compile-time error

namespace Banking
{
    public class Bank { ... }     // Okay
    internal class Bank { ... }   // Okay
    protected class Bank { ... }  // Compile-time error
    private class Bank { ... }    // Compile-time error
}
```

When you declare types in the global scope or in a namespace and do not specify an access modifier, the access defaults to internal:

```
/*internal */ class Bank { ... }

namespace Banking
{
    /*internal*/ class Bank { ... }
    ...
}
```

Nested Types

When you nest classes inside other classes, you can declare them with any of the five types of accessibility, as shown in the following code:

```
class Outer
{
    public class A { ... }
    protected class B { ... }
    protected internal class C { ... }
    internal class D { ... }
    private class E { ... }
}
```

You cannot declare any member of a **struct** with protected or protected internal accessibility because deriving from a **struct** will produce a compile-time error. The following code provides examples:

```
public struct S
{
    protected int x;            // Compile-time error
    protected internal int y;   // Compile-time error
}
```

Tip When you declare a protected internal member, the order of the keywords **protected** and **internal** is not significant. However, **protected internal** is recommended. The following code provides an example:

```
class BankAccount
{
    // Both versions are allowed
    protected internal BankAccount( ) { … }
    internal protected BankAccount(decimal balance) { … }
}
```

Note You cannot use access modifiers with destructors, so the following example will produce a compile-time error:

```
class BankAccount
{
    internal ~BankAccount( ) { ... } // Compile-time error
}
```

Internal Access Example

```
public interface IBankAccount { ... }

internal abstract class CommonBankAccount { ... }

internal class DepositAccount: CommonBankAccount,
                                IBankAccount { ... }
public class Bank
{
    public IBankAccount OpenAccount( )
    {
        return new DepositAccount( );
    }
}
```

To learn how to use internal access, consider the following example.

Scenario

In the banking example on the previous slide, there are three classes and an interface. The classes and interface are shown in the same source file for the sake of illustration. They could easily be in four separate source files. These four types would be physically compiled into a single assembly.

The **IBankAccount** interface and the **Bank** class are public and define how the assembly is used from the outside. The **CommonBankAccount** class and the **DepositAccount** class are implementation-only classes that are not intended to be used from outside the assembly and hence are not public. (Note that **Bank.OpenAccount** returns an **IBankAccount**.) However, they are not marked as private.

Note that the **CommonBankAccount** abstract base class is marked internal because the designer anticipates that new kinds of bank accounts might be added to the assembly in the future, and these new classes might reuse this abstract class. The following code provides an example:

```
internal class CheckingAccount:
                CommonBankAccount,
                IBankAccount
{
    ...
}
```

The **DepositAccount** class is slightly different. You can alternatively nest it inside the **Bank** class and make it private, as follows:

```
public class Bank
{
    ...
    private class DepositAccount:
                    CommonBankAccount,
                    IBankAccount
    {
        ...
    }
}
```

In the code on the slide, the access for the **DepositAccount** class is marked as internal, which is less restrictive than private access. You can achieve design flexibility by making this slight compromise because internal access provides the following:

- Logical separation

  DepositAccount can now be declared as a separate non-nested class. This logical separation makes both classes easier to read and understand.

- Physical separation

  DepositAccount can now be placed in its own source file. This physical separation means that **DepositAccount** maintenance will not affect other classes and can be performed at the same time as maintenance to other classes.

◆ Using Aggregation

- ■ **Objects Within Objects**
- ■ **Comparing Aggregation to Inheritance**
- ■ **Factories**
- ■ **Example Factory**

In this section, you will learn how to use aggregation to group objects together to form an object hierarchy. Aggregation specifies a relationship between objects, not classes. Aggregation offers the potential for creating reusable object configurations. Many of the most useful configurations have been documented as patterns. You will learn how to use the Factory pattern.

Objects Within Objects

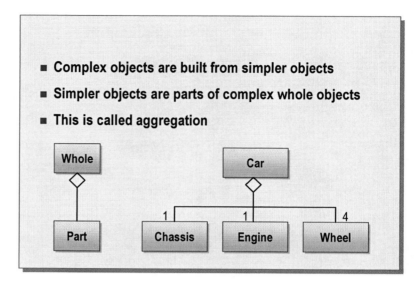

Aggregation represents a whole/part object relationship. You can see the Unified Modeling Language (UML) notation for aggregation in the slide. The diamond is placed on the "whole" class and a line links the whole to the "part" class. You can also place on an aggregation relationship a number that specifies the number of parts in the whole. For example, the slide depicts in UML that a car has one chassis, one engine, and four wheels. Informally, aggregation models the "has-a" relationship.

The words *aggregation* and *composition* are sometimes used as though they are synonyms. In UML, composition has a more restrictive meaning than aggregation:

- *Aggregation*

  Use aggregation to specify a whole/part relationship in which the lifetimes of the whole and the parts are not necessarily bound together, the parts can be traded for new parts, and parts can be shared. Aggregation in this sense is also known as *aggregation by reference*.

- *Composition*

  Use composition to specify a whole/part relationship in which the lifetimes of the whole and the parts is bound together, the parts cannot be traded for new parts, and the parts cannot be shared. Composition is also known as *aggregation by value*.

In an aggregation, the "whole class" is really just a class that is used to group and name the parts. In a sense, the whole class does not really exist at all. What is *car*? It is just the name that you use to describe an aggregation of specific parts that are arranged in a specific configuration. But it is much easier to just say *car*! In other cases, the whole class is conceptual—a family is an aggregation of people.

In programming, it is common for the whole class to simply forward the method calls to the appropriate part. This is called delegation. Aggregated objects form layered delegation hierarchies. Occasionally these hierarchies are referred to as assemblies (but the word *assemblies* can also refer to a Microsoft .NET-based physical assembly, as will be explained later in this module).

Comparing Aggregation to Inheritance

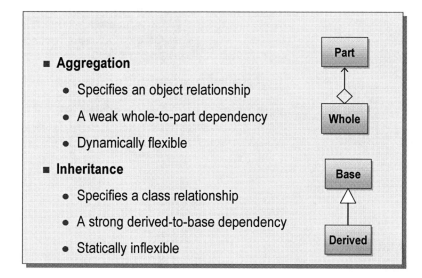

Aggregation and inheritance both provide ways to create larger classes from smaller classes, but they do this in completely different ways.

Aggregation

You can use aggregation with the following characteristics to create larger objects from smaller objects:

- An object relationship

    Aggregation specifies a relationship at the object level. The access control of the part can be public or non-public. The multiplicity can vary for different objects. For example, a computer is an aggregation of a monitor, a keyboard, and a CPU. However, some computers have two monitors (for remote debugging, for example). Some banks contain only a few bank account objects. More successful banks contain many more bank account objects. Aggregation can handle this variation at the object level because aggregation is an object-level relationship.

- Weak dependency from the whole to the part

    With aggregation, the methods of the part do not automatically become methods of the whole. A change to the part does not automatically become a change to the whole.

- Dynamically flexible

    The number of bank accounts contained in a bank can increase and decrease as bank accounts are opened and closed. If the whole object contains a reference to a part object, then at run time the actual object that this reference refers to can be derived from the part. The reference can even be dynamically rebound to objects of different derived types. Aggregation is a powerful and flexible structuring mechanism.

Inheritance

You use inheritance to create new classes from existing classes. The relationship between the existing class and the new class that extends it has the following characteristics:

■ A class relationship

Inheritance specifies a relationship at the class level. In C#, inheritance can only be public. It is impossible to specify the multiplicity for an inheritance. *Multiplicity* specifies the number of objects participating in an object relationship. But inheritance is fixed at the class level. There is no variation at the object level.

■ Strong dependency from the derived class to the base class

Inheritance creates a strong derived-to-base class dependency. The methods of the base class do automatically become methods of the derived class. A change to the base class does automatically become a change to all derived classes.

■ Statically inflexible

If a class is declared to have a particular base class, it always has that particular base class (and can only specify the base class as a base class once). Compare this to aggregation, in which the part reference can be dynamically rebound to objects of different derived classes. An object can never change its type. This inflexibility can create problems. For instance, consider a simple inheritance hierarchy with **Employee** as a base class and **Manager** and **Programmer** as parallel derived classes:

```
class Employee { ... }
class Manager: Employee { ... }
class Programmer: Employee { ... }
```

In this example, a **Programmer** object cannot be promoted to a **Manager** object!

Factories

- Creation is often complex and restricted
- Many objects are made only in specialist factories
- The factory encapsulates the complex creation
- Factories are useful patterns when modelling software

Newcomers to object orientation often ask how to create virtual constructors. The answer is that you cannot. A base class constructor is not inherited in a derived class and so cannot be virtual.

Analogy

However, the goal of abstracting away the details and responsibility of creation is a valid one. It happens in life all the time. For example, you cannot just create a phone. Creating a phone is a complicated process that involves the acquisition and configuration of all of the parts that make up a phone. Sometimes creation is illegal: you are not allowed to create your own money, for example. In these cases, the knowledge and responsibility for creation is delegated to another object—a factory—whose main responsibility is to create the product objects.

Encapsulating Construction

In software programs, you can also abstract away the details and responsibility of creation by encapsulating the construction of objects. Instead of attempting to create a virtual constructor in which delegation is automatic and moves down the class hierarchy, you can use manual delegation across an object hierarchy:

```
class Product
{
    public void Use( ) { ... }
    ...
    internal Product( ) { ... }
}

class Factory
{
    public Product CreateProduct( )
    {
        return new Product( );
    }
    ...
}
```

In this example, the **CreateProduct** method is known as a Factory Method pattern. (This definition is from *Design Patterns: Elements of Reusable Object-Oriented Software,* by E. Gamma, R. Helm, R. Johnson, and J. Vlissides.) It is a method of a factory that creates a product.

Encapsulating Destruction

Abstracting away the details and responsibility of destroying an object is also valid and useful. And again, it happens in real life. For example, if you open a bank account at a bank, you cannot destroy the bank account yourself. Only the bank can destroy the account. To provide another example, if a factory creates a product, the environmentally responsible way to destroy the product is to return it to the factory. The factory might be able to recycle some of the product's parts. The following code provides an example:

```
class Factory
{
    public Product CreateProduct( ) { ... }
    public void DestroyProduct(Product toDestroy) { ... }
    ...
}
```

In this example, the **DestroyProduct** method is known as a Disposal Method, another design pattern.

Using the Problem Vocabulary

In the preceding example, the Factory Method is called **CreateProduct**, and the Disposal Method is called **DestroyProduct**. In a real factory class, name these methods to correspond to the vocabulary of the factory. For example, in a **Bank** class (a factory for bank accounts), you might have a Factory Method called **OpenAccount** and a Disposal Method called **CloseAccount**.

Factory Example

```
public class Bank
{
    public BankAccount OpenAccount( )
    {
        BankAccount opened = new BankAccount( );
        accounts[opened.Number( )] = opened;
        return opened;
    }
    private Hashtable accounts = new Hashtable( );
}
public class BankAccount
{
    internal BankAccount( ) { ... }
    public long Number( ) { ... }
    public void Deposit(decimal amount) { ... }
}
```

To learn how to use the Factory pattern, consider an example of publicly useable, non-creatable objects being made and aggregated in a factory.

Scenario

In this example, the **BankAccount** class is public and has public methods. If you could create a **BankAccount** object, you could use its public methods. However, you cannot create a **BankAccount** object because its constructor is not public. This is a perfectly reasonable model. After all, you cannot just create a real bank account object. If you want a bank account, you need to go to a bank and ask a teller to open one. The bank creates the account for you.

This is exactly the model that the above code depicts. The **Bank** class has a public method called **OpenAccount**, the body of which creates the **BankAccount** object for you. In this case, the **Bank** and the **BankAccount** are in the same source file, and so will inevitably become part of the same assembly. Assemblies will be covered later in this module. However, even if the **Bank** class and the **BankAccount** classes were in separate source files, they could (and would) still be deployed in the same assembly, in which case the **Bank** would still have access to the internal **BankAccount** constructor. Notice also that the **Bank** aggregates the **BankAccount** objects that it creates. This is very common.

Design Alternatives

To restrict creation of **BankAccount** objects further, you can make **BankAccount** a private nested class of **Bank** with a public interface. The following code provides an example:

```
using System.Collections;

public interface IAccount
{
    long Number( );
    void Deposit(decimal amount);
    //...
}

public class Bank
{
    public IAccount OpenAccount( )
    {
        IAccount opened = new DepositAccount( );
        accounts[opened.Number( )] = opened;
        return opened;
    }

    private readonly Hashtable accounts = new Hashtable( );

    private sealed class DepositAccount: IAccount
    {
        public long Number( )
        {
            return number;
        }

        public void Deposit(decimal amount)
        {
            balance += amount;
        }
        //...
        // Class state
        private static long NextNumber( )
        {
            return nextNumber++;
        }
        private static long nextNumber = 123;

        // Object state
        private decimal balance = 0.0M;
        private readonly long number = NextNumber( );
    }
}
```

Alternatively, you can make the entire **BankAccount** concept private, and reveal only the bank account number, as shown in the following code:

```
using System.Collections;

public sealed class Bank
{
    public long OpenAccount( )
    {
        IAccount opened = new DepositAccount( );
        long number = opened.Number( );
        accounts[number] = opened;
        return number;
    }

    public void Deposit(long accountNumber, decimal amount)
    {
        IAccount account = (IAccount)accounts[accountNumber];
        if (account != null) {
            account.Deposit(amount);
        }
    }

    //...

    public void CloseAccount(long accountNumber)
    {
        IAccount closing = (IAccount)accounts[accountNumber];
        if (closing != null) {
            accounts.Remove(accountNumber);
            closing.Dispose( );
        }
    }

    private readonly Hashtable accounts = new Hashtable( );

    private interface IAccount
    {
        long Number( );
        void Deposit(decimal amount);
        void Dispose( );
        //...
    }

    private sealed class DepositAccount: IAccount
    {
        public long Number( )
        {
            return number;
        }

        public void Deposit(decimal amount)
        {
            balance += amount;
        }
```

Code continued on following page.

```
            public void Dispose( )
            {
                //...
                System.GC.SuppressFinalize(this);
            }


            private static long NextNumber( )
            {
                return nextNumber++;
            }
            private static long nextNumber = 123;

            private decimal balance = 0.0M;
            private readonly long number = NextNumber( );
        }
    }
```

Lab 11.1: Specifying Internal Access

Objectives

After completing this lab, you will be able to:

- Specify internal access for classes.
- Specify internal access for methods.

Prerequisites

Before working on this lab, you must be able to:

- Create classes.
- Use constructors and destructors.
- Use **private** and **public** access modifiers.

Estimated time to complete this lab: 30 minutes

Exercise 1
Creating a Bank

In this exercise, you will:

1. Create a new class called **Bank** that will act as the point of creation (a factory) for **BankAccount** objects.

2. Change the **BankAccount** constructors so that they use internal access.

3. Add to the **Bank** class overloaded **CreateAccount** factory methods that the customers can use to access accounts and to request the creation of accounts.

4. Make the **Bank** class "singleton-like" by making all of its methods static (and public) and adding a private constructor to prevent instances of the **Bank** class from being created accidentally.

5. Store **BankAccounts** in **Bank** by using a Hashtable (**System.Collections.Hashtable**).

6. Use a simple harness to test the functionality of the **Bank** class.

▶ **To create the Bank class**

1. Open the Bank.sln project in the *install folder*\Labs\Lab11\Exercise 1\Starter\Bank folder.

2. Review the four **BankAccount** constructors in the **BankAccount.cs** file.

   You will create four overloaded **CreateAccount** methods in the **Bank** class that will call each of these four constructors respectively.

3. Open the **Bank.cs** file and create a public non-static method of **Bank** called **CreateAccount** that expects no parameters and returns a **BankAccount**.

   The body of this method should return a newly created **BankAccount** object by calling the **BankAccount** constructor that expects no parameters.

4. Add the following statements to **Main** in the **CreateAccount.cs** file. This code tests your **CreateAccount** method.

```
Console.WriteLine("Sid's Account");
Bank bank = new Bank( );
BankAccount sids = bank.CreateAccount( );
TestDeposit(sids);
TestWithdraw(sids);
Write(sids);
sids.Dispose( );
```

5. In BankAccount.cs, change the accessibility of the **BankAccount** constructor that expects no parameters from public to internal.

6. Save your work.

7. Compile the program, correct any errors, and run the program.

   Verify that Sid's bank account is created and that the deposit and withdrawal appear in the transaction list if successful.

▶ **To make the Bank responsible for closing accounts**

Real bank accounts never leave their bank. Instead, bank accounts remain internal to their bank, and customers gain access to their accounts by using their unique bank account numbers. In the next few steps, you will modify the **Bank.CreateAccount** method in Bank.cs to reflect this.

1. Add a private static field called *accounts* of type **Hashtable** to the **Bank** class. Initialize it with a **new Hashtable** object. The **Hashtable** class is located inside the **System.Collections** namespace, so you will need an appropriate *using-directive*.

2. Modify the **Bank.CreateAccount** method so that it returns the **BankAccount** number (a **long**) and not the **BankAccount** itself. Change the body of the method so that it stores the newly created **BankAccount** object in the accounts **Hashtable**, using the bank account number as the key.

3. Add a public non-static **CloseAccount** method to the **Bank** class.

    This method will expect a single parameter of type **long** (the number of the account being closed) and will return a **bool**. The body of this method will access the **BankAccount** object from the accounts **Hashtable**, using the account number parameter as an indexer. It will then remove the **BankAccount** from the accounts **Hashtable** by calling the **Remove** method of the **Hashtable** class, and then dispose of the closing account by calling its **Dispose** method. The **CloseAccount** method will return **true** if the account number parameter successfully accesses a **BankAccount** inside the accounts **Hashtable**; otherwise it will return **false**.

    At this point, the **Bank** class should look as follows:

```
using System.Collections;

public class Bank
{
    public long CreateAccount( )
    {
        BankAccount newAcc = new BankAccount( );
        long accNo = newAcc.Number( );
        accounts[accNo] = newAcc;
        return accNo;
    }
    public bool CloseAccount(long accNo)
    {
        BankAccount closing = (BankAccount)accounts[accNo];
        if (closing != null) {
            accounts.Remove(accNo);
            closing.Dispose( );
            return true;
        }
        else {
            return false;
        }
    }
    private static Hashtable accounts = new Hashtable( );
}
```

4. Save your work.

5. Compile the program.

   It will not compile. The test harness in **CreateAccount.Main** now fails because **Bank.CreateAccount** returns a **long** rather than a **BankAccount**.

6. Add a public non-static method called **GetAccount** to the **Bank** class.

   It will expect a single parameter of type **long** that specifies a bank account number. It will return the **BankAccount** object stored in the accounts **Hashtable** that has this account number (or **null** if there is no account with this number). The **BankAccount** object can be retrieved by using the account number as an indexer parameter on accounts as shown below:

```
public class Bank
{
    ...
    public BankAccount GetAccount(long accNo)
    {
        return (BankAccount)accounts[accNo];
    }
}
```

7. Change **Main** in the CreateAccount.cs test harness so that it uses the new **Bank** methods, as follows:

```
public class CreateAccount
{
    static void Main ( )
    {
        Console.WriteLine("Sid's Account");
        Bank bank = new Bank( );
        long sidsAccNo = bank.CreateAccount( );
        BankAccount sids = bank.GetAccount(sidsAccNo);
        TestDeposit(sids);
        TestWithdraw(sids);
        Write(sids);
        if (bank.CloseAccount(sidsAccNo)) {
            Console.WriteLine("Account closed");
        } else {
            Console.WriteLine("Something went wrong closing
    ↪the account");
        }
    }
    ...
}
```

8. Save your work.

9. Compile the program, correct any errors, and run the program. Verify that Sid's bank account is created and that the deposit and withdrawal appear in the transaction list if they are successful.

▶ **To make all BankAccount constructors internal**

1. Find the **BankAccount** constructor that takes an **AccountType** and a **decimal** as parameters. Change it so that its access is internal rather than public.

2. Add another **CreateAccount** method to the **Bank** class.

   It will be identical to the existing **CreateAccount** method except that it will expect two parameters of type **AccountType** and **decimal** and will call the **BankAccount** constructor that expects these two parameters.

3. Find the **BankAccount** constructor that expects a single **AccountType** parameter. Change it so that its access is internal rather than public.

4. Add a third **CreateAccount** method to the **Bank** class.

   It will be identical to the two existing **CreateAccount** methods except that it will expect one parameter of type **AccountType** and will call the **BankAccount** constructor that expects this parameter.

5. Find the **BankAccount** constructor that expects a single **decimal** parameter. Change it so that its access is internal rather than public.

6. Add a fourth **CreateAccount** method to the **Bank** class.

   It will be identical to the three existing **CreateAccount** methods except that it will expect one parameter of type **decimal** and will call the **BankAccount** constructor that expects this parameter.

7. Save your work.

8. Compile the program and correct any errors.

▶ **To make the Bank class "singleton-like"**

1. Change the four overloaded **Bank.CreateAccount** methods so that they are static methods.

2. Change the **Bank.CloseAccount** method so that it is a static method.

3. Change the **Bank.GetAccount** method so that it is a static method.

4. Add a private **Bank** constructor to stop **Bank** objects from being created.

5. Modify **CreateAccount.Main** in CreateAccount.cs so that it uses the new static methods and does not create a bank object, as shown in the following code:

```
public class CreateAccount
{
    static void Main ( )
    {
        Console.WriteLine("Sid's Account");
        long sidsAccNo = Bank.CreateAccount( );
        BankAccount sids = Bank.GetAccount(sidsAccNo);
        TestDeposit(sids);
        TestWithdraw(sids);
        Write(sids);
        if (Bank.CloseAccount(sidsAccNo))
            Console.WriteLine("Account closed");
        else
            Console.WriteLine("Something went wrong closing
➥the account");
    }
    ...
}
```

6. Save your work.

7. Compile the program, correct any errors, and run the program. Verify that Sid's bank account is created and that the deposit and withdrawal appear in the transaction list if they are successful.

8. Open the Microsoft Visual Studio® .NET command prompt.

9. From the command prompt, run the Intermediate Language Disassembler (ILDASM) as follows:

```
c:\> ildasm
```

10. In the ILDASM, open the Bank.exe. Notice that the four classes and the **enum** are all listed.

11. Close ILDASM.

12. Close the Command window.

◆ Using Namespaces

- **Scope Revisited**
- **Resolving Name Clashes**
- **Declaring Namespaces**
- **Fully Qualified Names**
- **Declaring using-namespace-directives**
- **Declaring using-alias-directives**
- **Guidelines for Naming Namespaces**

In this section, you will learn about scope in the context of namespaces. You will learn how to resolve name clashes by using namespaces. (Name clashes occur when two or more classes in the same scope have the same name.) You will learn how to declare and use namespaces. Finally, you will learn some guidelines to follow when using namespaces.

Scope Revisited

■ **The scope of a name is the region of program text in which you can refer to the name without qualification**

```
public class Bank
{
    public class Account
    {
        public void Deposit(decimal amount)
        {
            balance += amount;
        }
        private decimal balance;
    }
    public Account OpenAccount( ) { ... }
}
```

In the code in the slide, there are effectively four scopes:

- The global scope. Inside this scope there is a single member declaration: the **Bank** class.

- The **Bank** class scope. Inside this scope there are two member declarations: the nested class called **Account** and the method called **OpenAccount**. Note that the return type of **OpenAccount** can be specified as **Account** and need not be **Bank.Account** because **OpenAccount** is in the same scope as **Account**.

- The **Account** class scope. Inside this scope there are two member declarations: the method called **Deposit** and the field called *balance*.

- The body of the **Account.Deposit** method. This scope contains a single declaration: the *amount* parameter.

When a name is not in scope, you cannot use it without qualification. This usually happens because the scope in which the name was declared has ended. However, it can also happen when the name is hidden. For example, a derived class member can hide a base class member, as shown in the following code:

```
class Top
{
    public void M( ) { ... }
}
class Bottom: Top
{
    new public void M( )
    {
        M( );        // Recursion
        base.M( );   // Needs qualification to avoid recursion
        ...
    }
}
```

A parameter name can hide a field name, as follows:

```
public struct Point
{
    public Point(int x, int y)
    {
        this.x = x; // Needs qualification
        this.y = y; // Needs qualification
    }
    private int x, y;
}
```

Resolving Name Clashes

- **Consider a large project that uses thousands of classes**
- **What if two classes have the same name?**
- **Do not add prefixes to all class names**

```
// From Vendor A
public class Widget
{ ... }

// From Vendor B
public class Widget
{ ... }
```

```
public class VendorAWidget
{ ... }

public class VendorBWidget
{ ... }
```

How can you handle the potential problem of two classes in the same scope having the same name? In C#, you can use namespaces to resolve name clashes. C# namespaces are similar to C++ namespaces and Java packages. Internal access is not dependent on namespaces.

Namespace Example

In the following example, the ability of each **Method** to call the internal **Hello** method in the other class is determined solely by whether the classes (which are located in different namespaces) are located in the same assembly.

```
// VendorA\Widget.cs file
namespace VendorA
{
    using System;

    public class Widget
    {
        internal void Hello( )
        {
            Console.WriteLine("Widget.Hello");
        }
        public void Method( )
        {
            new VendorB.ProcessMessage( ).Hello( );
        }
    }
}

// VendorB\ProcessMessage.cs file
namespace VendorB
{
    using System;

    public class ProcessMessage
    {
        internal void Hello( )
        {
            Console.WriteLine("ProcessMessage.Hello");
        }
        public void Method( )
        {
            new VendorA.Widget( ).Hello( );
        }
    }
}
```

What Happens If You Do Not Use Namespaces?

If you do not use namespaces, name clashes are likely to occur. For example, in a large project that has many small classes, you can easily make the mistake of giving two classes the same name.

Consider a large project that is split into a number of subsystems and that has separate teams working on the separate subsystems. Suppose the subsystems are divided according to architectural services, as follows:

- User services

  A means of allowing users to interact with the system.

- Business services

  Business logic used to retrieve, validate, and manipulate data according to specific business rules.

- Data services

  A data store of some type and the logic to manipulate the data.

In this multiple-team project, it is highly likely that name clashes will occur. After all, the three teams are working on the same project.

Using Prefixes As a Solution

Prefixing each class with a subsystem qualifier is not a good idea because the names become:

- Long and unmanageable.

  The class names quickly become very long. Even if this works at the first level of granularity, it cannot keep on working without class names becoming truly unwieldy.

- Complex.

  The class names simply become harder to read. Programs are a form of writing. People read programs. The easier a program is to read and comprehend, the easier it is to maintain.

Declaring Namespaces

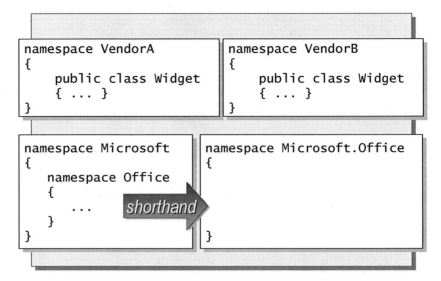

You can use namespaces to show the logical structure of classes in a way that can be interpreted by the compiler.

You need to specify the structure explicitly in the grammar of the language by using namespaces. For example, instead of writing

```
public class VendorAWidget { ... }
```

you would write

```
namespace VendorA
{
    public class Widget { ... }
}
```

Namespace Scope

A namespace, unlike a class, is an open scope. In other words, when you close a namespace, you are allowed to subsequently reopen it, even in a different source file, as shown in the following code:

```
// widget.cs
namespace VendorA
{
    public class Widget { ... }
}

// ProcessMessage.cs
namespace VendorA
{
    public class ProcessMessage { ... }
}
```

There are two important consequences of this:

- Multiple source files

  Collaborating classes that are located in a common namespace can still be implemented across several physical source files (typically one source file per class) rather than in one large source file. Compare this to nested classes, for which the definition of all nested classes and the outer class must be in the same physical source file.

- Extensible namespaces

  A new class can be added to a namespace without affecting any of the classes already inside the namespace. In contrast, adding a new method to an existing class requires the whole class to be recompiled.

Nesting Namespaces

You can nest a namespace inside another namespace, thus reflecting multiple levels of organization, as follows:

```
namespace Outer
{
    namespace Inner
    {
        class Widget { ... }
    }
}
```

This example is somewhat verbose, and takes a lot of white space, braces, and indentation. In C++, this syntax must be used. In C#, you can simplify it as follows:

```
namespace Outer.Inner
{
    class Widget { ... }
}
```

Access Levels for Namespaces

Namespaces are implicitly public. You cannot include any access modifiers when you declare a namespace, as is shown on the following code:

```
namespace Microsoft.Office // Okay
{
    ...
}

public namespace Microsoft.Office // Compile-time error
{
    ...
}

private namespace Microsoft.Office // Compile-time error
{
    ...
}
```

Fully Qualified Names

- A fully qualified class name includes its namespace
- Unqualified class names can only be used in scope

```
namespace VendorA
{
    public class Widget { ... }
    ...
}
class Application
{
    static void Main( )
    {
        Widget w = new Widget( );✗
        VendorA.Widget w = new VendorA.Widget( );✓
    }
}
```

When you use a class inside its namespace, you can use its short name, referred to as its *unqualified name*. However, if you use a class outside its namespace, it is out of scope and you must refer to it by its fully qualified name.

Fully Qualified Names

When you create a class that is located inside a namespace, you must use its fully qualified name if you want to use that class outside its namespace. The fully qualified name of a class includes the name of its namespace.

In the example on the slide, the class **Widget** is embedded inside the **VendorA** namespace. This means that you cannot use the unqualified name **Widget** outside the **VendorA** namespace. For example, the following code will not compile if you place it inside **Application.Main** because **Application.Main** is outside the **VendorA** namespace.

```
Widget w = new Widget( );
```

You can fix this code by using the fully qualified name for the **Widget** class, as follows:

```
VendorA.Widget w = new VendorA.Widget( );
```

As you can see, using fully qualified names makes code long and difficult to read. In the next topic, you will learn how to bring class names back into scope with *using-directives*.

Unqualified Names

You can use unqualified names such as **Widget** only when they are in scope. For example, the following code will compile successfully because the **Application** class has been moved to the **VendorA** namespace.

```
namespace VendorA
{
    public class Widget { ... }
}
namespace VendorA
{
    class Application
    {
        static void Main( )
        {
            Widget w = new Widget( ); // Okay
        }
    }
}
```

Important   Namespaces allow classes to be logically grouped together inside a named space. The name of the enclosing space becomes part of the full name of the class. However, there is no implicit relationship between a namespace and a project or assembly. An assembly can contain classes from different namespaces, and classes from the same namespace can be located in different assemblies.

Declaring using-namespace-directives

- **Effectively brings names back into scope**

```
namespace VendorA.SuiteB
{
    public class Widget { ... }
}
```

```
using VendorA.SuiteB;

class Application
{
    static void Main( )
    {
        Widget w = new Widget( );
    }
}
```

With namespace directives, you can use classes outside their namespaces without using their fully qualified names. In other words, you can make long names short again.

Using the Members of a Namespace

You use the *using-namespace-directives* to facilitate the use of namespaces and types defined in other namespaces. For example, the following code from the slide would not compile without the *using-namespace-directive*.

```
Widget w = new Widget( );
```

The compiler will return an error that would rightly indicate that there is no global class called **Widget**. However, with the using VendorA directive, the compiler is able to resolve **Widget** because there is a class called **Widget** inside the **VendorA** namespace.

Nested Namespaces

You can write a *using-directive* that uses a nested namespace. The following code provides an example:

```
namespace VendorA.SuiteB
{
    public class Widget { ... }
}

//...new file...
using VendorA.SuiteB;

class Application
{
    static void Main( )
    {
        Widget w = new Widget( );
        ...
    }
}
```

Declaring using-namespace-directives at Global Scope

The *using-namespace-directives* must appear before any member declarations when they are used in global scope, as follows:

```
//...new file...
class Widget
{
    ...
}
using VendorA;
// After class declaration: Compile-time error

//...new file...
namespace Microsoft.Office
{
    ...
}
using VendorA;
// After namespace declaration: Compile-time error
```

Declaring using-directives Inside a Namespace

You can also declare *using-directives* inside a namespace before any member declarations, as follows:

```
//...new file...
namespace Microsoft.Office
{
    using VendorA; // Okay

    public class Widget { ... }
}
namespace Microsoft.PowerPoint
{
    using VendorB; // Okay

    public class Widget { ... }
}
//...end of file...
```

When used like this, inside a namespace, the effect of a *using-namespace-directive* is strictly limited to the namespace body in which it appears.

using-namespace-directives Are Not Recursive

A *using-namespace-directive* allows unqualified access to the types contained in the given namespace, but specifically does not allow unqualified access to nested namespaces. For example, the following code fails to compile:

```
namespace Microsoft.PowerPoint
{
    public class Widget { ... }
}
namespace VendorB
{
    using Microsoft; // but not Microsoft.PowerPoint

    class SpecialWidget: Widget { ... }
    // Compile-time error
}
```

This code will not compile because the *using-namespace-directive* gives unqualified access to the types contained in **Microsoft**, but not to the namespaces nested in Microsoft. Thus, the reference to **PowerPoint.Widget** in **SpecialWidget** is in error because no members named **PowerPoint** are available.

Ambiguous Names

Consider the following example:

```
namespace VendorA
{
    public class Widget { ... }
}
namespace VendorB
{
    public class Widget { ... }
}
namespace Test
{
    using VendorA;
    using VendorB;

    class Application
    {
        static void Main( )
        {
            Widget w = new Widget( ); // Compile-time error
            ...
        }
    }
}
```

In this case, the compiler will return a compile-time error because it cannot resolve **Widget**. The problem is that there is a **Widget** class inside both namespaces, and both namespaces have *using-directives*. The compiler will not select **Widget** from **VendorA** rather than **VendorB** because A comes before B in the alphabet.

Note however, that the two **Widget** classes only clash when there is an attempt to actually use the unqualified name **Widget**. You can resolve the problem by using a fully qualified name for **Widget**, thus associating it with either **VendorA** or **VendorB**. You can also rewrite the code without using the name **Widget** at all, as follows, and there would be no error:

```
namespace Test
{
    using VendorA;
    using VendorB;

    // Okay. No error here.

    class Application
    {
        static void Main(string[ ] args)
        {
            VendorA.Widget w = new VendorA.Widget( );
        }
    }
}
```

Declaring using-alias-directives

■ **Creates an alias for a deeply nested namespace or type**

```
namespace VendorA.SuiteB
{
    public class Widget { ... }
}
```

```
using Widget = VendorA.SuiteB.Widget;

class Application
{
    static void Main( )
    {
        Widget w = new Widget( );
    }
}
```

The *using-namespace-directive* brings all the types inside the namespace into scope.

Creating Aliases for Types

You can use a *using-alias-directive* to facilitate the use of a type that is defined in another namespace. In the code on the slide, without the *using-alias-directive*, the line:

```
Widget w = new Widget( );
```

would, once again, fail to compile. The compiler would rightly indicate that there is no global class called **Widget**. However, with the `using Widget = ...` directive, the compiler is able to resolve **Widget** because **Widget** is now a name that is in scope. A *using-alias-directive* never creates a new type. It simply creates an alias for an existing type. In other words, the following three statements are identical:

```
Widget w = new Widget( );                 // 1
VendorA.SuiteB.Widget w = new Widget( );  // 2
Widget w = new VendorA.SuiteB.Widget( );  // 3
```

Creating Aliases for Namespaces

You can also use a *using-alias-directive* to facilitate the use of a namespace. For example, the code on the slide could be reworked slightly as follows:

```
namespace VendorA.SuiteB
{
    public class Widget { ... }
}

//... new file ...
using Suite = VendorA.SuiteB;

class Application
{
    static void Main( )
    {
        Suite.Widget w = new Suite.Widget( );
    }
}
```

Declaring using-alias-directives at Global Scope

When declaring *using-alias-directives* at global scope, you must place them before any member declarations. The following code provides an example:

```
//...new file...
public class Outer
{
    public class Inner
    {
        ...
    }
}
// After class declaration: Compile-time error
using Doppelganger = Outer.Inner;
...


//...new file...
namespace VendorA.SuiteB
{
    public class Outer
    {
        ...
    }
}
// After namespace declaration: Compile-time error
using Suite = VendorA.SuiteB;
...
```

Declaring using-alias-directives Inside a Namespace

You can also place *using-alias-directives* inside a namespace before any member declarations, as follows:

```
//...new file...
namespace Microsoft.Office
{
    using Suite = VendorA.SuiteB; // Okay

    public class SpecialWidget: Suite.Widget { ... }
}
...
namespace Microsoft.PowerPoint
{
    using Widget = VendorA.SuiteB.Widget; // Okay

    public class SpecialWidget: Widget { ... }
}
//...end of file...
```

When you declare a *using-alias-directive* inside a namespace, the effect is strictly limited to the namespace body in which it appears. The following code exemplifies this:

```
namespace N1.N2
{
    class A { }
}
namespace N3
{
    using R = N1.N2;
}
namespace N3
{
    class B: R.A { } // Compile-time error: R unknown here
}
```

Mixing using-directives

You can declare *using-namespace-directives* and *using-alias-directives* in any order. However, *using-directives* never affect each other; they only affect the member declarations that follow them, as is shown in the following code:

```
namespace VendorA.SuiteB
{
    using System;
    using TheConsole = Console; // Compile-time error

    class Test
    {
        static void Main( )
        {
            Console.WriteLine("OK");
        }
    }
}
```

Here the use of **Console** in **Test.Main** is allowed because it is part of the **Test** member declaration that follows the *using-directives*. However, the *using-alias-directive* will not compile because it is unaffected by the preceding *using-namespace-directive*. In other words it is not true that

```
using System;
using TheConsole = Console;
```

is the same as

```
using System;
using TheConsole = System.Console;
```

Note that this means that the order in which you write *using-directives* is not significant.

Guidelines for Naming Namespaces

- **Use PascalCasing to separate logical components**
  - Example: VendorA.SuiteB
- **Prefix namespace names with a company name or well-established brand**
  - Example: Microsoft.Office
- **Use plural names when appropriate**
  - Example: System.Collections
- **Avoid name clashes between namespaces and classes**

The following are guidelines that you should follow when naming your namespaces.

Using PascalCasing

Use PascalCasing rather than the camelCasing style when naming namespaces. Namespaces are implicitly public, so this follows the general guideline that all public names should use the PascalCasing notation.

Using Global Prefixes

In addition to providing a logical grouping, namespaces can also decrease the likelihood of name clashes. You can minimize the risk of name clashes by choosing a unique top-level namespace that effectively acts as a global prefix. The name of your company or organization is a good top-level namespace. Within this namespace, you can include sublevel namespaces if you want. For example, you could use the name of the project as a nested namespace within the company-name namespace.

Using Plural Names When Appropriate

Although it almost never makes sense to name a class with a plural name, it does sometimes make sense for a namespace. There is a namespace in the Microsoft .NET Framework software development kit (SDK) framework called **Collections** (which is located in the **System** namespace), for example. The name of a namespace should reflect its purpose, which is to collect together a group of related classes. Try to choose a name that corresponds to the collective task of these related classes. It is easy to name a namespace when its classes collaborate to achieve a clearly defined objective.

Avoiding Name Clashes

Avoid using namespaces and classes that have the same name. The following is allowed but not a good idea:

```
namespace Wibble
{
    class Wibble
    {
        ...
    }
}
```

◆ Using Modules and Assemblies

- ■ **Creating Modules**
- ■ **Using Assemblies**
- ■ **Creating Assemblies**
- ■ **Comparing Namespaces to Assemblies**
- ■ **Using Versioning**

In this section, you will learn how to create managed modules and assemblies and about the differences between namespaces and assemblies. Finally, you will learn about assembly versioning.

Using Modules

- **.cs files can be compiled into a (.netmodule) managed module**

```
csc /target:module Bank.cs
```

Creating a Managed Module

You can compile .cs source files into a managed module. You do this by using the **/target:module** switch on the CSC command-line compiler. Managed modules are compiled Microsoft Intermediate Language (MSIL) versions of source code files that contain enough metadata to make the module self-describing. At run time, a managed module is further compiled by means of the just-in-time (JIT) process to transform it into platform native code. When you build a source file into a module, the default extension for the module is .netmodule.

Use the following command-line option to create a module:

```
c:\> csc /target:module Bank.cs
```

The module will be called bank.netmodule.

Using Assemblies

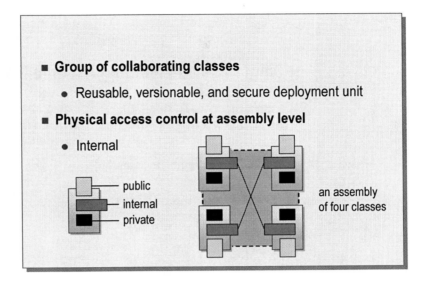

Executables can only use modules that have been added to an assembly.

What Is an Assembly?

You can physically deploy a group of collaborating classes in an assembly. You can think of an assembly as a logical DLL. Classes that are located inside the same assembly have access to each other's internal members (and classes located outside the assembly do not have access to these members).

An assembly is a reusable, versionable, secure, and self-describing deployment unit for types and resources; it is the primary building block of a .NET-based application. An assembly consists of two logical pieces: the set of types and resources that form some logical unit of functionality, and metadata that describes how these elements relate and what they depend on to work properly. The metadata that describes an assembly is called a *manifest*. The following information is captured in an assembly manifest:

- **Identity**. An assembly's identity includes its simple textual name, a version number, an optional culture if the assembly contains localized resources, and an optional public key used to guarantee name uniqueness and to protect the name from unwanted reuse.

- **Contents**. Assemblies contain types and resources. The manifest lists the names of all of the types and resources that are visible from outside the assembly, and information about where they can be found in the assembly.

- **Dependencies**. Each assembly explicitly describes other assemblies that it is dependent upon. Included in this dependency information is the version of each dependency that was present when the manifest was built and tested. In this way, you record a configuration that you know to be good, which you can revert to in the event of failures because of version mismatches.

In the simplest case, an assembly is a single-file assembly. This contains the code, resources, type metadata, and assembly metadata (manifest). In the more general case, however, assemblies consist of a number of files. In this case, the assembly manifest either exists as a stand-alone file or is contained in one of the PE files that contain types, resources, or a combination of the two.

Single-File and Multifile Assemblies

A single-file assembly is an assembly in which all the contents of the assembly are packaged into a single file. Predictably, the contents of a multifile assembly are arranged across multiple files. The manifest can be in a stand-alone file or incorporated into one of the managed module files in the assembly.

Single-file and multifile assemblies are shown in the following illustration.

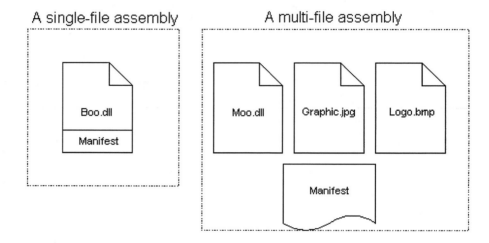

Creating Assemblies

- **Creating a single-file assembly**

```
csc /target:library /out:Bank.dll
                Bank.cs Account.cs
```

- **Creating multifile assembly**

```
csc /t:library /addmodule:Account.netmodule
              /out:Bank.dll Bank.cs
```

Creating a Single-File Assembly from Source Files

You can create an assembly directly from one or more .cs source files, as follows:

```
c:/> csc /target:library /out:Bank.dll Bank.cs Account.cs
```

You can inspect assembly files by using the Intermediate Language Disassembler (ILDASM) tool, as shown in the following code:

```
c:/> ildasm Bank.dll
```

In this case, the types declared in the .cs files are contained directly inside the assembly.

Creating a MultiFile Assembly

Suppose the Account type is located in a separate source file and has been compiled into an individual module called Account.netmodule. You can then create an assembly based on Bank.cs, and at the same time add the following in the module file:

```
c:/> csc /t:library /addmodule:Account.netmodule /out:Bank.dll
Bank.cs
```

You can inspect assembly files by using the Intermediate Language Disassembler (ILDASM) tool, as shown in the following code:

```
c:/> ildasm Bank.dll
```

For a complete list of command-line options, refer to Microsoft Visual Studio .NET Help.

Comparing Namespaces to Assemblies

- **Namespace: logical naming mechanism**
  - Classes from one namespace can reside in many assemblies
  - Classes from many namespaces can reside in one assembly
- **Assembly: physical grouping mechanism**
  - Assembly MSIL and manifest are contained directly
  - Assembly modules and resources can be external links

A namespace is a logical compile-time mechanism. Its purpose is to provide logical structure to the names of source code entities. Namespaces are not run-time entities.

An assembly is a physical run-time mechanism. Its purpose is to provide a physical structure to the run-time components that make up an executable.

Comparing Namespaces to Assemblies

You can deploy classes that are located in the same namespace into different assemblies. You can deploy classes that are located in different namespaces into one assembly. However, it is a good idea to maintain as close a logical-physical correspondence as possible.

Namespaces and assemblies are alike insofar as the physical locations of their elements:

- The elements of a namespace do not need to physically reside in a single source file. The elements of a namespace can (and, as a broad principle, should) be maintained in separate source files.

- The element references by an assembly do not need to reside directly inside the assembly. As you have seen, the modules inside a namespace are not physically contained inside the assembly. Instead, the assembly records a named link to the external module.

Using Versioning

- **Each assembly has a version number as part of its identity**
- **This version number is physically represented as a four-part number with the following format:**
  <major version>.<minor version>.<build number>.<revision>

Each assembly has a specific compatibility version number as part of its identity. Because of this, two assemblies that differ by version are completely different assemblies to the common language runtime class loader.

Version Number Format

The compatibility version number is physically represented as a four-part number with the following format:

<major version>.<minor version>.<build number>.<revision>

For example, version 1.5.1254.0 indicates 1 as the major version, 5 as the minor version, 1254 as the build number, and 0 as the revision number.

The runtime does not check references to private assemblies for version compatibility. This is because private assemblies are deployed along with the application and are placed in the same directory or subdirectory as the application, giving the author full control over the contents and distribution of these assemblies. In addition, private assemblies do not affect any applications other than the one which with they are deployed.

Shared assemblies and configuration files are beyond the scope of this course.

Lab 11.2: Using Namespaces and Assemblies

Objectives

After completing this lab, you will be able to:

- Use aggregation to group objects in a hierarchy.
- Organize classes into namespaces.

Prerequisites

Before working on this lab, you must be able to:

- Create classes.
- Use constructors and destructors.
- Use **private** and **public** access modifiers.

Estimated time to complete this lab: 30 minutes

Exercise 1
Organizing Classes

In this exercise, you will organize classes into a **Banking** namespace and create and reference an assembly. To do this, you will:

1. Place the **AccountType enum** and the **Bank**, **BankAccount**, and **BankTransaction** classes into the **Banking** namespace, and compile it as a library.

2. Modify the test harness. Initially, it will refer to the classes by using fully qualified names. You will then modify it with an appropriate *using-directive*.

3. Compile the test harness into an assembly that references the **Banking** library.

4. Use the ILDASM tool to verify that the test harness .exe refers to the Banking DLL and does not actually contain the **Bank** and **BankAccount** classes itself.

▶ **To place all of the classes into the Banking namespace**

1. Open the Bank.sln project in the *install folder*\Labs\Lab11\Exercise 2\Starter\Bank folder.

2. Edit the **AccountType enum** in AccountType.cs so that it is nested inside the **Banking** namespace, as follows:

```
namespace Banking
{
    public enum AccountType { ... }
}
```

3. Edit the **Bank** class in Bank.cs so that it is nested inside the **Banking** namespace, as follows:

```
namespace Banking
{
    public class Bank
    {
        ...
    }
}
```

4. Edit the **BankAccount** class in BankAccount.cs so that it is nested inside the **Banking** namespace, as follows:

```
namespace Banking
{
    sealed public class BankAccount
    {
        ...
    }
}
```

5. Edit the **BankTransaction** class in BankTransaction.cs so that it is nested inside the **Banking** namespace, as follows:

```
namespace Banking
{
    public class BankTransaction
    {
        ...
    }
}
```

6. Save your work.

7. Compile the program. It will fail to compile. The references to **Bank**, **BankAccount**, and **BankTransaction** in the CreateAccount.cs file cannot be resolved because these classes are now located inside the **Banking** namespace. Modify **CreateAccount.Main** to explicitly resolve all of these references. For example,

```
static void write(BankAccount acc) { ... }
```

will become:

```
static void write(Banking.BankAccount acc) { ... }
```

8. Save your work.

9. Compile the program and correct any errors. Verify that Sid's bank account is created and that the deposit and withdrawal appear in the transaction list if they are successful.

10. Open the Visual Studio .NET command prompt.

11. From the command prompt, run ILDASM.

12. Open Bank.exe using ILDASM. This file is located in the *install folder*\Labs\Lab11\Exercise2\Starter\Bank\bin\debug folder.

13. Notice that the three classes and the **enum** are now listed inside the **Banking** namespace and that the **CreateAccount** class is present.

14. Close ILDASM.

▶ **To create and use a Banking library**

1. Open a Visual Studio .NET command prompt, and navigate to the *install folder*\Labs\Lab11\Exercise2\Starter\Bank folder. From the command prompt, create the banking library as follows:

```
c:\> csc /target:library /out:bank.dll a*.cs b*.cs
c:\> dir
...
bank.dll
...
```

2. From the command prompt, run ILDASM, passing the name of the DLL as a command-line parameter, as follows:

```
c:\> ildasm bank.dll
```

3. Notice that the three "Bank*" classes and the **enum** are still listed inside the **Banking** namespace, but the **CreateAccount** class is no longer present. Close ILDASM.

4. From the command prompt, compile the test harness inside CreateAccount.cs into an assembly that references the **Banking** library bank.dll, as follows:

```
c:\> csc /reference:bank.dll createaccount.cs
c:\> dir
...
createaccount.exe
...
```

5. From the command prompt, run ILDASM, passing the name of the executable as a command-line parameter, as follows:

```
c:\> ildasm createaccount.exe
```

6. Notice that the four classes and the **enum** are no longer part of createaccount.exe. Double-click the MANIFEST item in ILDASM to open the **Manifest** window. Look at the manifest. Notice that the executable references, but does not contain, the banking library:

```
.assembly extern bank
```

7. Close ILDASM.

▶ **To simplify the test harness with a using-directive**

1. Edit CreateAccount.cs, and remove all occurrences of the **Banking** namespace. For example,

    ```
    static void write(Banking.BankAccount acc) { ... }
    ```

    will become

    ```
    static void write(BankAccount acc) { ... }
    ```

2. Save your work.

3. Attempt to compile the program. It will fail to compile. **Bank**, **BankAccount**, and **BankTransaction** still cannot be found.

4. Add to the beginning of CreateAccount.cs a *using-directive* that uses **Banking**, as follows:

    ```
    using Banking;
    ```

5. Compile the program, correct any errors, and run the program. Verify that Sid's bank account is created and that the deposit and withdrawal appear in the transaction list if they are successful.

▶ **To investigate internal methods**

1. Edit the **Main** method in the CreateAccount.cs test harness. Add a single statement that creates a new **BankTransaction** object, as follows:

```
static void Main( )
{
    new BankTransaction(0.0M);
    ...
}
```

2. Save your work.

3. Open a Command window, and navigate to the *install folder*\Labs\Lab11\Exercise2\Starter\Bank folder. From the command prompt, use the following line of code to verify that you can create an executable that does *not* use the banking library:

```
c:\> csc /out:createaccount.exe *.cs
```

4. From the command prompt, verify that you can create an executable that *does* use the banking library:

```
c:\> csc /target:library /out:bank.dll a*.cs b*.cs
c:\> csc /reference:bank.dll createaccount.cs
```

5. The extra statement in **Main** will not create problems in either case. This is because the **BankTransaction** constructor in BankTransaction.cs is currently public.

6. Edit the **BankTransaction** class in BankTransaction.cs so that its constructor has internal access.

7. Save your work.

8. From the command prompt, verify that you can *still* create an executable that does *not* use the banking library:

```
c:\> csc /out:createaccount.exe *.cs
```

9. From the command prompt, verify that you cannot create an executable that *does* use the banking library:

```
c:\> csc /target:library /out:bank.dll a*.cs b*.cs
c:\> csc /reference:bank.dll createaccount.cs
....error CS0122:
'Banking.BankTransaction.BankTransaction(decimal)' is
inaccessible due to its protection level
```

10. Remove from **CreateAccount.Main** the extra statement that creates a new **BankTransaction** object.

11. Save your work.

12. Verify that you can once again compile the test harness into an assembly that references the **Banking** library:

```
c:\> csc /target:library /out:bank.dll a*.cs b*.cs
c:\> csc /reference:bank.dll createaccount.cs
```

Review

- **Using Internal Classes, Methods, and Data**
- **Using Aggregation**
- **Using Namespaces**
- **Using Modules and Assemblies**

1. Imagine that you have two .cs files. The alpha.cs file contains a class called **Alpha** that contains an internal method called **Method**. The beta.cs file contains a class called **Beta** that also contains an internal method called **Method**. Can **Alpha.Method** be called from **Beta.Method**, and vice versa?

2. Is aggregation an object relationship or a class relationship?

3. Will the following code compile without error?

```
namespace Outer.Inner
{
    class Wibble { }
}
namespace Test
{
    using Outer.Inner;
    class SpecialWibble: Inner.Wibble { }
}
```

4. Can an executable program directly reference a managed module?

msdn training

Module 12: Operators, Delegates, and Events

Contents

Overview	1
Introduction to Operators	2
Operator Overloading	6
Lab 12.1: Defining Operators	19
Creating and Using Delegates	37
Defining and Using Events	47
Demonstration: Handling Events	53
Lab 12.2: Defining and Using Events	54
Review	63
Course Evaluation	65

Overview

- ■ **Introduction to Operators**
- ■ **Operator Overloading**
- ■ **Creating and Using Delegates**
- ■ **Defining and Using Events**

This module covers three areas of useful functionality: operators, delegates, and events.

Operators are the basic components of a language. You use operators to perform manipulations and comparisons between variables that may be logical, relational, or conditional in nature.

Delegates specify a contract between an object that issues calls to a function and an object that implements the called function.

Events provide the way for a class to notify its clients when a change occurs in the state of any of its objects.

After completing this module, you will be able to:

- ■ Define operators, to make a class or **struct** easier to use.

- ■ Use delegates to decouple a method call from a method implementation.

- ■ Add event specifications to a class to allow subscribing classes to be notified of changes in object state.

◆ Introduction to Operators

- Operators and Methods
- Predefined C# Operators

Operators are different from methods. They have special requirements that enable them to function as expected. C# has a number of predefined operators that you can use to manipulate the types and classes supplied with the Microsoft® .NET Framework.

After completing this lesson, you will be able to:

- Identify why C#, like most languages, has operators.
- Define operators, to make a class or **struct** easier to use.

Operators and Methods

- **Using methods**
  - Reduces clarity
  - Increases risk of errors, both syntactic and semantic

```
myIntVar1 = Int.Add(myIntVar2,
            Int.Add(Int.Add(myIntVar3,
                            myIntVar4), 33));
```

- **Using operators**
  - Makes expressions clear

```
myIntVar1 = myIntVar2 + myIntVar3 + myIntVar4 + 33;
```

The purpose of operators is to make expressions clear and easy to understand. It would be possible to have a language with no operators, relying instead on well-defined methods, but this would most likely have an adverse affect on the clarity of the language.

Using Methods

For example, suppose the arithmetic addition operator was not present, and the language instead provided an **Add** method of the **Int** class that took parameters and returned a result. Then, to add two variables, you would write code similar to the following:

```
myIntVar1 = Int.Add(myIntVar2, myIntVar3);
myIntvar2 = Int.Add(myIntVar2, 1);
```

Using Operators

By using the arithmetic addition operator, you can write the more concise lines of code that follow:

```
myIntVar1 = myIntVar2 + myIntVar3;
myIntVar2 = myIntVar2 + 1;
```

Code would become almost indecipherable if you were to add a series of values together by using the **Add** method, as in the following code:

```
myIntVar1 = Int.Add(myIntVar2, Int.Add(Int.Add(myIntVar3,
↪myIntVar4), 33));
```

If you use methods in this way, the likelihood of errors, both syntactic and semantic, is enormous. Operators are actually implemented as methods by C#, but their syntax is designed to make them easy to use. The C# compiler and runtime automatically convert expressions with operators into the correct series of method calls.

Predefined C# Operators

Operator Categories	
Arithmetic	Member access
Logical (Boolean and bitwise)	Indexing
String concatenation	Cast
Increment and decrement	Conditional
Shift	Delegate concatenation and removal
Relational	Object creation
Assignment	Type information
Overflow exception control	Indirection and address

The C# language provides a large set of predefined operators. Following is the complete list.

Operator category	Operators
Arithmetic	+, -, *, /, %
Logical (Boolean and bitwise)	&, |, ^, !, ~, &&, ||, true, false
String concatenation	+
Increment and decrement	++, --
Shift	<<, >>
Relational	==, !=, <, >, <=, >=
Assignment	=, +=, -=, *=, /=, %=, &=, |=, <<=, >>=
Member access	.
Indexing	[ ]
Cast	( )
Conditional	? :
Delegate concatenation and removal	+, -
Object creation	new
Type information	is, sizeof, typeof
Overflow exception control	checked, unchecked
Indirection and address	*, ->, [ ], &

You use operators for building expressions. The function of most operators is well understood. For example, the addition operator (+) in the expression 10 + 5 will perform arithmetic addition, and in this example the expression will yield the value of 15.

Some of the operators may not be as familiar as others, and some are defined as keywords rather than symbols, but their functionality with the data types and classes supplied with the .NET Framework is completely defined.

Operators with Multiple Definitions

A confusing aspect of operators is that the same symbol may have several different meanings. The + in the expression 10 + 5 is clearly the arithmetic addition operator. You can determine the meaning by the context in which it is used—no other meaning of + makes sense.

However, the following example uses the + operator to concatenate strings:

```
"Adam " + "Barr"
```

It is the function of the parser, when the program is compiled, to determine the meaning of an operator in any given context.

◆ Operator Overloading

■ **Introduction to Operator Overloading**

■ **Overloading Relational Operators**

■ **Overloading Logical Operators**

■ **Overloading Conversion Operators**

■ **Overloading Operators Multiple Times**

■ **Quiz: Spot the Bugs**

Many predefined operators in C# perform well-defined functions on classes and other data types. This clear definition widens the scope of expression for the user. You can redefine some of the operators provided by C# and use them as operators that work only with classes and structs that you have defined. In a sense, this is the same as defining your own operators. This process is known as operator overloading.

Not all predefined C# operators can be overloaded. The unary arithmetic and logic operators can be overloaded freely, as can the binary arithmetic operators. The assignment operators cannot be overloaded directly, but they are all evaluated using the arithmetic, logical, and shift operators, which in turn can be overloaded.

After completing this lesson, you will be able to:

■ Overload relational, logical, and conversion operators.

■ Overload an operator multiple times.

Introduction to Operator Overloading

- **Operator overloading**
  - Define your own operators only when appropriate
- **Operator syntax**
  - Operator**op**, where **op** is the operator being overloaded
- **Example**

```
public static Time operator+(Time t1, Time t2)
{
        int newHours = t1.hours + t2.hours;
        int newMinutes = t1.minutes + t2.minutes;
        return new Time(newHours, newMinutes);
}
```

Though operators make expressions simpler, you should only define operators when it makes sense to do so. Operators should only be overloaded when the class or **struct** is a piece of data (like a number), and will be used in that way. An operator should always be unambiguous in usage; there should be only one possible interpretation of what it means. For example, you should not define an increment operator (++) on an **Employee** class (emp1++;) because the semantics of such an operation on an **Employee** are not clear. What does it actually mean to "increment an employee"? Would you be likely to use this as part of a larger expression? If by increment you mean "give the employee a promotion," define a **Promote** method instead (emp1.Promote();).

Syntax for Overloading Operators

All operators are public static methods and their names follow a particular pattern. All operators are called operator**op**, where **op** specifies exactly which operator is being overloaded. For example, the method for overloading the addition operator is **operator+**.

The parameters that the operator takes and the types of parameters it returns must be well defined. All arithmetic operators return an instance of the class and manipulate objects of the class.

Example

As an example, consider the **Time struct** shown in the following code. A **Time** value consists of two parts: a number of hours and a number of minutes. The code in bold shows how to implement the binary addition operator (+) for adding two **Time**s together.

```
public struct Time
{
   public Time(int minutes) : this(0, minutes)
   {
   }

   public Time(int hours, int minutes)
   {
      this.hours = hours;
      this.minutes = minutes;
      Normalize( );
   }

   // Arithmetic

   public static Time operator+(Time lhs, Time rhs)
   {
      return new Time(lhs.hours + rhs.hours,
                        lhs.minutes + rhs.minutes
                      );
   }

   public static Time operator-(Time lhs, Time rhs)
   {
      ...
   }

   ...

   // Helper methods

   private void Normalize( )
   {
      if (hours < 0 || minutes < 0) {
          throw new ArgumentException("Time too small");
      }
      hours += (minutes / 60);
      minutes %= 60;
   }

   private int TotalMinutes( )
   {
      return hours * 60 + minutes;
   }

   private int hours;
   private int minutes;
}
```

Overloading Relational Operators

- **Relational operators must be paired**
  - < and >
  - <= and >=
  - == and !=
- **Override the Equals method if overloading == and !=**
- **Override the GetHashCode method if overriding equals method**

You must overload the relational or comparison operators in pairs. Each relational operator must be defined with its logical antonym. This means that if you overload <, you must also overload >, and vice versa. Similarly, != must be overloaded with ==, and <= must be overloaded with >=.

Tip For consistency, create a **Compare** method first and define all the relational operators by using **Compare**. The code example on the following page shows you how to do this.

Overriding the Equals Method

If you overload == and !=, you should also override the **Equals** virtual method that your class inherits from **Object**. This is to ensure consistency when two objects of this class are compared, whether by == or the **Equals** method, so that a situation in which == returns **true** and the **Equals** method returns **false** is avoided.

Overriding the GetHashCode Method

The **GetHashCode** method (also inherited from **Object**) is used to identify an instance of your class if it is stored in a hash table. Two instances of the same class for which **Equals** returns **true** should also hash to the same integer value. By default, this is not the case. Therefore, if you override the **Equals** method, you should also override the **GetHashCode** method.

Example

The following code shows how to implement the relational operators, the **Equals** method, and the **GetHashCode** method for the **Time struct**:

```
public struct Time
{

    ...

    // Equality

    public static bool operator==(Time lhs, Time rhs)
    {
        return lhs.Compare(rhs) == 0;
    }

    public static bool operator!=(Time lhs, Time rhs)
    {
        return lhs.Compare(rhs) != 0;
    }

    // Relational

    public static bool operator<(Time lhs, Time rhs)
    {
        return lhs.Compare(rhs) < 0;
    }

    public static bool operator>(Time lhs, Time rhs)
    {
        return lhs.Compare(rhs) > 0;
    }

    public static bool operator<=(Time lhs, Time rhs)
    {
        return lhs.Compare(rhs) <= 0;
    }

    public static bool operator>=(Time lhs, Time rhs)
    {
        return lhs.Compare(rhs) >= 0;
    }
```

Code continued on following page.

```csharp
        // Inherited virtual methods (from Object)

        public override bool Equals(object obj)
        {
            return obj is Time && Compare((Time)obj) == 0;
        }

        public override int GetHashCode( )
        {
            return TotalMinutes( );
        }

        private int Compare(Time other)
        {
            int lhs = TotalMinutes( );
            int rhs = other.TotalMinutes( );

            int result;
            if (lhs < rhs)
                result = -1;
            else if (lhs > rhs)
                result = +1;
            else
                result = 0;

            return result;
        }
        ...
}
```

Overloading Logical Operators

- **Operators && and || cannot be overloaded directly**
  - They are evaluated in terms of &, |, **true**, and **false**, which can be overloaded
  - **x && y** is evaluated as **T.false(x) ? x : T.&(x, y)**
  - **x || y** is evaluated as **T.true(x) ? x : T.|(x, y)**

You cannot overload the logical operators && and || directly. However, they are evaluated in terms of the &, |, **true**, and **false** operators, which you can overload.

If variables x and y are both of type **T**, the logical operators are evaluated as follows:

- **x && y** is evaluated as **T.false(x) ? x : T.&(x, y)**

  This expression translates as "if x is false as defined by the **false** operator of **T**, the result is x; otherwise it is the result of using the & operator of **T** over x and y."

- **x || y** is evaluated as **T.true(x) ? x : T.|(x, y)**

  This expression means "if x is true as defined by the **true** operator of **T**, the result is x; otherwise it is the result of using the | operator of **T** over x and y."

Overloading Conversion Operators

- **Overloaded conversion operators**

```
public static explicit operator Time (float hours)
{ ... }
public static explicit operator float (Time t1)
{ ... }
public static implicit operator string (Time t1)
{ ... }
```

- **If a class defines a string conversion operator**
  - The class should override ToString

You can define implicit and explicit conversion operators for your own classes and create programmer-defined cast operators that can be used to convert data from one type to another. Some examples of overloaded conversion operators are:

- `explicit operator Time (int minutes)`

  This operator converts an **int** into a **Time**. It is explicit because not all **int**s can be converted; a negative argument results in an exception being thrown.

- `explicit operator Time (float minutes)`

  This operator converts a **float** into a **Time**. Again, it is explicit because a negative parameter causes an exception to be thrown.

- `implicit operator int (Time t1)`

  This operator converts a **Time** into an **int**. It is implicit because all **Time** values can safely be converted to **int**.

- `explicit operator float (Time t1)`

  This operator converts a **Time** into a **float**. In this case the operator is explicit because, although all Times can be converted to **float**, the floating-point representation of some values may not be exact. (You always take this risk with computations involving floating-point values.)

- `implicit operator string (Time t1)`

  This operator converts a **Time** into a **string**. This is also implicit because there is no danger of losing any information in the conversion.

Overriding the ToString Method

Design guidelines recommend that, for consistency, if a class has a string conversion operator, it should override the **ToString** method, which should perform the same function. Many classes and methods in the **System** namespace – **Console.WriteLine** for example – use **ToString** to create a printable version of an object.

Example

The following code shows how to implement the conversion operators. It also shows one way to implement the **ToString** method. Note how the **Time struct** overrides **ToString**, which is inherited from **Object**.

```
public struct Time
{
  ...

  // Conversion operators
  public static explicit operator Time (int minutes)
  {
      return new Time(0, minutes);
  }

  public static explicit operator Time (float minutes)
  {
      return new Time(0, (int)minutes);
  }

  public static implicit operator int (Time t1)
  {
      return t1.TotalMinutes( );
  }

  public static explicit operator float (Time t1)
  {
      return t1.TotalMinutes( );
  }

  public static implicit operator string (Time t1)
  {
      return t1.ToString( );
  }

  // Inherited virtual methods (from Object)

  public override string ToString( )
  {
      return String.Format("{0}:{1:00}", hours, minutes);
  }
  ...
}
```

Tip If a conversion operator could throw an exception or return a partial result, make it explicit. If a conversion is guaranteed to work without any loss of data, you can make it implicit.

Overloading Operators Multiple Times

- **The same operator can be overloaded multiple times**

```
public static Time operator+(Time t1, int hours)
{...}

public static Time operator+(Time t1, float hours)
{...}

public static Time operator-(Time t1, int hours)
{...}

public static Time operator-(Time t1, float hours)
{...}
```

You can overload the same operator multiple times to provide alternative implementations that take different types as parameters. At compile time, the system establishes the method to be called depending upon the types of the parameters being used to invoke the operator.

Example

The following code shows more examples of how to implement the + and –
operators for the **Time struct**. Both examples add or subtract a specified
number of hours from the supplied **Time**:

```
public struct Time
{
    ...
    public static Time operator+(Time t1, int hours)
    {
        return t1 + new Time(hours, 0);
    }

    public static Time operator+(Time t1, float hours)
    {
        return t1 + new Time((int)hours, 0);
    }

    public static Time operator-(Time t1, int hours)
    {
        return t1 - new Time(hours, 0);
    }

    public static Time operator-(Time t1, float hours)
    {
        return t1 - new Time((int)hours, 0);
    }
    ...
}
```

Quiz: Spot the Bugs

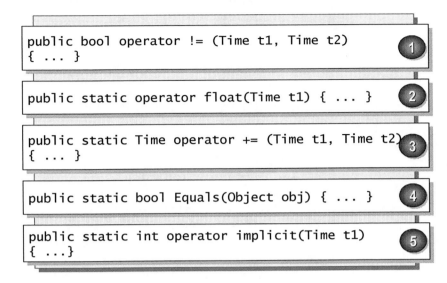

```
public bool operator != (Time t1, Time t2)
{ ... }
```
1

```
public static operator float(Time t1) { ... }
```
2

```
public static Time operator += (Time t1, Time t2)
{ ... }
```
3

```
public static bool Equals(Object obj) { ... }
```
4

```
public static int operator implicit(Time t1)
{ ...}
```
5

In this quiz, you can work with a partner to spot the bugs in the code on the slide. To see the answers to this quiz, turn the page.

Answers

1. Operators must be static because they belong to the class rather than an object. The definition for the != operator should be:

```
public static bool operator != (Time t1, Time t2) { ... }
```

2. The "type" is missing. Conversion operators must either be implicit or explicit. The code should be as follows:

```
public static implicit operator float (Time t1) { ... }
```

3. You cannot overload the += operator. However, += is evaluated by using the + operator, which you can overload.

4. The **Equals** method should be an instance method rather than a class method. However, if you remove the **static** keyword, this method will hide the virtual method inherited from **Object** and not be invoked as expected, so the code should use **override** instead, as follows:

```
public override bool Equals(Object obj) { ... }
```

5. The **int** and **implicit** keywords have been transposed. The name of the operator should be **int**, and its type should be implicit, as follows:

```
public static implicit operator int(Time t1) { ... }
```

Note All the cases listed above will result in compile-time errors.

Lab 12.1: Defining Operators

Objectives

After completing this lab, you will be able to:

- Create operators for addition, subtraction, equality testing, multiplication, division, and casting.
- Override the **Equals**, **ToString**, and **GetHashCode** methods.

Prerequisites

Before working on this lab, you must be familiar with the following:

- Using inheritance in C#
- Defining constructors and destructors
- Compiling and using assemblies
- Basic C# operators

Estimated time to complete this lab: 30 minutes

Exercise 1
Defining Operators for the BankAccount Class

In previous labs, you created classes for a banking system. The **BankAccount** class holds customer bank account details, including the account number and balance. You also created a **Bank** class that acts as a factory for creating and managing **BankAccount** objects.

In this exercise, you will define the == and != operators in the **BankAccount** class. The default implementation of these operators, which is inherited from **Object**, tests to check whether the references are the same. You will redefine them to examine and compare the information in two accounts.

You will then override the **Equals** and **ToString** methods. The **Equals** method is used by many parts of the runtime and should exhibit the same behavior as the equality operators. Many classes in the .NET Framework use the **ToString** method when they need a string representation of an object. Use the starter file provided for this lab.

▶ **To define the == and != operators**

1. Open the Bank.sln project in the *install folder*\Labs\Lab12\Starter\Bank folder.

2. Add the following method to the **BankAccount** class:

   ```
   public static bool operator == (BankAccount acc1,
   BankAccount acc2)
   {
       ...
   }
   ```

3. In the body of **operator ==**, add statements to compare the two **BankAccount** objects. If the account number, type, and balance of both accounts are the same, return **true**; otherwise return **false**.

4. Compile the project. You will receive an error.

   (Why will you receive an error when you compile the project?)

5. Add the following method to the **BankAccount** class:

   ```
   public static bool operator != (BankAccount acc1,
   BankAccount acc2)
   {
       ...
   }
   ```

6. Add statements in the body of **operator !=** to compare the contents of the two **BankAccount** objects. If the account number, type, and balance of both accounts are the same, return **false**; otherwise return **true**. You can achieve this by calling **operator ==** and inverting the result.

7. Save and compile the project. The project should now compile successfully. The previous error was caused by having an unmatched **operator ==** method. (If you define **operator ==**, you must also define **operator !=**, and vice versa.)

The complete code for both of the operators is as follows:

```
public class BankAccount
{
    ...
    public static bool operator == (BankAccount acc1,
⇥BankAccount acc2)

    {
        if ((acc1.accNo == acc2.accNo) &&
            (acc1.accType == acc2.accType) &&
            (acc1.accBal == acc2.accBal)) {
            return true;
        } else {
            return false;
        }
    }

    public static bool operator != (BankAccount acc1,
⇥BankAccount acc2)

    {
        return !(acc1 == acc2);
    }
    ...
}
```

▶ **To test the operators**

1. Open the TestHarness.sln project in the *install folder*\Labs\Lab12\Starter\TestHarness folder.

2. Create a reference to the **Bank** component that you created in the previous labs. To do this:

   a. Expand the TestHarness project in Solution Explorer.

   b. Right-click **References**, and then click **Add Reference**.

   c. Click **Browse**, and navigate to the *install folder*\Labs\Lab12\Starter\Bank\bin\debug folder.

   d. Click **Bank.dll**, and then click **Open**.

   e. Click **OK**.

3. Create two **BankAccount** objects in the **Main** method of the **CreateAccount** class. To do this:

   a. Use **Bank.CreateAccount()**, and instantiate the **BankAccount** objects with the same balance and account type.

   b. Store the account numbers generated in two long variables called *accNo1* and *accNo2*.

4. Create two **BankAccount** variables called *acc1* and *acc2*. Populate them with the two accounts created in the previous step by calling **Bank.GetAccount()**.

5. Compare *acc1* and *acc2* by using the == operator. This test should return **false** because the two accounts will have different account numbers.

6. Compare *acc1* and *acc2* by using the != operator. This test should return **true**.

7. Create a third **BankAccount** variable called *acc3*. Populate it with the account that you used to populate *acc1* by calling **Bank.GetAccount()**, using *accNo1* as the parameter.

8. Compare *acc1* and *acc3* by using the == operator. This test should return **true**, because the two accounts will have the same data.

9. Compare *acc1* and *acc3* by using the != operator. This test should return **false**.

   If you have problems, a utility function called **Write** is available that you can use to display the contents of a **BankAccount** that is passed in as a parameter.

   Your completed code for the test harness should be as follows:

```
class CreateAccount
{
    static void Main( )
    {


        long accNo1 = Bank.CreateAccount(AccountType.Checking,
                                                   100);
        long accNo2 = Bank.CreateAccount(AccountType.Checking,
                                                   100);


            BankAccount acc1 = Bank.GetAccount(accNo1);
        BankAccount acc2 = Bank.GetAccount(accNo2);

        if (acc1 == acc2) {
            Console.WriteLine(
        ↪   "Both accounts are the same. They should not be!");
        } else {
            Console.WriteLine(
        ↪    "The accounts are different. Good!");
        }

        if (acc1 != acc2) {
            Console.WriteLine(
        ↪    "The accounts are different. Good!");
        } else {
            Console.WriteLine(
        ↪    "Both accounts are the same. They should not be!");
        }
```

```
Code continued on following page.
```

```
            BankAccount acc3 = Bank.GetAccount(accNo1);
            if (acc1 == acc3) {
                Console.WriteLine(
            ↪    "The accounts are the same. Good!");
            } else {
                Console.WriteLine(
            ↪    "The accounts are different. They should not be!");
            }

            if (acc1 != acc3) {
                Console.WriteLine(
            ↪    "The accounts are different. They should not be!");
            } else {
                Console.WriteLine(
            ↪    "The accounts are the same. Good!");
            }
        }
}
```

10. Compile and run the test harness.

▶ **To override the Equals, ToString, and GetHashCode methods**

1. Open the Bank.sln project in the *install folder*\Labs\Lab12\Starter\Bank
    folder.

2. Add the **Equals** method to the **BankAccount** class:

    ```
    public override bool Equals(object acc1)
    {
        ...
    }
    ```

    The **Equals** method should perform the same function as the == operator,
    except that it is an instance rather than a class method. Use the == operator
    to compare **this** to *acc1*.

3. Add the **ToString** method as follows:

    ```
    public override string ToString( )
    {
        ...
    }
    ```

    The body of the **ToString** method should return a string representation of
    the instance.

4. Add the **GetHashCode** method as follows:

    ```
    public override int GetHashCode( )
    {
        ...
    }
    ```

    The **GetHashCode** method should return a unique value for each different
    account, but different references to the same account should return the same
    value. The easiest solution is to return the account number. (You will need
    to cast it to an **int** first.)

5. The completed code for **Equals**, **ToString**, and **GetHashCode** is as follows:

```
public override bool Equals(Object acc1)
{
    return this == (BankAccount)acc1;
}

public override string ToString( )
{
    string retVal =  "Number: " + this.accNo + "\tType: ";
    retVal += (this.accType == AccountType.Checking) ?
↪"Checking" : "Deposit";
    retVal += "\tBalance: " + this.accBal;

    return retVal;
}

public override int GetHashCode( )
{
    return (int)this.accNo;
}
```

6. Save and compile the project. Correct any errors.

▶ **To test the Equals and ToString methods**

1. Open the TestHarness.sln project in the
   install folder\Labs\Lab12\Starter\TestHarness folder.

2. In the **Main** method of the **CreateAccount** class, replace the use of == and
   != with **Equals**, as follows:

```
if (acc1.Equals(acc2)) {
    ...
}

if (!acc1.Equals(acc2)) {
    ...
}
```

3. After the **if** statements, add three **WriteLine** statements that print the
   contents of *acc1*, *acc2*, and *acc3*, as shown in the following code. The
   WriteLine method uses **ToString** to format its arguments as strings.

```
Console.WriteLine("acc1 - {0}", acc1);
Console.WriteLine("acc2 - {0}", acc2);
Console.WriteLine("acc3 - {0}", acc3);
```

4. Call the **Dispose** method for each account object.

5. Compile and run the test harness. Check the results.

Exercise 2
Handling Rational Numbers

In this exercise, you will create an entirely new class for handling rational numbers. This is a brief respite from the world of banking.

A rational number is a number that can be written as a ratio of two integers. (Examples of rational numbers include ½, ¾, and -17.) You will create a **Rational** class, which will consist of a pair of private integer instance variables (called *dividend* and *divisor*) and operators for performing calculations and comparisons on them. The following operators and methods will be defined:

- Rational(**int** dividend)

  This is a constructor that sets the dividend to the supplied value and the divisor to 1.

- Rational(**int** dividend, **int** divisor)

  This is a constructor that sets the dividend and the divisor.

- == and !=

  These will perform comparisons based upon the calculated numeric value of the two operands (for example, `Rational(6, 8) == Rational(3, 4)`). You must override the **Equals( )** methods to perform the same comparison.

- <, >, <=, >=

  These will perform the appropriate relational comparisons between two rational numbers (for example, `Rational(6, 8) > Rational(1, 2)`).

- binary + and –

  These will add one rational number to or subtract one rational number from another.

- ++ and --

  These will increment and decrement the rational number.

▶ **To create the constructors and the ToString method**

1. Open the Rational.sln project in the *install folder*\Labs\Lab12\Starter\Rational folder.

2. The **Rational** class contains two private instance variables called *dividend* and *divisor*. They are initialized to 0 and 1, respectively. Add a constructor that takes a single integer and uses it to set *dividend*, leaving *divisor* with the value 1.

3. Add another constructor that takes two integers. The first is assigned to *dividend*, and the second is assigned to *divisor*. Check to ensure that *divisor* is not set to zero. Throw an exception if this occurs and raise **ArgumentOutOfRangeException**.

4. Create a third constructor that takes a *Rational* as a parameter and copies the values it contains.

Note C++ developers will recognize the third constructor as a copy constructor. You will use this constructor later in this lab.

The completed code for all three constructors is as follows:

```
public Rational(int dividend)
{
    this.dividend = dividend;
    this.divisor = 1;
}

public Rational(int dividend, int divisor)
{
    if (divisor == 0) {
        throw new ArgumentOutOfRangeException(
                            "Divisor cannot be zero");
    } else {
        this.dividend = dividend;
        this.divisor = divisor;
    }
}

public Rational(Rational r1)
{
    this.dividend = r1.dividend;
    this.divisor = r1.divisor;
}
```

5. Override the **ToString** method that returns a **string** version of the *Rational*, as follows:

```
public override string ToString( )
{
    return String.Format("{0}/{1}", dividend, divisor);
}
```

6. Compile the project and correct any errors.

▶ **To define the relational operators**

1. In the **Rational** class, create the == operator as follows:

```
public static bool operator == (Rational r1, Rational r2)
{
    ...
}
```

2. The == operator will:

   a. Establish the decimal value of *r1* by using the following formula.

   ```
   decimalValue1 = r1.dividend / r1.divisor
   ```

   b. Establish the decimal value of *r2* by using a similar formula.

   c. Compare the two decimal values and return **true** or **false**, as appropriate. The completed code is as follows:

   ```
   public static bool operator == (Rational r1, Rational
   r2)
   {
       decimal decimalValue1 =
                   (decimal)r1.dividend / r1.divisor;
       decimal decimalValue2 =
                   (decimal)r2.dividend / r2.divisor;
       return decimalValue1 == decimalValue2;
   }
   ```

Note   This code can be reduced to:

```
public static bool operator== (Rational r1, Rational r2)
{
    return (r1.dividend * r2.divisor ) == (r2.dividend *
r1.divisor);
}
```

Why are the decimal casts necessary when performing the division?

3. Create and define the != operator by using the == operator, as follows:

```
public static bool operator != (Rational r1, Rational r2)
{
    return !(r1 == r2);
}
```

4. Override the **Equals** method. Use the == operator, as follows:

```
public override bool Equals(Object r1)
{
    return (this == (Rational)r1);
}
```

5. Define the < operator. Use a strategy similar to that used for the ==
   operator, as follows:

```
public static bool operator < (Rational r1, Rational r2)
{
    return (r1.dividend * r2.divisor) < (r2.dividend *
➥r1.divisor);
}
```

6. Create the > operator, using == and <, as shown in the following code. Be
   sure that you understand the Boolean logic used by the expression in the
   return statement.

```
public static bool operator > (Rational r1, Rational r2)
{
    return !((r1 < r2) || (r1 == r2));
}
```

7. Define the <= and >= operators in terms of > and <, as shown in the
   following code:

```
public static bool operator <= (Rational r1, Rational r2)
{
    return !(r1 > r2);
}
```

```
public static bool operator >= (Rational r1, Rational r2)
{
    return !(r1 < r2);
}
```

8. Compile the project and correct any errors.

▶ **To test the constructors, the ToString method, and the relational
operators**

1. In the **Main** method of the **TestRational** class of the Rational project, create
   two **Rational** variables, *r1* and *r2*, and instantiate them with the value pairs
   (1,2) and (1,3), respectively.

2. Print them by using **WriteLine** to test the **ToString** method.

3. Perform the following comparisons, and print a message indicating the
   results:

   a. Is *r1* > *r2*?

   b. Is *r1* <= *r2*?

   c. Is *r1* != *r2*?

4. Compile and run the program. Check the results.

5. Change *r2* and instantiate it with the value pair (2,4).

6. Compile and run the program again. Check the results.

▶ **To create the binary additive operators**

1. In the **Rational** class, create the binary + operator. Create two versions for:

   a. Adding two **Rationals** together.

   Tip   To add two rational numbers together, you need to establish a common divisor. Unless both divisors are the same (if they are you can skip this step and the next), do this by multiplying the divisors together. For example, assume you want to add 1/4 to 2/3. The common divisor is 12 (4 * 3). The next step is to multiply the dividend of each number by the divisor of the other. Hence, 1/4 would become (1 * 3)/12, or 3/12, and 2/3 would become (4 * 2)/12, or 8/12. Finally, you add the two dividends together and use the common divisor. So 3/12 + 8/12 = 11/12, and hence 1/4 + 2/3 = 11/12. If you use this algorithm, you will need to make copies of the parameters passed in (using the copy constructor defined earlier) to the + operator. If you modify the formal parameters, you will find that the actual parameters will also be changed because of the way in which reference types are passed.

   ---

   b. Adding a rational number and an integer.

   Tip   To add an integer to a rational number, convert the integer to a rational number that has the same divisor. For example, to add 2 and 3/8, convert 2 into 16/8, and then perform the addition.

   Both versions should return a **Rational**. (Do not worry about producing a normalized result.)

2. Create the binary – operator. Create two versions, one each for:

    a. Subtracting one rational number from another.

    b. Subtracting an integer from a rational number.

    Both versions should return a **Rational** (non-normalized). The completed code for the + and – operators is as follows:

```
public static Rational operator + (Rational r1, Rational
r2)
{
    // Make working copies of r1 and r2
    Rational tempR1 = new Rational(r1);
    Rational tempR2 = new Rational(r2);

    // Determine a common divisor.
    // That is, to add 1/4 and 2/3, convert to 3/12 and 8/12
    int commonDivisor;
    if (tempR1.divisor != tempR2.divisor) {
        commonDivisor = tempR1.divisor * tempR2.divisor;

        // Multiply out the dividends of each rational
        tempR1.dividend *= tempR2.divisor;
        tempR2.dividend *= tempR1.divisor;
    } else {
        commonDivisor = tempR1.divisor;
    }

    // Create a new Rational.
    // For example, 1/4 + 2/3 = 3/12 + 8/12 = 11/12.

    Rational result = new Rational(tempR1.dividend +
                            tempR2.dividend, commonDivisor);
    return result;
}

public static Rational operator + (Rational r1, int i1)
{
    // Convert i1 into a Rational
    Rational r2 = new Rational(i1 * r1.divisor,
                                    r1.divisor);

    return r1 + r2;
}
```

Code continued on following page.

```
// Perform Rational addition
public static Rational operator - (Rational r1, Rational
r2)
{
   // Make working copies of r1 and r2
   Rational tempR1 = new Rational(r1);
   Rational tempR2 = new Rational(r2);

   // Determine a common divisor.
   // For example, to subtract 2/3 from 1/4,
   // convert to 8/12 and 3/12.
   int commonDivisor;
   if (tempR1.divisor != tempR2.divisor) {
      commonDivisor = tempR1.divisor * tempR2.divisor;

      // Multiply the dividends of each rational
      tempR1.dividend *= tempR2.divisor;
      tempR2.dividend *= tempR1.divisor;
   } else {
      commonDivisor = tempR1.divisor;
   }

   // Create a new Rational.
   // For example, 2/3 - 1/4 = 8/12 - 3/12 = 5/12.

   Rational result = new Rational(tempR1.dividend -
                          tempR2.dividend, commonDivisor);
   return result;
}

public static Rational operator - (Rational r1, int i1)
{
   // Convert i1 into a Rational
   Rational r2 = new Rational(i1 * r1.divisor, r1.divisor);

   // Perform Rational subtraction
   return r1 - r2;
}
```

▶ **To define the increment and decrement operators**

1. In the **Rational** class, create the unary ++ operator.

Tip Use the + operator that you defined earlier. Use it to add 1 to the parameter passed to the ++ operator.

---

2. In the **Rational** class, create the unary -- operator. The completed code for both operators is as follows:

```
public static Rational operator ++ (Rational r1)
{
    return r1 + 1;
}

public static Rational operator -- (Rational r1)
{
    return r1 - 1;
}
```

▶ **To test the additive operators**

1. In the **Main** method of the **TestRational** class, add statements to:

   a. Add *r2* to *r1* and print the result.

   b. Add 5 to *r2* (use +=) and print the result.

   c. Subtract *r1* from *r2* (use -=) and print the result.

   d. Subtract 2 from *r2* and print the result.

   e. Increment *r1* and print the result.

   f. Decrement *r2* and print the result.

2. Compile and run the program. Check the results.

If Time Permits
Creating Additional Rational Number Operators

In this exercise, you will create the following additional operators for the **Rational** class:

- Explicit and implicit casts

  These casts are for conversion between **Rational, float**, and **int** types.

- *, /, %

  These binary multiplicative operators are for multiplying, for dividing, and for extracting the remainder after integer division of two rational numbers.

▶ **To define the cast operators**

1. Define an explicit cast operator for converting a rational number to a floating-point number, as follows:

   ```
   public static explicit operator float (Rational r1)
   {
       ...
   }
   ```

2. In the body of the of the **float** cast operator, return the result of dividing *dividend* by *divisor*. Ensure that floating-point division is performed.

3. Create an explicit cast operator for converting a rational number to an integer, as follows:

   ```
   public static explicit operator int (Rational r1)
   {
       ...
   }
   ```

   Note   This operator is explicit because information loss is likely to occur.

4. In the body of the **int** cast operator, divide *dividend* by *divisor*. Ensure that floating-point division is performed. Truncate the result to an **int** and return it.

5. Create an implicit cast operator for converting an integer to a rational number, as follows:

   ```
   public static implicit operator Rational (int i1)
   {
       ...
   }
   ```

   Note   It is safe to make this operator implicit.

6. In the body of the **Rational** cast operator, create a new **Rational** with *dividend* set to *i1* and *divisor* set to 1. Return this **Rational**. The complete code for all three cast operators is as follows:

```
public static implicit operator float (Rational r1)
{
    float temp;
    temp = (float)r1.dividend / r1.divisor;
    return (int)temp;
}

public static explicit operator int (Rational r1)
{
    float temp;
    temp = (float)r1.dividend / r1.divisor;
    return (int) temp;
}

public static implicit operator Rational (int i1)
{
    Rational temp = new Rational(i1, 1);
    return temp;
}
```

7. Add statements to the test harness to test these operators.

▶ **To define the multiplicative operators**

1. Define the multiplication operator (*) to multiply two rational numbers, as follows:

```
public static Rational operator * (Rational r1, Rational r2)
{
    ...
}
```

Tip To multiply two rational numbers, you multiply the dividend and the divisor of both rational numbers together.

---

2. Define the division operator (/) to divide one rational number by another, as follows:

```
public static Rational operator / (Rational r1, Rational
r2)
{
    ...
}
```

Tip To divide **Rational** *r1* by **Rational** *r2*, multiply *r1* by the reciprocal of *r2*. In other words, exchange the *dividend* and *divisor* of *r2*, and then perform multiplication. (1/3 / 2/5 is the same as 1/3 * 5/2.)

---

3. Define the modulus operator (%). (The modulus is the remainder after division.) It returns the remainder after dividing by an integer:

```
public static Rational operator % (Rational r1, int i1)
{
   ...
}
```

Tip   Convert *r1* to an **int** called *temp*, and determine the difference between *r1* and *temp*, storing the result in a **Rational** called *diff*. Perform *temp* % *i1*, and store the result in an **int** called *remainder*. Add *diff* and *remainder* together.

The completed code for the operators is as follows:

```
public static Rational operator * (Rational r1, Rational r2)
{
   int dividend = r1.dividend * r2.dividend;
   int divisor = r1.divisor * r2.divisor;
   Rational temp = new Rational(dividend, divisor);
   return temp;
}

public static Rational operator / (Rational r1, Rational r2)
{
   // Create the reciprocal of r2, and then multiply
   Rational temp = new Rational(r2.divisor, r2.dividend);
   return r1 * temp;
}

public static Rational operator % (Rational r1, int i1)
{
   // Convert r1 to an int
   int temp = (int)r1;

   // Compute the rounding difference between temp and r1
   Rational diff = r1 - temp;

   // Perform % on temp and i1
   int remainder = temp % i1;

   // Add remainder and diff together to get the
   // complete result
   diff += remainder;
   return diff;
}
```

4. Add statements to the test harness to test these operators.

◆ Creating and Using Delegates

- ■ **Scenario: Power Station**
- ■ **Analyzing the Problem**
- ■ **Creating Delegates**
- ■ **Using Delegates**

Delegates allow you to write code that can dynamically change the methods that it calls. This is a flexible feature that allows a method to vary independently of the code that invokes it.

After completing this lesson, you will be able to:

- ■ Analyze a scenario for which delegates prove useful.
- ■ Define and use delegates.

Scenario: Power Station

- ■ **The problem**
  - How to respond to temperature events in a power station
  - Specifically, if the temperature of the reactor core rises above a certain temperature, coolant pumps need to be alerted and switched on
- ■ **Possible solutions**
  - Should all coolant pumps monitor the core temperature?
  - Should a component that monitors the core turn on the appropriate pumps when the temperature changes?

To understand how to use delegates, consider a power station example for which using a delegate is a good solution.

The Problem

In a power station, the temperature of the nuclear reactor must be kept below a critical temperature. Probes inside the core constantly monitor the temperature. If the temperature rises significantly, various pumps need to be started to increase the flow of coolant throughout the core. The software controlling the working of the nuclear reactor must start the appropriate pumps at the appropriate time.

Possible Solutions

The controlling software could be designed in many ways that would meet these criteria, two of which are listed below:

- ■ The software driving the coolant pumps could constantly measure the temperature of the nuclear core and increase the flow of coolant as the temperature requires.

- ■ The component monitoring the core temperature could start the appropriate coolant pumps every time the temperature changes.

Both of these techniques have drawbacks. In the first technique, the frequency with which the temperature must be measured needs to be determined. Measuring too frequently could affect the operation of the pumps because the software has to drive the pumps as well as monitor the core temperature. Measuring infrequently could mean that a very rapid rise in temperature could be missed until it is too late.

In the second technique, there may be many dozens of pumps and controllers that need to be alerted about each temperature change. The programming required to achieve this could be complex and difficult to maintain, especially if there are different types of pumps in the system that need to be alerted in different ways.

Analyzing the Problem

■ **Existing concerns**

 ● There may be several types of pumps, supplied by different manufacturers

 ● Each pump could have its own method for activation

■ **Future concerns**

 ● To add a new pump, the entire code will need to change

 ● A high overhead cost will result with every such addition

■ **A solution**

 ● Use delegates in your code

To start solving the problem, consider the dynamics involved in implementing a solution in the power station scenario.

Existing Concerns

The major issue is that there could be several different types of pumps supplied by different manufacturers, each with its own controlling software. The component monitoring the core temperature will have to recognize, for each type of pump, which method to call to turn the pump on.

For this example, suppose that there are two types of pumps: electric and pneumatic. Each type of pump has its own software driver that contains a method to switch the pump on, as follows:

```
public class ElectricPumpDriver
{
  ...
  public void StartElectricPumpRunning( )
  {
  ...
  }
}

public class PneumaticPumpDriver
{
  ...
  public void SwitchOn( )
  {
    ...
  }
}
```

The component monitoring the core temperature will switch the pumps on. The following code shows the main part of this component, the **CoreTempMonitor** class. It creates a number of pumps and stores them in an **ArrayList**, a collection class that implements a variable-length array. The **SwitchOnAllPumps** method iterates through the **ArrayList**, determines the type of pump, and calls the appropriate method to turn the pump on:

```
public class CoreTempMonitor
{
  public void Add(object pump)
  {
    pumps.Add(pump);
  }

  public void SwitchOnAllPumps()
  {
    foreach (object pump in pumps) {
      if (pump is ElectricPumpDriver) {
       ((ElectricPumpDriver)pump).StartElectricPumpRunning();
      }
      if (pump is PneumaticPumpDriver) {
       ((PneumaticPumpDriver)pump).SwitchOn();
      }
      ...
    }
  }
  ...
  private ArrayList pumps = new ArrayList();
}

public class ExampleOfUse
{
  public static void Main( )
  {
    CoreTempMonitor ctm = new CoreTempMonitor();

    ElectricPumpDriver ed1 = new ElectricPumpDriver();
    ctm.Add(ed1);

    PneumaticPumpDriver pd1 = new PneumaticPumpDriver();
    ctm.Add(pd1);

    ctm.SwitchOnAllPumps();
  }
}
```

Future Concerns

Using the structure as described has a serious drawback. If a new type of pump is installed later, you will need to change the **SwitchOnAllPumps** method to incorporate the new pump. This would also mean that the entire code would need to be thoroughly retested, with all the associated downtime and costs, since this is a crucial piece of software.

A Solution

To solve this problem, you can use a mechanism referred to as a *delegate*. The **SwitchOnAllPumps** method can use the delegate to call the appropriate method to turn on a pump without needing to determine the type of pump.

Creating Delegates

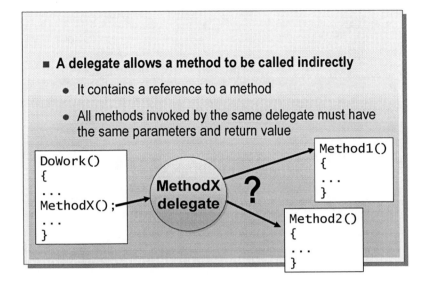

- **A delegate allows a method to be called indirectly**
  - It contains a reference to a method
  - All methods invoked by the same delegate must have the same parameters and return value

```
DoWork()
{
...
MethodX();
...
}
```

MethodX delegate ?

```
Method1()
{
...
}
```

```
Method2()
{
...
}
```

A delegate contains a reference to a method rather than the method name. By using delegates, you can invoke a method without knowing its name. Calling the delegate will actually execute the method referenced by the delegate.

In the power station example, rather than use an **ArrayList** to hold pump objects, you can use it to hold delegates that refer to the methods required to start each pump.

A delegate is a similar to an interface. It specifies a contract between a caller and an implementer. A delegate associates a name with the specification of a method. An implementation of the method can be attached to this name, and a component can call the method by using this name. The primary requirement of the implementing methods is that they must all have the same signature and return the same type of parameters. In the case of the power station scenario, the **StartElectricPumpRunning** and **SwitchOn** methods are both **void**, and neither takes any parameters.

To use a delegate, you must first define it and then instantiate it.

Defining Delegates

A delegate specifies the return type and parameters that each method must provide. You use the following syntax to define a delegate:

```
public delegate void StartPumpCallback( );
```

Note that the syntax for defining a delegate is similar to the syntax for defining a method. In this example, you define the delegate **StartPumpCallback** as being for a method that returns no value (**void**) and takes no parameters. This matches the specifications of the methods **StartElectricPumpRunning** and **SwitchOn** in the two pump driver classes.

Instantiating Delegates

After you define a delegate, you must instantiate it and make it refer to a method. To instantiate a delegate, use the delegate constructor and supply the object method it should invoke when it is called. In the following example, an **ElectricPumpDriver**, **ed1**, is created, and then a delegate, **callback**, is instantiated, referencing the **StartElectricPumpRunning** method of **ed1**:

```
public delegate void StartPumpCallback( );

void Example()
{
    ElectricPumpDriver ed1 = new ElectricPumpDriver( );

    StartPumpCallback callback;
    callback =
      ↪new StartPumpCallback(ed1.StartElectricPumpRunning);
    ...
}
```

Using Delegates

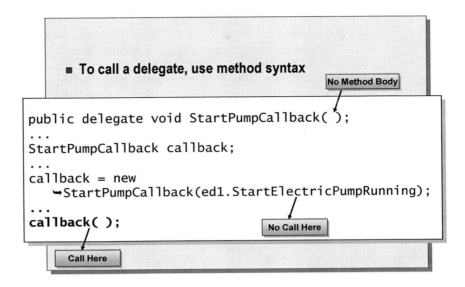

A delegate is a variable that invokes a method. You call it in the same way you would call a method, except that the delegate replaces the method name.

Example

The following code shows how to define, create, and call delegates for use by the power station. It populates an **ArrayList** named *callbacks* with instances of delegates that refer to the methods used to start each pump. The **SwitchOnAllPumps** method iterates through this **ArrayList** and calls each delegate in turn. With delegates, the method need not perform type checking and is much simpler than the previous solution.

```
public delegate void StartPumpCallback( );

public class CoreTempMonitor2
{
    public void Add(StartPumpCallback callback)
    {
        callbacks.Add(callback);
    }

    public void SwitchOnAllPumps( )
    {
        foreach(StartPumpCallback callback in callbacks)
        {
            callback( );
        }
    }

    private ArrayList callbacks = new ArrayList( );
}

class ExampleOfUse
{
    public static void Main( )
    {
        CoreTempMonitor2 ctm = new CoreTempMonitor2( );

        ElectricPumpDriver ed1 = new ElectricPumpDriver( );
        ctm.Add(
          new StartPumpCallback(ed1.StartElectricPumpRunning)
        );

        PneumaticPumpDriver pd1 = new PneumaticPumpDriver( );
        ctm.Add(
          new StartPumpCallback(pd1.SwitchOn)
        );

        ctm.SwitchOnAllPumps( );
    }
}
```

◆ Defining and Using Events

- ■ **How Events Work**
- ■ **Defining Events**
- ■ **Passing Event Parameters**
- ■ **Demonstration: Handling Events**

In the power station example, you learned how to use a delegate to solve the problem of how to start different types of pumps in a generic manner. However, the component that monitors the temperature of the reactor core is still responsible for notifying each of the pumps in turn that they need to start. You can address the issue of notification by using events.

Events allow an object to notify other objects that a change has occurred. The other objects can register an interest in an event, and they will be notified when the event occurs.

After completing this lesson, you will be able to:

- ■ Define events.
- ■ Handle events.

How Events Work

- **Publisher**
  - Raises an event to alert all interested objects (subscribers)
- **Subscriber**
  - Provides a method to be called when the event is raised

Events allow objects to *register an interest* in changes to other objects. In other words, events allow objects to register that they need to be notified about changes to other objects. Events use the publisher and subscriber model.

Publisher

A publisher is an object that maintains its internal state. However, when its state changes, it can raise an event to alert other interested objects about the change.

Subscriber

A subscriber is an object that registers an interest in an event. It is alerted when a publisher raises the event. An event can have zero or more subscribers.

Events can be quite complex. To make them easier to understand and maintain, there are guidelines that you should follow when using them.

Defining Events

- **Defining an event**

```
public delegate void StartPumpCallback( );
private event StartPumpCallback CoreOverheating;
```

- **Subscribing to an event**

```
PneumaticPumpDriver pd1 = new PneumaticPumpDriver( );
...
CoreOverheating += new StartPumpCallback(pd1.SwitchOn);
```

- **Notifying subscribers to an event**

```
public void SwitchOnAllPumps( ) {
  if (CoreOverheating != null) {
      CoreOverheating( );
  }
}
```

Events in C# use delegates to call methods in subscribing objects. They are multicast. This means that when a publisher raises an event, it may result in many delegates being called. However, you cannot rely on the order in which the delegates are invoked. If one of the delegates throws an exception, it could halt the event processing altogether, resulting in the other delegates not being called at all.

Defining an Event

To define an event, a publisher first defines a delegate and bases the event on it. The following code defines a delegate named **StartPumpCallback** and an event named **CoreOverheating** that invokes the **StartPumpCallback** delegate when it is raised:

```
public delegate void StartPumpCallback( );
private event StartPumpCallback CoreOverheating;
```

Subscribing to an Event

Subscribing objects specify a method to be called when the event is raised. If the event has not yet been instantiated, subscribing objects specify a delegate that refers to the method when creating the event. If the event exists, subscribing objects add a delegate that calls a method when the event is raised.

For example, in the power station scenario, you could create two pump drivers and have them both subscribe to the **CoreOverheating** event:

```
ElectricPumpDriver ed1 = new ElectricPumpDriver( );
PneumaticPumpDriver pd1 = new PneumaticPumpDriver( );
...
CoreOverheating = new StartPumpCallback(
↪ed1.StartElectricPumpRunning);
CoreOverheating += new StartPumpCallback(pd1.SwitchOn);
```

Note   You must declare delegates (and methods) that are used to subscribe to an event as **void**. This restriction does not apply when a delegate is used without an event.

Notifying Subscribers to an Event

To notify the subscribers, you must *raise* the event. The syntax you use is the same as that for calling a method or a delegate. In the power station example, the **SwitchOnAllPumps** method of the core-temperature monitoring component no longer needs to iterate through a list of delegates:

```
public void SwitchOnAllPumps( )
{
  if (CoreOverheating != null) {
     CoreOverheating( );
  }
}
```

Executing the event in this way will cause all of the delegates to be invoked, and, in this example, all of the pumps that subscribe to the event will be activated. Notice that the code first checks that the event has at least one subscribing delegate. Without this check, the code would throw an exception if there were no subscribers.

For information about guidelines and best practices to follow when using events, search for "event guidelines" in the .NET Framework SDK Help documents.

Passing Event Parameters

- **Parameters for events should be passed as EventArgs**
  - Define a class descended from EventArgs to act as a container for event parameters
- **The same subscribing method may be called by several events**
  - Always pass the event publisher (sender) as the first parameter to the method

Event Parameter Guidelines

To pass parameters to a subscribing method, enclose the parameters in a single class that supplies accessor methods to retrieve them. Derive this class from **System.EventArgs**.

For example, in the power station scenario, assume that the methods that start the pumps, **StartElectricPumpRunning** and **SwitchOn**, need the current core temperature to determine the speed at which the pumps should run. To address this issue, you create the following class to pass the core temperature from the core-monitoring component to the pump objects:

```
public class CoreOverheatingEventArgs: EventArgs
{
    private readonly int temperature;

    public CoreOverheatingEventArgs(int temperature)
    {
        this.temperature = temperature;
    }

    public int GetTemperature( )
    {
        return temperature;
    }
}
```

The **CoreOverheatingEventArgs** class contains an integer parameter. The constructor stores the temperature internally, and you use the method **GetTemperature** to retrieve it.

The sender Object

An object may subscribe to more than one event from different publishers and could use the same method in each case. Therefore, it is customary for an event to pass information about the publisher that raised it to the subscribers. By convention, this is the first parameter passed to the subscribing method, and it is usually called *sender*. The following code shows the new versions of the **StartElectricPumpRunning** and **SwitchOn** methods, modified to expect *sender* as the first parameter and the temperature as the second parameter:

```
public class ElectricPumpDriver
{
  ...

  public void StartElectricPumpRunning(object sender,
➥CoreOverheatingEventArgs args)
  {
      // Examine the temperature
      int currentTemperature = args.GetTemperature( );

      // Start the pump at the required speed for
      // this temperature
      ...
  }
  ...
}


public class PneumaticPumpDriver
{
  ...

  public void SwitchOn(object sender,
➥CoreOverheatingEventArgs args)
  {
      // Examine the temperature
      int currentTemperature = args.GetTemperature( );

      // Start the pump at the required speed for
      // this temperature
      ...
  }
  ...
}
```

Note You will also need to modify the delegate in the core-temperature monitoring component. In the power station example, the delegate will become:

```
public delegate void StartPumpCallback(object sender,
➥CoreOverheatingEventArgs args);
```

Demonstration: Handling Events

In this demonstration, you will see an example of how you can use events to communicate information between objects.

Lab 12.2: Defining and Using Events

Objectives

After completing this lab, you will be able to:

- Publish events.
- Subscribe to events.
- Pass parameters to events.

Prerequisites

Before working on this lab, you must be familiar with the following:

- Creating classes in C#
- Defining constructors and destructors
- Compiling and using assemblies

Estimated time to complete this lab: 30 minutes

Exercise 1
Auditing Bank Transactions

This exercise extends the bank example used in earlier labs. In this exercise, you will create a class called **Audit**. The purpose of this class is to record the changes made to account balances in a text file. The account will be notified of changes by an event published by the **BankAccount** class.

You will use the **Deposit** and **Withdraw** methods of the **BankAccount** class to raise the event, called **Auditing**, which is subscribed to by an **Audit** object.

The **Auditing** event will take a parameter containing a **BankTransaction** object. If you completed the earlier labs, you will recall that the **BankTransaction** class contains the details of a transaction, such as the amount of the transaction, the date it was created, and so on. A **BankTransaction** object is created whenever a deposit or withdrawal is made by using a **BankAccount**.

You will make full use of the event-handling guidelines discussed in the module.

▶ **To define the event parameter class**

In this exercise, the event that will be raised will be passed a **BankTransaction** object as a parameter. Event parameters should be derived from **System.EventArgs**, so a new class will be created that contains a **BankTransaction**.

1. Open the Audit.sln project in the *install folder*\Labs\Lab12\Starter\Audit folder.

2. Create a new class by using **Add New Item** on the **Project** menu. Make sure that you create a **New C# Class**, and name it **AuditEventArgs.cs**.

3. Change the namespace to **Banking**.

4. Change the definition of **AuditEventArgs** so that it is derived from **System.EventArgs**, as follows:

```
public class AuditEventArgs : System.EventArgs
{
    ...
}
```

5. Create a private readonly **BankTransaction** variable called *transData*, and initialize it to **null**, as follows:

```
private readonly BankTransaction transData = null;
```

6. Modify the default constructor to take a single **BankTransaction** parameter called *transaction* and set **this.transData** to this parameter. The code for the constructor is as follows:

```
public AuditEventArgs(BankTransaction transaction)
{
    this.transData = transaction;
}
```

7. Provide a public accessor method called **getTransaction** that returns the value of **this.transData**, as follows:

```
public BankTransaction getTransaction( )
{
    return this.transData;
}
```

8. Compile the project and correct any errors.

▶ **To define the Audit class**

1. In the **Audit** project, create a new class by using **Add New Item** from the **Project** menu. Make sure that you create a **New C# Class**, and name it **Audit.cs**. This is the class that will subscribe to the **Auditing** event and write details of transactions to a file on disk.

2. When the class has been created, add a comment that summarizes the purpose of the **Audit** class. Use the exercise description to help you.

3. Change the namespace to **Banking**.

4. Add a **using** directive that refers to **System.IO**.

5. Add a private **string** variable called *filename* to the **Audit** class.

6. Add a private **StreamWriter** variable called *auditFile* to the **Audit** class.

Note   A **StreamWriter** allows you to write data to a file. You used **StreamReader** for reading from a file in Lab 6. In this exercise, you will use the **AppendText** method of the **StreamWriter** class.

The **AppendText** method opens a named file to append text to that file. It writes data to the end of the file. You use the **WriteLine** method to actually write data to the file once it is open (just like the **Console** class).

---

7. Modify the default constructor in the **Audit** class to take a single string parameter called *fileToUse*. In the constructor:

   • Set **this.filename** to *fileToUse*.

   • Open this named file in AppendText mode and store the file descriptor in *auditFile*.

   The completed code for the constructor is as follows:

```
private string filename;
private StreamWriter auditFile;

public Audit(string fileToUse)
{
    this.filename = fileToUse;
    this.auditFile = File.AppendText(fileToUse);
}
```

8. In the **Audit** class, add the method that will be used to subscribe to the **Auditing** event of the **BankTransaction** class. It will be executed when a **BankTransaction** object raises the event. This method should be public **void** and called **RecordTransaction**. It will take two parameters: an **object** called *sender*, and an **AuditEventArgs** parameter called *eventData*.

9. In the **RecordTransaction** method, add code to:

- Create a **BankTransaction** variable called *tempTrans*.

- Execute **eventData.getTransaction( )** and assign the result to *tempTrans*.

- If *tempTrans* is not **null**, use the **WriteLine** method of **this.auditFile** to append the amount of *tempTrans* (use the **Amount( )** method) and the date created (use the **When( )** method) to the end of the audit file. Do not close the file.

Note The *sender* parameter is not used by this method, but by convention all event-handling methods expect the sender of the event as the first parameter.

The completed code for this method is as follows:

```
public void RecordTransaction(object sender,
                              AuditEventArgs eventData)
{
   BankTransaction tempTrans = eventData.getTransaction( );
   if (tempTrans != null)
      this.auditFile.WriteLine("Amount: {0}\tDate: {1}",
            tempTrans.Amount( ), tempTrans.When( ));
}
```

10. Add a private bool variable named **closed** to the Audit class and initialize it to false.

11. In the **Audit** class, create a public **void Close** method that closes **this.auditFile**. The code for the Close method is as follows:

```
public void Close()
{
   if (!closed)
   {
   this.auditFile.Close();
   closed = true;
   }
}
```

12. Compile the project and correct any errors.

▶ **To test the Audit class**

1. Open the AuditTestHarness.sln project in the
   install folder\Labs\Lab12\Starter\AuditTestHarness folder.

2. Perform the following steps to add a reference to the library containing your
   compiled **Audit** class. It will be in a dynamic-link library (DLL) called
   Audit.dll in *install folder*\Labs\Lab12\Starter\Audit\bin\Debug.

   a. In Solution Explorer, expand the **AuditTestHarness** project tree.

   b. Right-click **References**.

   c. Click **Add Reference**.

   d. Click **Browse**.

   e. Navigate to *install folder*\Labs\Lab12\Starter\Audit\bin\Debug.

   f. Click **Audit.dll**.

   g. Click **Open**, and then click **OK**.

3. In the **Test** class, review the **Main** method. This class:

   a. Creates an instance of the **Audit** class, using the name AuditTrail.dat for
      the file name in which it stores the audit information.

   b. Creates a new **BankTransaction** object for an amount of 500 dollars.

   c. Creates an **AuditEventArgs** object that uses the **BankTransaction**
      object.

   d. Invokes the **RecordTransaction** method of the **Audit** object.

   The test is repeated with a second transaction for –200 dollars.

   After the second test, the **Close** method is called to ensure that audit records
   are stored on the disk.

4. Compile the project.

5. Open a Command window and navigate to the folder
   install folder\Labs\Lab12\Starter\AuditTestHarness\bin\Debug. This folder
   will contain the AuditTestHarness.exe and Audit.dll files. It will also
   contain the files AuditTestHarness.pdb and Audit.pdb, which you can
   ignore.

6. Execute **AuditTestHarness**.

7. Using a text editor of your choice (for example, WordPad), navigate to the
   folder *install folder*\Labs\Lab12\Starter\AuditTestHarness\bin\Debug and
   examine the contents of the file AuditTrail.dat. It should contain the data for
   the two transactions.

▶ **To define the Auditing event**

1. Open the Audit.sln project in the *install folder*\Labs\Lab12\Starter\Audit folder.

2. In the BankAccount.cs file, above the **BankAccount** class, declare a public delegate of type **void** that is called **AuditEventHandler** and takes two parameters—an **Object** called *sender* and an **AuditEventArgs** called *data*—as shown:

```
public delegate void AuditEventHandler(Object sender,
↪AuditEventArgs data);
```

3. In the **BankAccount** class, declare a private event of type **AuditEventHandler** called **AuditingTransaction**, and initialize it to **null**, as follows:

```
  private event AuditEventHandler AuditingTransaction =
↪null;
```

4. Add a public **void** method called **AddOnAuditingTransaction**. This method will take a single **AuditEventHandler** parameter called *handler*. The purpose of the method is to add *handler* to the list of delegates that subscribe to the **AuditingTransaction** event. The method will look as follows:

```
public void AddOnAuditingTransaction(AuditEventHandler
↪handler)
{
    this.AuditingTransaction += handler;
}
```

5. Add another public **void** method called **RemoveOnAuditingTransaction**. This method will also take a single **AuditEventHandler** parameter called *handler*. The purpose of this method is to remove *handler* from the list of delegates that subscribe to the **AuditingTransaction** event. The method will look as follows:

```
public void RemoveOnAuditingTransaction(AuditEventHandler
↪handler)
{
    this.AuditingTransaction -= handler;
}
```

6. Add a third method that the **BankAccount** object will use to raise the event and alert all subscribers. The method should be protected **void** and should be called **OnAuditingTransaction**. This method will take a **BankTransaction** parameter called *bankTrans*. The method will examine the event **this.AuditingTransaction**. If it contains any delegates, it will create an **AuditEventArgs** object called *auditTrans*, which will be constructed by using *bankTrans*. It will then cause the delegates to be executed, passing itself in as the sender of the event along with the *auditTrans* parameter as the data. The code for this method will look as follows:

```
protected void OnAuditingTransaction(BankTransaction
bankTrans)
{
    if (this.AuditingTransaction != null) {
        AuditEventArgs auditTrans = new
                        AuditEventArgs(bankTrans);
        this.AuditingTransaction(this, auditTrans);
    }
}
```

7. In the **Withdraw** method of **BankAccount**, add a statement that will call **OnAuditingTransaction**. Pass in the transaction object created by the **Withdraw** method. This statement should be placed just prior to the return statement at the end of the method. The completed code for **Withdraw** is as follows:

```
public bool Withdraw(decimal amount)
{
    bool sufficientFunds = accBal >= amount;
    if (sufficientFunds) {
        accBal -= amount;
        BankTransaction tran =
    ↪new BankTransaction(-amount);
        tranQueue.Enqueue(tran);
        this.OnAuditingTransaction(tran);
    }
    return sufficientFunds;
}
```

8. Add a similar statement to the **Deposit** method. The completed code for **Deposit** is as follows:

```
public decimal Deposit(decimal amount)
{
    accBal += amount;
    BankTransaction tran = new BankTransaction(amount);
    tranQueue.Enqueue(tran);
    this.OnAuditingTransaction(tran);
    return accBal;
}
```

9. Compile the project and correct any errors.

▶ **To subscribe to the Auditing event**

1. The final stage is to create the **Audit** object that will subscribe to the **Auditing** event. This **Audit** object will be part of the **BankAccount** class, and will be created when the **BankAccount** is instantiated, so that each account will get its own audit trail.

   Define a private **Audit** variable called *accountAudit* in the **BankAccount** class, as follows:

   ```
   private Audit accountAudit;
   ```

2. Add a public **void** method to **BankAccount** called **AuditTrail**. This method will create an **Audit** object and subscribe to the **Auditing** event. It will take a **string** parameter, which will be the name of a file to use for the audit trail. The method will:

   - Instantiate *accountAudit* by using this **string**.

   - Create an **AuditEventHandler** variable called *doAuditing* and instantiate it by using the **RecordTransaction** method of *accountAudit*.

   - Add *doAuditing* to the list of subscribers to the **Auditing** event. Use the **AddOnAuditingTransaction** method, passing *doAuditing* as the parameter.

   The completed code for this method is as follows:

   ```
   public void AuditTrail(string auditFileName)
   {
       this.accountAudit = new Audit(auditFileName);
       AuditEventHandler doAuditing = new
   ↪AuditEventHandler(this.accountAudit.RecordTransaction);
       this.AddOnAuditingTransaction(doAuditing);
   }
   ```

3. In the destructor for the **BankAccount** class, add a statement that invokes the **Dispose** method. (This is to ensure that all audit records are correctly written to disk.)

4. In the Dispose method of the **BankAccount** class add the following line of code inside the if statement:

   ```
   accountAudit.Close();
   ```

5. Compile the project and correct any errors.

▶ **To test the Auditing event**

1. Open the EventTestHarness.sln project in the
   install folder\Labs\Lab12\Starter\EventTestHarness folder.

2. Perform the following steps to add a reference to the DLL Audit.dll)
   containing your compiled **Audit** and **BankAccount** classes. The Audit.dll is
   located in *install folder*\Labs\Lab12\Starter\Audit\bin\Debug.

   a. In Solution Explorer, expand the **EventTestHarness** project tree.

   b. Right-click **References**.

   c. Click **Add Reference**.

   d. Click **Browse**.

   e. Navigate to *install folder*\Labs\Lab12\Starter\Audit\bin\Debug.

   f. Click **Audit.dll**.

   g. Click **Open**, and then click **OK**.

3. In the **Test** class, review the **Main** method. This class:

   a. Creates two bank accounts.

   b. Uses the **AuditTrail** method to cause the embedded **Audit** objects in
      each account to be created and to subscribe to the **Auditing** event.

   c. Performs a number of deposits and withdrawals on each account.

   d. Closes both accounts.

4. Compile the project and correct any errors.

5. Open a Command window and navigate to the
   install folder\Labs\Lab12\Starter\EventTestHarness\bin\Debug folder. This
   folder will contain the EventTestHarness.exe and Audit.dll files. It will also
   contain the files EventTestHarness.pdb and Audit.pdb, which you can
   ignore.

6. Execute EventTestHarness.

7. Using a text editor of your choice, examine the contents of the Account1.dat
   and Account2.dat files. They should contain the data for the transactions
   performed on the two accounts.

Review

■ **Introduction to Operators**

■ **Operator Overloading**

■ **Creating and Using Delegates**

■ **Defining and Using Events**

1. Can the arithmetic compound assignment operators (+=, -=, *=, /=, and %=) be overloaded?

2. Under what circumstances should a conversion operator be explicit?

3. How are explicit conversion operators invoked?

4. What is a delegate?

5. How do you subscribe to an event?

6. In what order are the methods that subscribe to an event called? Will all methods that subscribe to an event always be executed?

Course Evaluation

Your evaluation of this course will help Microsoft understand the quality of your learning experience.

At a convenient time between now and the end of the course, please complete a course evaluation, which is available at http://www.metricsthatmatter.com/survey.

Microsoft will keep your evaluation strictly confidential and will use your responses to improve your future learning experience.

msdn training

Module 13: Properties and Indexers

Contents

Overview	1
Using Properties	2
Using Indexers	17
Lab 13.1: Using Properties and Indexers	33
Review	42

Overview

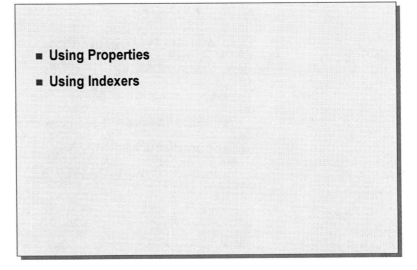

■ **Using Properties**

■ **Using Indexers**

You can expose the named attributes for a class by using either fields or properties. Fields are implemented as member variables with private access. In C#, properties appear to be fields to the user of a class, but they use methods to get and set values.

C# provides an indexer feature that allows objects to be indexed in the same way as an array.

In this module, you will learn how to use properties and indexers. You will learn how to use properties to enable field-like access and indexers to enable array-like access.

After completing this module, you will be able to:

■ Create properties to encapsulate data within a class.

■ Define indexers to gain access to classes by using array-like notation.

◆ Using Properties

- **Why Use Properties?**
- **Using Accessors**
- **Comparing Properties to Fields**
- **Comparing Properties to Methods**
- **Property Types**
- **Property Example**

After completing this lesson, you will be able to:

- Use properties to encapsulate data in a class.
- Use properties to access data in a class.

Why Use Properties?

- ■ **Properties provide:**
  - A useful way to encapsulate information inside a class
  - Concise syntax
  - Flexibility

Properties provide a useful way to encapsulate data within a class. Examples of properties include the length of a string, the size of a font, the caption of a window, the name of a customer, and so on.

Concise Syntax

C# adds properties as first-class elements of the language. Many existing languages, such as Microsoft® Visual Basic®, already have properties as first-class elements of the language. If you think of a property as a field, it can help you to focus on the application logic. Compare, for example, the following two statements. The first statement does not use properties, whereas and the second does use properties.

```
o.SetValue(o.GetValue( ) + 1);

o.Value++;
```

The statement that uses a property is certainly easier to understand and much less error prone.

Flexibility

To read or write the value of a property, you use field-like syntax. (In particular, you do not use parentheses.) However, the compiler translates this field-like syntax into encapsulated method-like **get** and **set** accessors. For example, **Value** could be a property of the object **o** in the expression **o.Value**, which will cause the statements inside the **get** accessor "method" for the **Value** property to be executed. This separation allows the statements inside the **get** and **set** accessors of a property to be modified without affecting the use of the property, which retains its field-like syntax. Because of this flexibility, you should use properties instead of fields whenever possible.

When you expose state through a property, your code is potentially less efficient than when you expose state directly through a field. However, when a property contains only a small amount of code and is non-virtual (which is frequently the case), the execution environment can replace calls to an accessor with the actual code of the accessor. This process is known as *inlining*, and it makes property access as efficient as field access, yet it preserves the increased flexibility of properties.

Using Accessors

> ■ **Properties provide field-like access**
>
>   ● Use **get** accessor statements to provide read access
>
>   ● Use **set** accessor statements to provide write access

```
class Button
{
    public string Caption // Property
    {
        get { return caption; }
        set { caption = value; }
    }
    private string caption; // Field
}
```

A property is a class member that provides access to a field of an object. You use a property to associate actions with the reading and writing of an object's attribute. A property declaration consists of a type and a name and has either one or two pieces of code referred to as accessors. These accessors are as follows:

■ **get** accessor

■ **set** accessor

Accessors have no parameters. A property does not need to have both a **get** accessor and a **set** accessor. For example, a read-only property will provide only a **get** accessor. You will learn more about read-only properties later in this section.

Using the get Accessor

The **get** accessor of a property returns the value of the property. The following code provides an example:

```
public string Caption
{
    get { return caption; }
    ...
}
```

You implicitly call a property's **get** accessor when you use that property in a read context. The following code provides an example:

```
Button myButton;
...
string cap = myButton.Caption; // Calls "myButton.Caption.get"
```

Notice that you do not use parentheses after the property name. In this example, the statement `return caption;` returns a string. This string is returned whenever the value of the **Caption** property is read.

Reading a property should not change the object's data. When you invoke a **get** accessor, it is conceptually equivalent to reading the value of a field. A **get** accessor should not have observable side effects.

Using the set Accessor

The **set** accessor of a property modifies the value of a property.

```
public string Caption
{
    ...
    set { caption = value; }
}
```

You implicitly call a property's **set** accessor when you use that property in a write context—that is, when you use it in an assignment. The following code provides an example:

```
Button myButton;
...
myButton.Caption = "OK"; // Calls "myButton.Caption.set"
```

Notice again that you do not use parentheses. The variable *value* contains the value that you are assigning and is created automatically by the compiler. Inside the **set** accessor for the **Caption** property, *value* can be thought of as a string variable that contains the string "OK." A **set** accessor cannot return a **value**.

Invoking a **set** accessor is syntactically identical to a simple assignment, so you should limit its observable side effects. For example, it would be somewhat unexpected for the following statement to change both the speed and the color of the **thing** object.

```
thing.speed = 5;
```

However, sometimes **set** accessor side effects can be useful. For example, a shopping basket object could update its total whenever the item count in the basket is changed.

Comparing Properties to Fields

- **Properties are "logical fields"**
  - The **get** accessor can return a computed value
- **Similarities**
  - Syntax for creation and use is the same
- **Differences**
  - Properties are not values; they have no address
  - Properties cannot be used as **ref** or **out** parameters to methods

As an experienced developer, you already know how to use fields. Because of the similarities between fields and properties, it is useful to compare these two programming elements.

Properties Are Logical Fields

You can use the **get** accessor of a property to calculate a value rather than return the value of a field directly. Think of properties as logical fields—that is, fields that do not necessarily have a direct physical implementation. For example, a **Person** class might contain a field for the person's date of birth and a property for the person's age that calculates the person's age:

```
class Person
{
    public Person(DateTime born)
    {
        this.born = born;
    }

    public int Age
    {
        // Simplified...
        get { return DateTime.UtcNow.Year - born.Year; }
    }
    ...
    private readonly DateTime born;
}
```

Similarities with Fields

Properties are a natural extension of fields. Like fields, they:

- Specify a name with an associated non-void type, as shown:

```
class Example
{
    int field;
    int Property { ... }
}
```

- Can be declared with any access modifier, as shown:

```
class Example
{
    private int field;
    public int Property { ... }
}
```

- Can be static, as shown:

```
class Example
{
    static private int field;
    static public int Property { ... }
}
```

- Can hide base class members of the same name, as shown:

```
class Base
{
    public int field;
    public int Property { ... }
}
class Example: Base
{
    public int field;
    new public int Property { ... }
}
```

- Are assigned to or read from by means of field syntax, as shown:

```
Example o = new Example( );
o.field = 42;
o.Property = 42;
```

Differences from Fields

Unlike fields, properties do not correspond directly to storage locations. Even though you use the same syntax to access a property that you would use to access a field, a property is not classified as a variable. So you cannot pass a property as a **ref** or **out** parameter without getting compile-time errors. The following code provides an example:

```
class Example
{
    public string Property
    {
        get { ... }
        set { ... }
    }
    public string Field;
}
class Test
{
    static void Main( )
    {
        Example eg = new Example( );

        ByRef(ref eg.Property); // Compile-time error
        ByOut(out eg.Property); // Compile-time error

        ByRef(ref eg.Field); // Okay
        ByOut(out eg.Field); // Okay
    }
    static void ByRef(ref string name) { ... }
    static void ByOut(out string name) { ... }
}
```

Comparing Properties to Methods

- **Similarities**
  - Both contain code to be executed
  - Both can be used to hide implementation details
  - Both can be virtual, abstract, or override
- **Differences**
  - Syntactic – properties do not use parentheses
  - Semantic – properties cannot be **void** or take arbitrary parameters

Similarities with Methods

With both properties and methods, you can:

- Specify statements to be executed.
- Specify a return type that must be at least as accessible as the property itself.
- Mark them as virtual, abstract, or override.
- Introduce them in an interface.
- Provide a separation between an object's internal state and its public interface (which you cannot do with a field).

This last point is perhaps the most important. You can change the implementation of a property without affecting the syntax of how you use the property. For example, in the following code, notice that the **TopLeft** property of the **Label** class is implemented directly with a **Point** field.

```
struct Point{
    public Point(int x, int y)
    {
        this.x = x;
        this.y = y;
    }
    public int x, y;
}
class Label
{
    ...
    public Point TopLeft
    {
        get { return topLeft; }
        set { topLeft = value; }
    }
    private Point topLeft;
}
class Use
{
    static void Main( )
    {
        Label text = new Label(...);
        Point oldPosition = text.TopLeft;
        Point newPosition = new Point(10,10);
        text.TopLeft = newPosition;
    }
    ...
}
```

Because **TopLeft** is implemented as a property, you can also implement it without changing the syntax of how you use the property, as shown in this example, which uses two **int** fields named *x* and *y* instead of the **Point** field named *topLeft*:

```
class Label
{
    public Point TopLeft
    {
        get { return new Point(x,y); }
        set { x = value.x; y = value.y; }
    }
    private int x, y;
}
class Use
{
    static void Main( )
    {
        Label text = new Label(...);
        // Exactly the same
        Point oldPosition = text.TopLeft;
        Point newPosition = new Point(10,10);
        text.TopLeft = newPosition;
        ...
    }
}
```

Differences from Methods

Properties and methods differ in a few important ways, as summarized in the following table.

Feature	Properties	Methods
Use parentheses	No	Yes
Specify arbitrary parameters	No	Yes
Use void type	No	Yes

Consider the following examples:

- Properties do not use parentheses, although methods do.

```
class Example
{
    public int Property { ... }
    public int Method( ) { ... }
}
```

- Properties cannot specify arbitrary parameters, although methods can.

```
class Example
{
    public int Property { ... }
    public int Method(double d1, decimal d2) { ... }
}
```

- Properties cannot be of type **void**, although methods can.

```
class Example
{
    public void Property { ... }  // Compile-time error
    public void Method( ) { ... } // Okay
}
```

Property Types

- **Read/write properties**
  - Have both **get** and **set** accessors
- **Read-only properties**
  - Have **get** accessor only
  - Are not constants
- **Write-only properties – very limited use**
  - Have **set** accessor only
- **Static properties**
  - Apply to the class and can access only static data

When using properties, you can define which operations are allowed for each property. The operations are defined as follows:

- Read/write properties

  When you implement both **get** and **set**, you have both read and write access to the property.

- Read-only properties

  When you implement only **get**, you have read-only access to the property.

- Write-only properties

  When you implement only **set**, you have write-only access to the property.

Using Read-Only Properties

Properties that only have a **get** accessor are called read-only properties. In the example below, the **BankAccount** class has a **Balance** property with a **get** accessor but no **set** accessor. Therefore, **Balance** is a read-only property.

```
class BankAccount
{
    private decimal balance;
    public decimal Balance
    {
        get { return balance; } // But no set
    }
}
```

You cannot assign a value to a read-only property. For example, if you add the statements below to the previous example, you will get a compile-time error.

```
BankAccount acc = new BankAccount( );
acc.Balance = 1000000M; // Compile-time error
```

A common mistake is to think that a read-only property specifies a constant value. This is not the case. In the following example, the **Balance** property is read-only, meaning you can only read the value of the balance. However, the value of the balance can change over time. For example, the balance will increase when a deposit is made.

```
class BankAccount
{
    private decimal balance;
    public decimal Balance
    {
        get { return balance; }
    }
    public void Deposit(decimal amount)
    {
        balance += amount;
    }
    ...
}
```

Using Write-Only Properties

Properties that only have a **set** accessor are called write-only properties. In general, you should avoid using write-only properties.

If a property does not have a **get** accessor, you cannot read its value; you can only assign a value to it. If you attempt to read from a property that does not have a **get** accessor, you will get a compile-time error.

Static Properties

A static property, like a static field and a static method, is associated with the class and not with an object. Because a static property is not associated with a specific instance, it can access only static data and cannot refer to **this** or instance data. Following is an example:

```
class MyClass
{
    private int MyData = 0;

    public static int ClassData
    {
        get {
            return this.MyData; // Compile-time error
        }
    }
}
```

You cannot include a **virtual**, **abstract**, or **override** modifier on a static property.

Property Example

```
public class Console
{
    public static TextReader In
    {
        get {
            if (reader == null) {
                reader = new StreamReader(...);
            }
            return reader;
        }
    }
    ...
    private static TextReader reader = null;
}
```

Just-in-Time Creation

You can use properties to delay the initialization of a resource until the moment it is first referenced. This technique is referred to as *lazy creation*, *lazy instantiation*, or *just-in-time creation*. The following code shows an example from the Microsoft .NET Framework SDK of just-in-time creation (simplified and not thread-safe):

```
public class Console
{
    public static TextReader In
    {
        get {
            if (reader == null) {
                reader = new StreamReader(...);
            }
            return reader;
        }
    }
    ...
    private static TextReader reader = null;
}
```

In the code, notice that:

■ The underlying field called *reader* is initialized to **null**.

■ Only the first read access will execute the body of the **if** statement inside the **get** accessor, thus creating the **new StreamReader** object. (**StreamReader** is derived from **TextReader**.)

◆ Using Indexers

- ■ **What Is an Indexer?**
- ■ **Comparing Indexers to Arrays**
- ■ **Comparing Indexers to Properties**
- ■ **Using Parameters to Define Indexers**
- ■ **String Example**
- ■ **BitArray Example**

An *indexer* is a member that enables an object to be indexed in the same way as an array. Whereas you can use properties to enable field-like access to the data in your class, you can use indexers to enable array-like access to the members of your class.

After completing this lesson, you will be able to:

- ■ Define indexers.
- ■ Use indexers.

What Is an Indexer?

- **An indexer provides array-like access to an object**
  - Useful if a property can have multiple values
- **To define an indexer**
  - Create a property called *this*
  - Specify the index type
- **To use an indexer**
  - Use array notation to read or write the indexed property

An object is composed of a number of subitems. (For example, a list box is composed of a number of strings.) Indexers allow you to access the subitems by using array-like notation.

Defining Indexers

The following code shows how to implement an indexer that provides access to a private array of strings called **list**:

```
class StringList
{
    private string[ ] list;

    public string this[int index]
    {
        get { return list[index]; }
        set { list[index] = value; }
    }
    ...
    // Other code and constructors to initialize list
}
```

The indexer is a property called **this** and is denoted by square brackets containing the type of index it uses. (Indexers must always be called **this**; they never have names of their own. They are accessed by means of the object they belong to.) In this case, the indexer requires that an **int** be supplied to identify the value to be returned or modified by the accessors.

Using Indexers

You can use the indexer of the **StringList** class to gain both read and write access to the members of **myList**, as shown in the following code:

```
...
StringList myList = new StringList( );
...
myList[3] = "o";              // Indexer write
...
string myString = myList[3];   // Indexer read
...
```

Notice that the syntax for reading or writing the indexer is very similar to the syntax for using an array. Referencing **myList** with an **int** in square brackets causes the indexer to be used. Either the **get** accessor or the **set** accessor will be invoked, depending upon whether you are reading or writing the indexer.

Comparing Indexers to Arrays

- **Similarities**
  - Both use array notation
- **Differences**
  - Indexers can use non-integer subscripts
  - Indexers can be overloaded—you can define several indexers, each using a different index type
  - Indexers are not variables, so they do not denote storage locations—you cannot pass an indexer as a **ref** or an **out** parameter

Although indexers use array notation, there are some important differences between indexers and arrays.

Defining Index Types

The type of the index used to access an array must be integer. You can define indexers to accept other types of indexes. For example, the following code shows how to use a string indexer:

```
class NickNames
{
    private Hashtable names = new Hashtable( );

    public string this[string realName]
    {
        get { return (string)names[realName]; }
        set { names[realName] = value; }
    }
    ...
}
```

In the following example, the **NickNames** class stores real name and nickname pairs. You can store a nickname and associate it with a real name, and then later request the nickname for a given real name.

```
...
NickNames myNames = new NickNames( );
...
myNames["John"] = "Cuddles";
...
string myNickName = myNames["John"];
...
```

Overloading

A class can have multiple indexers, if they use different index types. You could extend the **NickNames** class to create an indexer that takes an integer index. The indexer could iterate through the Hashtable the specified number of times and return the value found there. Following is an example:

```
class NickNames
{
    private Hashtable names = new Hashtable( );

    public string this[string realName]
    {
        get { return (string)names[realName]; }
        set { names[realName] = value; }
    }

    public string this[int nameNumber]
    {
        get
        {
            string nameFound;
            // Code that iterates through the Hashtable
            // and populates nameFound
            return nameFound;
        }
    }
    ...

}
```

Indexers Are Not Variables

Unlike arrays, indexers do not correspond directly to storage locations. Instead, indexers have **get** and **set** accessors that specify the statements to execute in order to read or write their values. This means that even though you use the same syntax for accessing an indexer that you use to access an array (you use square brackets in both cases), an indexer is not classified as a variable.

If you pass an indexer as a **ref** or **out** parameter, you will get compile-time errors, as the following example shows:

```
class Example
{
    public string[ ] array;

    public string this[int index]
    {
        get { ... }
        set { ... }
    }
}

class Test
{
    static void Main( )
    {
        Example eg = new Example( );

        ByRef(ref eg[0]); // Compile-time error
        ByOut(out eg[0]); // Compile-time error

        ByRef(ref eg.array[0]); // Okay
        ByOut(out eg.array[0]); // Okay
    }
    static void ByRef(ref string name) { ... }
    static void ByOut(out string name) { ... }
}
```

Comparing Indexers to Properties

- **Similarities**
  - Both use **get** and **set** accessors
  - Neither have an address
  - Neither can be void
- **Differences**
  - Indexers can be overloaded
  - Indexers cannot be static

Indexers are based on properties, and indexers share many of the features of properties. Indexers also differ from properties in certain ways. To understand indexers fully, it is helpful to compare them to properties.

Similarities with Properties

Indexers are similar to properties in many ways:

- Both use **get** and **set** accessors.

- Neither denote physical storage locations; therefore neither can be used as **ref** or **out** parameters.

```
class Dictionary
{
    public string this[string index]
    {
        get { ... }
        set { ... }
    }
}
Dictionary oed = new Dictionary( );
...
ByRef(ref oed["life"]); // Compile-time error
ByOut(out oed["life"]); // Compile-time error
```

- Neither can specify a **void** type.

  For example, in the code above, oed["life"] is an expression of type **string** and could not be an expression of type **void**.

Differences from Properties

It is also important to understand how indexers and properties differ:

- Identification

  A property is identified only by its name. An indexer is identified by its signature; that is, by the square brackets and the type of the indexing parameters.

- Overloading

  Since a property is identified only by its name, it cannot be overloaded. However, since an indexer's signature includes the types of its parameters, an indexer can be overloaded.

- Static or dynamic

  A property can be a static member, whereas an indexer is always an instance member.

Using Parameters to Define Indexers

- **When defining indexers**
  - Specify at least one indexer parameter
  - Specify a value for each parameter you specify
  - Do not use **ref** or **out** parameter modifiers

There are three rules that you must follow to define indexers:

- Specify at least one indexer parameter.
- Specify a value for each parameter.
- Do not use **ref** or **out** as parameter modifiers.

Syntax Rules for Indexer Parameters

When defining an indexer, you must specify at least one parameter (index) for the indexer. You have seen examples of this already. There are some restrictions on the storage class of the parameter. For example, you cannot use **ref** and **out** parameter modifiers:

```
class BadParameter
{
    // Compile-time error
    public string this[ref int index] { ... }
    public string this[out string index] { ... }
}
```

Multiple Parameters

You can specify more than one parameter in an indexer. The following code provides an example:

```
class MultipleParameters
{
    public string this[int one, int two]
    {
        get { ... }
        set { ... }
    }
    ...
}
```

To use the indexer of the **MultipleParameters** class, you must specify two values, as shown in the following code:

```
...
MultipleParameters mp = new MultipleParameters( );
string s = mp[2,3];
...
```

This is the indexer equivalent of a multidimensional array.

String Example

> ■ **The String class**
>
> - Is an immutable class
>
> - Uses an indexer (**get** accessor but no **set** accessor)

```
class String
{
    public char this[int index]
    {
        get {
            if (index < 0 || index >= Length)
                throw new IndexOutOfRangeException( );
            ...
        }
    }
    ...
}
```

The **string** type is a fundamental type in C#. It is a keyword that is an alias for the **System.String** class in the same way that **int** is an alias for the **System.Int32** struct.

The String Class

The **String** class is an immutable, sealed class. This means that when you call a method on a **string** object, you are guaranteed that the method will not change that **string** object. If a **string** method returns a string, it will be a new string.

The Trim Method

To remove trailing white space from a string, use the **Trim** method:

```
public sealed class String
{
    ...
    public String Trim( ) { ... }
    ...
}
```

The **Trim** method returns a new trimmed string, but the string used to call **Trim** remains untrimmed. The following code provides an example:

```
string s = "   Trim me   ";
string t = s.Trim( );
Console.WriteLine(s); // Writes "   Trim me   "
Console.WriteLine(t); // Writes "Trim me"
```

The String Class Indexer

No method of the **String** class ever changes the string used to call the method. You define the value of a string when it is created, and the value never changes.

Because of this design decision, the **String** class has an indexer that is declared with a **get** accessor but no **set** accessor, as shown in the following example:

```
class String
{
    public char this[int index]
    {
        get {
          if (index < 0 || index >= Length)
              throw new IndexOutOfRangeException( );
          ...
        }
    }
    ...
}
```

If you attempt to use a string indexer to write to the string, you will get a compile-time error:

```
string s = "Sharp";
Console.WriteLine(s[0]); // Okay
s[0] = 'S'; // Compile-time error
s[4] = 'k'; // Compile-time error
```

The **String** class has a companion class called **StringBuilder** that has a read-write indexer.

BitArray Example

```
class BitArray
{
    public bool this[int index]
    {
        get {
            BoundsCheck(index);
            return (bits[index >> 5] & (1 << index)) != 0;
        }
        set {
            BoundsCheck(index);
            if (value) {
                bits[index >> 5] |= (1 << index);
            } else {
                bits[index >> 5] &= ~(1 << index);
            }
        }
    }
    private int[ ] bits;
}
```

This is a more complex example of indexers, based on the **BitArray** class from the .NET Framework SDK. By implementing indexers, the **BitArray** class uses less memory than the corresponding Boolean array.

Comparing the BitArray Class to a Boolean Array

The following example shows how to create an array of Boolean flags:

```
bool[ ] flags = new bool[32];
flags[12] = false;
```

This code works, but unfortunately it uses a single byte to store each **bool**. The state of a Boolean flag (**true** or **false**) can be stored in a single bit, but a byte is eight bits wide. Therefore, an array of bools uses eight times more memory than it needs.

To address this memory issue, the .NET Framework SDK provides the **BitArray** class, which implements indexers and also uses less memory than the corresponding bool array. Following is an example:

```
class BitArray
{
    public bool this[int index]
    {
      get {
         BoundsCheck(index);
         return (bits[index >> 5] & (1 << index)) != 0;
      }
      set {
         BoundsCheck(index);
         if (value) {
            bits[index >> 5] |= (1 << index);
         } else {
            bits[index >> 5] &= ~(1 << index);
         }
      }
    }
    ...
    private int[ ] bits;
}
```

How BitArray Works

To learn how the **BitArray** class works, consider step-by-step what the code is doing:

1. Store 32 **bool**s in one **int**.

    BitArray uses substantially less memory than a corresponding bool array by storing the state for 32 **bool**s in one **int**. (Remember that **int** is an alias for **Int32**.)

2. Implement an indexer:

    ```
    public bool this[int index]
    ```

    The **BitArray** class contains an indexer to allow a **BitArray** object to be used in an array-like manner. In fact, a **BitArray** can be used exactly like a **bool** [ ].

    ```
    BitArray flags = new BitArray(32);
    flags[12] = false;
    ```

3. Extract the individual bits.

    To extract the individual bits, you must shift the bits. For example, the following expression appears frequently because shifting right by 5 bits is equivalent to dividing by 32, because $2*2*2*2*2 == 2^5 == 32$. Therefore, the following shift expression locates the **int** that holds the bit at position index:

    ```
    index >> 5
    ```

4. Determine the value of the correct bit.

    After the correct **int** is found, the individual bit (out of all 32) still needs to be determined. You can do this by using the following expression:

    ```
    1 << index
    ```

    To understand how this works, you need to know that when you shift an **int** left only the lowest 5 bits of the second argument are used. (Again, only 5 bits are used because the **int** being shifted has 32 bits.) In other words, the above shift-left expression is semantically the same as the following:

    ```
    1 << (index % 32)
    ```

More Details About BitArray

Following is the **BitArray** class in more detail:

```
class BitArray
{
    public BitArray(int length)
    {
        if (length < 0)
            throw new ArgumentOutOfRangeException(...);
        this.bits = new int[((length - 1) >> 5) + 1];
        this.length = length;
    }

    public int Length
    {
        get { return length; }
    }

    public bool this[int index]
    {
        get {
            BoundsCheck(index);
            return (bits[index >> 5] & (1 << index)) != 0;
        }
        set {
            BoundsCheck(index);
            if (value) {
                bits[index >> 5] |= (1 << index);
            } else {
                bits[index >> 5] &= ~(1 << index);
            }
        }
    }

    private void BoundsCheck(int index)
    {
        if (index < 0 || index >= length) {
            throw new ArgumentOutOfRangeException(...);
        }
    }

    private int[ ] bits;
    private int length;
}
```

Lab 13.1: Using Properties and Indexers

Objectives

After completing this lab, you will be able to:

- Create properties to encapsulate data within a class.
- Define indexers for accessing classes by using array-like notation.

Prerequisites

Before working on this lab, you must be able to:

- Create and use classes.
- Use arrays and collections.

Estimated time to complete this lab: 30 minutes

Exercise 1
Enhancing the Account Class

In this exercise, you will remove the bank account number and bank account type methods from the **BankAccount** class and replace them with read-only properties. You will also add to the **BankAccount** class a read/write string property for the account holder's name.

▶ **To change the account number and type methods into read-only properties**

1. Open the Bank.sln project in the *install folder*\Labs\Lab13\Exercise1\Starter\Bank folder.

2. In the **BankAccount** class, replace the method called **Number** with a read-only property (a property that has a **get** accessor but no **set** accessor). This is shown in the following code:

```
public long Number
{
   get { return accNo; }
}
```

3. Compile the project.

    You will receive error messages. This is because **BankAccount.Number** is still being used as a method in the four overloaded **Bank.CreateAccount** methods.

4. Change these four **Bank.CreateAccount** methods to access the bank account number as a property.

    For example, change

    ```
    long accNo = newAcc.Number( );
    ```

    to:

    ```
    long accNo = newAcc.Number;
    ```

5. Save and compile the project.

6. In the **BankAccount** class, replace the method called **Type** with a read-only property whose **get** accessor returns **accType.ToString**.

7. Save and compile the project.

▶ **To add to the BankAccount class a read/write property for the account holder**

1. Add a private field called *holder* of type **string** to the **BankAccount** class.

2. Add a public read/write property called **Holder** (note the capital "H") of type **string** to the **BankAccount** class.

   The **get** and **set** accessors of this property will use the holder string you have just created:

   ```
   public string Holder
   {
     get { return holder; }
     set { holder = value; }
   }
   ```

3. Modify the **BankAccount.ToString** method so that the string it returns contains the account holder's name in addition to the account number, type, and balance.

4. Save your work, compile the project, and correct any errors.

▶ **To test the properties**

1. Open the TestHarness.sln test harness in the *install folder*\Labs\Lab13\Exercise1\Starter\TestHarness folder.

2. Add a reference to the Bank library (the DLL that contains the components that you worked on in the previous two procedures) by performing the following steps:

   a. Expand the project in Solution Explorer.

   b. Right-click **References**, and then click **Add Reference**.

   c. Click **Browse**.

   d. Navigate to the *install folder*\Labs\Lab13\Exercise1\Starter\Bank\bin\Debug folder.

   e. Click **Bank.dll**, click **Open**, and then click **OK**.

3. Add two statements to the **Main** method of the **CreateAccount** class, as follows:

   - Set the name of the holder of *acc1* to "Sid."

   - Set the name of the holder of *acc2* to "Ted."

4. Add statements that retrieve and print the number and type of each account.

5. Save your work, compile the project, and correct any errors.

6. Run the project and verify that the account numbers, the account types, and the names "Sid" and "Ted" appear.

Exercise 2
Modifying the Transaction Class

In this exercise, you will modify the **BankTransaction** class (which you developed in previous labs and which is provided here). As you may recall, the **BankTransaction** class was created for holding information about a financial transaction pertaining to a **BankAccount** object.

You will replace the methods **When** and **Amount** with a pair of read-only properties. (**When** returns the date of the transaction, **Amount** returns the transaction amount.)

▶ **To change the When method into a read-only property**

1. Open the Bank.sln project in the
   install folder\Labs\Lab13\Exercise2\Starter\Bank folder.

2. In the **BankTransaction** class, replace the method called **When** with a read-only property of the same name.

3. Compile the project.

   You will receive an error message. This is because **BankTransaction.When** is still being used as a method in **Audit.RecordTransaction**. (The **Audit** class records an audit trail of transaction information, so it uses the **When** and **Amount** methods to find the date and amount of each transaction.)

4. Change the **Audit.RecordTransaction** method so that it accesses the **When** member as a property.

5. Save your work, compile the project, and correct any errors.

▶ **To change Amount into a read-only property**

1. In the **BankTransaction** class, replace the method called **Amount** with a read-only property.

2. Compile the project.

   You will receive error messages. This is because **BankTransaction.Amount** is still being used as a method in **Audit.RecordTransaction**.

3. Change the **Audit.RecordTransaction** method so that it accesses the **Amount** member as a property.

4. Save your work, compile the project, and correct any errors.

▶ **To test the properties**

1. Open the TestHarness.sln test harness in the
   install folder\Labs\Lab13\Exercise2\Starter\TestHarness folder.

2. Add a reference to the Bank library (the DLL that contains the components
   that you worked on in the previous procedures) by performing the following
   steps:

   a. Expand the project in Solution Explorer.

   b. Right-click **References**, and then click **Add Reference**.

   c. Click **Browse**.

   d. Navigate to the
      install folder\Labs\Lab13\Exercise2\Starter\Bank\bin\Debug folder.

   e. Click **Bank.dll**, click **Open**, and then click **OK**.

3. Add statements to the **Main** method of the **CreateAccount** class that will:

   a. Deposit money into accounts *acc1* and *acc2*. (Use the **Deposit** method,
      and make up your own numbers.)

   b. Withdraw money from accounts *acc1* and *acc2*. (Use the **Withdraw**
      method.)

   c. Print the transaction history for each account. A method called **Write**
      has been supplied at the end of the test harness. You pass it an account
      whose transaction history you want to display. It uses and tests the
      When and **Amount** properties of the **BankTransaction** class.
      Following is an example:

      ```
      Write(acc1);
      ```

4. Save your work, compile the project, and correct any errors.

5. Run the project, and verify that the transaction details appear as expected.

Exercise 3
Creating and Using an Indexer

In this exercise, you will add an indexer to the **BankAccount** class to provide access to any of the **BankTransaction** objects cached in the internal array.

The transactions that belong to an account are accessible by means of a queue (**System.Collections.Queue**) that is in the **BankAccount** object itself.

You will define an indexer on the **BankAccount** class that retrieves the transaction at the specified point in the queue or returns **null** if no transaction exists at that point. For example,

```
myAcc.AccountTransactions[2]
```

will return transaction number 2, the third one in the queue.

The **GetEnumerator** method of **System.Collections.Queue** will be useful in this exercise.

▶ **To declare a read-only BankAccount indexer**

1. Open the Bank.sln project in the
    install folder\Labs\Lab13\Exercise3\Starter\Bank folder.

2. In the **BankAccount** class, declare a public indexer that returns a **BankTransaction** and takes a single **int** parameter called **index**, as follows:

```
public BankTransaction this[int index]
{
  ...
}
```

3. Add a **get** accessor to the body of the indexer, and implement it with a single
    ```
    return new BankTransaction(99);
    ```
    statement, as follows:

```
public BankTransaction this[int index]
{
  get { return new BankTransaction(99); }
}
```

The purpose of this step is only to test the syntax of the indexer. Later, you will implement the indexer properly.

4. Save your work, compile the project, and correct any errors.

▶ **To create transactions**

1. Open the TestHarness.sln test harness in the
   install folder\Labs\Lab13\Exercise3\Starter\TestHarness folder.

2. Add a reference to the Bank library (the DLL that contains the components
   that you worked on in the previous stage) by performing the following
   steps:

   a. Expand the project in Solution Explorer.

   b. Right-click **References**, and then click **Add Reference**.

   c. Click **Browse**.

   d. Navigate to the
      install folder\Labs\Lab13\Exercise3\Starter\Bank\bin\Debug folder.

   e. Click **Bank.dll**, click **Open**, and then click **OK**.

3. Create some transactions by adding the following statements to the end of
   the **CreateAccount.Main** method:

   ```
   for (int i = 0; i < 5; i++) {
       acc1.Deposit(100);
       acc1.Withdraw(50);
   }
   Write(acc1);
   ```

   The calls to **Deposit** and **Withdraw** create transactions.

4. Save your work, compile the project, and correct any errors.

   Run the project, and verify that the **Deposit** and **Withdraw** transactions are
   correctly displayed.

▶ **To call the BankAccount indexer**

1. The last few statements of the **CreateAccount.Write** method currently display the transactions using by a **foreach** statement, as follows:

```
Queue tranQueue = acc.Transactions( );
foreach (BankTransaction tran in tranQueue) {
    Console.WriteLine("Date: {0}\tAmount: {1}", tran.When,
↪tran.Amount);
}
```

2. Change the way transactions are displayed as follows:

   a. Replace this **foreach** statement with a **for** statement that increments an **int** variable called *counter* from zero to the value returned from **tranQueue.Count**.

   b. Inside the **for** statement, call the **BankAccount** indexer that you declared in the previous procedure. Use *counter* as the subscript parameter, and save the returned **BankTransaction** in a local variable called *tran*.

   c. Print the details from *tran*:

```
for (int counter = 0; counter < tranQueue.Count;
↪counter++) {
  BankTransaction tran = acc[counter];
    Console.WriteLine("Date: {0}\tAmount: {1}", tran.When,
↪tran.Amount);
}
```

3. Save your work, compile the project, and correct any errors.

4. Run the project.

   It will display a series of transactions with a value of 99 (the temporary test value that you used earlier) because the indexer has not yet been fully implemented.

▶ **To complete the BankAccount indexer**

1. Return to the Bank project (Bank.sln in the
   install folder\Labs\Lab13\Exercise3\Starter\Bank folder).

2. In the **BankAccount** class, delete the
   `return new BankTransaction(99);`
   statement from the body of the indexer.

3. The **BankAccount** transactions are held in a private field called *tranQueue*
   of type **System.Collections.Queue**. This **Queue** class does not have an
   indexer, so to access a given element you will need to manually iterate
   through the class. The process for doing this is as follows:

   a. Declare a variable of type *IEnumerator* and initialize it by using the
      GetEnumerator method of *tranQueue*. (All queues provide an
      enumerator to allow you to step through them.)

   b. Iterate through the queue *n* times, using the **MoveNext** method of the
      IEnumerator variable to move to the next item in the queue.

   c. Return the **BankTransaction** found at the *n*th location.

   Your code should look as follows:

```
IEnumerator ie = tranQueue.GetEnumerator( );
for (int i = 0; i <= index; i++) {
    ie.MoveNext( );
}
BankTransaction tran = (BankTransaction)ie.Current;
return tran;
```

4. Check that the **int** parameter *index* is neither greater than **tranQueue.Count**
   nor less than zero.

   Check for this before iterating through **tranQueue**.

5. The complete code for the indexer should look as follows:

```
public BankTransaction this[int index]
{
  get
  {
      if (index < 0 || index >= tranQueue.Count)
          return null;

      IEnumerator ie = tranQueue.GetEnumerator( );
      for (int i = 0; i <= index; i++)  {
          ie.MoveNext( );
      }
      BankTransaction tran = (BankTransaction)ie.Current;
      return tran;
    }
  }
}
```

6. Save your work, compile the project, and correct any errors.

7. Return to TestHarness and execute it.

   Verify that all ten transactions appear correctly.

Review

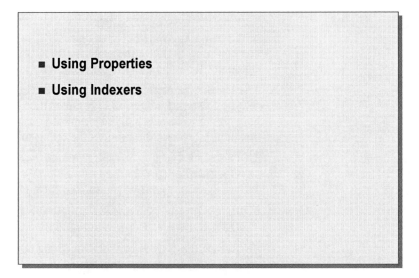

■ Using Properties

■ Using Indexers

1. Declare a **Font** class that contains a read-only property called **Name** of type **string**.

2. Declare a **DialogBox** class that contains a read/write property called **Caption** of type **string**.

3. Declare a **MutableString** class that contains a read/write indexer of type **char** that expects a single **int** parameter.

4. Declare a **Graph** class that contains a read-only indexer of type **double** that expects a single parameter of type **Point**.

msdn training

Module 14: Attributes

Contents

Overview	1
Overview of Attributes	2
Defining Custom Attributes	13
Retrieving Attribute Values	22
Lab 14.1: Defining and Using Attributes	26
Review	34
Course Evaluation	36

Overview

- **Overview of Attributes**
- **Defining Custom Attributes**
- **Retrieving Attribute Values**

Attributes are a simple technique for adding metadata to classes. They can be useful when you need to build components.

In this module, you will learn the purpose of attributes and the function that they perform in C# applications. You will learn about attribute syntax and how to use some of the predefined attributes in the Microsoft® .NET Framework environment. You will also learn to create custom user-defined attributes. Finally, you will learn how classes and other object types can implement and use these custom attributes to query attribute information at run time.

After completing this module, you will be able to:

- Use common predefined attributes.

- Create simple custom attributes.

- Query attribute information at run time.

◆ Overview of Attributes

- ■ **Introduction to Attributes**
- ■ **Applying Attributes**
- ■ **Common Predefined Attributes**
- ■ **Using the Conditional Attribute**
- ■ **Using the DllImport Attribute**
- ■ **Using the Transaction Attribute**

With the introduction of attributes, the C# language provides a convenient technique that will help handle tasks such as changing the behavior of the runtime, obtaining transaction information about an object, conveying organizational information to a designer, and handling unmanaged code.

After completing this lesson, you will be able to:

- ■ Identify which tasks you can perform with attributes.
- ■ Use the syntax for using attributes in your code.
- ■ Identify some of the predefined attributes that are available in the .NET Framework.

Introduction to Attributes

- ■ **Attributes are:**
  - Declarative tags that convey information to the runtime
  - Stored with the metadata of the element

- ■ **.NET Framework provides predefined attributes**
  - The runtime contains code to examine values of attributes and act on them

---

The .NET Framework provides attributes so that you can extend the capabilities of the C# language. An attribute is a declarative tag that you use to convey information to the runtime about the behavior of programmatic elements such as classes, enumerators, and assemblies.

You can think of attributes as annotations that your programs can store and use. In most cases, you write the code that retrieves the values of an attribute in addition to the code that performs a change in behavior at run time. In its simplest form, an attribute is an extended way to document your code.

You can apply attributes to many elements of the source code. Information about the attributes is stored with the metadata of the elements they are associated with.

The .NET Framework is equipped with a number of predefined attributes. The code to examine them and act upon the values they contain is also incorporated as a part of the runtime and .NET Framework SDK.

Applying Attributes

■ **Syntax: Use square brackets to specify an attribute**

```
[attribute(positional_parameters,named_parameter=value, ...)]
element
```

■ **To apply multiple attributes to an element, you can:**

- Specify multiple attributes in separate square brackets

- Use a single square bracket and separate attributes with commas

- For some elements such as assemblies, specify the element name associated with the attribute explicitly

---

You can apply attributes to different kinds of programming elements. These elements include assemblies, modules, classes, structs, enums, constructors, methods, properties, fields, events, interfaces, parameters, return values, and delegates.

Attribute Syntax

To specify an attribute and associate it with a programming element, use the following general syntax:

```
[attribute(positional_parameters,name_parameter=value, ...)]
element
```

You specify an attribute name and its values within square brackets ([and]) before the programmatic element to which you want to apply the attribute. Most attributes take one or more parameters, which can be either *positional* or *named*.

You specify a positional parameter in a defined position in the parameter list, as you would specify parameters for methods. Any named parameter values follow the positional parameters. Positional parameters are used to specify essential information, whereas named parameters are used to convey optional information in an attribute.

Tip   Before using an unfamiliar attribute, it is a good practice to check the documentation for the attribute to find out which parameters are available and whether they should be positional or named.

Example

As an example of using attributes, consider the following code, in which the **DefaultEvent** attribute is applied on a class by using a positional **string** parameter, **ShowResult**:

```
using System.ComponentModel;
...
[DefaultEvent("ShowResult")]
public class Calculator: System.Windows.Forms.UserControl
{
    ...
}
```

Applying Multiple Attributes

You can apply more than one attribute to an element. You can enclose each attribute in its own set of square brackets, although you can also enclose multiple attributes, separated with commas, in the same set of square brackets.

In some circumstances, you must specify exactly which element an attribute is associated with. For example, in the case of assembly attributes, place them after any **using** clauses but before any code, and explicitly specify them as attributes of the assembly.

The following example shows how to use the **CLSCompliant** assembly attribute. This attribute indicates whether or not an assembly strictly conforms to the Common Language Specification.

```
using System;
[assembly:CLSCompliant(true)]

class MyClass
{
    ...
}
```

Common Predefined Attributes

- **.NET provides many predefined attributes**
  - General attributes
  - COM interoperability attributes
  - Transaction handling attributes
  - Visual designer component building attributes

The capabilities of predefined attributes in the .NET Framework encompass a wide range of areas, from interoperability with COM to compatibility with visual design tools.

This topic describes some of the common predefined attributes that are provided by the .NET Framework. However, it is not intended to be comprehensive. For more information about predefined attributes, refer to the Microsoft Visual Studio® .NET Help documents.

General Attributes

The following list summarizes some of the general attributes that are provided by the .NET Framework.

Attribute	Applicable to	Description
Conditional	Method	Tests to see whether a named symbol is defined. If it is defined, any calls to the method are executed normally. If the symbol is not defined, the call is not generated.
DllImport	Method	Indicates that the method is implemented in unmanaged code, in the specified DLL. It causes the DLL to be loaded at run time and the named method to execute.

COM Interoperability Attributes

When using the attributes to provide interoperability with COM, the goal is to ensure that using COM components from the managed .NET Framework environment is as seamless as possible. The .NET Framework has many attributes relating to COM interoperability. Some of these are listed in the following table.

Attribute	Applicable to	Description
ComImport	Class/Interface	Indicates that a class or interface definition was imported from a COM type library.
ComRegisterFunction	Method	Specifies the method to be called when a .NET Framework assembly is registered for use from COM.
ComUnregisterFunction	Method	Specifies the method to be called when a .NET assembly is unregistered for use from COM.
DispId	Method, field, property	Indicates which dispatch ID is to be used for the method, field or property.
In	parameter	Indicates that the data should be marshaled from the caller to the callee.
MarshalAs	Field, parameter, return values	Specifies how data should be marshaled between COM and the managed environment.
ProgId	Class	Specifies which prog ID is to be used for the class.
Out	parameter	Indicates that data should be marshaled from the callee back to caller.
InterfaceType	Interface	Specifies whether a managed interface is **IDispatch**, **IUnknown**, or dual when it is exposed to COM.

For more information about COM interoperability, search for "Microsoft ComServices" in the .NET Framework SDK Help documents.

Transaction Handling Attributes

Components running in a COM+ environment use transaction management. The attribute you use for this purpose is shown in the following table.

Attribute	Applicable to	Description
Transaction	Class	Specify the type of transaction that should be available to this object.

Visual Designer Component-Building Attributes

Developers who build components for a visual designer use the attributes listed in the following table.

Attribute	Applicable to	Description
Bindable	Property	Specifies whether a property is typically used for binding.
DefaultProperty	Class	Specifies the default property for the component.
DefaultValue	Property	Indicates that the property is the default value for the component.
Localizable	Property	When code is generated for a component, members that are marked with **Localizable(true)** have their property values saved in resource files. You can localize these resource files without modifying the code.
DefaultEvent	Class	Specifies the default event for the component.
Category	Property, event	Specifies the category into which the visual designer should place this property or event in the property window.
Description	Property, event	Defines a brief piece of text to be displayed at the bottom of the property window in the visual designer when this property or event is selected.

Using the Conditional Attribute

- **Serves as a debugging tool**
  - Causes conditional compilation of method calls, depending on the value of a programmer-defined symbol
  - Does not cause conditional compilation of the method itself

```
using System.Diagnostics;
...
class MyClass
{
  [Conditional ("DEBUGGING")]
  public static void MyMethod( )
  {
    ...
  }
}
```

- **Restrictions on methods**
  - Must have return type of **void**
  - Must not be declared as **override**
  - Must not be from an inherited interface

You can use the **Conditional** attribute as a debugging aid in your C# code. This attribute causes conditional compilation of method calls, depending on the value of a symbol that you define. It lets you invoke methods that, for example, display the values of variables, while you test and debug code. After you have debugged your program, you can "undefine" the symbol and recompile your code without changing anything else. (Or you can simply remove the symbol from the command line, and not change anything.)

Example

The following example shows how to use the **Conditional** attribute. In this example, the **MyMethod** method in **MyClass** is tagged with the **Conditional** attribute by the symbol DEBUGGING:

```
using System.Diagnostics;
...
class MyClass
{
  [Conditional ("DEBUGGING")]
  public static void MyMethod( )
  {
    ...
  }
}
```

The symbol DEBUGGING is defined as follows:

```
#define DEBUGGING

class AnotherClass
{
  public static void Test( )
  {
    MyClass.MyMethod( );
  }
}
```

As long as the symbol DEBUGGING remains defined when the method call is compiled, the method call will operate normally. When DEBUGGING is undefined, the compiler will omit calls to the method. Therefore, when you run the program, it will be treated as though that line of code does not exist.

You can define the symbol in one of two ways. You can either add a **#define** directive to the code as shown in the preceding example, or define the symbol from the command line when you compile your program.

Restrictions on Methods

The methods to which you can apply a **Conditional** attribute are subject to a number of restrictions. In particular, they must have a return type of **void**, they must not be marked as **override**, and they must not be the implementation of a method from an inherited interface.

Note   The **Conditional** attribute does not cause conditional compilation of the method itself. The attribute only determines the action that will occur when the method is called. If you require conditional compilation of a method, then you must use the **#if** and **#endif** directives in your code.

Using the DllImport Attribute

- **With the DllImport attribute, you can:**
  - Invoke unmanaged code in DLLs from a C# environment
  - Tag an external method to show that it resides in an unmanaged DLL

```
using System.Runtime.InteropServices;
...
public class MyClass( )
{
  [DllImport("MyDLL.dll", EntryPoint="MyFunction")]
  public static extern int MyFunction(string param1);
  ...
  int result = MyFunction("Hello Unmanaged Code");
  ...
}
```

You can use the **DllImport** attribute to invoke unmanaged code in your C# programs. *Unmanaged code* is the term used for code that has been developed outside the .NET environment (that is, standard C compiled into DLL files). By using the **DllImport** attribute, you can invoke unmanaged code residing in dynamic-link libraries (DLLs) from your managed C# environment.

Invoking Unmanaged Code

The **DllImport** attribute allows you to tag an **extern** method as residing in an unmanaged DLL. When your code calls this method, the common language runtime locates the DLL, loads it into the memory of your process, marshals parameters as necessary, and transfers control to the address at the beginning of the unmanaged code. This is unlike a normal program, which does not have direct access to the memory that is allocated to it. The following code provides an example of how to invoke unmanaged code:

```
using System.Runtime.InteropServices;
...
public class MyClass( )
{
  [DllImport("MyDLL.dll", EntryPoint="MyFunction")]
  public static extern int MyFunction(string param1);
  ...
  int result = MyFunction("Hello Unmanaged Code");
  ...
}
```

Using the Transaction Attribute

- **To manage transactions in COM+**
  - Specify that your component be included when a transaction commit is requested
  - Use a Transaction attribute on the class that implements the component

```
using System.EnterpriseServices;
...
[Transaction(TransactionOption.Required)]
public class MyTransactionalComponent
{
  ...
}
```

It is likely that, as a Microsoft Visual Basic® or C++ developer working in a Microsoft environment, you are familiar with technologies such as COM+. An important feature of COM+ is that it allows you to develop components that can participate in distributed transactions, which are transactions that can span multiple databases, machines, and components.

Managing Transactions in COM+

Writing code to guarantee a correct transaction commit in a distributed environment is difficult. However, if you use COM+, it takes care of managing the transactional integrity of the system and coordinating events on the network.

In this case, you only need to specify that your component be included when an application that uses your component requests a transaction commit. To make this specification, you can use a **Transaction** attribute on the class that implements the component, as follows:

```
using System.EnterpriseServices;
...
[Transaction(TransactionOption.Required)]
public class MyTransactionalComponent
{
  ...
}
```

The **Transaction** attribute is one of the predefined .NET Framework attributes that the .NET Framework runtime interprets automatically.

◆ Defining Custom Attributes

- **Defining Custom Attribute Scope**
- **Defining an Attribute Class**
- **Processing a Custom Attribute**
- **Using Multiple Attributes**

When you encounter a situation in which none of the predefined .NET Framework attributes satisfy your requirements, you can create your own attribute. Such a custom attribute will provide properties that allow you to store and retrieve information from the attribute.

Like predefined attributes, custom attributes are objects that are associated with one or more programmatic elements. They are stored with the metadata of their associated elements, and they provide mechanisms for a program to retrieve their values.

After completing this lesson, you will be able to:

- Define your own custom attributes.
- Use your own custom attributes.

Defining Custom Attribute Scope

- **Use the AttributeUsage tag to define scope**
  - Example

```
[AttributeUsage(AttributeTargets.Method)]
public class MyAttribute: System.Attribute
{ ... }
```

- **Use the bitwise "or" operator (|) to specify multiple elements**
  - Example

```
[AttributeUsage(AttributeTargets.Class | AttributeTargets.Struct)]
public class MyAttribute: System.Attribute
{ ... }
```

As with some predefined attributes, you must explicitly specify the programming element to which you want to apply a custom attribute. To do so, you annotate your custom attribute with an **AttributeUsage** tag as shown in the following example:

```
[AttributeUsage(target_elements)]
public class MyAttribute: System.Attribute
{ ... }
```

Defining Attribute Scope

The parameter to **AttributeUsage** contains values from the **System.AttributeTargets** enumeration to specify how the custom attribute can be used. The members of this enumeration are summarized in the following table.

Member name	Attribute can be applied to
Class	class
Constructor	constructor
Delegate	delegate
Enum	enum
Event	event
Field	field
Interface	interface
Method	method
Module	module

(continued)

Member name	Attribute can be applied to
Parameter	parameter
Property	property
ReturnValue	return value
Struct	struct
Assembly	assembly
All	Any element

Example of Using Custom Attributes

To specify that the **MyAttribute** custom attribute can be applied only to methods, use the following code:

```
[AttributeUsage(AttributeTargets.Method)]
public class MyAttribute: System.Attribute
{
...
}
```

Specifying Multiple Elements

If the attribute can be applied to more than one element type, use the bitwise "or" operator (|) to specify multiple target types. For example, if **MyAttribute** can also be applied to constructors, the earlier code will be modified as follows:

```
[AttributeUsage(AttributeTargets.Method |
➥AttributeTargets.Constructor)]
public class MyAttribute: System.Attribute
{
...
}
```

If a developer attempts to use the **MyAttribute** in a context different from that which is defined by **AttributeUsage**, the developer's code will not compile.

Defining an Attribute Class

- **Deriving an attribute class**
  - All attribute classes must derive from System.Attribute, directly or indirectly
  - Suffix name of attribute class with "Attribute"
- **Components of an attribute class**
  - Define a single constructor for each attribute class by using a positional parameter
  - Use properties to set an optional value by using a named parameter

After you define the scope of a custom attribute, you need to specify the way you want the custom attribute to behave. For this purpose, you must define an attribute class. Such a class will define the name of the attribute, how it can be created, and the information that it will store.

The .NET Framework SDK provides a base class, **System.Attribute**, that you must use to derive custom attribute classes and to access the values held in custom attributes.

Deriving an Attribute Class

All custom attribute classes must derive from **System.Attribute**, either directly or indirectly. The following code provides an example:

```
public class DeveloperInfoAttribute: System.Attribute
{
    ...
    public DeveloperInfoAttribute(string developer)
    {
        ...
    }
    public string Date
    {
        get { ... }
        set { ... }
    }
}
```

It is a good practice to append the name of a custom attribute class with the suffix "Attribute," as in **DeveloperInfoAttribute**. This makes it easier to distinguish the attribute classes from the non-attribute classes.

Components of an Attribute Class

All attribute classes must have a constructor. For example, if the **DeveloperInfo** attribute expects the name of the developer as a string parameter, it must have a constructor that accepts a string parameter.

A custom attribute must define a single constructor that sets the mandatory information. The positional parameter or parameters of the attribute pass this information to the constructor. If an attribute has optional data, then it is attempting to overload the constructor. This is not a good practice to adopt. Use named parameters to provide optional data.

An attribute class can, however, provide properties to get and set data. Therefore, you must use properties to set optional values, if required. Then a developer can specify the optional values as named parameters when using the attribute.

For example, the **DeveloperInfoAttribute** provides a **Date** property. You can call the **set** method of the **Date** property to set the named parameter: *Date*. The developer name, *Bert*, for example, is the positional parameter that is passed to the constructor of the attribute:

```
[DeveloperInfoAttribute("Bert", Date="08-28-2001")]
public class MyClass
{
    ...
}
```

Processing a Custom Attribute

The Compilation Process

1. **Searches for the attribute class**

2. **Checks the scope of the attribute**

3. **Checks for a constructor in the attribute**

4. **Creates an instance of the object**

5. **Checks for a named parameter**

6. **Sets field or property to named parameter value**

7. **Saves current state of attribute class**

When the compiler encounters an attribute on a programming element, the compiler uses the following process to determine how to apply the attribute:

1. Searches for the attribute class

2. Checks the scope of the attribute

3. Checks for a constructor in the attribute

4. Creates an instance of the object

5. Checks for a named parameter

6. Sets the field or property to a named parameter value

7. Saves the current state of the attribute class

To be completely accurate, the compiler actually verifies that it *could* apply the attribute, and then stores the information to do so in the metadata. The compiler does not create attribute instances at compile time.

Example

To learn more about how the compiler handles attributes, consider the following example:

```
[AttributeUsage(AttributeTargets.Class)]
public class DeveloperInfoAttribute: System.Attribute
{
    ...
}
.....
{
.....
}

[DeveloperInfo("Bert", Date="08-28-2001")]
public class MyClass
{
...
}
```

Note As is mentioned in the previous topic, it is a good practice to add the suffix "Attribute" to the name of an attribute class. Strictly speaking, it is not necessary to do so. Even if you omit the Attribute suffix as shown in the example, your code will still compile correctly. However, without the Attribute suffix there are potential issues concerning how the compiler searches for classes. Always use the Attribute suffix.

The Compilation Process

In the preceding example, when **MyClass** is compiled, the compiler will search for an attribute class called **DevloperInfoAttribute**. If the class cannot be located, the compiler will then search for **DeveloperInfo**.

After it finds **DeveloperInfo**, the compiler will check whether the attribute is allowed on a class. Then it will check for a constructor that matches the parameters specified in the attribute use. If it finds one, it creates an instance of the object by calling the constructor with the specified values.

If there is a named parameter, the compiler matches the name of the parameter with a field or property in the attribute class, and then sets the field or property to the specified value. Then the current state of the attribute class is saved to the metadata for the program element on which it is applied.

Using Multiple Attributes

- **An element can have more than one attribute**
  - Define both attributes separately

- **An element can have more than one instance of the same attribute**
  - Use AllowMultiple = true

You can apply more than one attribute to a programming element, and you can use multiple instances of the same attribute in an application.

Using Multiple Attributes

You can apply more than one attribute to a programming element. For example, the following code shows how you can tag the **FinancialComponent** class with two attributes: **Transaction** and **DefaultProperty**.

```
[Transaction(TransactionOption.Required)]
[DefaultProperty("Balance")]
public class FinancialComponent: System.Attribute
{
  ...
  public long Balance
  {
    ...
  }
}
```

Using the Same Attribute Multiple Times

The default behavior of a custom attribute does not permit multiple instances of the attribute. However, under some circumstances it might make sense to allow an attribute to be used on the same element more than once.

An example of this is the custom attribute **DeveloperInfo**. This attribute allows you to record the name of the developer that wrote a class. If more than one developer was involved in the development, you need to use the **DeveloperInfo** attribute more than once. For an attribute to permit this, you must mark it as **AllowMultiple** in the **AttributeUsage** attribute, as follows:

```
[AttributeUsage(AttributeTargets.Class, AllowMultiple=true)]
public class DeveloperInfoAttribute: System.Attribute
{
  ...
}
```

◆ Retrieving Attribute Values

- **Examining Class Metadata**
- **Querying for Attribute Information**

After you have applied attributes to programming elements in your code, it is useful to be able to determine the values of the attributes. In this section, you will learn how to use reflection to examine the attribute metadata of a class and query classes for attribute information.

After completing this lesson, you will be able to:

- Use reflection to examine the attribute metadata of a class.
- Query classes for attribute information.

Examining Class Metadata

- **To query class metadata information:**
  - Use the MemberInfo class in System.Reflection
  - Populate a MemberInfo object by using System.Type
  - Create a System.Type object by using the typeof operator
- **Example**

```
System.Reflection.MemberInfo typeInfo;
typeInfo = typeof(MyClass);
```

The .NET Framework runtime supplies a mechanism called *reflection* that allows you to query information held in metadata. Metadata is where attribute information is stored.

Using the MemberInfo Class

The .NET Framework provides a namespace named **System.Reflection**, which contains classes that you can use for examining metadata. One particular class in this namespace—the **MemberInfo** class—is very useful if you need to find out about the attributes of a class.

To populate a **MemberInfo** array, you can use the **GetMembers** method of the **System.Type** object. To create this object, you use the **typeof** operator with a class or any other element, as shown in the following code:

```
System.Reflection.MemberInfo[ ] memberInfoArray;
memberInfoArray = typeof(MyClass).GetMembers( );
...
```

Once created, the *typeInfo* variable can be queried for metadata information about the class **MyClass**.

Tip If you need more detailed information, for example, if you want to discover the values of attributes that a method has, you can use a **MethodInfo** object. In addition, there are other "Info" classes: **ConstructorInfo**, **EventInfo**, **FieldInfo**, **ParameterInfo**, and **PropertyInfo**. Detailed information about how to use these classes is beyond the scope of this course, but you can find out more by searching for "System.Reflection namespace" in the .NET Framework SDK Help documents.

Note **MemberInfo** is actually the abstract base class of the other "Info" types.

Querying for Attribute Information

■ **To retrieve attribute information:**

- Use **GetCustomAttributes** to retrieve all attribute information as an array

```
System.Reflection.MemberInfo typeInfo;
typeInfo = typeof(MyClass);
object[ ] attrs = typeInfo.GetCustomAttributes(false);
```

- Iterate through the array and examine the values of each element in the array

- Use the **IsDefined** method to determine whether a particular attribute has been defined for a class

---

After you create the *typeInfo* variable, you can query it to get information about the attributes applied to its associated class.

Retrieving Attribute Information

The **MemberInfo** object has a method called **GetCustomAttributes**. This method retrieves the information about all attributes of a class and stores it in an array, as shown in the following code:

```
System.Reflection.MemberInfo typeInfo;
typeInfo = typeof(MyClass);
object [ ] attrs = typeInfo.GetCustomAttributes(false);
```

You can then iterate through the array to find the values of the attributes that you are interested in.

Iterating Through Attributes

You can iterate through the array of attributes and examine the value of each one in turn. In the following code, the only attribute of interest is **DeveloperInfoAttribute**, and all the others are ignored. For each **DeveloperInfoAttribute** found, the values of the **Developer** and **Date** properties are displayed as follows:

```
...
object [ ] attrs = typeInfo.GetCustomAttributes(false);
foreach(Attribute atr in attrs) {
  if (atr is DeveloperInfoAttribute) {
    DeveloperInfoAttribute dia = (DeveloperInfoAttribute)atr;
    Console.WriteLine("{0}  {1}", dia.Developer, dia.Date);
  }
}
...
```

Tip **GetCustomAttributes** is an overloaded method. If you only want values for that one attribute type, you can invoke this method by passing the type of the custom attribute you are looking for through it, as shown in the following code:

```
object [ ] attrs =
typeInfo.GetCustomAttributes(typeof(DeveloperInfoAttribute),
                                                     false);
```

Using the IsDefined Method

If there are no matching attributes for a class, **GetCustomAttributes** returns a **null** object reference. However, to find out whether a particular attribute has been defined for a class, you can use the **IsDefined** method of **MemberInfo** as follows:

```
Type devInfoAttrType = typeof(DeveloperInfoAttribute);
if (typeInfo.IsDefined(devInfoAttrType, false)) {
  object [ ] attrs =
        typeInfo.GetCustomAttributes(devInfoAttrType, false);
  ...
}
```

Note You can use Intermediate Language Disassembler (ILDASM) to see these attributes inside the assembly.

Lab 14.1: Defining and Using Attributes

Objectives

After completing this lab, you will be able to:

- Use the predefined **Conditional** attribute.
- Create a custom attribute.
- Add a custom attribute value to a class.
- Use reflection to query attribute values.

Prerequisites

Before working on this lab, you should be familiar with the following:

- Creating classes in C#
- Defining constructors and methods
- Using the **typeof** operator
- Using properties and indexers in C#

Estimated time to complete this lab: 45 minutes

Exercise 1
Using the Conditional Attribute

In this exercise, you will use the predefined **Conditional** attribute to conditionally execute your code.

Conditional execution is a useful technique if you want to incorporate testing or debugging code into a project but do not want to edit the project and remove the debugging code after the system is complete and functioning correctly.

During this exercise, you will add a method called **DumpToScreen** to the **BankAccount** class (which was created in earlier labs). This method will display the details of the account. You will use the **Conditional** attribute to execute this method depending on the value of a symbol called **DEBUG_ACCOUNT**.

▶ **To apply the Conditional attribute**

1. Open the Bank.sln project in the *install folder*\Labs\Lab14\Starter\Bank folder.

2. In the **BankAccount** class, add a public void method called **DumpToScreen** that takes no parameters.

   The method must display the contents of the account: account number, account holder, account type, and account balance. The following code shows a possible example of the method:

   ```
   public void DumpToScreen( )
   {
     Console.WriteLine("Debugging account {0}. Holder is {1}.
   ↪Type is {2}. Balance is {3}",
       this.accNo, this.holder, this.accType, this.accBal);
   }
   ```

3. Make use of the method's dependence on the **DEBUG_ACCOUNT** symbol.

   Add the following **Conditional** attribute before the method as follows:

   ```
   [Conditional("DEBUG_ACCOUNT")]
   ```

4. Add a **using** directive for the **System.Diagnostics** namespace.

5. Compile your code and correct any errors.

▶ **To test the Conditional attribute**

1. Open the TestHarness.sln project in the
   install folder\Labs\Lab14\Starter\TestHarness folder.

2. Add a reference to the **Bank** library.

   a. In Solution Explorer, expand the **TestHarness** tree.

   b. Right-click **References**, and then click **Add Reference**.

   c. Click **Browse**, and then navigate to
      install folder\Labs\Lab14\Starter\Bank\Bin\Debug.

   d. Click **Bank.dll**, click **Open**, and then click **OK**.

3. Review the **Main** method of the **CreateAccount** class. Notice that it creates
   a new bank account.

4. Add the following line of code to **Main** to call the **DumpToScreen** method
   of **myAccount**:

   ```
   myAccount.DumpToScreen( );
   ```

5. Save your work, compile the project, and correct any errors.

6. Run the test harness.

   Notice that nothing happens. This is because the **DumpToScreen** method
   has not been called.

7. From the Microsoft Windows® command prompt, use the ILDASM utility
   (ildasm) to examine
   install folder\Labs\Lab14\Starter\Bank\Bin\Debug\Bank.dll.

   You will see that the **DumpToScreen** method is present in the
   BankAccount class.

8. Double-click the **DumpToScreen** method to display the Microsoft
   intermediate language (MSIL) code.

   You will see the **ConditionalAttribute** at the beginning of the method. The
   problem is in the test harness. Because of the **ConditionalAttribute** on
   DumpToScreen, the runtime will effectively ignore calls made to that
   method if the **DEBUG_ACCOUNT** symbol is not defined when the calling
   program is compiled. The call is made, but because **DEBUG_ACCOUNT**
   is not defined, the runtime finishes the call immediately.

9. Close ILDASM.

10. Return to the test harness. At the top of the CreateAccount.cs file, before the
    first **using** directive, add the following code:

    ```
    #define DEBUG_ACCOUNT
    ```

    This defines the **DEBUG_ACCOUNT** symbol.

11. Save and compile the test harness, correcting any errors.

12. Run the test harness.

    Notice that the **DumpToScreen** method displays the information from
    myAccount.

Exercise 2
Defining and Using a Custom Attribute

In this exercise, you will create a custom attribute called
DeveloperInfoAttribute. This attribute will allow the name of the developer
and, optionally, the creation date of a class to be stored in the metadata of that
class. This attribute will permit multiple use because more than one developer
might be involved in the coding of a class.

You will then write a method that retrieves and displays all of the
DeveloperInfoAttribute values for a class.

▶ **To define a custom attribute class**

1. Using Visual Studio .NET, create a new Microsoft Visual C#™ project,
   using the information shown in the following table.

Element	Value
Project Type	Visual C# Projects
Template	Class Library
Name	CustomAttribute
Location	*install folder*\Labs\Lab14\Starter

2. Change the name and file name of class **Class1** to **DeveloperInfoAttribute**.

   Make sure that you also change the name of the constructor.

3. Specify that the **DeveloperInfoAttribute** class is derived from
   System.Attribute.

   This attribute will be applicable to classes, enums, and structs only. It will
   also be allowed to occur more than once when it is used.

4. Add the following **AttributeUsage** attribute before the class definition:

   ```
   [AttributeUsage(AttributeTargets.Class |
   ↪AttributeTargets.Enum | AttributeTargets.Struct,
   ↪AllowMultiple=true)]
   ```

5. Document your attribute with a meaningful summary (between the
   <summary> tags). Use the exercise description to help you.

6. The **DeveloperInfoAttribute** attribute requires the name of the developer of
   the class as a mandatory parameter and takes the date that the class was
   written as an optional string parameter. Add private instance variables to
   hold this information, as follows:

   ```
   private string developerName;
   private string dateCreated;
   ```

7. Modify the constructor so that it takes a single string parameter that is also
   called **developerName**, and add a line of code to the constructor that
   assigns this parameter to **this.developerName**.

8. Add a public **string** read-only property called **Developer** that can be used to
   get the value of **developerName**. Do not write a **set** accessor.

9. Add another public **string** property that is called **Date**. This property should have a **get** accessor that reads **dateCreated** and a **set** accessor that writes **dateCreated**.

10. Compile the class and correct any errors.

Because the class is in a class library, the compilation process will produce a DLL (CustomAttribute.dll) rather than a stand-alone executable program. The complete code for the **DeveloperInfoAttribute** class follows:

```
namespace CustomAttribute
{
  using System;
  /// <summary>
  ///  This class is a custom attribute that allows
  ///  the name of the developer of a class to be stored
  ///  with the metadata of that class.
  /// </summary>
  [AttributeUsage(AttributeTargets.Class |
  ↪AttributeTargets.Enum | AttributeTargets.Struct,
  ↪AllowMultiple=true)]
  public class DeveloperInfoAttribute: System.Attribute

  {
    private string developerName;
    private string dateCreated;

    // Constructor. Developer name is the only
    // mandatory parameter for this attribute.
    public DeveloperInfoAttribute(string developerName)
    {
      this.developerName = developerName;
    }
    public string Developer
    {
      get
      {
        return developerName;
      }
    }

    // Optional parameter
    public string Date
    {
      get
      {
        return dateCreated;
      }
      set
      {
        dateCreated = value;
      }
    }
  }
}
```

▶ **To add a custom attribute to a class**

1. You will now use the **DeveloperInfo** attribute to record the name of the developer of the **Rational** number class. (This class was created in an earlier lab, but it is provided here for your convenience.) Open the Rational.sln project in the *install folder*\Labs\Lab14\Starter\Rational folder.

2. Perform the following steps to add a reference to the **CustomAttribute** library that you created earlier:

   a. In Solution Explorer, expand the **Rational** tree.

   b. Right-click **References**, and then click **Add Reference**.

   c. In the **Add Reference** dialog box, click **Browse**.

   d. Navigate to the *install folder*\Labs\Lab14\Starter\CustomAttribute\Bin\Debug folder, and click **CustomAttribute.dll**.

   e. Click **Open**, and then click **OK**.

3. Add a **CustomAttribute.DeveloperInfo** attribute to the **Rational** class, specifying your name as the developer and the current date as the optional date parameter, as follows:

   ```
   [CustomAttribute.DeveloperInfo("Your Name",
   ↪Date="Today")]
   ```

4. Add a second developer to the **Rational** class.

5. Compile the **Rational** project and correct any errors.

6. Open a Command window and navigate to the *install folder*\Labs\Lab14\Starter\Rational\Bin\Debug folder.

   This folder should contain your Rational.exe executable.

7. Run ILDASM and open Rational.exe.

8. Expand the **Rational** namespace in the tree view.

9. Expand the **Rational** class.

10. Near the top of the class, notice your custom attribute and the values that you supplied.

11. Close ILDASM.

▶ **To use reflection to query attribute values**

Using ILDASM is only one way to examine attribute values. You can also use reflection in C# programs. Return to Visual Studio .NET, and edit the **TestRational** class in the **Rational** project.

1. In the **Main** method, create a variable called *attrInfo* of type **System.Reflection.MemberInfo**, as shown in the following code:

```
public static void Main( )
{
  System.Reflection.MemberInfo attrInfo;
...
```

2. You can use a **MemberInfo** object to hold information about the members of a class. Assign the **Rational** type to the **MemberInfo** object by using the **typeof** operator, as follows:

```
attrInfo = typeof(Rational);
```

3. The attributes of a class are held as part of the class information. You can retrieve the attribute values by using the **GetCustomAttributes** method. Create an object array called **attrs**, and use the **GetCustomAttributes** method of **attrInfo** to find all of the custom attributes used by the **Rational** class, as shown in the following code:

```
object[ ] attrs = attrInfo.GetCustomAttributes(false);
```

4. Now you need to extract the attribute information that is stored in the **attrs** array and print it. Create a variable called *developerAttr* of type **CustomAttribute.DeveloperInfoAttribute**, and assign it the first element in the **attrs** array, casting as appropriate, as shown in the following code:

```
CustomAttribute.DeveloperInfoAttribute developerAttr;
developerAttr =
  ↪(CustomAttribute.DeveloperInfoAttribute)attrs[0];
```

Note In production code, you would use reflection rather than a cast to determine the type of the attribute.

---

5. Use the **get** accessor of the **DeveloperInfoAttribute** attribute to retrieve the **Developer** and **Date** attributes and print them out as follows:

```
Console.WriteLine("Developer: {0}\tDate: {1}",
  ↪developerAttr.Developer, developerAttr.Date);
```

6. Repeat steps 4 and 5 for element 1 of the **attrs** array.

   You can use a loop if you want to be able to retrieve the values of more than two attributes.

7. Compile the project and correct any errors.

   The completed code for the **Main** method is shown in the following code:

```
namespace Rational
{
using System;

// Test harness
public class TestRational
{
  public static void Main( )
  {
    System.Reflection.MemberInfo attrInfo;
    attrInfo = typeof(Rational);
    object[ ] attrs = attrInfo.GetCustomAttributes(false);
    CustomAttribute.DeveloperInfoAttribute developerAttr;
    developerAttr =
      ↪(CustomAttribute.DeveloperInfoAttribute)attrs[0];
    Console.WriteLine("Developer: {0}\tDate: {1}",
      ↪developerAttr.Developer, developerAttr.Date);
    developerAttr =
      ↪(CustomAttribute.DeveloperInfoAttribute)attrs[1];
    Console.WriteLine("Developer: {0}\tDate: {1}",
      ↪developerAttr.Developer, developerAttr.Date);
  }
}
}
```

Here is an alternative **Main** that uses a **foreach** loop:

```
  public static void Main( )
  {
    System.Reflection.MemberInfo attrInfo;
    attrInfo = typeof(Rational);
    object[ ] attrs = attrInfo.GetCustomAttributes(false);

    foreach (CustomAttribute.DeveloperInfoAttribute
      ↪ devAttr in attrs)
    {
      Console.WriteLine("Developer: {0}\tDate: {1}",
        ↪devAttr.Developer, devAttr.Date);
    }
  }
```

8. When you run this program, it will display the names and dates that you supplied as **DeveloperInfoAttribute** information to the **Rational** class.

Review

- Overview of Attributes
- Defining Custom Attributes
- Retrieving Attribute Values

1. Can you tag individual objects by using attributes?

2. Where are attribute values stored?

3. What mechanism is used to determine the value of an attribute at run time?

4. Define an attribute class called **CodeTestAttributes** that is applicable only to classes. It should have no positional parameters and two named parameters called **Reviewed** and **HasTestSuite**. These parameters should be of type **bool** and should be implemented by using read/write properties.

5. Define a class called **Widget,** and use **CodeTestAttributes** from the previous question to mark that **Widget** has been reviewed but has no test suite.

6. Suppose that **Widget** from the previous question had a method called **LogBug**. Could **CodeTestAttributes** be used to mark only this method?

Course Evaluation

Your evaluation of this course will help Microsoft understand the quality of your learning experience.

To complete a course evaluation, go to http://www.metricsthatmatter.com/survey.

Microsoft will keep your evaluation strictly confidential and will use your responses to improve your future learning experience.

msdn training

Appendix A: Resources for Further Study

Microsoft

◆ Resources for C#

- **Books About C# Programming**
- **C# Development Resources**
- **.NET Development Resources**

You can use this appendix as a resource to help you locate the latest news and information about C# and the Microsoft® .NET Framework. It provides you with book titles and links to key locations of interest to developers:

- Books about C# programming
- C# development resources
- .NET Framework development resources

Books About C# Programming

- **Microsoft Visual C# Step By Step**
- **A Programmer's Introduction to C# (2nd Edition)**
- **Inside C#**
- **C# Unleashed**
- **Programming C#**
- **C# Developer's Headstart**
- **C# and the .NET Platform**

To learn more about programming in C#, try the following books:

- *Microsoft Visual C# Step By Step*, by John Sharp and Jon Jagger, Microsoft Press®, 2002
- *A Programmer's Introduction to C# (2nd Edition)*, by Eric Gunnerson, Apress, 2001.
- *Inside C#*, by Tom Archer, Microsoft Press, 2001.
- *C# Unleashed*, by Joe Mayo, Sams Publishing, 2001.
- *Programming C#*, by Jesse Liberty, O'Reilly and Associates, 2001.
- *C# Developer's Headstart*, by Mark Michaelis and Philip Spokas, Osborne McGraw-Hill, 2001.
- *C# and the .NET Platform*, by Andrew Troelsen, Apress, 2001.

To find information about other C# books and publications, visit:

- http://www.microsoft.com/mspress/devtools/csharp
- http://www.dotnetbooks.com

C# Development Resources

- http://www.dotnetwire.com
- http://www.csharphelp.com
- http://www.csharp-station.com
- http://www.csharpindex.com
- http://www.codehound.com/csharp
- http://www.c-sharpcorner.com

You can find valuable information about developing C# applications at the following Web sites:

- To access the premier Microsoft site for .NET news, visit http://www.dotnetwire.com

- To access articles, information, and feedback about C#, visit http://www.csharphelp.com

- To access information about C# programming, visit http://www.csharp-station.com

- To access reference information about C#, visit http://www.csharpindex.com

- To access a C# search engine, visit http://www.codehound.com/csharp

- To access a C# and .NET developer's network, visit http://www.c-sharpcorner.com

.NET Framework Development Resources

- **Resources**
  - http://www.microsoft.com/net
  - http://msdn.microsoft.com/net
  - http://www.gotnet.com
- **Articles**

Information about developing solutions for the .NET Framework is available from Microsoft Web sites. The following sites include information about the C# programming language:

- http://www.microsoft.com/net/
- http://msdn.microsoft.com/net/
- http://www.gotnet.com

The following articles provide further insight into the .NET Framework and related technologies:

- "Microsoft .NET: Realizing the Next Generation Business Integration," at http://www.microsoft.com/net/use/nextgenbiz.asp
- "Microsoft .NET Framework FAQ," at http://msdn.microsoft.com/library/techart/faq111700.htm
- "C# Language Specification," at http://msdn.microsoft.com/vstudio/nextgen/technology/csharpdownload.asp
- "C# Introduction and Overview," at http://msdn.microsoft.com/vstudio/nextgen/technology/csharpintro.asp

Notes

Notes

Notes

Notes

Notes

Notes

Notes

Notes